Telegrams from the Soul:
Peter Altenberg and the Culture of fin-de-siècle Vienna

Andrew Barker

Telegrams from the Soul

Peter Altenberg and the Culture of fin-de-siècle Vienna

Camden House

Copyright © 1996 by
CAMDEN HOUSE, INC.

Published by Camden House, Inc.
Drawer 2025
Columbia, SC 29202 USA

Printed on acid-free paper.
Binding materials are chosen for strength and
durability.

ISBN:1–57113–079–9

Library of Congress Cataloging-in-Publication Data

Barker, Andrew.
    Telegrams from the soul: Peter Altenberg and the culture of fin-
de-siècle Vienna / Andrew Barker.
        p.   cm.   -- (Studies in German literature, linguistics, and
    culture)
    Includes bibliographical references and index.
    ISBN 1–57113–079–9 (alk. paper)
    Altenberg, Peter, 1859–1919. 2. Authors, Austrian--19th
century--Biography. 3. Authors, Austrian--20th century--Biography.
4. Vienna (Austria)--Intellectual life. I. Title. II. Series:
Studies in German literature, linguistics. and culture (Unnumbered)
PT2601.L78Z57   1996
831'.912—dc20
    [B]   96-6260
                                                                        CIP

Contents

Acknowledgments   vii
    A note on translations   viii

List of Primary Texts and Abbreviations   ix

Introduction — The "little genius"   xi

1: The Making of Peter Altenberg   1
    Richard Engländer and Peter Altenberg   1
    Family Album of a Viennese Merchant's Son   5
    The Naming of Peter Altenberg   9

2: The Birth of the Writer   18
    "Young Vienna"   18
    First Steps in Print   24
    "Ich hasse die Retouche": Altenberg's letter to Schnitzler,
    July 1894.   30

3: The Early Work: 1896–1903   38
    Altenberg and Impressionism   38
    Wie ich es sehe   48
    Ashantee: the "People from Paradise"   63
    Femmes fatales and the flight to Munich   74
    Was der Tag mir zuträgt: Wagner, Women and bouillon-cubes   86
    Kunst and other catastrophes   94

4: New Directions, Old Habits   107
    Pròdromos: Poetry and Hygiene   107
    Cabaret and Commemoration: *Märchen des Lebens; Die
    Auswahl aus meinen Büchern; Bilderbögen des kleinen Lebens*   119

5: Madness and Confinement   140
    Neues Altes: Something old, something new   140
    Return to Paradise?: *"Semmering 1912"*   150

6: Musical Postcards and Talking Apes   166
    Altenberg and the "New Music" in Vienna   166
    Franz Kafka and Peter Altenberg   174

7: War and Late Loves   186
   Fechsung   186
   Nachfechsung   196

8: The Final Years   205
   Vita Ipsa   205
   The Evening of my Life: *Mein Lebensabend*   215

9: Epilogue   224
   Death in Vienna   224
   Dead, but not forgotten   231

Appendix 1   237

Appendix 2   238

Works Cited   241

Index   253

Acknowledgments

Whatever it says on the cover, a book such as this can never be the product of a single author. In this instance thanks must go first and foremost to my friend, colleague and mentor Leo Lensing, whose generosity, scholarship and critical acumen have informed this work more than any simple acknowledgment could possibly indicate. Hardly less important has been the impetus provided by Jane Kallir and Hildegard Bachert, directors of the Galerie St. Etienne in New York, who allowed me to mine the treasures of Altenberg's unpublished papers now in their safe guardianship. I am also indebted to the Institut für Zeitungsforschung in Dortmund whose director permitted unrestricted access to their unique holdings at a time when the Institute was officially closed. Like so many others who delve into the unprinted sources of Viennese culture, I have gained immeasurably from the tolerant understanding of the staff of the Vienna Stadt- und Landesbibliothek, and in particular of Karl Misar. For permission to reproduce the portrait of Altenberg on the dust-cover I am grateful to the Leo Baeck Institute in New York. My thanks are also due to the following institutions, from all of which I received much kindness and help:

> Historisches Museum der Stadt Wien; Österreichische Nationalbibliothek, Vienna; Österreichisches Theatermuseum, Vienna; Dokumentationsstelle für neuere österreichische Literatur, Vienna; Städtische Bibliothek, Munich; Bayerische Staatsbibliothek (Munich); Staatsbibliothek Preußischer Kulturbesitz (West Berlin); Deutsche Staatsbibliothek (East Berlin); RIAS Berlin; Deutsches Literatur Archiv (Marbach am Neckar); Werner Kraft-Archiv; Biblioteka Jagiellonska (Kraków); The National Library of Scotland; The Lilly Library (Indiana University, Bloomington, Indiana); The Houghton Library (Harvard University); New York City Public Library; The Arnold Schoenberg Institute (University of Southern California, Los Angeles). I wish also to record my special thanks to the staff of Inter-library loans at Edinburgh University Library, who did their utmost to track down my outlandish requests.

No work so reliant upon archival material in both the Old and the New World could have flourished without considerable financial support, and it gives me pleasure to record my gratitude to The Carnegie Trust for the Universities of Scotland; The British Academy; The University of Edinburgh; Wesleyan University, Middletown, Connecticut. In addition I am particularly grateful to the Carnegie Trust and to the Moray Endowment Fund for further grants enabling publication of this work.

Many individuals have given of their time and wisdom in the preparation of this book, and I am grateful to them all. At the risk of offending those whose names have been omitted, I should nevertheless like to thank in particular the following: Gregor Ackermann, Iain Boyd-Whyte, Juliane Brand, the late Hans Gal, Christopher Hailey, Volker Kahmen, Hannes Krauss, Heinz Lunzer, Victoria Lunzer-Talos, Alasdair Macdonald, Paul Salmon, Wendelin Schmidt-Dengler, George Schoolfield, Josephine Simpson, and Margaret Stone.

During the final stages of preparation, Jim Hardin's efficiency and sagacity were much appreciated, as was also the astute critical reading of the manuscript by Steve Dowden. Throughout the many years in which "Peter" demanded my attention, often at the cost of more important things, Sheila, Euan and Rachel looked on with tolerance and good humour, and I thank them profoundly for their forbearance.

A note on translations:

As Altenberg's idiom is unique and his texts often difficult to obtain, I have provided readers with numerous examples of his writing in the original German, along with a translation into English. In some instances, however, although I felt it appropriate to quote Altenberg, I have felt that an English translation alone would suffice to convey the substance and flavour of the text. Except where stated otherwise, I am responsible for all translations. Unless the phraseology of the original was deemed especially noteworthy or ambiguous, quotations from other German-language authors are generally given in English translation only.

Andrew Barker
Edinburgh, January 1996

List of Primary Texts and Abbreviations

Works by Peter Altenberg:

Wie ich es sehe (1896)
Ashantee (1897)
Was der Tag mir zuträgt (1901)
Pròdròmŏs (1905)
Märchen des Lebens (1908)
Die Auswahl aus meinen Büchern (1908)
Bilderbögen des kleinen Lebens (1909)
Neues Altes (1911)
"Semmering 1912" (1913)
Fechsung (1915)
Nachfechsung (1916)
Vita Ipsa (1918)
Mein Lebensabend (1919)
Das Altenbergbuch (1921)
Der Nachlaß (1925)
Nachlese (1930)

The following editions and abbreviations are used:

A	*Ashantee*, (Berlin: Fischer, 1897), 204pp.
AB	*Das Altenbergbuch*, ed. Egon Friedell, (Leipzig, Vienna and Zürich: Verlag der Wiener Graphischen Werkstätte, 1921), 425pp.
AL	*Die Auswahl aus meinen Büchern*, (Berlin: Fischer 1908), 147pp.
B	*Bilderbögen des kleinen Lebens*, (Berlin: Reiß ,1909), 221pp.
F	*Fechsung*, (Berlin: Fischer, 1915), 280pp.
LA	*Mein Lebensabend*, (Berlin: Fischer, 1919), 364pp.
ML	*Märchen des Lebens*, (Berlin: Fischer, 1908), 213pp.

ML[3]	*Märchen des Lebens*, 3. veränderte und vermehrte Auflage, (Berlin: Fischer, 1911), 239pp.
N	*Der Nachlaß*, ed. Alfred Polgar, (Berlin: Fischer, 1925), 158pp.
NA	*Neues Altes*, (Berlin: Fischer, 1911), 214pp.
NE	*Nachlese*, ed. Marie M(authner), (Vienna: Lányi, 1930), 67pp.
NF	*Nachfechsung*, (Berlin: Fischer, 1916), 351pp.
P	*Pròdrŏmŏs*, (Berlin: Fischer, 1905), 204pp.
S	*"Semmering 1912"*, (Berlin: Fischer, 1913), 217pp.
S[3]	*"Semmering 1912"*, 3. vermehrte Auflage, (Berlin: Fischer. 1913), 248pp.
VI	*Vita Ipsa*, (Berlin: Fischer, 1918), 317pp.
WS	*Wie ich es sehe*, 4. veränderte und vermehrte Auflage, (Berlin: Fischer, 1904), 332pp.
WT	*Was der Tag mir zuträgt*, 2. veränderte und vermehrte Auflage, (Berlin: Fischer, 1902), 327pp.

Further abbreviations:

GSE:	Altenberg's papers in the private collection administered by the Galerie St. Etienne, New York.
LBI:	Altenberg's papers in the Leo Baeck Institute, New York.
SPK:	Staatsbibliothek Preußischer Kulturbesitz, Berlin.
WKA:	Werner Kraft-Archiv
WSB:	Wiener Stadt- und Landesbibliothek, Vienna.

Introduction

The "little genius"

Peter Altenberg, anti-modern modernist and misogynistic feminist, anti-Semitic Jew and drug-addicted health fanatic, was the very embodiment of the Janus-faced culture of fin de siècle Vienna. He inspired some of his most talented contemporaries not just in literature, but across the entire gamut of the arts: Oskar Kokoschka and Alban Berg, Adolf Loos and Arthur Schnitzler, Franz Kafka and Robert Musil all responded personally and creatively to this "Verlaine of the Ringstraße,"[1] once described as Vienna's most popular figure.[2] Altenberg's life, like that of his fellow Viennese Gustav Klimt, framed more or less exactly the last phase of Hapsburg hegemony in Central Europe, from the setting up of the first quasi-representative parliament in 1861 to the collapse of 1918. Altenberg and Klimt were good friends, but they shared something else: in the opinion of Alfred Polgar at least, Altenberg was the strongest erotic talent ever to have written in German.[3] Forty years after the demise of the Dual Monarchy, which Altenberg survived by barely two months, reading this now virtually forgotten author proved seminal in the emergence of Uwe Johnson as a major writer.[4] In the 1960s Jürgen Habermas pointed to Altenberg's lasting significance for T. W. Adorno as an example of "individuation pushed to extremes" who, through his uncompromising stance, anticipated a freer humanity.[5]

Both during his lifetime and in the eyes of posterity, Altenberg was at least as famous for his eccentricity as for his writing. When in the 1980s Felix Mitterer turned his attention to Altenberg, the resultant work highlighted

---

[1] Alfred Kerr, "Dem toten Peter Altenberg," *Die neue Rundschau* 30, no. 3 (1919): 332. Altenberg's own extravagant regard for Kerr, whom he met but once, was published in Paul Cassirer's journal *Pan*, 1 (1910): 482.

[2] Kurt Pinthus, "Peter Altenberg, '*Semmering 1912*'," *Beiblatt der Zeitschrift für Bücherfreunde* 5, no. 2 (1913): 71–72. See also Werner Riemerschmied, "Peter Altenberg," *Literatur und Kritik* 12, no. 120 (1977): 593.

[3] *Peter Altenberg: Leben und Werk in Texten und Bildern*, ed. Hans Christian Kosler, (Munich: Matthes and Seitz, 1981), 54.

[4] Uwe Johnson, *"Wo ist der Erzähler auffindbar?" Gutachten für Verlage 1956–1958*, ed. Bernd Neumann, (Frankfurt: Suhrkamp, 1992), 81–116, 182–188.

[5] Jürgen Habermas, "Ein philosophischer Intellektueller," *Über T. W. Adorno*, ed. J. W. Adorno, (Frankfurt: Suhrkamp 1968), 35–36. See Jacques Le Rider, *Modernity and crises of identity. Culture and society in fin-de-siècle Vienna*, trans. Rosemary Morris, (New York: Continuum, 1993), 298.

the writer's foolishness.[6] Altenberg himself accepted no distinction between his work and his persona, which was projected as intensely in public life as it was in his art. Yet as we shall see, the creation of that persona was itself a creative response to the problem of being born Jewish in a hostile intellectual, social and cultural environment. Deeply loved in Vienna, he could inspire profound antipathy elsewhere. Bert Brecht claimed an "iron curtain" descended when reading Altenberg,[7] and for many years critics took a similarly jaundiced view. Although Altenberg produced twelve books in a career of just twenty-two years — a thirteenth was at proof stage when he died — Arnold Schoenberg's biographer called him an idler. Others have considered him variously a dropout and a coffee-shop scribbler, while a critic of the 1970s attacked his use of language as nothing short of criminal.[8]

Altenberg's major formal contribution to Austro-German letters lies in his development of the modern prose-poem, yet when the first scholarly book on this topic appeared in 1970, his name was barely mentioned.[9] By 1980 he was hailed as the single-handed creator of the German prose poem in its modern guise,[10] and by 1985 *Die Zeit* trumpeted him as "die wahre Eminenz Wiens" [Vienna's true eminence.][11] Those disputing this claim may be surprised to learn that no less a figure than Robert Musil found it impossible to decide who was the greater writer, Goethe or Altenberg.[12] Questions of relative rank apart, I believe that the phenomenon of Peter Altenberg, poet and fool, exemplifies the creative tensions in the dynamic triad of life, art, and artist in a way which renders him the most *representative* figure in the hot-house world of Vienna's Indian summer.

Altenberg's work and life lie at the very heart of *fin de siècle* Vienna, yet only lately has he attracted the critical attention long since accorded other major figures of the period. Given Vienna's fashionability, it is no surprise that there have recently been several extended studies of Altenberg, and as

---

[6] Felix Mitterer, *Der Narr von Wien: Aus dem Leben des Dichters Peter Altenberg. Ein Drehbuch*, (Salzburg: Residenz, 1982).

[7] Kosler, *Peter Altenberg*, (fn. 3) 193. Brecht may nonetheless have responded to Altenberg in spite of himself. Compare "Prodromos" (F 226) with Brecht's "Wenn die Haifische Menschen wären." The Brecht disciple Hanns Eisler included texts by both Altenberg and Brecht in his song-cycle *Hollywood-Liederbuch* (Opus 78.)

[8] Hans Heinz Stuckenschmidt, *Arnold Schoenberg . His Life, Work and World*, trans. Humphrey Searle, (New York: Schirmer, 1978), 23; Roy Pascal, *From Naturalism to Expressionism. German Literature and Society 1880–1918*, (London: Weidenfeld and Nicholson, 1973), 57; Jost Hermand, *Der Schein des schönen Lebens. Studien zur Jahrhundertwende*, (Frankfurt: Athenäum, 1972), 181; Klaus G. Just, *Von der Gründerzeit bis zur Jahrhundertwende. Geschichte der deutschen Literatur seit 1871*, (Bern: Francke, 1973), 215.

[9] Ulrich Fülleborn, *Das deutsche Prosagedicht: Zur Theorie und Geschichte einer Gattung*, (Munich: Wilhelm Fink, 1970, 55–56).

[10] Viktor Žmegač, *Geschichte der deutschen Literatur vom 18. Jahrhundert bis zur Gegenwart*, vol. 2, 2, (Königstein/Taunus: Athenäum, 1980), 387.

[11] *Die Zeit* (Magazin), 14 (1985): 28.

[12] Robert Musil, *Prosa, Dramen, Späte Briefe*, ed. Adolf Frisé (Reinbek bei Hamburg: Rowohlt, 1957), 712.

will become apparent, I am indebted to all of them.[13] Few, however, take more than cursory steps toward examining his role in the larger fabric of Viennese society and culture in the last decades of the Dual Monarchy.[14] Most survey thematic aspects of his work or discuss minutiae of literary taxonomy. Few delve into the astonishingly rich literature, not all of it anecdotal, which the author himself inspired from his contemporaries.[15] Fewer still consult the abundant manuscript material in Austria, Germany, Poland and the United States. Much of Altenberg's work first came out in the popular press and literary journals: a trawl through them reveals a host of other long-forgotten texts.[16] The present study will draw frequently upon these unrecorded or disregarded sources and will attempt to examine Altenberg in more than a narrowly literary sense. Only by so doing will the extent of his significance across the culture as a whole become apparent.

By the end of the 1920s Altenberg's reputation had gone into steep decline, as if his work could not survive his physical demise. The extended nature of his eclipse is shown by the fact that almost seven decades had elapsed from Altenberg's death before his long-time publisher Fischer finally made an edition of his works available to modern readers. Sadly, the venture collapsed after only two volumes of the projected five had appeared. Moreover, it transpires that these "Collected Works" are merely another of the antholo-

---

[13] Geoffrey Broad, "The Didactic Element in the Works of Peter Altenberg," Ph.D diss., Otago, 1980; Barbara Z. Schoenberg, "The Art of Peter Altenberg. Bedside Chronicles of a Dying World," Ph.D diss., U. C. L. A., 1984; Stefan Nienhaus, *Das Prosagedicht im Wien der Jahrhundertwende. Altenberg — Hofmannsthal — Polgar*, (Berlin and New York: de Gruyter, 1986); Irene Köwer, *Peter Altenberg als Autor der literarischen Kleinform*, (Frankfurt: Peter Lang, 1987); Josephine M. N. Simpson, *Peter Altenberg: A neglected writer of the Viennese Jahrhundertwende*, (Frankfurt: Peter Lang, 1987); Burckhard Spinnen, *Schriftbilder. Studien zu einer Geschichte emblematischer Kurzprosa*, (Münster: Aschendorff, 1991).

[14] See, however: Edward Timms, "Peter Altenberg — authenticity or pose?," *Fin de siècle Vienna*, ed. Gilbert J. Carr and Eda Sagarra, (Dublin: Trinity College, 1985) 126–142; Susanne Rode, *Alban Berg und Karl Kraus: Zur geistigen Biographie des Komponisten der "Lulu"*, (Frankfurt: Peter Lang, 1988), esp. 18–35; Hans Bisanz, *Mein äußerstes Ideal: Altenbergs Photosammlung von geliebten Frauen, Freunden und Orten*, (Vienna and Munich: Christian Brandstätter, 1987); Barbara Z. Schoenberg, "'Woman Defender' and 'Woman Offender'. Peter Altenberg and Otto Weininger. Two Literary Stances vis-à-vis bourgeois Culture in the Viennese 'Belle Epoque'," *Modern Austrian Literature* 20, no. 2 (1987): 51–69; Barbara Z. Schoenberg, "The influence of the French prose poem on Peter Altenberg," *Modern Austrian Literature* 22, nos. 3–4 (1989): 15–32. Ian Foster, "Altenberg's African Spectacle *Ashantee*," *Theatre and Performance in Austria. From Mozart to Jellinek*, ed. Ritchie Robertson and Edward Timms, (Edinburgh: Edinburgh University Press, 1993), 29–60; Andrew Barker and Leo A. Lensing, *Peter Altenberg: Rezept die Welt zu sehen*, (Vienna: Braumüller, 1995).

[15] For generally reliable biographical material written in a semi-popular vein see Camillo Schaefer, *Peter Altenberg. Ein biographischer Essay*, (Vienna: Freibord, 1980); Camillo Schaefer, *Peter Altenberg, oder, Die Geburt der modernen Seele*, (Vienna: Amalthea, 1992).

[16] Among newspapers which regularly published Altenberg are: *Neues Wiener Tagblatt; Neues Wiener Journal; Wiener Allgemeine Zeitung; Prager Tagblatt.* See Appendix 1 for a list of periodicals in which Altenberg's work appeared.

gies to which Altenberg's work now seems condemned.[17] It was, however, Altenberg himself who first anthologized his writings as early as 1900 and subsequently in 1908. Early in the Great War Karl Kraus first thought of his own anthology, this evoking from Altenberg an outraged letter to Fischer.[18] In 1925 the poet Oskar Loerke began work on an anthology which never appeared, and it was only in 1932, after much unseemly wrangling, that Kraus finally brought out his collection independently of Fischer. Since then the anthology is the sole form in which Altenberg's works have been published. Though invaluable as introductions, they are no substitute for texts in authentic format. The originals, now increasingly difficult — and expensive — to come by, naturally permit an overview of the developments within his art which no anthology could possibly accomplish.

As he grew older, Altenberg could indeed be obsessively repetitive, but this was not exclusively an indication of declining artistic powers. It represented also a deliberate and conscious stylistic effect, sought by the author in an increasingly desperate attempt to weld together the ethical and the aesthetic aspects of his view of life. As early as 1905 he exclaimed in *Pròdròmòs* that people should not accuse him of repeating himself: perhaps after the ten-thousandth repetition they might be justified, but only if they were prepared to grasp and follow his teachings (P 45). For many of his contemporary readers, the very predictability of Altenberg's work was a major source of its attraction.

With just one exception, all the books published during his lifetime came out with the S. Fischer Verlag, the pre-eminent German publisher of literary modernism. Altenberg, keenly aware of the status and presentation of his texts, was initially happy with their performance, boasting that in the whole of his first book *Wie ich es sehe* (1896) there was but a single misprint. By 1909, however, he had grown so disaffected with Fischer that the beautifully produced *Bilderbögen des kleinen Lebens* came out with Erich Reiss, publisher of the radical theatre journal *Die Schaubühne*. Altenberg soon made up with Fischer, but in August 1918 the poet, novelist and dramatist Franz Werfel was sounding out Kurt Wolff, his own and Kafka's publisher, as a possible alternative.[19] Altenberg was doubtless paranoid, but his exasperation with Fischer seems justified, for especially in the later collections signs of sloppy production abound.

Besides being a prolific and innovative producer of prose miniatures, some bearing the stamp of genius, Altenberg was also a copious and inspired writer of letters. A year after Altenberg's death Stefan Großmann announced that a collection of letters, edited by Altenberg's brother Georg Engländer, would appear imminently with Fischer. Nothing emerged. Later in the

---

[17] Peter Altenberg, *Gesammelte Werke in 5 Bänden*, ed. Werner J. Schweiger, (Vienna and Frankfurt: Löcker and Fischer, 1987), vol. 1, *Expedition in den Alltag: Gesammelte Skizzen 1895–1898*; vol. 2, *Extrakte des Lebens: Gesammelte Skizzen 1898–1919*.

[18] WSB 199.208, 1–5. For a list of abbreviations see p. ix.

[19] *Kurt Wolff: Briefwechsel eines Verlegers 1911–1963*, ed. Bernhard Zeller and Ellen Otten, (Frankfurt: Heinrich Scheffler, 1966), 117–118.

1920s vain attempts were undertaken to persuade the publisher of the Innsbruck periodical *Der Brenner* to bring out a selection of his correspondence.[20] Some bibliographies and studies quote the existence of Altenberg's letters in an edition by Franz Glück, purportedly published in 1947. This edition is a fiction, although a selection of Altenberg's letters was extant in unpublished form as early as 1932, when Glück announced in a letter to Alban Berg that he already had gathered a great deal of material for his forthcoming edition.[21] Early in January 1934 Berg's colleague Willi Reich, a pupil of Schoenberg, attended a reading where Glück declaimed from Altenberg's correspondence, due to be published in the autumn. He reported in a letter to Berg that the planned volume would be a vital addition to the published sketches.[22] It is a major loss to Austrian literature that this collection never saw the light of day.

Reich's high opinion of the letters was shared by Altenberg himself. Writing to Adolf Loos's long-time lover Bessie Bruce, he exclaimed in his touching English: "My *letter*, dearest, is my *soul*."[23] On the penultimate page of *Pròdromòs* Altenberg has a fictitious girl say that in his correspondence he is "wirklich der einzige Peter, wie er leibt und lebt" [the only real living, breathing Peter: P 204]. Altenberg knew his letters were contiguous with his imaginative work, and at the time of his first major anthology in 1908 he was also negotiating for the publication of his correspondence. He even received an advance of 1,000 marks from Fischer. In preparation he recovered many letters from their addressees, promising strictest discretion when it came to publication, but this edition too never transpired.

After the venture folded, Altenberg touted the letters around in bundles, selling them according to length and content for ten, fifteen, or twenty crowns to anyone prepared to part with the cash.[24] Not surprisingly, much was lost, but much also remains, both in public libraries and personal collections. Over the years some correspondence has been published, most notably the complete letters to Karl Kraus,[25] but despite the bulk of the material in Glück's abortive edition surviving intact in private hands, imminent publication appears unlikely.

---

[20] "Briefe an St. Gr.," *Das Tagebuch* 1, no. 48 (1920): 1543–44. See also Gerald Stieg, *Der Brenner und Die Fackel*, (Salzburg: Otto Müller, 1976), 20.

[21] Rode, *Alban Berg*, (fn. 14), 27. Glück read from Altenberg letters on 8 January 1934 at the Vienna Architects' Association. The proceeds of the reading were for a headstone for Adolf Loos. The flier announced the autumn appearance of "Peter Altenberg. Die Briefsammlung, herausgegeben von Franz Glück. Mit vielen Bildern und Facsimiles." The publisher was to have been Anton Schroll, who had already brought out Kraus's anthology. Approximately 480pp long, it was to cost 7.50 Marks.

[22] Rode, *Alban Berg*, 27.

[23] WSB 137.034.

[24] "Briefe Peter Altenbergs. Mitgeteilt und eingeleitet von Arthur Roessler," WSB 156.465. It is not known whether this typescript was ever published. Roessler was close to Egon Schiele.

[25] Barker and Lensing, *Rezept* (fn. 14), 209–268.

In his *Unpolitische Erinnerungen* (1927) the German anarchist writer Erich Mühsam pondered on Altenberg's fast-waning star, echoing the arch-conservative Hofmannsthal on what constitutes the essence of the "Austrian" as opposed to the "German." Mühsam concludes that with his love of the specific, Altenberg has to be accounted the most Viennese of writers. He considers him the most concrete writer ever to have written in German, capturing the essence of Vienna in both its negative and positive aspects. For Mühsam, "Viennese" is the absence of abstraction, it is sensual but it is also limited, and hence he perceives a direct line from Altenberg's mode of thought via Karl Kraus and Alfred Polgar to the "concretisation of souls by the Viennese Sigmund Freud."[26] Altenberg's neglect had been bemoaned, however, long before Mühsam joined the chorus. It was already underway in 1904, when Kraus mocked a history of German literature for its neglect of his friend. Complaints continued in subsequent issues of *Die Fackel*, culminating in Kraus's cry of despair that the situation was grotesque but only to be expected in Austria.[27] The paradoxical nature of Altenberg's standing prior to World War I — universally known, widely read and considerably neglected — was further reinforced by his co-nomination with Arthur Schnitzler for the 1914 Nobel literature prize. The outbreak of war led to the suspension of the award, and when resumed in 1915 it went to neither Austrian, but to Romain Rolland.

Literary reputations are neither created nor destroyed by creative artists themselves, and Altenberg's work has not, in general, appealed to the academics and critics who remain the chief arbiters of literary merit. And in any case, Austrian letters have often, until quite recently, made slower headway in the consciousness of such critics than strictly "German" literature. In the Third Reich Altenberg's Jewishness put paid to whatever standing he still had, yet as the examples of Kafka and Schnitzler suggest, not all Austro-Jewish writers suffered the eclipse which Altenberg's reputation was already suffering well before Hitler came to power.[28] While his being both Austrian and Jewish may have worked against Altenberg's reputation, such factors do not alone explain his long confinement to the shadows of literary history.

As Mühsam well appreciated, Altenberg's work is uneven, but as he also realised, artists must be judged by their best and most original work. The self-styled impressionist Altenberg may sometimes have found it too easy to produce instant art, and as his health deteriorated, so his talent appeared increasingly diluted. Nevertheless, his capacity to rediscover the poetry in everyday existence, the "Märchen des Lebens" as he entitled one of his books, made an impact across the German-speaking world and indeed far beyond. The Paris-based Emil Szittya recalled how in the first decade of this century

---

[26] Erich Mühsam, *Ausgewählte Werke*, vol. 2, *Publizistik, Unpolitische Erinnerungen*, ed. Christlieb Hirte, (Berlin: Volk und Welt, 1978), 576.

[27] Karl Kraus, *Die Fackel*, 171 (1904): 24; 189 (1905): 21–22.

[28] Immediately after the end of the Second World War Alfred Döblin, author of *Berlin Alexanderplatz*, put Altenberg on his list of writers to be readmitted to the German pantheon (*Schriften zu Ästhetik, Poetik und Literatur*, [Olten and Freiburg: Walter, 1989], 391, 451.)

Altenberg was worshipped in Russia,[29] and Stanisław Przybyszewski recalls a similar Altenberg mania in Poland at the turn of the century.[30] By the time of his death, Altenberg had, by his own tally, been translated into a dozen or more languages.

What has probably determined the comparative neglect of Altenberg's work, given the importance of academic critics — rather than creative artists — in deciding relative merit, is his choice of genre. As early as 1922 the Viennese expressionist Albert Ehrenstein, lamenting the inequitable treatment of Austrian compared with German writers, reacted scathingly to the "half-blind critics" whose prejudices fostered the appalling anonymity which had befallen a writer who, together with Raimund and Nestroy, was one of the three original geniuses nineteenth-century Austria had produced. Crucial to this critical neglect, Ehrenstein claimed, was Altenberg's adherence to short forms instead of fabricating classical sonnets, tragedies in iambic pentameter or idiotic *Bildungsromane.*[31]

Altenberg's chief medium was the prose narrative, a vehicle traditional aesthetics had long considered inferior to other forms. Tragedy came first, followed by poetry. The upstart prose narrative was felt to degenerate too easily into mere entertainment.[32] Among the various prose forms, the novel garners most critical respect; the shorter forms are not generally considered so highly. At the very bottom comes the prose sketch, which Altenberg made his own.[33] Almost as disregarded as the prose sketch is the prose poem, a genre recognized today as being of central importance to European letters in the later nineteenth and early twentieth centuries. In January 1904, the poet Richard Dehmel complained of the failure to include Altenberg and other Viennese writers in a planned anthology of modern writing. Initially, however, Dehmel is less concerned with the omission of such deserving individual cases than with the failure to include the genre of prose poem per se.[34]

To dub Peter Altenberg predominantly a writer of prose poems is, however, to undervalue his sketches, anecdotes, aphorisms, miniature dramas,

---

[29] Emil Szittya, *Das Kuriositätenkabinett*, (Leipzig: Kurt Wolff, 1922), 286.

[30] Stanisław Przybyszewski, *Ferne komm ich her . . .* , (Leipzig and Weimar: Gustav Kiepenheuer, 1985), 283–284.

[31] *Juden in der deutschen Literatur*, ed. Gustav Krojanker, (Berlin: Welt-Verlag, 1922), 193. Reading this essay, Schnitzler wondered why authors writing about Altenberg always felt it necessary to attack his contemporaries in Vienna, (*Tagebuch 1920–1922*, [Vienna: Akademie der Wissenschaften, 1992], 381.)

[32] Charles Dickens writes ironically of the "superior poetic geniuses who scorn to take prose pains" in "Mugby Junction," *Christmas Stories*, (London: Chapman and Hall, 1894), 342.

[33] Typical of this dogmatically hierarchical approach to literature is that of Hamann and Hermand, writing forty years after Ehrenstein's strictures. They contend that the collapse of traditional genres, with its attendant disdain for thought, planning and composition, reaches its nadir in Altenberg. His sketches are devoid of anything novelistic or anecdotal, consisting merely of an entertaining fragment, an aphorism, or a series of snapshots: Richard Hamann and Jost Hermand, *Impressionismus*, (Munich: Nymphenburger Verlagshandlung, 1972), 219.

[34] Richard Dehmel, *Ausgewählte Briefe aus den Jahren 1902 bis 1920*, (Berlin: Fischer, 1923), 40.

homilies and diatribes. The vast majority are no more than a page or two long, the preferred style is the "Telegramm-Stil der Seele" [telegram style of the soul], a style meant to portray a person in a sentence, a spiritual experience on a page, a landscape in a word. Egon Friedell perceives in this brevity the very essence of Altenberg's quality as an artist: for Altenberg it is never a question of saying something as beautifully as possible, but as precisely and concisely as possible. He is interested not in beauty but in truth, being convinced that truth always contains beauty anyhow (B 211).

Altenberg frequently described his pieces as *Skizzen* or *Studien*, labels which hardly convey the flavour of these intensely compact vignettes at their best. Maybe they are better understood not in terms of conventional literary classification, but rather in the context of Schoenberg's miniatures from 1910 and 1911, composed when he was avidly reading Altenberg.[35] Along with the late piano compositions of Brahms, Altenberg's prose miniatures mark the very first examples of that aesthetic minimalism which was rapidly to become so marked a feature of Viennese art and thought around the turn of the century. Kraus, though not unbiased, once contended that a single piece of Altenberg's prose was worth as much as an entire Viennese novel.[36]

While at differing times and to differing degrees Altenberg's Jewishness, his Austrianness, his uneven output and his unconventional choice of genre have led to critical neglect, other, non-literary, factors may also be at work. One concerns the personal impression he made upon everyone he came into contact with. The fastidious Hofmannsthal may have found him hard to stomach, Schnitzler may have considered him a "Schubiak" [rogue],[37] but Altenberg was enormously well-liked. This is obvious from tributes in *Das Altenbergbuch*, where people sometimes bound only by deep and mutual loathing joined in homage to the dead artist.[38] What, however, had impressed many of them more than the caliber of Altenberg's writing was his quality as a personality, and over and beyond that, his representative status *qua* artist. What he stood for seemed often more important than his achievements as a writer. An extreme example of this attitude is shown in the reminiscences of the poet Richard von Schaukal. Strange as it may sound, he contends, there are poets without words, and he considers Altenberg as such a poet, existing beyond the bounds of language.[39]

[35] Kraus confirmed the affinity between the two by printing on opposite pages an Altenberg sketch and one of Schoenberg's settings of Stefan George's poetry from *Das Buch der hängenden Gärten*, *Die Fackel*, 300 (1910): 8–9. Schoenberg himself never set Altenberg to music.
[36] Kraus says he would swap a few lines of Altenberg for all the novels in a lending library (*Die Fackel*, 274 [1909]: 3.)
[37] Arthur Schnitzler, *Tagebuch 1920–1922*, (Vienna: Akademie der Wissenschaften, 1993), 381. In the same diary entry he also acknowledges that Altenberg was "ein außerordentlicher und wundervoller Dichter" [an extraordinary and wonderful poet].
[38] Here too Schnitzler strikes a dissenting note, remarking that neither Altenberg nor those around him come across particularly well in *Das Altenbergbuch* (*Tagebuch 1920–1922*, 270.)
[39] Richard Schaukal, *Über Dichter*, (Munich and Vienna: Langen and Müller, 1966), 84. At the back of his mind may have been Werther's assertion in the letter of 10 May that although he was

Altenberg's quirkiness did his standing little good either in his own day or in the eyes of posterity. Critics of Austro-German high art are not noted for their frivolity, and the Bohemian cult in Austria and Germany at the turn of the century has met with a very different response from that accorded *la Bohème* in France. Critical opinion has found it hard to credit someone as unusual and occasionally demented as Altenberg with producing important literature. Fittingly for one who lived, worked and died in the city of Freud, Altenberg has probably also met with critical disapproval because aspects of his personal behavior failed to meet accepted standards of social and sexual decorum. Not only did he eschew the comfortable bourgeois life to which he was born, his addiction to drugs and alcohol was common knowledge, as was his predilection for prostitutes and an openly expressed taste for young girls.

All too often the Altenberg legend has obscured his real achievement, but given the congruence between the public performance which was his life and the projection of this persona in literary texts, it is understandable how this has come about. Schaukal contended that Peter Altenberg the man was indistinguishable from Peter Altenberg the poet;[40] for Franz Blei Altenberg was a poet not only when he was writing, but in every aspect of his life. Yet because it was an artist's life led in an ostentatiously public fashion, it was an object of comic amusement for the bourgeois public. Out-of-kilter though this eccentric existence was with the norms of middle-class existence, neither Altenberg's life nor his art can be abstracted from their historical and cultural milieu. Kurt Hiller, an early leader of the expressionist movement in Germany, had no doubt as to Altenberg's significance for German letters as a whole, remarking he had more philosophy in one earlobe than Hegel had in his entire skull.[41] Less acerbically, Franz Blei asserted that only when there was nobody left to recall the sound of his wooden clogs on the paving stones of the Graben, when there was nobody who broke into a grin on hearing the name Peter Altenberg, would the "gentle humaneness of this figure celebrate its resurrection."[42] The goal of the book is to assist in this resurrection and to

---

unable to draw a line there had never been a greater painter (*Goethes Werke in zwei Bänden*, vol. 2, ed. Richard Friedenthal, [Munich: Knaur, 1953], 10).

[40] Schaukal, *Über Dichter*, 85.

[41] Kurt Hiller, *Leben gegen die Zeit*, vol. 1, *Logos*, (Reinbek bei Hamburg: Rowohlt, 1969), 101.

[42] Franz Blei, *Schriften in Auswahl*, (Munich: Biederstein, 1960), 282.

restore the artist styled by Georg Brandes as the "little genius"[43] to his proper place on the canvas of Viennese culture at the turn of the century.

---

[43] "Lille Genius" was how Brandes designated Altenberg in an essay of 1912. See *Georg Brandes und Arthur Schnitzler. Ein Briefwechsel,* ed. Kurt Bergel, (Bern: Francke, 1956), 177.

1: The Making of Peter Altenberg

Richard Engländer and Peter Altenberg

Peter Altenberg only officially came into being in 1896 when the thirty-seven year old Richard Engländer published his first book *Wie ich es sehe* under this pseudonym. Around this time the author continued signing letters with various permutations of the names Peter Altenberg and Richard Engländer, but in June 1896 a letter to S. Fischer was signed with the name which had appeared on the title page of *Wie ich es sehe* some two months earlier.[1] Thereafter Richard Engländer remained Peter Altenberg, for with the publication of his first book, the artist had conclusively displaced the burgher.

A month or so after the appearance of *Wie ich es sehe* Schnitzler muses in his diary on the book and the identity of its author. He is complimentary about the work, noting that Peter Altenberg was the same as "Richard E.," a man in whom people had earlier observed certain similarities with himself.[2] Although Schnitzler adjusted rapidly to the new name, he never forgot that Peter Altenberg was a fiction, the creation of a man who had found scant satisfaction in his given name and identity. Like Oscar Wilde, who was extremely popular in Vienna in the early 1890s, Altenberg regarded the manipulation of his persona as an art form in its own right, certainly one to stand comparison with his published writings. Indeed, so successful a creation was Peter Altenberg that it soon cast a shadow over the appreciation of the literature bearing the pseudonym.

The rejection of an earlier, given identity reveals much about the author's desire to shed the irksome trappings of a bourgeois background that meant little to his life as an artist. It is also symptomatic of a deeper trend within Austro-German letters around the turn of the century, when the constitution of the identity was a major theme and the adoption of a new name commonplace. Max Nordau, Felix Salten, Felix Dörmann, Egon Friedell, Alfred Polgar, Alfred Kerr, Maximilian Harden, Herwarth Walden, Max Reinhardt and Otto Brahm are all pseudonyms, and this list is by no means exhaustive. What all have in common is their Jewish ancestry, and for these writers it was more than a question of finding a name which sounded better for publication purposes. It has been well observed by Edward Timms that it was a matter of choosing a name which excluded those Jewish associations which

---

[1] Edward Timms, "Peter Altenberg — Authenticity or Pose," *Fin de Siècle Vienna*, ed. Gilbert J. Carr & Eda Sagarra, (Dublin: Trinity College, 1985), 131–132.

[2] Arthur Schnitzler, *Tagebuch 1893–1902*, (Vienna: Akademie der Wissenschaften, 1989), 192.

attached to their original names. The choice of a new name was thus part of a 'life-plan': to distance themselves from the Jewish community into which they had been born and to become assimilated into German culture. In many cases the change of name coincided with a formal renunciation of membership of the Jewish religious community and even with the decision to be received into the Catholic Church. The name Engländer (curious though this may seem to the English reader) had unmistakable Jewish associations, from which Altenberg was clearly distancing himself through the adoption of a new name."[3]

Altenberg's formal conversion took place in April 1900, but after his death an obituary in the German-nationalist anti-Semitic Viennese newspaper *Das Neue Reich* was quick to seize upon the change from a name which though Jewish-sounding had at least, it contended, been honest. Kraus published a collection of these obituaries,[4] but failed to remark that Altenberg's relationship with his Jewish antecedents had long been a source of inner tension for the writer himself. Stefan Großmann recalled that nothing was more calculated to give rise to one of Altenberg's temper tantrums than to remind him that he had been born Richard Engländer. These outbursts were virulently anti-Semitic in tone.[5]

Early published evidence of Altenberg's reactions to Judaism emerges in "Semitische Rasse," a title that reveals not so much a religious position as a socio-biological one: Jews have a *"perfide Lebens-Sehnsucht"* [*perfidious longing for life*: WT 275]. Life is for them simply a form of capital, but whereas others are content with a return of three percent, they want one hundred percent. Criticism of a "Jewish" attitude towards living is here expressed in the unmistakable language of a Christian anti-Semitism that goes back to Jesus' expulsion of the money lenders from the temple. Evidence of Altenberg's anti-Semitism emerges later in a letter to the actress Mitzi Thumb excoriating all his friends, with the exception of Egon Friedell, as either "Judenbuben ärgster Sorte oder verjudete Christen" [Jew-boys of the worst kind or jewified Christians].[6]

That Altenberg was well aware of the ambivalent position of the assimilated Jew emerges in "Rassenprobleme," a text which remained unpublished until after his death. In it he registers his puzzlement at the paradox of Viennese anti-Semitism. Vienna is the "Metropole des *organischen Antisemitismus der Welt*" [world metropolis of *organic anti-Semitism*], where Jewish artists in the variety theaters and cabarets who consciously accentuate their racial difference are genuinely popular. Altenberg ponders whether this may be because Jews stress their "otherness" in an amusing manner. For this they are liked by the "Viennese" (Altenberg's own quotation marks,) who do not like

---

[3] Timms, "Peter Altenberg — Authenticity or Pose", 131–132.

[4] Karl Kraus, *Die Fackel*, 546–550 (1920): 41–44.

[5] Stefan Großmann, *Ich war begeistert. Eine Lebensgeschichte*, (Berlin: Fischer, 1930), 109.

[6] *Kraus Hefte* 30, (1984): 88.

having to admit that they are just like themselves.[7] Thus Altenberg appears to see the problem of Viennese Jewry as residing in the fact that they are the same as the Gentile population yet different.[8] The Viennese wanted the Jews to be different, and obviously different, yet when they showed their difference in real life, as did the immigrant Jews in the Leopoldstadt, exotically dressed and speaking Yiddish, they were widely rejected. The Jews would never be totally assimilated even when they were completely acculturated. Peter Altenberg, the "fool" of *fin de siècle* Vienna, the Jew who elected to parody the artist as outsider rather than choose the protective clothing of the Viennese bourgeoisie, thus shows himself closer in his analysis to Theodor Herzl, the founding father of Zionism, than he would probably have appreciated.[9]

An intriguing light on Altenberg's relationship with Judaism is cast in the early sketch "Die Primitive" when the "revolutionary" Albert Königsberg, a semi-autobiographical figure, takes a prostitute back to his rooms. Whereas in later sketches Altenberg often refers to a reproduction of Klimt's "Schubert" which hung over his bed, the autobiographical revolutionary has a print of E. von Gebhardt's painting of the Last Supper over his. In this picture, Judas peers round a half-open door, but where Judas's face should be there is instead a gold medallion bearing the features of the Jewish philosopher Spinoza. The revolutionary comments that Spinoza wipes out Judas's disgrace and makes amends for things by covering him with pure gold ["deckt ihn mit seinem puren Golde, wetzt die Scharte aus": WS 123]. As she prepares to leave, the prostitute asks for the medallion, the revolutionary complies, and as he releases the medallion she sees Judas underneath. She reacts instantly, with the words "Auch ein Zerstörer" [Also a destroyer]. To which Königsberg retorts that everyone has a Judas in him, betraying, selling and killing the "Other," the ideal human being within us all. After she has departed with the Spinoza medallion, he hangs the picture back on the wall:

> Und Judas stand bleich in der halbgeöffneten Thüre, durch welche dämmerndes Frühlicht schimmerte. Der Morgen brach an - - -.
> Es war aber nicht der Morgen, der anbrach - - es war die Nacht, die hereinbrach! (WS 128)

> [And Judas stood pale in the half-open doorway, through which the first rays of early light shone. Morning was breaking - - -
> But it was not morning which broke - - it was the night which was falling!]

Despite this intriguing example, Altenberg only rarely confronts the problem of Jewishness in his published writings. In correspondence, or in the scabrous pseudo-obituary "Leo Ebermann, à Kritische Studie" it is a differ-

---

[7] Barker and Lensing, *Rezept*, 36.

[8] Marthe Robert, *From Oedipus to Moses. Freud's Jewish Identity*, trans. Ralph Mannheim, (New York: Anchor Press, 1976), 17–18.

[9] Nike Wagner, "Theodor Herzl oder das befreite Wien," *Die Zeit*, 5 April 1985, 73–74.

ent story.[10] Here we meet a man neurotically hostile to Jews and Jewishness. Nonetheless, in contrast to the anti-Semitism of the private Altenberg, his books mostly portray the world of the well-to-do middle classes in which secular Viennese Jews pursue a life-style indistinguishable from that of their Gentile fellow-citizens. In his memoirs the music critic Max Graf, father of Freud's Young Hans, recalls that besides making the acquaintance of Schoenberg and Zemlinsky, Altenberg-Engländer had drawn attention to himself in the cafés of Vienna in the early 1890s through his penchant for delivering Christian homilies at the top of his voice.[11]

This is reflected in the sketch "Wahrheit" from the early cycle "Aus einem Skizzenbuch" where Christ fits into Altenberg's quasi-Haeckelian evolutionary philosophy not just as the pinnacle of what has been achieved, but also as an example of what can be aimed for. Christ, the most humane God, the most divine human being, is quite simply the way, the truth and the life.[12] Such statements may indicate that Altenberg's conversion was more than a matter of convenience.[13]

Whatever Altenberg's deepest beliefs may have entailed, it was not merely anti-Semites who never forgot his origins. For fellow-Jews also he remained Jewish. Albert Ehrenstein considered Altenberg's Christian burial his last, bitter joke;[14] and what is one to make of the municipal grave of honour that Altenberg's non-Jewish friend Adolf Loos designed for him in Vienna's Zentralfriedhof? The ostentatiously large wooden crucifix, still towering to-day above adjacent monuments, is intended to make a public statement which none should overlook. Yet what Peter Gay noted in his consideration of Jewish culture in Berlin counted equally for Vienna:

> Everyone understood — everyone, philo-Semite and anti-Semite alike — that even those former Jews who had repudiated Judaism by religious conversion to Christianity, or legal disaffiliation from the Jewish community, were still somehow Jews."[15]

---

[10] First published in Barker and Lensing, *Rezept*, 36.

[11] Max Graf, *Jede Stunde war erfüllt*, (Vienna and Frankfurt: Forum, n. d.), 149.

[12] Barker and Lensing, *Rezept*, 69.

[13] In his panoramic novel *Barbara oder die Frömmigkeit* (Berlin, Vienna and Leipzig: Paul Zsolnay, 1929) Franz Werfel chose as one of his central figures a tortured intellectual named Engländer. Riven between the rival claims of Judaism and Christianity, out of which he desires to create a grand synthesis, Alfred Engländer, like Peter Altenberg, suffers a mental breakdown, and ends up as did his namesake in the Steinhof asylum in Vienna.

[14] Albert Ehrenstein, "Peter Altenberg," *Juden in der deutschen Literatur*, ed. Gustav Krojanker, (Berlin: Welt-Verlag, 1922), 197.

[15] Peter Gay, *Freud, Jews and other Germans: Masters and Victims in modernist Culture*, (New York: Oxford University Press, 1978), 174. The widest ranging and most acute discussion of the problems of Jewish identity in Vienna is found in Jacques Le Rider, *Modernity and crises of identity. Culture and society in fin-de-siècle Vienna*, trans. Rosemary Morris, (New York: Continuum, 1993).

Family Album of a Viennese Merchant's Son

Although Peter Altenberg only came about with the creation of works bearing that name, he never turned his back entirely on his life as Richard Engländer. Indeed, he frequently wrote about pre-Altenberg days, but to what extent this results in a fragmentary autobiography of Richard Engländer, and to what extent it provides only a stylized biography of the Altenberg persona is difficult to determine. Whatever the exact relationship between poetry and truth, Altenberg's autobiographical writings are a form he excelled in and they constitute a significant part of his oeuvre. Noting the request by an important newspaper that he should write his memoirs, he pointed out that the myriad impressions in his books already constituted such a work (LA 1).

Richard Engländer was born on 3 March 1859 in the second district of Vienna where the majority of Jewish families then lived. Peter Altenberg was, however, at pains to show he came from an established and integrated family, not to be confused with immigrants from the east. His father Moriz Engländer was a "k. u. k. Großhändler" [wholesale merchant by appointment to the court] and Richard's early life outwardly conformed to that of other wealthy Jewish merchants' sons who figured so prominently in Viennese cultural and intellectual life from the late 1880s until the destruction of their community began in the 1930s. At no point in his autobiographical writings, randomly scattered across many books, does Altenberg openly admit to a Jewish heritage. On the other hand, regular recourse to Yiddish suggests a willingness to reveal his linguistic heritage in the interest of creative expression.

Altenberg retained a life-long affection for his father, an unconventional man whom some of Altenberg's contemporaries considered far more original than the poet himself. Siegfried Trebitsch, a writer who was responsible for introducing George Bernard Shaw to German-speaking audiences, considered Altenberg but a pale imitation of Moriz Engländer:

> He was almost always in the highest of spirits. But once he said to me, not without making a deep impression on me: 'My son Peter goes and prints all the things I have been saying all these years . . . . If I had dreamt that the things I say and write to my friends would ever be worth so much, I would have published them under my own name. It's all very well for a son — for plagiarism of one's own father doesn't really count as plagiarism. The son is only making his father's arm longer when he touches upon the same things.'[16]

Peter Altenberg, on the other hand, records how wags would point out Herr Engländer in the street and declare that the old man was suffering from a congenital condition passed down from his son (WT 9).

Stefan Großmann recalls that for all his family's creature comforts, Moriz was hardly a thrusting businessman, while his son portrays him as anything

---

[16] Siegfried Trebitsch, *Chronicle of a Life*, trans. Eithne Wilkins and Ernst Kaiser, (London: Heinemann, 1953), 80.

but a ruthlessly ambitious or overweening figure from the Victorian stereotype. A voracious consumer of French literature, the father encouraged his son's artistic development in the most conventional of ways, through music lessons (LA 7–8). Consistent with the family's wealthy life-style, young Richard was taught violin by Rudolf Zöllner, later to become mayor of Baden near Vienna, but then still a fiddle player in the Court Opera Orchestra. There even seems to have been a hint of Franz Grillparzer's "Der arme Spielmann" about the young Engländer, for he was marvellously expressive in his playing but also utterly lacking in technique (LA 8).[17] Altenberg recounts his teacher declaring of him that he was "Ein Genie ohne Fähigkeiten" [A genius with no abilities: LA 8], lacking everything that was needed for life.

As recalled by the sick and aging poet, the freedom allowed Richard by his father was more reminiscent of the later twentieth than the nineteenth century. When asked whether he was proud of his son, Moriz Engländer reportedly replied that as he was not particularly upset that he had been a good-for-nothing for thirty years, he did not feel particularly honored now he was a poet: "Ich gab ihm Freiheit. Ich wusste, dass es ein Va-banque-Spiel sei. Ich rechnete auf seine Seele!" [I gave him freedom. I knew it was all or nothing. I counted on his soul!: WT 5].

Suspicion that Altenberg's later autobiographical sketches err on the side of poetry rather than truth is confirmed by the "Revolutionary" cycle in *Wie ich es sehe*. There he evokes the more radical alter ego of Albert Königsberg, which is in all likelihood rather closer to the reality of Richard Engländer than the personality depicted by the older Peter Altenberg. Most revealing of all is the sketch "Familienleben." This appears only in the first edition of *Wie ich es sehe* and reproduces the familial constellations of the Engländer family in a way apparently too close for comfort. The father comes across as a man of conventional tastes, uncomprehending of his son's work, wishing simply that he would write a decent feuilleton. The mother is described as a waspish, disappointed woman with indestructibly fine features whose beauty had petrified into an "aristocratic look" (WS 108). She has a low opinion of her eldest son, a figure who can confidently be identified as Richard Engländer-Peter Altenberg. He in turn makes no attempt to veil his contempt for polite society with its superficiality, self-deception and lack of introspection. The open tensions revealed here are more concealed in later works, where an increasingly sanitized version of real events prevails. It can be no accident, however, that "Familienleben," at nearly eight pages the longest of all Altenberg's published sketches, was excised from subsequent editions of *Wie ich es sehe*.

Nowhere is this sanitization more obvious than when Altenberg sketches (or invents?) his relationship with the delicate, frequently ailing, gazelle-slim Paulina Engländer. During childhood his feelings for her were fanatical, eat-

[17] The title of one of Altenberg's last sketches "Sunti certi denique fines <Horaz>" (N 126) is also cited in Grillparzer's novella about the artist who is all soul and no technique. Horace's line can be translated as "Everything has its limits."

ing away at him as though he was an unhappy suitor pining for his beloved. Already over fifty when he recalled this incestuously-tinged mother-worship, the very act of writing turns him into a frightened child, crying out to her beyond the grave:

> Ich sah sie an und war voll übertriebener Zärtlichkeit, als ob ich noch überhaupt bewußtlos in ihrem Schoße läge, von ihren Kräften innerlichst behütet, genährt, gepflegt, so vorzeitig herausgestellt in eine Welt, in die ich *noch nicht* hineingehörte! Mama! Mama! (S 41)

> [I looked at her and was full of exaggerated tenderness, as though I still lay unconscious in her womb, guarded to the depths of my being by her powers, fed, nurtured, so prematurely ejected into a world in which I did *not yet* belong! Mama! Mama!]

In a sense Altenberg never stopped being a child, as was demonstrated by his feelings for the teenaged Paula Schweitzer. His first contact with her came on his birthday in 1914, and almost to the end she remained central to his emotional life, even after her marriage and move to Innsbruck in 1917. In "An Paula," published in 1916, he writes of himself as "ein merkwürdig zartes altes Kindchen" [remarkably gentle old child] and of Paula as "eine merkwürdig liebvolle junge Mama!" [a remarkably loving young mama!: NF 13]. He was then fifty-six, Paula nineteen. Such passages lay bare the emotional retardation, infantilism even, of the adult who despite numerous infatuations never found a woman to replace his mother.

Paulina Engländer's feelings for her eldest seem to have been almost as intense as his for her. When ten years old, Richard succumbed to a foot infection which dragged on for a year, and for which he was treated by Theodor Billroth, the great surgeon and intimate of Johannes Brahms, recently appointed to the Chair of Surgery at Vienna. During the entire illness, so Altenberg claims, his mother kept her bed in his room and slept beside him. In the afternoons she would sing Schubert songs in the room next door. As an adult he idolized Schubert, and it has been suggested that when composing his early prose poems in cyclical form, he was trying to emulate the compositional techniques of the Schubert song-cycles.[18]

In a way reminiscent of young Törless at the end of Musil's first novel, the smell of the mother's perfume haunted Altenberg in adulthood, acting as a barrier between the poet and fulfilled relationships with other women (NA 159). Sometime after his mother's death at the age of sixty-five on 3 November 1902, Altenberg revisited his birthplace and imagined her agony as she gave birth to him. The attempt to reconstruct her sufferings induced guilt in the son, whose relationship with his once-adored mother had come to grief many years before. In "Das Sterben" (P 186) he makes no attempt to hide his contempt for his dying mother's irredeemably bourgeois outlook,

---

[18] Peter Wagner, "Peter Altenbergs Prosadichtung. Untersuchungen zur Thematik und Struktur des Frühwerks," Dr.phil diss., Münster, 1965. Altenberg himself draws attention to another link between himself and Schubert, for he believed the source of Schubert's creativity lay like his own in an unrequited love for a young girl (B 73).

but here the poet too betrays an inability to slough off the expectations of family and class. The forty-eight year old Altenberg, bald as an egg and gone to seed, displays in the remembrance of the mother who had given him his intelligence, his soul and a healthy body a guilt similar to that which Kafka felt in respect to his father. He asks that peace may be with her.

Losing his mother's love plainly disturbed him and explains why in later recollection childhood so often assumes the status of a lost paradise. *Märchen des Lebens* was published at a time of increasing gloom, yet "Die Kinderzeit" (ML 55) is a gem of selective observation and recollection, the product of an increasingly haunted and disappointed man looking back not on an age of innocence — he remains too clear-minded to idealize the past completely — but at least on a time when happiness was possible. Happiness, perhaps revealingly, was found not in the city but in the alpine forests and meadows of the Semmering, far from the cares and demands of everyday living.[19] And woven into all these apparently disparate fond memories is the figure of his mother. That happiness cannot be forever is the final import of the piece. Everyday existence is deadening both for the child and the mother (ML 59).

Paulina Engländer's cosy relationship with her son ended abruptly in 1883 when the psychiatrist Ludwig Schlager diagnosed Richard's constitutional incapability of fulfilling the norms of middle-class life, advising the family against exposing him to undue stress. He then rapidly grew away from his family, sleeping by day with the window wide open so that the noise from the street would dampen the domestic sounds which so disturbed him. He also began drinking, not from any great desire for alcohol, but simply to enable him to sleep during the daylight hours. Altenberg-Engländer's bat-like existence had now begun.[20]

As Altenberg grew increasingly anxious about his own mortality, the more he felt he had to make his peace with the remaining members of his family — his brother Georg and sisters Gretl and Marie. These sketches are, however, frequently overshadowed by despair about the future, and a depressed awareness of what he considered his own failure. As he grew older, it was to his misogynistic younger brother Georg that he probably remained closest. They even shared living quarters for a time between 1898 and 1902, although their relationship became strained when the gift of a large dog from Adolf Loos was more than Georg Engländer could stand.[21] At this point Altenberg took up residence in the Hotel London, an institution in the Wallnerstraße in the First District of Vienna. Little better than a brothel, it remained his address for years. Georg Engländer had by now taken over the family business, but he was as inept as his brother and father, and his bank-

[19] The Munich writer Max Halbe considered Altenberg the most urban writer who ever lived and an "enemy of nature" (*Jahrhundertwende*, [Munich and Vienna: Langen and Müller, 1976], 211.) See also W. G. Sebald, "Le Paysan de Vienne. Über Peter Altenberg," *Die Neue Rundschau* 100, no. 1 (1989): 75–95.

[20] A caricature of Altenberg as a bat by Richard Beer-Hofmann and sent to Arthur Schnitzler survives in Beer-Hofmann's papers at the State University of New York, Binghamton.

[21] Camillo Schaefer, *Peter Altenberg. Ein biographischer Essay*, (Vienna: Freibord, 1981), 26.

ruptcy in 1904 would cause Altenberg severe financial embarrassment. With it his most regular source of income dried up.[22] An avid reader of his brother's works, Georg Engländer was the dedicatee of *Was der Tag mir zuträgt*, and to the end of his life Altenberg trumpeted his praises.

That reality was occasionally different from poetic recollection emerges from the circumstances of Altenberg's confinement in the Steinhof asylum in 1912–13. Georg Engländer was instrumental in having him removed from everyday life, and became the butt of Altenberg's wrath and frustration. Yet once Altenberg was released in the spring of 1913 and taken to Venice by Adolf Loos, postcard after postcard to Georg Engländer revealed the depth of Altenberg's affection.[23] A posthumously-published sketch reveals his feelings about the family as an institution, as opposed to his affection for individual family members, and records his final debt of gratitude to his younger brother. Without recourse to "den althergebrachten stupiden Familien-Unsinn" [silly traditional family nonsense] Altenberg records how Georg has always been a gentleman towards him, but can only put this down to a "eine *brüderliche Krankheit*. Daß er existiert, genügt mir . . . " [a *fraternal sickness*. That he exists is sufficient for me: N 93].

This contrasts starkly with one of the last pieces Altenberg ever wrote, dated 23 December 1918 and committed to paper just an hour before Christmas Eve was ushered in. He acknowledges the end of his life as a poet and human being before launching into an indictment of his parents, which at the eleventh hour articulates what he perceives as the truth of his family affairs. No longer wishing to protest a public fiction which improved on reality, the dying poet apostrophizes his parents as the source of all his woes: "O kranke Eltern eines kränkeren Sohnes" [Oh sick parents of a sicker son: N 141]. His life and fate had been inescapably determined by what he inherited from each of them. The curse of being different and his pathological brain were the accursed gifts of pathological parents, people who should never have been permitted to put children onto this earth. His inheritance was the compulsive search for truth and romanticism which had consumed all his energies, turning him into a living corpse before the sixtieth birthday he would never see. His parents had made him the poet he was (N 140).

The Naming of Peter Altenberg

As the son of a wealthy and assimilated Jewish family, Richard Engländer received an education typical of the monied classes in late nineteenth-century Austria. Instead of attending primary school, he was educated by tutors at home. For his secondary education he went to the Wiener Akademische Gymnasium, where Grillparzer had gone to school and which shortly after

---

[22] Großmann, *Ich war begeistert*, 107.

[23] Over twenty postcards to Georg are preserved in the Galerie St. Etienne (GSE). Extensive correspondence in the private Werner Kraft-Archiv (WKA) demonstrates the centrality of Georg in Altenberg's life.

Engländer was there had on its roll not only Schnitzler but also Hof-mannsthal, Friedell and Beer-Hofmann. By Altenberg's own admission, his school career was undistinguished. Asked to write an essay in his *Matura* examination on the influence of the New World upon the Old, he claims to have answered in one word: potatoes (LA 2). This early foray into miniaturism did not impress his teachers and he failed the exam, eventually passing it a year later at the Theresianum, another of Vienna's outstanding schools.

After Engländer obtained his Matura in 1878 there followed years of inconclusive study — medicine and botany in Vienna, the book trade in Stuttgart, law in Graz — culminating in his father's seeking medical help to determine the causes of his son's lack of purposeful endeavor. The doctor pronounced him a wreck, though his official diagnosis was over-excitability of the nervous system. At the end of his life, looking back on earlier times, Altenberg called on a favorite piece of pseudo-medical jargon to explain his failure to achieve academic respectability: his inability to learn, he claimed, was "pathological" (LA 3).

Early in this period of desultory failure a decisive episode occurred in Richard Engländer's life. When aged about twenty, he spent some time with an intellectually gifted school friend in Altenberg, a small settlement on the Danube near St. Andrä-Wördern, a few miles upstream from Vienna. There the he met his friend's thirteen-year-old sister Bertha, the daughter of Zacharias Konrad Lecher, editor of Vienna's leading newspaper the *Neue Freie Presse*, president of the writers' organization Concordia, and host to one of Vienna's most prestigious Carnival balls. Lecher's wife Luise was a formidable bluestocking who wrote weepy installment novels for Peter Rosegger's *Heimgarten* and generally encouraged the presence of budding young artists at the summer establishment they kept in Altenberg. The Lechers had three sons and four daughters, all of them younger than the boys, and of the girls, Bertha was herself the youngest.[24]

The way the boys treated their sisters was probably an accurate reflection of current assumptions about the role and status of women, something Altenberg would challenge in the *Frauenkult* which features strongly in his early writing. They expected the girls to act as servants, removing their shoes, making their beds and serving them their meals, all for a few pennies a week. Not content with this, the young gentlemen considered it beneath their dignity to be served by mere females. A gentleman required a gentleman's gentleman, therefore they gave their sisters male monickers: Emma, Hedwig and Hilda were dubbed Emmlinger, Hedlinger and Hildinger, while Bertha became Peter. The young Engländer, who in the meanwhile had fallen in love with Bertha-Peter, was outraged both at her treatment by one of his school friends and by the denial of her identity and gender by the males around her. He reacted in two ways, one of which was conventional and predictable: he composed poems full of wrathful indignation.

---

[24] Albert Lorenz, *Wenn der Vater mit dem Sohne*, (Vienna: Deuticke, 1952), 79, suggests there were nine children but names only four daughters and three sons. Altenberg's sister Marie Mauthner mentions five girls (NE 16).

His other reaction was the first and most decisive step in the forging of a new identity through which to confront the world around him, not least in matters of sexual identity. By casting aside Richard Engländer for the mask of Peter Altenberg, a mask which was eventually to become more of a "reality" than Richard Engländer ever had been, the artist confirmed his solidarity with the female victims of his society. The name Altenberg he settled upon as a lasting reminder of the place where this act of identification first took place; Peter he adopted out of sympathy for the object of that humiliation and an awareness of the plight of women in a male-dominated world. The fact that the name Peter was first carried by a woman rather than a man points, however, to underlying ambiguities in the sexual constitution of the person who became Peter Altenberg.

Around this time there was a similar case in a very different cultural milieu to Hapsburg Vienna, that of late Victorian Britain, where the Scottish author William Sharp was publishing his successful Celtic tales under the pseudonym Fiona Macleod. Although it was common knowledge that Sharp and Macleod were one and the same, Sharp never admitted to his dual identity. Richard Engländer did not go so far as to adopt such an unambiguously feminine literary identity as Sharp; nevertheless, a decade before Wilhelm Fließ and Otto Weininger stressed the fundamental bisexuality of all humans, Richard Engländer responded to the sexual ambiguities both within himself and his society by adopting a pseudonym which, though it was to outward appearances masculine and eminently Gentile, nevertheless concealed a self-acknowledged feminine component. Many years later in a letter to Karl Kraus he would express his longing to possess female genitalia,[25] while even in his review of Wie ich es sehe Hofmannsthal hinted at something ambiguous in Altenberg's sexuality (AB 155). Apostrophizing Altenberg after his death, Adolf Loos exclaimed that in his male body he bore a feminine soul.[26] Altenberg himself acknowledged this feminine component in a letter to Kraus, exclaiming that in him both a man and a woman had gone missing: a hermaphrodite with no external characteristics, he nevertheless felt that both sexes were present in him in their "besten tiefsten Essenzen vorhanden, ohne je zu Kraft und Friede zu gelangen" [best, deepest essentials, without ever achieving power and contentment].[27]

Late in life Altenberg told the young Stella Klein-Löw, later prominent in Austrian Socialist educational politics, that he adopted his artistic name because he did not care to be associated with the English. Unlike him, they laid great stress on external appearances. Asked why he settled on the name Altenberg, he replied that it was because there had been a House of Altenberg whose permission he had sought before adopting their title.[28] This, of course, is sheer whimsy. In reality, the adoption of the name Peter Altenberg indi-

[25] Barker and Lensing, Rezept, 243.

[26] Ibid., 333.

[27] Ibid., 243.

[28] "Im Gespräch mit Stella Klein-Löw," Falter 12, 16 August 1984.

cates a wish to mythologize the days of his childhood and youth and to avoid
the social, financial and sexual responsibilities of the adult male as understood
by the community into which he was born. He came to detest the male role
in heterosexual encounters, calling it an artistically worthless "Pissoir-Ange-
legenheit" [urinal affair]. Altenberg was equally cynical about the institution
of marriage, and in an (unsent) letter to Karl Kraus he imagines how a bourgeois husband would blithely reveal his attitude towards women:

> Ausspruch eines glücklichen Ehegatten: "Mein lieber Altenberg, *eine jede
> Frau* ist eine *perfecte Hure*, bis auf die *wenigen Ausnahmen*, die es *nicht*
> sind! Und *Die* sind es *erst recht*."[29]

> [Saying of a happy husband: "My dear Altenberg, *each and every woman* is
> a perfect whore, except for the *few exceptions* who are not. And precisely
> *those* are the ones *who are*."]

For there to be male happiness within marriage, woman has to be down-
graded into a function of the market economy. The radical feminism manifested in this contemptuous depiction of the "happily married man" is,
however, by no means the whole story.

Although Altenberg despises the masculinism of bourgeois culture, both
in its social and sexual guises, and although his sympathy for exploited
women is genuine, it would be facile to regard him as a spokesman for
women's rights as understood today. Despite his veneration of "Gottes
Kunstwerk 'Frauenleib'" [the divine work of art which is a 'woman's body':
WT 7], Altenberg's love of woman is not primarily for her own sake. Hers is
a specific role in an evolutionary concept of society, geared to bringing to
perfection not her own existence, but that of the "New Man," the antithesis
of the detested bourgeois male: a decent woman ought to know at every
moment how she might help the male in his "tragically difficult" existence.
That should be her sole "womanly honor." Everything else is merely the
massaging of vanity, selfishness, lack of shame, idiocy and whoredom. It is
the sacred mission of woman to help and serve the man wrestling in the
"labyrinth of this life." Everything else about her is "*teuflisch* und *hinderlich*"
[a *diabolical hindrance*], for the world is thought out according to "God's
most inspired plans," and not according to "der *Frauen teuflisch rückständi-
gen Plänen!*" [the *diabolically retrograde plans of women!*] August Strindberg
succumbed to woman, the poet concludes, but not Peter Altenberg! (VI 26–
27).

This perception of woman as body rather than intellect is most reminiscent of the writer who epitomises Viennese misogyny: Otto Weininger. Yet
Weininger's *Geschlecht und Charakter* did not appear until 1903, so rather
than Altenberg reflecting the impact of Weininger, as Friedell suggests when
calling Altenberg's *Frauenkult* the positive side of Weininger's philosophy, it
may be that Weininger learned something from Altenberg.[30] Given Alten-

---

[29] Barker and Lensing, *Rezept*, 27.

[30] Egon Friedell, *Ecce Poeta*, (Berlin: Fischer, 1912), 178.

berg's widespread impact, this would not be surprising. Later in his career Altenberg had not only read Weininger's work, but had thoroughly assimilated his ideas on women. In *Vita Ipsa* Altenberg quotes directly (albeit inaccurately) from *Geschlecht und Charakter*,[31] and in an undated letter to Kraus he writes that he was inescapably a pupil of Strindberg and Weininger, with whom he was of a like mind.[32] Many to whom Altenberg was closest, such as Kraus, responded equally positively to Weininger's ideas.[33] Adolf Loos's first wife, the actress Lina Loos, wrote that far from venerating women, Altenberg hated them in the same way he hated rich people who did not know how to spend their riches. In their turn, women passed him by, thus he was compelled to cast in letters those things which remained beyond his actual experience.[34]

Weininger claims that all people have two antithetical sides to them, the essentially positive male aspect, and the negative feminine one, which in Weininger's terms is synonymous with the Jewish. According to Weininger, his day was not only the most Jewish, but also the most effeminate of all time.[35] The apparently widespread association of Jew and Woman was seen by Freud as ensuing from the Gentile view of the Jew as "female" insofar as circumcision was a symbolic castration. The misogynist in Altenberg may thus be a form of self-hatred, hatred of himself as Jew, to apply Theodor Lessing's notion of "Jewish Self-hatred." Altenberg's misogyny would in this case represent a complex reaction to his original Jewish identity while it was also a feature of the masculinist non-Jewish bourgeoisie to which, through his choice of pseudonym, he aspired. His devastation at Weininger's suicide in 1903 is vividly portrayed in the memoirs of the Polish-German *décadent* Stanisław Przybyszewski who recounts how Altenberg apparently rampaged through the cafés of Vienna, calling him a criminal and accusing him, or rather the influence of his *Totenmesse*, of causing Weininger's suicide.[36]

Altenberg's sister Marie Mauthner recalled how until the end of his life her brother kept a picture in his room of the adolescent Bertha-Peter. The effect was of a shrine, for in front of the icon, reminiscent of a Holbein madonna, was a small lamp illuminating Bertha's face and reminding Altenberg of his gratitude to the girl who had triggered the poet in him (NE 18). The religious symbolism of this shrine to his lost love — but also in a very real sense to *himself*— is striking. In his necrologue, Alfred Kerr remarked that

[31] VI 206–207. Compare also VI 158 with Otto Weininger, *Geschlecht und Charakter*, (Vienna and Leipzig: Braumüller, 1903), 142.

[32] Barker and Lensing, *Rezept*, 262.

[33] Nike Wagner, *Karl Kraus und die Erotik der Wiener Moderne*, (Frankfurt: Suhrkamp, 1982).

[34] Kosler, *Peter Altenberg*, 107–108.

[35] Cited in Barbara Z. Schoenberg, "'Woman-Defender' and 'Woman-Offender', Peter Altenberg and Otto Weininger. Two literary stances vis-à-vis Bourgeois Culture in the Viennese 'Belle Epoque'," *Modern Austrian Literature* 20, no. 2 (1987): 63.

[36] Stanisław Przybyzcewski, *Ferne komme ich her . . .* , (Leipzig and Weimar: Gustav Kiepenheuer, 1985), 191.

Altenberg's coffin should only have been carried by fifteen-year old girls.[37] Altenberg's love of adolescent girls with markedly "boyish" features points to a barely concealed homosexual pedophile response, confirmed by the existence in typescript of a pornographic poem celebrating the pleasures of "des Knaben Schwänzlein" [the lad's little prick].[38]

Simultaneously with his seminal emotional experience with Bertha-Peter, Richard Engländer developed other quirks central to his self-perception as a writer. Mauthner recalled how he adopted a milk-based diet and ate large quantities of raw eggs, all the while making propaganda for his diet. Such crazes were then commonplace, especially among young Wagnerites. She also remembered how in 1883, the year of the *Wagner Feier* in Vienna to mark the composer's death, Altenberg-Engländer not only followed Wagner's nutritional fads, but sang *fortissimo* tunes from Wagner's operas. His lasting enthusiasm was reflected in the many Wagnerian references in later works. Like lots of other young Jews in Vienna, Engländer seems to have been unperturbed by the growing anti-Semitism of the pro-Wagner, pro-German factions, a racial hostility encouraged by Wagner's own well-advertised dislike of Jews. Just as Engländer's infatuation with Bertha Lecher provided a matrix for subsequent passions, and explains much about the work of the man presenting himself as Peter Altenberg, so too his early views on eating reform grew into an *idée fixe*, reaching their apogee in *Pròdròmòs* (1906).

In keeping with the "fiction" of Peter Altenberg as opposed to the "reality" of Richard Engländer, the later writer happily stylized these early days when writing what purported to be an autobiography. With characteristic sense of failure, he recounts how at the at the age of twenty-three he idolized a wonderful girl of thirteen, wept his nights away, got engaged to her, became a bookseller in Stuttgart to earn quick money in order to look after her. But it all came to nothing, for nothing ever became of his dreams (WT 10). In an intriguing parallel with Altenberg, the founding father of Zionism Theodor Herzl, (b. 1860) also fell in love at the age of twenty-three with a girl of thirteen. It has been suggested that for him too this experience was a determining factor in his whole subsequent development, in his case away from literature and journalism. Herzl even wrote about this experience in prose reminiscent of Altenberg.[39]

An inscribed photograph of Bertha in Altenberg's hand reveals she was thirteen in 1880, making him not twenty-three but twenty-one at the time of his infatuation. His stay in Stuttgart was probably related to his sexual fantasies rather than his scholastic calamities, and hence it has a poetic rather than prosaic truth. In fact, the chronology of Engländer's life around this period is not obvious. The most plausible sequence is that he fell in love with

---

[37] Alfred Kerr, "Dem toten Peter Altenberg," *Die Neue Rundschau* 30, no. 3 (1919): 335.

[38] GSE

[39] Nike Wagner, "Theodor Herzl und Karl Kraus," *Theodor Herzl und das Wien des Fin de Siècle*, ed. Norbert Leser, (Vienna: Böhlau, 1987), 168.

Bertha in 1879, and went to Stuttgart later that year. The details are not important: what counts is the emotional experience, affecting Richard Engländer to the extent that it became linked in his psyche with the very notion of his identity as a person and artist.

Although there may be doubts about the chronology of Engländer's infatuation with Bertha-Peter, there should be none about his capacity to feel misery and disappointment. In the biographical memoir in *Was der Tag mir zuträgt*, as so often elsewhere, we gain a strong impression that the writer regards unhappiness as a source of strength and as a means to greater intensity of feeling and imagination. Later he was to remark of a nephew that he lacked "das Glück, unglücklich zu sein" [the good fortune of being unhappy: ML 120].

The loss of innocence with the onset of maturity and its accompanying social expectations were themes which always exercised Altenberg. His infatuation with Bertha-Peter marked the end of childhood and youth, though Engländer's theoretical innocence had ended at the age of fourteen when he was seduced in time-honored manner by a beautiful twenty-one year old maidservant (NF 114). For the later writer, childhood remained the time when the self and nature were in wondrous and innocent accord, above all in the mountains and meadows of Lower Austria, at Payerbach and Reichenau, on the sides of the Raxalpe and the Schneeberg.[40]

The early 1880s were hard times for Richard Engländer. Although he was well-thought of by the Lechers, a long-term relationship with Bertha was out of the question. For a family like the Lechers marriage was a serious matter, and for all their regard for the arts, a neurasthenic young Jew was not a potential son-in-law. More to their tastes was Adolf Lorenz, who married their daughter Emma. He was a Silesian immigrant to Vienna, who achieved world fame as an orthopaedic surgeon, had his memoirs commissioned by Scribner's in New York, and came within a hair's breadth of winning the Nobel Prize by devising a cure for children with congenital dislocation of the hip.[41] Bertha Lecher married the anti-clerical pedagogue Eduard Jordan, a man almost twenty years older than herself and a thorn in the side of the Viennese Christian Social leader Karl Lueger.[42] Bertha Jordan became a teacher, and for a time taught her celebrated nephew, the Nobel laureate Konrad Lorenz. She died in 1953.

[40] A few decades later this same area meant much to the Viennese novelist Heimito von Doderer, one of whose very earliest works, "Fortunatina und die Löwin. Ein Märchen" is a reworking of Altenberg's "Der Hofmeister" (A 5). See: Heimito von Doderer, *Die sibirische Klarheit: Texte aus der Gefangenschaft*, ed. Wendelin Schmidt-Dengler and Martin Loew-Cadonna, (Munich: Biederstein, 1991), 87–97.

[41] Lorenz built a grandiloquent Viennese town house as well as a country retreat in Altenberg, where the Tyrolean dramatist Karl Schönherr wrote his most celebrated work *Erde* (1907). It was reviewed by Altenberg in *Bilderbögen des kleinen Lebens* (B 51).

[42] See John W. Boyer, *Cultural and political crisis in Vienna. Christian Socialism in power, 1897–1918*, (Chicago and London: The University of Chicago Press 1995), 50, 63.

Richard Engländer's sojourn in Stuttgart after his failure as a medical student was not a success, and he fled once again to the scene of his childhood idylls: the uplands around the Semmering pass. There at the Hotel Thalhof he struck up a relationship with the proprietress Olga Waisnix, greatly to Schnitzler's later displeasure: although he was to have a far more serious fling with her, he was suspicious and jealous of Engländer. After Stuttgart, Engländer became a relatively successful student in Graz, even passing the first part of his law degree. However, he did not forget Bertha-Peter and kept up a correspondence with her. A letter of 30 December 1881 survives, its form of address "L. P." (L[iebe] P[eter]) betraying that despite his sympathy for the denial of self which the masculinization of Bertha implied, Engländer too had taken to using her pseudonym.

In a sense, then, the very first Peter Altenberg was not Richard Engländer, the bourgeois Jew turned avant-garde artist, but Bertha Lecher. His letter also makes plain that their relationship was already more familial than sexual (he says how happy he is that she now calls him one of her brothers!) Presumably it was not the strains of their love life which led him to abandon the study of law, which he continued in Vienna from the summer semester of 1882 through to the following summer.

His failure to move towards professional respectability inevitably hastened Engländer's exit from the world his parents had mapped out for him. In *Mein Lebensabend* Altenberg summed up his attempted integration into the world of middle-class learning and attainments with an expression of contempt for what other people did. His life had at least been of his own making, and not others'. The contrast with the dark musings of 23 December 1918, where he blames everything on his parents (N 140), could hardly be more pronounced. Here he recounts leaving Stuttgart on borrowed money and fleeing to his beloved Thalhof with its autumnal forests, damp moss, mountain mists and the splashing of the little fountain at night: "Ich steuerte in die Almen des Schneebergs. Wohin steuern die andern? Pfui!" [I headed for the meadows of the Schneeberg. Where are the others heading? Who cares!: LA 3].

Following the relocation of the family home from the Walfischgasse to the Mölkerbastei in 1886, Engländer left home for good. His first independent lodgings were a tiny cell in an ancient house in the Tiefer Graben, in the heart of Vienna's inner city.[43] In what was to become the heartland of Peter Altenberg, recorder of the psychopathology of everyday life in Vienna, Richard Engländer was already consorting with the prostitutes, serving girls, and dancers, for whose lives he had unique sympathy. For the next thirty years

[43] For further details on Altenberg's early life see Camillo Schaefer, *Peter Altenberg: oder die Geburt der modernen Seele*, (Vienna: Amalthea 1992).

and more, most of his waking and sleeping life would be spent in the parks, piazzas and narrow old streets of central Vienna.

2: The Birth of the Writer

"Young Vienna"

In *Mein Lebensabend* Altenberg declared that in his thirty-sixth year he suddenly became a writer (LA 238). This bald conclusion is one of his last recorded statements as to how, after years of doing very little, he had emerged as a consistently productive artist. As a schoolboy he had written verse, but there were few other signs of literary precocity. In her memoir, however, Marie Mauthner recalled receiving a puzzling letter from her brother when he was a student in Graz. At first she believed its contents corresponded to reality, learning only later that the letter recounted a dream sequence featuring her brother, a young countess, and a little shrine in a mossy forest. Intoxicated with the vision of the slender aristocrat and the woodland scents, he had written a naive little poem about march violets (NE 25). This chiefly reflects the ongoing influence in the 1880s of the Romantic tradition, most prominently perpetuated by Gustav Mahler in his preoccupation with the poems of *Des Knaben Wunderhorn*.

More significantly for future developments, the outlines of this dream narrative already contain much that is recognizably Altenbergian: the poet captivated by the slender body of the young woman, the poet as supplicant who resorts to the written word to express his feelings, and the poet as nature worshipper. Mauthner also recalled, possibly only with hindsight, that despite his purposeful lack of activity, her brother was convinced that some day, somehow, his hour would come (NE 24). If Altenberg himself is to be believed, the very earliest extant example of his writing is a poem composed when he was eight, but not published until the writer was in his late fifties (NF 16).[1] Possibly influenced by Mauthner's recollections, Lorenz claimed that Altenberg had already composed a volume of verse when he met Bertha Lecher.[2]

By the early 1890s Richard Engländer was known to several of the generation of young writers then emerging in Vienna. Felix Salten recalls him representing a firm selling exotic Egyptian cigarettes, but did not regard him as a writer; Stefan Großmann was struck at their first meeting by the shine of Engländer's prematurely bald pate and the inordinate pride he took in his finely manicured hands and delicate feet.[3] Others recall his nocturnal tirades

---

[1] See also "Mutterliebe" (NE 10).

[2] Albert Lorenz, *Wenn der Vater mit dem Sohne*, (Vienna: Deuticke, 1952), 79.

[3] Altenberg's interest in hands, and especially those of women, was obsessive, with references abounding throughout his work. Alban Berg recalls him as a nailbiter like himself (*Alban Berg*.

in cafés, his *forte voce* evangelical Christianity, his outrageous dress and the strange company he kept. Lina Loos highlights the litheness of his movements, and how his body, indeed his whole being, conveyed the impression of something hovering.[4]

Richard Engländer appears in Schnitzler's diaries as early as April 1886, not for any literary achievement, but because of their shared interest in Olga Waisnix.[5] She later assured Schnitzler that her relationship with Engländer had been platonic and that their friendship focused on a shared love of books. Herr Waisnix, however, threatened to shoot Engländer should he show his face again at the Thalhof, and he sensibly left. This spelled the end of his association with Olga, if not with the Thalhof, where he kept turning up for many years to come. Looking back on the early years of his relationship with Engländer, before either of them had published a word, Schnitzler recalls how a girl named Ännie Holitscher reacted favorably towards him because his looks reminded her of Engländer. Schnitzler sardonically remarks that just as all negroes superficially look the same to European eyes, so a young girl may initially find one poet much like the next.[6]

Holitscher's importance to Engländer emerges from the letters he addressed to her over a period from 1885 until August 1896.[7] These record both his love and the neuroses which had forced such a wedge between him and his family. Constantly bemoaning his physical and spiritual malaise, he informs Holitscher that he would like to marry her, but happiness, insofar as he can conceive of it, only exists on the basis of complete material security, and this she cannot give him (!). This, we must assume, is the closest Engländer or Altenberg ever came to the conventional state of matrimony. To the end, Ännie Holitscher remained single and considered herself to be Peter Altenberg's "Braut," his "Betrothed."[8]

That Schnitzler was not flattered by any comparison with Engländer is plain. He considered Engländer a "geistreicher Sonderling" [witty oddity], and something of a professional neurotic.[9] He made no secret of his feelings,

Briefe an seine Frau, [Munich and Vienna: Albert Langen and Georg Müller, 1965], 132.) The most striking public manifestation of this interest in hands emerges in 1903 when as editor of his own journal *Kunst,* he gave pride of place to photographs of the hands of Risa Horn to illustrate his views on the nature of art itself. See Andrew Barker and Leo Lensing, *Peter Altenberg. Rezept die Welt zu sehen,* (Vienna: Braumüller 1995), 161–165.

[4] *Peter Altenberg. Leben und Werk in Texten und Bildern,* ed. Hans Christian Kosler, (Munich: Matthes and Seitz 1981), 231.

[5] Arthur Schnitzler, *Tagebuch 1879–1892,* (Vienna: Akademie der Wissenschaften, 1987), 192.

[6] Arthur Schnitzler, *Jugend in Wien: Eine Autobiographie,* (Vienna, Munich, Zürich: Molden, 1968), 212.

[7] See Ursula Weyrer, *"Das Silberboot": Eine österreichische Literaturzeitschrift (1935–36, 1946–52),* (Innsbruck: Innsbruck University Press, 1984). These letters, now in the Wiener Stadt- und Landesbibliothek, were formerly in the possession of Ernst Schönwiese.

[8] Käthe Braun Prager, "Seien Sie barmherzig mit mir . . . Ungedruckte Briefe Peter Altenbergs an seine erste Braut Aennie Holitscher," *Neues Österreich,* 3 August 1958, 13–14, 10 August 1958, 19. Also Kosler, *Peter Altenberg,* 164–167.

[9] Schnitzler, *Jugend in Wien,* 213.

but apparently Engländer did not take this amiss. Strangely, when Schnitzler first grew close to Olga Waisnix she too, like Ännie Holitscher, remarked upon the similarity between the two men.[10] After Waisnix's death in 1897, Altenberg wrote a maudlin poem to her memory, eventually published in *Märchen des Lebens* under the title "Die Jugendzeit" (ML 40). In the first edition of *Wie ich es sehe*, one of the most wistful prose poems is a miniature epic of unfulfilled love entitled "Wie wunderbar - - - ," a story which opens with the ending of a couple's relationship. As originally published it could have stood for any man losing a lover and compensating for his loss through thoughts imputed to the beloved: "Wie wunderbar! Es hat kein Ende - -." [How wonderful! It has no end - - : WS 211], thoughts then turned into poetry which defies reality. In the 1904 edition of *Wie ich es sehe*, however, Altenberg unveils the personal substance of the piece by a short dedication to the "noble departed Madame Olga Waisnix" (WS 210). Two decades on from their relationship, the poet finally felt able to put their love on the record.

By the early 1890s Engländer was acquainted with Salten and Hofmannsthal as well as Schnitzler. Evidence in *Die Fackel* suggests that Kraus too first met Engländer around 1891. In 1906 the satirist recounted his fifteen years of association with Altenberg, though Altenberg dated their first meeting some three years later, in 1894.[11] Altenberg admits that when first moving in artistic circles he was "der 'reine Niemand'" [a 'complete nobody': VI 165], and in a seminal letter to Schnitzler of July 1894, examined in the final section of this chapter, records his appreciation that this circle of cultured young men, soon to be known to the wider literary world as *Jung Wien* [Young Vienna], treated one of "life's invalids" with such benevolence and kindness.

Schnitzler's diary for 25 February 1894 records a literary gathering at Richard Beer-Hofmann's where the host read a "novellette" by Richard Engländer,[12] whilst, in the correspondence between Schnitzler and Hofmannsthal, Engländer is mentioned as the author of an essay on Solness, the main figure in Ibsen's *The Master Builder*, first performed early in 1893.[13] How typical of Altenberg, that amongst the very earliest of his works should be one dealing with an older man's obsession with a much younger woman! Unlike any subsequent commentator, Marie Mauthner dates Altenberg's first serious work back to 1892, and unlike other writers, she also believes he had the major say in putting together *Wie ich es sehe*, which appeared in April 1896 (NE 27). She may well be correct in both assertions. Whatever the precise date of his earliest texts, however, it is obvious that Altenberg was

---

[10] Ibid., 219.

[11] Karl Kraus, *Die Fackel*, 203 (1906): 21. Kraus mentions his fifteen years of acquaintance with Altenberg.

[12] Arthur Schnitzler, *Tagebuch 1893–1902*, (Vienna: Akademie der Wissenschaften, 1989), 71.

[13] *Hugo von Hofmannsthal, Arthur Schnitzler: Briefwechsel*, ed. Therese Nickl and Heinrich Schnitzler, (Frankfurt: Fischer, 1964), 34.

drawn to literary life precisely when the other members of Young Vienna — most notably Hofmannsthal, Schnitzler, Beer-Hofmann, Salten and Bahr — were re-establishing the city not just within German letters, but on the wider literary map of Europe as well.

To speak of the Young Vienna writers as belonging to a group is misleading: they worked and sometimes played together, but apart from Hermann Bahr as the original organizing spirit, no one figure was dominant. In later years the ties grew increasingly loose, Beer-Hofmann (as reported by Salten) even going so far as to deny any real friendship between them. They consorted together only because they did not make each other feel anxious.[14] What these often strongly differentiated authors had in common — Hofmannsthal in the lyric, Schnitzler in the drama, Bahr as critic and wheeler-dealer with the German firms who published the Young Viennese — was a shared awareness of their part in the renewal of Austrian letters from a cosmopolitan perspective. Exposed to the multicultural environment of the Hapsburg empire, they displayed a constant openness to foreign literatures, whose innovations and developments they were pleased to incorporate into their own work. They were anything but chauvinistic, unlike their contemporaries, the German Naturalists Holz and Schlaf, who in the preface to *Die Familie Selicke* (1889) trumpeted (rather hollowly in fact) their independence from all foreign models. Like Tosca, the Young Viennese lived overwhelmingly for art, but for a wit like Karl Kraus it was all too easy to mock their preciousness, over-refined sensibilities, tired affectations and obsession with the psyche.

Although *fin de siècle* Vienna is seen today as a cultural Golden Age, literary production was distinguished by the crass discrepancy between the perceptions the artists had of themselves and their actual reception by an audience which often reacted to the new writing with incomprehension.[15] The revolutionary atonal music of the Second Viennese School of composers, led by Arnold Schoenberg and his pupils Alban Berg and Anton Webern, would soon come up against the similar paradox of a music-hungry public whose tastes did not stretch beyond what they already knew and loved. Amongst the writers there emerged an understandable tendency to counter incomprehension by retreating into literary cliques: consorting with like minds was the best antidote to a world on which their work had in any case so often turned its back. Amidst friends, the isolation at least seemed more bearable, and the place where the lonely avant-garde met to form what has been called their "sub-society"[16] was that long-established Viennese refuge, the coffee house. Already in self-elected exile from bourgeois society, Altenberg was to become the poet par excellence of the Viennese café. In

[14] Felix Salten, "Aus den Anfängen. Erinnerungsskizzen," *Jahrbuch deutscher Bibliophilen und Literaturfreunde*, 18–19 (1932–1933): 45.

[15] Stefan Nienhaus, *Das Prosagedicht im Wien der Jahrhundertwende: Altenberg — Hofmannsthal — Polgar*, (Berlin: de Gruyter, 1986), 13.

[16] Jens Malte Fischer, *Fin de Siècle: Kommentar zu einer Epoche*, (Munich: Winkler, 1978), 22.

Mein Lebensabend he pays full tribute to the institution which nurtured his art and sustained him in his many hours of need:

> You've got worries, be they this, be they that - - - into the café!
> She cannot come to you, for whatever reason, and be it ever so
> plausible - - - into the café!
> You've got holes in your boots - - - into the café!
> You're properly careful and don't pamper yourself - - - café!
>
> You're a civil servant and would rather have been a doctor - - - café!
> You can't find a girl to suit you - - - café!
> You're mentally on the brink of suicide - - - cafe!
> You loathe and despise people but you cannot do without them - - - café!
> You've run out of credit everywhere else - - - café!
>
> (VI 186)[17]

The lonely hothouse Altenberg had now entered attracted the collective name *Jung Wien* in ironic acknowledgement of the revolution they had wrought in the provincial world of late nineteenth century Austrian letters. The title was directly analogous to the name *Jung Deutschland*, borne by the politically active young German writers in the run up to the revolution of 1848. But whereas an obsession with the realities of the day had been a common feature of the Young Germans, the Young Viennese were on the whole apolitical, despite their living in an empire and a city with more than their share of political troubles. Interestingly, many political activists in Vienna in the 1890s (it should not be forgotten that Vienna was a hotbed of politicking at that period) came from the same social background as the writers who in the main so consciously rejected political involvement.[18]

Initially at least, Altenberg was regarded as a member of this Young Viennese clique, but as he did not publish his first book until the age of thirty-seven his membership shows a fairly broad definition of youth. The Young Viennese writers were all habitués of the Café Griensteidl until it closed early in 1897, moving Karl Kraus to exclaim that Vienna had been demolished into a metropolis.[19] Though initially well-received by this collection of exquisitely educated young men, Altenberg always kept his own table apart from the others, and subsequently maintained closer links only with Schnitzler. After the Café Griensteidl closed he moved to the Café Central, where his wax effigy today serves as a reminder of the days when Peter Altenberg was its most famous patron.

---

[17] An alternative translation is provided in Hilde Spiel, *Vienna's Golden Autumn, 1866–1938*, (London: Weidenfeld and Nicolson, 1987), 58–59. See Gilbert C. Carr, "Großstadt und Kaffeehaus in der Wiener Literatur um 1900," *Deutsche Literatur in sozialgeschichtlicher Perspektive*, ed. Eda Sagarra, (Dublin: Trinity College, 1989), 146–162.

[18] See William McGrath, *Dionysian art and populist politics in Austria*, (New Haven: Yale University Press, 1974).

[19] Karl Kraus, *Die demolirte Literatur*, (Vienna: Bauer, 1897), 5.

Viennese artistic and intellectual communities around the turn of the century were tight-knit, and thanks to their intense coffee house existence everyone seemed to know not only everyone else but also everyone else's business. In Polgar's phrase, the café was an organization for the disorganised,[20] where young aesthetes renowned for their sensitivity felt safe from the threatening world outside. It was, however, an institution where they could not only socialise, but also read and write. In addition, they could read about themselves: Vienna had long been famed for its capacity to produce and consume art, and public fascination with artists meant that their doings regularly made the newspaper headlines of the popular press, as they still do in a city neurotically aware of and sensitive to its artistic traditions.

While the young, and preponderantly Jewish, generation of the 1890s responded with creative vigor to the need for the "modern," it was also weighed down, prematurely exhausted even, by the psychological demands of a glorious cultural tradition in which Jews had not generally played much of a role. Yet as Stefan Zweig points out, nine-tenths of what we today celebrate as Viennese culture of the *fin de siècle* was furthered, nurtured and created by Viennese Jews. Of the Young Viennese only Hermann Bahr was neither Jewish nor, as were Andrian and Hofmannsthal, of partly Jewish extraction. Writing in 1894 about Gabriele d'Annunzio the twenty-year-old Hofmannsthal expressed to perfection the anomalous situation of a gilded youth burdened down with the cares of centuries:

> We have made idols of our dead, all they have they have from us . . . we have equipped these shadows with a higher beauty and more wondrous strength than life can bear . . . Yes, all our thoughts of beauty and happiness have run away from us and moved in with the fairer being of an artificial existence . . . with us, there is nothing left but freezing life, stale and bleak reality, broken-winged reality.[21]

To elicit why Jews were the standard bearers of a culture which weighed so heavily upon them has elicited many studies, but of overwhelming significance were clearly the socio-economic conditions in Austria during the second half of the nineteenth century. Enterprise capitalism was the economic factor which in Austria, as elsewhere in Europe, had fueled the forces of change, but circumstances there were rather different. Austria was later than most European countries in coming to terms with industrialization, a major factor being the reluctance of the nobility, whose status was enormous, to descend from their baronial estates and go into the market-place. Because of its delayed emergence into the modern world economy, Austria had been slow in developing an urban middle class to service the economy when growth did eventually come. So when in the 1860s the modern world finally began to catch up with the Hapsburg realms, there was a glaring gap to be closed. When filled, it was not primarily by the hegemonically superior

---

[20] Irene Köwer, *Peter Altenberg als Autor der literarischen Kleinform: Untersuchungen zu seinem Werk unter gattungstypologischem Aspekt*, (Frankfurt: Peter Lang, 1987), 67.

[21] Spiel, *Vienna's Golden Autumn*, 87.

"German" Austrians, but by Jews who, given economic emancipation in 1848 (full emancipation finally arrived in 1867) seized their chance with acuity, habituated as they were by tradition to skills in handling money.

There thus grew very rapidly a Jewish middle class which had accrued great wealth in a relatively short time, attracting to the city many thousands of hopeful immigrants. Censuses reveal that in 1880 there were 72,000 Jews living in Vienna, but by 1910 there were 175,000, giving it, after Warsaw, Europe's second largest Jewish population. Many of these Jews did not, however, belong to the established Jewish bourgeoisie, a class which, though small in number, had been relatively long-established in Vienna. Instead, they were immigrant "Kaftan Jews" from the eastern provinces and beyond, attracted by Vienna's bourgeoning economy and the opportunities its relatively tolerant attitudes supposedly afforded Jews.[22]

With the entry of increasing numbers of Jews into the relatively small but rapidly expanding Austrian bourgeoisie came also their growing desire to identify culturally with not only the middle class but with traditional Austrian aesthetic concerns. This meant above all patronage of the arts and the espousal of Classical German culture. By the 1880s, parents who had grown rich in the *Gründerzeit* had produced children who were able to enter and become predominant in professions previously the preserve of non-Jews. Hence Jews came to play an ever-increasing part in law, medicine and journalism in Vienna. Also, however, as a result of assimilation, a generation of children was born which saw the fulfilment of its career ambitions not in the world of commerce, which had founded their families' fortunes, nor in the professions, which traditionally have been the way in which "outsiders" attempt to confirm their place in society, but in the world of art itself, a world of unique status within the Austrian tradition.

To become an artist was the ultimate affirmation of acculturation, if not assimilation. It was the recognition that the offspring of Jews only a couple of generations away from the ghetto had thrown in their lot with the mainstream of a predominantly Roman Catholic society not noted for its tolerance towards children of Israel. It was also at precisely this time, when newly emancipated and increasingly wealthy middle class Jews were bidding for an entrée into Germanic culture, that German Nationalists in the Austrian Empire were fueling the political anti-Semitism that would spell the end of that creative Jewish-German cultural symbiosis, the product of nineteenth-century economic and social liberalism.

First Steps in Print

An unreliable narrator of his own literary history, Altenberg claims in *Mein Lebensabend* that his career only started in late September 1894. "Wie ich 'Schriftsteller' wurde," written with a quarter century's hindsight, gives a

[22] Harry Zohn, "*... ich bin ein Sohn der deutschen Sprache nur ...* " *Jüdisches Erbe in der österreichischen Literatur*," (Vienna and Munich: Amalthea, 1986), 17.

quasi-official version of his debut: in 1894 two delightful little girls aged nine and eleven had become infatuated with him whilst spending the summer in Gmunden, a holiday resort in the Salzkammergut. At the end of September the family returned to Vienna, whereupon at the age of thirty-five, during the night of the tearful separation from the girls Alice and Auguste, Altenberg composed his first-ever sketch. Entitled "Neun und elf," this became the opening sketch of his first book *Wie ich es sehe* (LA 9). Given Altenberg's penchant for young girls, what could be more fitting than that two should have provided the stimulus for this sudden flowering at such a relatively ripe age? By this point in our examination of Altenberg, however, we may suspect a typically stylized autobiographical, not to say fictional, account. For even if elements of this report are accurate, by elevating Alice and Auguste to the inspiration for his whole career, Altenberg promotes a convenient myth, tailored to underpin an image of himself projected unswervingly over the preceding twenty years. In reality, his writing career was already well underway by the autumn of 1894.

In 1913, spurred on perhaps by the considerable number of friends and acquaintances claiming a role in launching his career, Altenberg published a sardonic account of how the newly creative writer was discovered, pen in hand, in the Café Central by a covey of young Viennese writers. "So wurde ich" is revealing not only for the light it sheds on numerous literary luminaries of the Hapsburg sunset, but also for the writer's own self-assessment at a time when mental illness and alcohol threatened not just his career but his life. Of particular interest is the use of language identifying him unmistakably as a Jewish writer. He describes how in his thirty-fourth year — he long maintained the fiction of 1860 as his birth-year — he was sitting in the Café Central, reading a newspaper carrying the photograph of a girl called Johanna W. who had disappeared on the way to her piano lesson. Shaken by her fate, he wrote the sketch "Lokale Chronik." Who should then enter but Schnitzler, Hofmannsthal, Salten, Beer-Hofmann, and Bahr. Schnitzler expressed surprise that Altenberg-Engländer was a writer and took the sketch away with him.

The following Sunday Richard Beer-Hofmann put on a literary supper and read out the sketch for dessert. Three days later Bahr, having been present at the reading, wrote to Engländer-Altenberg asking for contributions to his new periodical *Die Zeit*. Later, Karl Kraus sent a packet of sketches to S. Fischer in Berlin. In Altenberg's later recollection, Kraus recommended the new author as an original genius "der anders sei, nebbich. S. Fischer druckte mich, und so wurde ich!" [who was different, nebbich. S. Fischer printed me, that's how I became me!: S 35]. What the linguistic purist Kraus made of Altenberg putting Yiddish into his mouth is easily guessed. Nevertheless, as Altenberg later remembered, it was this series of chance events which "made" him. Had he instead been paying his long-overdue bill in the café, Schnitzler would not have taken him up, Beer-Hofmann would not have put on his soirée, and Bahr would not have contacted him. Altenberg believed there was no way in which Karl Kraus would have failed to send off the bundle of sketches to S. Fischer, for Kraus was his own man, and utterly incorruptible:

> Alle zusammen jedoch haben mich 'gemacht'. Und was bin ich geworden?!
> Ein Schnorrer!
>
> [All together, however, they 'made' me. And what have I become?! A
> schnorrer!: S 35]

In response to Altenberg's quizzical self-assessment as a schnorrer, a familiar figure in Jewish communities "who did not so much ask for alms as claim them,"[23] the nationalistic critic Adolf Bartels, unaware that "Schnorrer" has a humorous connotation in Yiddish, wrote that Altenberg had thus done nothing more than many another Jew.[24]

In this stock-taking Altenberg's narration of time is unreliable, for he was not in his thirty-fourth year when his secret came out, and Felix Salten for one recalls events very differently.[25] In *Vita Ipsa* Altenberg himself tried to redress the balance of "So wurde ich" by laying greater weight upon the influence of Kraus, with whom relations were then somewhat strained. Whatever Altenberg's motives for composing "Wie ich mir Karl Kraus 'gewann',"it vividly reveals the chaos of his life, a chaos which is anything but a feature of his early prose poetry. The insouciant description of his personal mess seems, however, to have lodged itself in the minds of many critics. In reality Altenberg simply wrote up to the popular image many of his contemporaries had long held of him. In this sketch Altenberg claims that he had met Kraus in Ebensee, and out of boredom had started singing "Heini von Steyr." That, he claims, is how he won over a man who was otherwise unwinnable. Behind his back Kraus later sent off to S. Fischer the manuscripts of *Wie ich es sehe* which were scattered around in his bedside cabinet, drawers and wardrobe (VI 166).

Few apart from Altenberg would have cheerfully and publicly acknowledged being bored in the presence of Kraus, nor does the aging poet's memory of the satirist shipping off the manuscripts to Berlin square with Salten's account. However, letters from Altenberg to Kraus in the summer of 1895 reveal the debutant author's worries about Fischer's reactions to his book, which must therefore already have been at the publisher. When he nervously asks his friend whether he has received Job's comfort from the publisher, it is clear that Kraus must have played a significant role in the proceedings.[26] Kraus thought so too when recalling their long acquaintance in

---

[23] Leo Rosten, *The Joys of Yiddish*, (London: Penguin, 1976), 369. Rosten defines the word as 1. A beggar, a panhandler, a moocher. 2. A cheapskate, a chiseller. 3. A bum, a drifter. 4. A compulsive bargain hunter and bargainer. 5. An impudent indigent.

[24] Adolf Bartels, *Deutsches Schrifttum* 2, (1914): 95–96, cited in Hedwig Prohaska, "Peter Altenberg. Versuch einer Monographie," Dr.phil diss., Vienna, 1948, 31.

[25] Felix Salten, "Aus den Anfängen," 46.

[26] Barker and Lensing, *Rezept*, 220.

Die Fackel in May 1906. There he stated simply that it was he who had had Altenberg's first sketches printed.[27]

Salten, no friend of Kraus, whose ears he had boxed after the publication of *Die demolirte Literatur*, recalls a meeting at Beer-Hofmann's (the same as that of February 1894 noted in Schnitzler's diary?) when the host announced he would read from a manuscript which, he swore, he had not himself authored. Furthermore, Beer-Hofmann had given his word not to reveal the author's identity until the assembled company had given their verdict upon what they had heard. He then read the "See-Ufer" cycle, which had been sent to him at Ischl by the author himself.[28] The reception of these texts, which eventually formed the opening sequence of *Wie ich es sehe*, was tumultuous. All agreed they had heard masterpieces with a novel kind of beauty and "einem ganz besonderen Duft" [a very special scent]. Salten then relates how astonished they all were when Beer-Hofmann joyously informed them that the creator of these prose poems was none other than Richard Engländer, the cigarette salesman from the night café. It was decided to send all the manuscripts to the publisher, who then declared himself ready at once to publish the book. Salten concludes by saying that they had discovered a poet: Peter Altenberg.[29]

Published nearly four decades after the events related, Salten's account is noticeable both for writing out Kraus and elevating Beer-Hofmann into a crucial figure. It also eliminates Schnitzler from the proceedings, whereas in a letter to the dramatist in 1897 Altenberg pays tribute to him as being the first to recognize his talents.[30] Before long, Beer-Hofmann had grown critical of what he considered Altenberg's posturing, but Altenberg's proximity to Karl Kraus would in any case have done little for his standing amongst the Young Viennese who so loathed their public tormenter.

For all his long association with the satirist, Altenberg considered himself the creation in turn of various of the Young Viennese, of Karl Kraus and indeed of S. Fischer. Significantly, in the text of the same name, the phrase "so wurde ich" occurs in direct connection with the name of S. Fischer. Indeed, the publisher's wife Hedwig herself competes with Kraus, Schnitzler, Salten et al. for the honor of having discovered Peter Altenberg. In her unpublished account of the Fischer Verlag she too recalls her pride at finding the new author.[31] In her early married life Frau Fischer worked as a reader for the publishing house and remembered receiving the first of Altenberg's manuscripts which arrived unbound in a large cardboard box in summer 1895. The handwriting reminded her at first glance of a woman's, but she warmed instantly to the short, loosely linked sketches. Her husband found her in tears

---

[27] Karl Kraus, *Die Fackel*, 203 (1906): 21.

[28] Letter from Richard Engländer to Richard Beer-Hofmann at Eglmoos 22, Ischl. Houghton Library, Harvard, bMS Ger 183 (9).

[29] Salten, "Aus den Anfängen," 45–46.

[30] Arthur Schnitzler, *Das Wort*, ed. Kurt Bergel, (Frankfurt: Fischer, 1966), 8.

[31] Peter de Mendelssohn, *S. Fischer und sein Verlag*, (Frankfurt: Fischer, 1970), 214.

over the manuscript, and that was recommendation enough for him to publish it.[32]

Thereafter, thanks to this stroke of luck, and a happy choice of pseudonym, Peter Altenberg's name came first in the catalog of the Fischer Verlag. Indeed, a satirical item in *Die Schaubühne* reckoned that Engländer only adopted the name Altenberg so that his name could stand at the head of German literature.[33] The official chronicler of the Fischer Verlag failed to share Frau Fischer's enthusiasm for Altenberg, noting that once Altenberg had become part of Fischer's publishing empire, his cardboard boxes arrived every two years with the sort of regularity of which only the completely slovenly are capable.[34]

As if the Fischers, Salten, Bahr and Kraus were not enough, yet another of Kraus's enemies, Stefan Großmann — in his memoirs he calls the satirist a "tragic dwarf" — claims that the real discovery of Altenberg's talent fell to Fritz Eckstein, friend of Hugo Wolf and unofficial secretary to Anton Bruckner. Though not a writer, Eckstein was one of the Café Griensteidl's most impassioned debaters, and a considerable personality in his own right. A member of the same monied bourgeoisie as most of the Griensteidl set, he was a manufacturer of parchment paper and had an obsession for Indian philosophy. Like many another merchant's son in Vienna, however, he was half-hearted at best in his approach to commerce, preferring to clamber to the top of his factory chimney to read his books undisturbed by customers or by intrusive new inventions like the telephone. That such a man would find Engländer congenial is scarcely surprising. Altenberg found Eckstein's wife Bertha congenial too, dedicating to her the so-called *Novelle* "Paulina" in *Ashantee*. Bertha herself soon embarked on a literary career under the pseudonym of Sir Galahad, writing Altenberg-like sketches for the Munich periodical *März* and sharing with him an obsession with diet and slimness.[35]

Who actually "discovered" Altenberg is now hard to ascertain, given that the competing claims came from people who were often themselves engaged in literary feuds. That Altenberg's emergence is claimed by a variety of wildly incompatible figures is good indication of his ability to draw people together across the divides of literary enmity. Whoever was responsible for his discovery — and the probability must be that it was a variety of people who in later life simply wished to have nothing to do with each other — once launched into the literary life Altenberg produced books with a regularity that gainsays the fecklessness often ascribed to him. In the mêlée of everyday existence, the act of writing was the one thing he adhered to with unshaking purpose. The more he wrote, the more he came to live out the persona "Peter Altenberg."

Whatever Altenberg's first written sketch may have been, his first *published* work was "Lokale Chronik." This appeared on 21 January 1896 in the

---

[32] Ibid., 214.

[33] Köwer, *Peter Altenberg*, 276.

[34] de Mendelssohn, *S. Fischer*, 215.

[35] Sibylle Mulot-Déri, *Sir Galahad. Portrait einer Veschollenen*, (Frankfurt: Fischer, 1987).

periodical *Liebelei*, a journal whose title bore tribute to the success of Schnitzler's innovative social drama of the same name. Published by Rudolf Strauß and Rolf Baron Brockdorff, *Liebelei* only survived from 4 January until 20 March, just a few days before the publication of *Wie ich es sehe*. Egon Friedell recalls how with its mixture of lyric poetry and polemics *Liebelei* was regarded during its brief lifetime as the organ for the young Turks in Vienna. Although it succeeded in giving all sorts of offense, the greatest umbrage of all, Friedell recalls, was caused by some "confused sketches," the work of a first-time author previously known only for causing commotions in cafés with revolutionary pro-feminist and contra-philistine diatribes. His dress was reckoned as outlandish as his views. Though never known to mount a horse, he sported leather riding leggings, while his nocturnal habits, courtliness towards streetwalkers, and connections with cabbies, pimps and waiters were already the cause of much comment. Unlike *Liebelei*, the author of these pieces did not cease production almost as soon as he had begun, and soon his name had become a byword for every sort of modern paranoia and sensationalism.[36]

Like "Neun und elf," "Lokale Chronik" was inspired by an adolescent girl, but the circumstances of its inspiration were infinitely sadder. Narrated in the third person, it tells how, when reading a newspaper in the café on 21 November 1894, the writer learned of a fifteen-year-old girl named as Johanna H. who had disappeared while on the way to her piano lesson. Her picture appeared in the paper, and everything about her, her age, her coloration and looks — reddish blond hair, brown eyes, slender build — might have been calculated to arouse the writer's interest (A 197). As the narrator readily admits, she meets his ideal and he confesses instant love. The intensely visual nature of Altenberg's inspiration is marked, but in his imagination he already begins to "improve" the color of her hair from "rotblond" to "rotgolden" [golden red], her physical appearance and his concern at her fate combining to unleash the free flow of his fantasy. This strategy, too, is already typical of Altenberg's penchant for making art "improve" on life, and placing his own emotions and reactions at the pivot of his writing. That the object of his instant love is also unobtainable not only through her age but by virtue of her fate, is equally typical of Altenberg's relationship with his many love-objects.

Perhaps most arresting about the sketch, however, is the way Altenberg's sympathy for adolescent girls permits insight into the presumed thought processes not just of the abducted girl but also of the abductor. It is an intensely self-conscious narration, as the writer fantasizes on his rôle as her potential saviour. However, he is always ironically aware that his instant feelings for her, based merely on a picture and a prosaic newspaper story, are inspired to a large extent not by reality but by literature and an awareness of contem-

---

[36] Egon Friedell, *Kleine Porträtgalerie*, (Munich: Beck, 1953), 9.

porary psychology.[37] This readiness to self-parody would remain an appealing trait, though on a diminishing scale as Altenberg's personal plight deteriorated. Soon, however, he would make no attempt at hiding the reactions of "P.A." through use of a third-person narrator; indeed he revelled in the projection of an increasingly famous persona.

It rapidly became a truism that Altenberg's art was instant, unmeditated and unrevised, "impressionistic" in the worst sense. Yet the evidence of this first published piece should raise doubt about this often-repeated view. From the opening with its introduction "Er las im Café diese Notiz aus dem 'Extrablatt' vom 21. November" [He was in the café reading this item from the 'Extrablatt' of 21 November] and its subsequent use of the past tense, it is clear that a process of recollection is taking, and has taken, place. The realization that the prose is precisely considered, and not the spontaneous outpourings of an "arch-impressionist," is strengthened by the sketch's sardonic coda, addressed to the readers and drawing attention to their disappointed reactions. Through an abrupt change in style, the heady fantasy of the poet's relationship with Johanna, which reaches its apogee with his association of himself with Christ and of Johanna with Mary Magdalena, is destroyed by the prosaic intrusion of quotidian reality. The narrator draws attention to the techniques of writing themselves, a "feiner Schriftsteller-Tric, das Heraustreiben von Gegensätzen" [neat authorial trick, emphasising contrasts] before confessing to life's inability to keep up with art: life is tactless; it fails to see the finer points (A 203).

In the last resort, the poet's work is a "holde Phantasie" [blessed fantasy], no matter how much the very real fate of Johanna H., which after all he only partook of thanks to the lithographer's art and printer's ink, inspired genuine feeling. Johanna H. was lost, and remained lost. As Alfred Polgar recalled a quarter of a century after the piece appeared, the sign of genius was already apparent in this sketch. It was like nothing which had gone before: no stale smell from some literary kitchen clung to it. New words, animated by a new breath, spoke in a new rhythm. Out of half-tones there emerged the sweetest uncloying melody.[38]

"Ich hasse die Retouche": Altenberg's letter to Schnitzler, July 1894.[39]

A new, more critical perception of Altenberg's role and status in the culture of fin de siècle Vienna may be gaining ground beyond literary-critical cir-

---

[37] Werner J. Schweiger, "Wiener Literatencafés. VI. Ein Dichter wird entdeckt," *Die Pestsäule*, 10 (1974): 947. Barker and Lensing, *Rezept*, 134.

[38] Alfred Polgar, *Kleine Schriften*, vol. 4, ed. Marcel Reich Ranicki and Ulrich Weinzierl, (Reinbek bei Hamburg: Rowohlt, 1984), 10.

[39] This section is adapted from my essay of the same title in *Modern Austrian Literature* 25, nos. 3–4 (1992): 256–272.

cles,[40] but some long-cherished assumptions about his literary performance, based overwhelmingly on the author's own statements, are proving hard to dislodge. In the age of sophisticated literary theory it is particularly surprising that Altenberg's reliability as the narrator of his own life and practices should go widely unquestioned.[41] Despite attempts to show that received opinion does not always coincide with his practice, the view has persisted that Altenberg was an obsessive impressionist who never reconsidered what he wrote, whose instantaneous inspiration remained his final inspiration; whose works, in short, lack constructive discipline.[42]

This view is epitomized by Altenberg's companion Helga Malmberg in her reminiscences of the poet, published over forty years after his death. She claimed that when the mood took him he would write for hours at a time in his telegram style, seemingly oblivious of what was going on around him. Afterwards, he would not even bother reading through his work, the sketches eventually migrating into a big old suitcase in the corner of his little room. Once a year he would take them out and send them off to the Fischer Verlag. There they were sorted, arranged and ordered, but nobody interfered with these highly original manuscripts.[43]

Of all the documents contributing to the coincidence of the critical consensus on Altenberg with the myths he merrily propagated, none has been more influential than a letter to Schnitzler in July 1894, first published by Friedell in *Das Altenbergbuch*. In this letter Altenberg is glad to inform the apparently curious Schnitzler how he sets about composing his texts, claiming that everything he writes is produced absolutely freely and spontaneously, and that he never knows his subject in advance. He simply takes some paper and writes, starting with the title and hoping that something will transpire which connects with it. What then emerges, he reckons, is what is truly and deeply within him. Hence he regards writing as a natural organic release of the self, with all its strengths and weaknesses. He stresses that he abhors "die Retouche," that is, "touching up" his material. All that matters is to get the thing down on paper and then let it be. He realises that because of this spontaneous approach, his works will be regarded as little more than experiments. In fact, they represent all that that he is capable of producing, but this is of no great concern to him. More important is that in a circle of refined and educated young people he can show that he possesses a certain spark. He concludes with considerable irony that as he is already one of life's invalids, someone with no job, no money, no position and hardly any hair, thus to be acknowledged by someone like Schnitzler is a very pleasant experience:

[40] For example the two RIAS Berlin broadcasts: "Jahrhundertwende-Hippie. Radio Portrait des Wiener Dichters Peter Altenberg," RIAS 1, Berlin, 21 November 1986; "'Ein Toilettespiegel und kein Weltspiegel', Anja Kempe über Peter Altenberg," RIAS 1, Berlin, 2 April 1991.

[41] See, however, Peter Wagner, "Peter Altenbergs Prosadichtung. Untersuchungen zur Thematik und Struktur des Frühwerks," Dr.phil. diss., Münster, 1965; Irene Köwer, *Peter Altenberg*.

[42] Gisela Wysocki, *Peter Altenberg: Bilder und Geschichten des befreiten Lebens*, (Munich and Vienna: Hanser, 1979), 9.

[43] Kosler, *Peter Altenberg*, 118–119.

> Deshalb bin und bleibe ich doch nur ein Schreiber von "Muster ohne Wert" und die Ware kommt alleweil nicht. Ich bin so ein kleiner Hand-spiegel, Toilettespiegel, kein Welten-Spiegel.

> [That's why I am, and shall remain, merely a writer of "samples without commercial value" and fail to come up with the goods. I am a little hand-mirror, a boudoir mirror, no mirror on the world.]

The influence of this self-deprecatory reply to Schnitzler's enquiry, with its final ironic allusion to Goethe, the "Weltspiegel," has been considerable. Yet while it has proved one of Altenberg's most durable texts, helping cast the fledgling author in a mold which surely must be recast, it has also been neglected when examining Altenberg's literary beginnings and his relation-ship with Young Vienna. By examining the pre- and post-publication history of a range of Altenberg texts, this section will attempt to scotch the deeply embedded cliché of the "instant artist" which Altenberg himself projected not infrequently.

Although Altenberg's first published work was "Lokale Chronik," the letter reveals that, despite being unpublished, Altenberg's writing was already circulating to positive effect amongst the writers of Young Vienna by the summer of 1894. Furthermore, the observation that his works "immer für kleine Proben betrachtet werden" [are always regarded as little experiments] suggests he was already quite prolific. The approval of the circle of well-educated young men is obviously of importance, suggesting perhaps a tem-peramental proximity to writers he later grew away from. What the letter conclusively disproves is Altenberg's own account of his literary debut. In "Wie ich 'Schriftsteller' wurde," written with a quarter century's hindsight, Altenberg gives a quasi-official version of his writing debut, but in reality plays up to his popular image, propagated on numerous occasions over the intervening years. For example, when replying to a Nürnberg manuscript collector in 1901, he was happy to reinforce what had obviously become an accepted fact about the way he produced his texts. The initial disclaimer should not fool us:

> Wenige wollen es mir glauben, dennoch ist es so: mein Gehirn ist nicht fähig, sich dem Nachdenken über irgendeine Sache hinzugeben ... Ich denke nie nach — nie vor. Ich habe nie auch die geringste Ahnung von dem, was ich schreibe. Die Ereignisse des Tages scheinen sich, mir un-bewußt, in mir selbst abzuphotographieren.[44]

> [Few will believe me, but it is the case. My brain is not capable of reflecting upon anything ... I have no prior thoughts, and no afterthoughts. I never have the slightest inkling what I am writing about. The day's events seem, without my being conscious of it, to register themselves photographically inside me.]

---

[44] "Unveröffentlichte Briefe über die dichterische Inspiration," *Die literarische Welt* 8, no. 23 (1932): 3.

Four years later in *Pròdròmòs*, Altenberg consciously uses the language of impressionism to denote this attitude to the world, but this should not be equated automatically with his attitude to writing. Obviously, however, Altenberg subscribes to the Machian notion of "das unrettbare Ich" [the irrecoverable self] which Bahr so forcefully popularised in his *Dialog vom Tragischen* (1904),[45] stating the belief that our nervous system bears absolutely no responsibility for the impressions of the moment. Every minute has its own laws. Ask someone at six o'clock what sort of a being he was an hour before and he will answer that perhaps he was a higher being, but it is equally possible that he was a lower one (P 181).

When at the end of his letter to Schnitzler Altenberg characterizes himself as a mirror, he places himself in the context of a traditional mimetic aesthetic. In the most striking formulation in the letter, however, he emphasizes how he hates "die Retouche" [touching up], a phrase which seems to confirm the unreflected nature of Altenberg's literary practice. This apparently programmatic utterance is taken, however, not from the realm of literature, but from contemporary photographic practice and refers to the touching-up process in which the photographer in his darkroom artfully adapts the initial evidence of the camera lens in the interests of aesthetic presentation. This may confirm the strongly visual nature of Altenberg's inspiration, but, as a statement of artistic practice, ought not to be taken at face value. For, contrary to received opinion, evidence abounds that Altenberg constantly worked on his "prints," just as the skilled photographer can achieve strikingly different effects from the same negative. In "Kunst" (WS 293) Altenberg draws an analogy between his artistic ideal and a Kodak camera, and in 1902 he produced a catalog for the twelfth Vienna Secession exhibition where he makes an important statement in view of his pioneering relationship to photography. Responding to Bruno Liljefors's painting *Eidervogelstrich* Altenberg declares:

> Endlich, endlich erhält der Künstler das Auge des Momentphotographen-Apparates, endlich! Immer wird ja unsere Seele von selbst hinzukommen als *Retoucheur* . . . *Moment-Photographen* wollen wir werden und unsere *Seele* wirke von selbst als *Retoucheur.*[46]

> [At last, at last the artist receives the eye of the instant camera, at last! Our soul will always come to it by itself as a *retoucher* . . . Let us become *instant photographers* and our soul shall act by itself as a *retoucher.*]

The notion of Altenberg as loathe to revise what he had put down on paper, incapable of putting work together in any semblance of order, grew out of the chaos affecting his everyday existence as it was known to friends and acquaintances. Yet just as we know that the Young Viennese obsession with the figure of the aesthete does not of necessity mean that the Young Vi-

---

[45] Hermann Bahr, *Dialog vom Tragischen*, (Berlin: Fischer, 1904), 181.

[46] "P. Altenbergs Katalog: XII. Ausstellung," *Ver Sacrum*, 2 (1902): 31. The migration of immense numbers of Eider ducks remains one of the great natural spectacles along the Southern Swedish coast.

ennese were themselves aesthetes, so Altenberg's obvious interest in impressionism, and even his view of himself as a typical "impressionist," should not blind us to the realities of his writing. Evidence of the care with which Altenberg conceived and executed his work exists from the outset of his career. Proof lies not only in the architecture of individual items, but in the conception of the prose poem cycles as published in *Wie ich es sehe, Ashantee* and *Was der Tag mir zuträgt.* Unwilling to distinguish between the persona of Peter Altenberg and the evidence of the texts themselves, many of which are highly consciously structured,[47] commentators have been more than happy to seize upon such personal statements in order to denigrate Altenberg's artistic achievement.

Examination of manuscript sources reveals that from the start Altenberg worked and reworked his texts. Material in the first two editions of *Wie ich es sehe* (1896–98) is based upon manuscripts "Aus einem Skizzenbuch von Peter Altenberg," five very early sketches which may well date back to when Altenberg wrote to Schnitzler. They refute much of what he claims in the letter. Comparing a text like "Nacht-Café" as published in *Wie ich es sehe* with its earlier form in the "Skizzenbuch" shows how little credence should be placed in Altenberg's assertion that he hated "die Retouche."[48] However, whereas the example of "Nacht-Café" reveals the probable revision of work prior to publication, it can be demonstrated that "Roman am Lande" (WS 26) underwent revision in the course of successive editions of *Wie ich es sehe.* What such an adaptation of previously published work demonstrates is not just that Altenberg continued working at his material even after publication, it also confirms that in some ways his works were indeed what his earliest critics in Young Vienna had contended: "kleine Proben," little experiments, containing within their structures the capacity for change and growth.

Much of Altenberg's work appeared initially in journals and newspapers before being collected for publication in book form. Here too comparison of the various versions shows Altenberg continuing to work at his "prints" long after their first appearance. For instance, on 28 February 1910 the Munich-based satirical journal *Simplicissimus* published a short sketch entitled "Der Dichter" which was subsequently republished in *Neues Altes* (NA 77). Comparing the two versions of this autobiographical text reveals that although they are not extensive, the additions and deletions are more than cosmetic. They point to a hardening of the poet's attitude towards the woman who has spurned him: time has not proved a great healer. The revised text exhibits a narrator more embittered and more accusatory than in the original version. The woman's actions have become "fast heimtückisch" [almost malicious] and "schnöde" [despicable], she herself has developed into a "Teufeline" [she-devil] whose actions alone have occasioned the poet's misery. *Neues Altes* appeared in November 1911, eighteen months after the first publication of "Der Dichter," during which time Altenberg had spent many months in

---

[47] Stefan Nienhaus, *Das Prosagedicht,* 31–139.

[48] Barker and Lensing, *Rezept,* 47–56.

the Inzersdorf sanatorium under treatment for clinical paranoia. Abandoned by the long-suffering Helga Malmberg, who had returned to her native Hamburg to rescue her own sanity, Altenberg's mood is reflected in the vastly increased self-pity of the revised version.

From this same period comes an especially telling example of Altenberg's textual manipulation. In the first volume of Herwarth Walden's journal *Das Theater* (1909–10) Altenberg presented the text "Pro domo" in which he discusses his unique series of playlets entitled "Fünf-Minuten Szenen." These were apparently conceived as a cycle, analogous perhaps to the practice in his earlier work of writing *Studien-Reihen*. In reality they were published in no fewer than three different collections, *Märchen des Lebens, Bilderbögen des kleinen Lebens* and *Neues Altes*. Any notion of a cycle was thus well and truly destroyed. In "Pro domo" Altenberg lists seven playlets, adding that he will have to write a further fourteen and perform them consecutively on one evening. His notion of the reader as an indispensable co-creator of the texts, first formulated in *Was der Tag mir zuträgt*, has a very modern ring to it:

> *Extrakte von Ereignissen*! Der Zuschauer wirkt mit, indem er ergänzt. In ihm erst wird es zu einem Ganzen. Er wird geehrt, indem man ihn selbst zum Dramatiker erhöht.[49]

> [*Extracts of events*! The spectator collaborates by filling them out. Only in him does the thing become a whole. He is honoured by being elevated into a dramatist.]

As an example, Altenberg produces a very short text, "Station Unter-purkersdorf," whose extensive "stage directions," with their strongly narrative-psychological content, are reminiscent of the conventions of the Naturalist theater of Gerhart Hauptmann. A young village schoolmaster, in the company of a young lady, awaits the arrival of her husband from Vienna. The teacher is on the verge of being in love with her; she is on the verge of allowing herself to be loved. The train steams in, the husband, despite business worries, comes laden with gifts for his wife. Deeply moved, the teacher says he must go. There is a pause. He remains alone on the station bench. His favourite pupil, a fourteen-year old girl, comes by, and only then does dramatic dialogue ensue. She asks him what is wrong, to which he replies that everything is fine. He was merely thinking about which train to take on his vacation trip the following day. The vacation comes as news to the girl, who was under the impression that the teacher had no intention of going away. She then goes down on her knees before the teacher, telling him that her prayers for his safety would go with him as he climbed in his beloved mountains.

The title of this text is virtually identical with "Station Unter-Purkersdorf," a miniature drama published first in 1908 in *Märchen des Lebens* (ML 159). Any comparison of the text above with "Station Unter-Purkersdorf" must give the lie to Altenberg's self-assessment as a writer who

---

[49] Peter Altenberg, "Pro domo," *Das Theater* 1, no. 1 (1909–10): 72.

never had second thoughts. "Station Unterpurkersdorf" in "Pro domo" is barely a quarter the length of "Station Unter-Purkersdorf" in *Märchen des Lebens*. The 1910 text is, however, patently a resumé of the earlier one. Entirely rewritten, it has the same list of personae, in the same constellation, with an identical sequence of events. It represents a self-conscious application of Altenberg's own "Extrakt-Theorie," the programmatic explication of his artistic method first set out in *Was der Tag mir zuträgt* and alluded to in his introduction to the "Fünf-Minuten-Szene" when he talks of "*Extrakte von Ereignissen*":

> Denn sind meine kleinen Sachen Dichtungen?! Keineswegs. Es sind Extracte! Extracte des Lebens. Das Leben der Seele und des zufälligen Tages, in 2–3 Seiten eingedampft, vom Überflüssigen befreit wie das Rind im Liebig-Tiegel! Dem Leser bleibe es überlassen, diese Extracte aus eigenen Kräften wieder aufzulösen. (WT 6)

> [For are my little things literature?! Not at all. They are extracts! Extract of life. The life of the soul and the happenstance of the day, condensed into 2–3 pages, liberated from the superfluous like the beef in the stockpot. It is up to the reader to reconstitute these extracts on his own.]

In "Pro domo" an already condensed text has been put once more through Altenberg's artistic strainer, producing in effect an extract of an extract. The transformation of "Station Unterpurkersdorf" into "Station Unter-Purkersdorf" can hence be seen as providing a practical illustration of Altenberg's growing linguistic skepticism, which in his later works led to a further reduction in the length of his already attenuated sketches. Two programmatic aphorisms published in 1916 make this process particularly clear. In one he remarks that that his thought processes are getting shorter and shorter, and that means better and better, because they take up less time. In the end he will not say anything, and that will be best of all (NF 104). In the other he asks what his sketches are. The answer is that they are extracts of novellas, just as his aphorisms are extracts of his sketches. Asking what would happen if he ceased writing altogether, he concludes that it would represent "Extrakte meines Heiligen Schweigens!" [extracts of my sacred silence!: NF 113].

Vita Ipsa was the last book whose production Altenberg oversaw, yet here too an examination of the printed text with extant manuscripts reveals the ailing and depressed author still making amendments between the manuscript and the printed stages of his work. One example is found in the two sketches entitled "Buchenwälder" (VI 33) and "Die Buchen" (VI 45). Apart from its opening line "Buchenwälder" bears no resemblance whatsoever to a manuscript version with the same title, whereas a manuscript entitled "Buchenwälder" is essentially the same as the material appearing under the title "Die Buchen."[50] Rather more substantial changes are evident from items reprinted in the posthumous *Mein Lebensabend*, for which some of Alten-

---

[50] LBI

berg's manuscript additions to the printed newspaper items have been preserved.[51] For this, two examples will suffice: "Anständigkeit" (LA 50) and
"Lucie Höflich" (LA 68). In each instance, far from reducing his material, as
may have been expected from both earlier practice and aphorisms in *Nachfechsung*, Altenberg expanded his work by about a quarter before submitting
it to Fischer. In both cases the newspaper clipping was glued to the notepaper headed "Graben-Hotel" upon which much of Altenberg's later work was
written. The changes take chiefly the form of an addendum at the end of
each item. In both cases the additional material strengthens the impact of the
narratorial comment, making a more universal point compared to the earlier
concentration on the individual incident which had occasioned the piece.
Comparing this with the subsequent versions in *Mein Lebensabend*, it will be
found that at the proof stage Altenberg has added further minor adjust-
ments. These changes are, admittedly, on a very small scale but they serve
further to reinforce the need to revise our view of Altenberg's writing praxis.

When Altenberg told Schnitzler he hated "die Retouche," he barely
stood on the threshold of a publishing career, and perhaps at this earliest
stage in his artistic life he did indeed hate to touch up the products of a fresh
and original imagination. However, recourse to both printed and manuscript
sources demonstrates that if ever a statement of aesthetic intention needed
treating with caution in the light of subsequent practice, it is this phrase. Altenberg may have been an "impressionist" in his love of nuance, his fascination with the world of the psyche, and in his unquestioned ability to react
with great rapidity to an aesthetic impulse, but he was also an infinitely more
reflective and collected writer than the subsequent myth, which he did much
to promote, has permitted us to realize.

[51] GSE

3: The Early Work: 1896–1903

Altenberg and Impressionism

When *Wie ich es sehe* appeared in April 1896, it created a sensation in Vienna, not least because of the reputation already enjoyed by its author. Hugo von Hofmannsthal, still only twenty-two, responded at length to the challenge of *Wie ich es sehe* in an essay, published in the autumn of 1896, with the disarmingly simple title "Ein neues Wiener Buch." What Hofmannsthal was reviewing was indeed a new book from a new Viennese author, one that had fresh things to say about life both in Vienna and the Salzkammergut, a favorite stomping ground of the Viennese monied classes. But it was not just a new book from a new author, whom Hofmannsthal surprisingly never names. It was, as was pointed out immediately and not just by Hofmannsthal, a book unlike any other hitherto published in German. As Friedell later commented, it was written not so much in German as in that very special dialect which was all Altenberg's own.[1]

That for all his praise of the work Hofmannsthal did not consider its author a genius rankled Altenberg. In a review of *Die Hochzeit der Sobeide* in March 1899,[2] he made a barbed reference to Hofmannsthal's remark, a rare occasion when Altenberg took public notice of criticism of his writing:

> Der Autor dieser Sachen, der tiefe Dichter von wunderbaren Gedichten, hat einmal in einem sehr schönen Essay über einen "Neuen" geschrieben: "Merkwürdig, *so tiefe Dinge* von einem, der *kein Genie ist*!" Jetzt könnte man über ihn sagen, "*Merkwürdig so flache Dinge* von einem, der ein Genie ist!!"

> [In a very fine essay the author of these pieces, the profound poet of wonderful poems, once wrote about a "newcomer": "Strange, *such profound things* from someone who *is not a genius*!" Now one could say about him: "Strange, such *shallow things* from someone who is a genius!!"]

Never more than a few pages long, the items in *Wie ich es sehe* were externally and superficially reminiscent of the many feuilletons in the Viennese press; what was different about *Wie ich es sehe* was its tenor, its particular way of seeing things. As Bahr remarked in May 1896, it had its own tone

---

[1] Egon Friedell, *Ecce Poeta,* (Berlin: Fischer, 1912), 159.

[2] Robert Werba, "Ein Außenseiter der Theaterkritik. Peter Altenberg und das Wiener Theaterjahr 1898–99," *Maske und Kothurn* 20, (1974): 181.

through and through.[3] More than two decades after *Wie ich es sehe* appeared, Polgar could still recall the freshness of form and perception in a debut which already contained several of the main emphases in Altenberg's later work: a love of young women, children and nature, and a programmatic call for a "New Man," not dissimilar to the calls which more than a decade later the fledgling expressionist movement would make (N 149–154).

Many of the sixty-eight items in *Wie ich es sehe* were prose poems, a genre not in itself new to German letters. In the 1770s Goethe's translations of Macpherson's *Ossian* in *Die Leiden des jungen Werthers* had brought the form to the widest audience yet seen for a German prose narrative, and in Goethe's wake Romantic poets such as Novalis, a writer much in vogue at the turn of the nineteenth century, continued to cultivate the form. Egon Friedell wrote and published his doctoral dissertation on Novalis, whose call to find poetry in everyday life found an echo not only in Altenberg's practice but even in the title of one of his later collections, *Märchen des Lebens.* In the course of the nineteenth century the prose poem had been pursued with the greatest success not in Germany but in France, first by Baudelaire, then by Mallarmé and Rimbaud, writers who were conscious that the barriers which classical aesthetics had for so long maintained between the lyric, the narrative and the drama had effectively collapsed. Viennese writers in the 1890s were acutely sensitive to developments in France, and Altenberg was not the only one to cultivate the prose poem, but in his early work he did it in the most sustained manner and to greatest effect.[4]

For all his success with small forms — prose poems, feuilleton-like sketches and aphorisms — Altenberg never went on to experiment with larger-scale genres. In avoiding more extended structures, Altenberg was typical of an age which, in its complex reactions to developments in biology, psychology, and politics, as well as to the gargantuanism of the nineteenth-century novel and the music dramas of Wagner, turned increasingly to miniaturism. In the drama one-acters became a favored form; short-stories, feuilletons and aphorisms blossomed, while the *fin de siècle* became a great age of lyric poetry at a juncture when technological man seemed on the brink of conquering the world. The widely-felt urge to re-poeticise literature encouraged forms which responded to the subjective impulse, an impulse strengthened by artists grappling with the challenge of literary naturalism. The more their awareness dawned of how questionable the very notion of the autonomous self might be, the more artists questioned the constitution of the personality. Hence the greater the potential for mass movements and behavior became in the wake of urban industrialization, the greater the subjective reaction against these developments in many branches of the arts.

At the same time, a feeling grew that, with the new century looming, mankind stood not just on the brink of something totally different, but of

[3] *Das junge Wien: Österreichische Literatur- und Kunstkritik,* ed. Gotthart Wunberg, vol. 1, (Tübingen: Niemeyer, 1976), 588.

[4] Barbara Z. Schoenberg, "The influence of the French prose poem on Peter Altenberg," *Modern Austrian Literature* 22, nos. 3–4 (1989): 15–32.

something terrifyingly complex too. Faced with the imminence of the new
and unknown, old certainties faded fast. Darwin, Marx, and Nietzsche con-
spired together in various combinations to unsettle thinkers and artists alike
at the end of the nineteenth century. Progress was trumpeted everywhere,
but that very technology which was the engine of progress seemed constantly
to bring into question basic presuppositions and procedures within the arts,
the most obvious being the response of the visual arts to the spread of the
camera. To many the world no longer appeared as a unity which could be
grasped and portrayed, instead it loomed as a series of images, sometimes
fragmented, chaotic and threatening. Thus Altenberg's comparison of life
with an "ideal cinema" is a representative statement of a pointillistic feeling
for life in which the world around splits into a myriad of stimuli.[5]

In short, this was the age of impressionism, which in the Vienna of the
1890s was simply known as "die Moderne" [modernism], a term not coined
by Bahr, but certainly popularized by him. In literature at least, Viennese
modernism had its roots in naturalism, which the young Viennese writers in
particular are so often held to reject. For as soon as naturalistic techniques are
turned away from the examination of the mechanics of society and are projected onto the workings of the psyche, a new sort of subjectivity arises. Society fragments into individuals; the novel, the societal epic, dissolves into the
Studien and *Skizzen* which are the hallmarks of Altenberg's writing. Hence in
the years after 1890, virtually as soon as German naturalism had celebrated
its first triumph with Hauptmann's *Vor Sonnenaufgang* in 1889, it was already being challenged outright by the symbolist poetry of Stefan George in
Munich, and significantly modified by the Young Viennese in the wake of
Hermann Bahr's persuasive essays, first collected in the book *Zur Überwindung des Naturalismus* (1891). Indeed, there is plenty of evidence to
show that Bahr's theoretical stance had already moved beyond consequential
naturalism even before Hauptmann's epoch-making drama.[6] To claim, as
histories of literature have often done, that naturalism never came to Vienna,
shows a fundamental misunderstanding of the nature of the literary debate in
the city in the early 1890s, where the response to naturalism was a major
topic amongst the new generation. Karl Kraus saw this quite clearly when he
wrote in *Die demolirte Literatur*, his personal demolition of the writers of
Young Vienna, of the triumphant path of naturalism in the early 1890s.[7]

With the effects of science and technology now making themselves felt as
much in Vienna as anywhere, the world was changing at an astonishing rate,
and with it people's perception of time changed too. Cities grew as industry
spawned industry, and with the bustle of the city, life itself appeared speeded

[5] Irene Köwer, *Peter Altenberg als Autor der literarischen Kleinform*, (Frankfurt: Peter Lang, 1987), 62.

[6] Andrew Barker, "'Der große Überwinder'. Hermann Bahr and the Rejection of Naturalism," *The Modern Language Review* 78, no. 3 (1983): 617–630; Andrew Barker, "Hermann Bahr und die Überwindung des Naturalismus," *Hermann Bahr Symposion; "Der Herr Aus Linz,"* ed. Margret Dietrich, (Linz: LIVA, 1987), 9–14.

[7] Karl Kraus, *Die demolirte Literatur*, (Vienna: Bauer 1897), 7.

up as impression heaped upon impression. Yet as Baudelaire had shown, the city was not without poetry. For him, indeed, modern poetry would be urban poetry. Impressionism thus found fertile soil in the never-ending stimuli of the cities. In "Idylle" Altenberg attempts the pose of Baudelaire's *parfait flâneur* to convey the overwhelming nature of urban experience even when one is taking one's time:[8]

> Sie gingen langsam durch die stillen warmen Straßen.
> Alle schwiegen.
> Albert ging neben dem jungen Mädchen dahin.
> Strasse, Strassenecke, Strasse, Strassenecke, Strasse,
> Strassenecke, Hausthor. Stiller Hausflur, stille Stiege,
> brim, brim, brim, brim, stilles Vorzimmer, stilles
> Wohnzimmer. (WS 58–59)

> [They walked slowly through the quiet warm streets.
> Nobody spoke.
> Albert walked along beside the young girl.
> Street, street-corner, street, street-corner, street,
> street-corner, house door. Quiet entry-way, quiet stairway,
> brim, brim, brim, brim, quiet vestibule, quiet living room.]

Yet time also seemed to shrink as communications quickened: telephones, express trains, mass-circulation newspapers and moving pictures all made the world seem smaller, and as the world shrank, so apparently did mankind's disposable time. The patriarchal cigar, redolent of a slower age, was now replaced by the machine-age cigarette. Women too began smoking, as Altenberg was quick to point out.[9] Time, now subsumed into the vocabulary of commerce, came at a premium. The consequences for artistic perception and production were considerable. The short forms were now often held to be those which best suited a new age, one which would no longer have the time to consume 500-page novels. Newspapers became the chief reading matter of the literate classes, and especially in Vienna, which lacked a proper network of publishing houses, writers would come increasingly to look upon newspaper publication as a vital outlet for their talents.

As Friedell indicated, the temptation and pressure to opt for short forms of a journalistic nature thus had practical and financial as well as philosophical and historical roots (B 209–210). In fact, though Altenberg's art was perceived by early critics as coming from nowhere, at least one of its antecedents, for there is no rootless art, lay precisely in the journalistic world of Vienna, more precisely in the "Wiener Spaziergänge" of Daniel Spitzer, for so long an integral part of the *Neue Freie Presse*. As he watched the world go

---

[8] Josephine N. M. Simpson, *Peter Altenberg: A neglected writer of the Viennese Jahrhundertwende*, (Frankfurt: Peter Lang, 1987), 3–4.

[9] Roman Sandgruber, "Wiener Alltag um 1900," *Ornament und Askese im Zeitgeist des Wien der Jahrhundertwende*, ed. Alfred Pfabigan, (Vienna: Christian Brandstätter, 1985), 33–36.

by from his café table or strolled through his favorite Volksgarten, it is clear that Altenberg also often saw himself in the role of the *flâneur*. And in his perceptions of life, which often changed from day to day, we perceive the very essence of that "jour-nalism" for whose despised practitioners Karl Kraus would coin the term "journaille." When *Wie ich es sehe* appeared, however, Kraus had yet to sever finally his links with the popular press. Equally, though, he was moving away rapidly from the world of the Café Griensteidl where he too had once sat; the great respect in which Kraus held the new author is nowhere better reflected than in his decision not to parody him in *Die demolirte Literatur*. Kraus's decision was not shared by others, however, who found Altenberg an irresistible target.[10]

Though Altenberg later chose to remember differently, his debut created keen debate amongst the literati of Vienna and beyond, the discussion revolving not least around the precise meaning of the title of *Wie ich es sehe*. Altenberg himself never wavered in his conviction that to stress the "I" would be to inflate the function of the poet: the poet is never the "only" one to experience, he is however the first, from whom others will then learn.[11] In good impressionistic manner, and in congruence with the ideas of Ernst Mach, who in that same year 1896 took up a chair at Vienna University, Altenberg thus stresses the supremacy of sensory perception over the claims of the self. For Mach, indeed, the self was famously chimeric — "Das Ich ist unrettbar" [the ego is irrecoverable], as Hermann Bahr put it in the essay of 1904.[12]

In his interpretation of his own work's title Altenberg firmly places the book in the context of a Viennese impressionism which has been dubbed epistemological, an impressionism in which the "self is dissolved into a succession of discrete moments, which remain unconnected by any unifying ego. This egoless, floating sensibility becomes atomized into a thousand selves, each one lacking a goal or permanent convictions."[13] Although this form of impressionism can often give rise to literature obsessed with such "decadent" themes as transience, disease and death, Altenberg's early collections frequently display great vigor. For this same "cult of evanescence"[14] means that the artist who is aware of flux is at pains to capture the uniqueness of each and every changing vista, sensation, mood or experience. This was not obvious to all commentators at the time *Wie ich es sehe* appeared. Writing to Johannes Schlaf in June 1898, Richard Dehmel, who was aware of the Jewish contribution to the new literature, reckoned that with the ex-

---

[10] See A. F. Seligmann's parodies in Hans E. Goldschmidt, *Quer Sacrum: Wiener Parodien und Karikaturen der Jahrhundertwende*, (Vienna and Munich: Jugend und Volk, 1976), 96–98.

[11] For the interpretational possibilities of the title see Stefan Nienhaus, *Das Prosagedicht im Wien der Jahrhundertwende: Altenberg — Hofmannsthal — Polgar*, (Berlin: de Gruyter, 1986), 31.

[12] *Die Wiener Moderne. Literatur, Kunst und Musik zwischen 1890 und 1910*, ed. Gotthart Wunberg and Johannes J. Braakenburg, (Stuttgart: Reclam, 1981), 147–148.

[13] William M. Johnston, "Viennese Impressionism: A reappraisal of a once fashionable category," *Focus on Vienna 1900*, ed. Erika Nielsen, (Munich: Wilhelm Fink, 1982), 4.

[14] Ibid.

ception of Alfred Mombert the rest of the Jewish writers from Heine through to Hofmannsthal and Altenberg displayed clear signs of being tired of life.[15]

The very existence of Peter Altenberg was, however, a conscious attempt to create a persona which, in the face of the irrecoverable self, would have a permanence which the "reality" of Richard Engländer had never established. In the creation of the persona, whose reformatory zeal transcended the flux of impressionism, Peter Altenberg was able partially at least to refute Arnold Hauser's characterisation of Viennese Impressionism as the art of the sons of rich bourgeois, the expression of joyless hedonism of that "second generation" which lives on the fruits of its father's work. They are nervous and melancholy, tired and aimless, sceptical and ironic about themselves, these poets of exquisite moods, which evaporate in a trice and leave nothing behind but the feeling of evanescence, of having missed one's opportunities, and the consciousness of being unfit for life.[16]

The creation of a definite persona, based on a program of reform, was Richard Engländer's way of tackling the problems inherited from his Jewish bourgeois background. To that extent he fails to fit into Hauser's sociologically-conceived pattern of the Viennese impressionist as an effete and world-weary *décadent*. What is nonetheless typical of impressionism in Altenberg's writing is its openness to a myriad of stimuli, with the consequence that his work often seems like a kaleidoscopic review of bourgeois life in late nineteenth-century Austria. Friedell believed that Altenberg had provided a topography of contemporary society which later generations would find far more comprehensive and exact than any novel of the period.[17]

In the pseudo-biographical preface to *Was der Tag mir zuträgt*, Altenberg again stresses the supreme importance of visual perception as he exclaims "*Auge, Auge, Rothschild-Besitz des Menschen*" [*Eye, eye, humanity's Rothschild fortune*: WT 8]. It has been observed that this not unambiguous statement shows how an artist like Altenberg prospers from the investment of his visual perception in things in the same way as a Rothschild from the interest accruing on his capital.[18] That such a conspicuous non-participator in the world of business and finance, and with an ambivalent relationship with Jewry to boot, should have chosen precisely this analogy raises at least as many questions as it is meant to clear up. What Altenberg's insistence on the primacy of visual perception in the creation of his art does reveal, of course, is a close relationship with literary impressionism, although this may be disputed because of the consistently didactic streak in his writing. Egon Friedell is convinced of Altenberg's position as a radical literary impressionist, meaning by impressionism a heightened receptivity towards sensory stimuli, linked

[15] Richard Dehmel, *Ausgewählte Briefe aus den Jahren 1883 bis 1902*, (Berlin: Fischer, 1923), 280.

[16] Johnston, "Viennese Impressionism," 5.

[17] Friedell, *Ecce Poeta*, 170.

[18] Eckhardt Köhn, "Stenograph des Wiener Lebens. Großstadterfahrung im Werk Peter Altenbergs," *Sprachkunst*, 17 (1986): 24.

with the basic tendency to convey nothing other than those physiological impressions.[19]

What Friedell fails to note is how Altenberg, true to the parallel he draws with Rothschild, returns what he sees not in mirror-fashion,[20] but with interest added. Where interest accrues is in the subjective modifications of these direct sensory impressions. The nature of Altenberg's impressionism consists in a subjective reforming of the perceived object, consciously rejecting exactitude in the recording of these perceptions in favor of the imagination. Hence Altenberg's own analogy of the artistic ideal with a Kodak camera. For him nature is the greatest artist, and with a Kodak "in einer wirklich menschlich-zärtlichen Hand" [in a really humane and gentle hand] one can effortlessly recovers its treasures (WS 293). We realize there is a close relationship not only between Altenberg's view of art and that of the naturalists, but also with that of Adolf Loos and Karl Kraus, both of whom were convinced of nature's supremacy as artist. It will be recalled how the German naturalists saw art as "nature minus X," and how they called for art to mirror nature as closely as possible. In this light, the motto of *Was der Tag mir zuträgt* can be seen as an almost crypto-naturalistic programmatic statement; Friedell considered Altenberg a naturalist through and through.[21]

In a posthumous article published in 1915 in Franz Pfemfert's periodical *Die Aktion*, Hans Leybold had no hesitation in placing Altenberg's writing, as with all literary impressionists, in direct line of descent from the naturalists.[22] Yet despite Altenberg's call for art to hold the mirror to nature, and despite his encomium to the Kodak camera, it is plain that with Altenberg results do not always conform with intentions. As Köhn remarks, if the analogy with photography is at all valid, it is akin to the use of a filter which serves to blur the outlines and to destroy the sharpness of focus.[23]

For Leybold too, some seventy-odd years before Köhn, Altenberg cannot be classed as an impressionist because impressionism, if it can be defined at all, is the pure, unadulterated reproduction of sense impressions. Taking Zola's famous dictum that a work of art is an aspect of nature "vu à travers un tempérament" [seen through the filter of a temperament], Leybold regards consequential naturalism as fulfilling the first half of the statement: for the naturalists, a work of art is as close to nature as possible. The George circle on the other hand, Leybold contends, sees only the second half of Zola's proposition, namely the decisive role of the artistic temperament. Peter Altenberg, however, Leybold regards as the embodiment of the polar opposites

---

[19] Friedell, *Ecce Poeta*, 163.

[20] The motto to *Was der Tag mir zuträgt* is "Ein Spiegel sei der Dinge um dich her!" [Be a mirror of the things around you!]

[21] Friedell, *Ecce Poeta*, 170. Altenberg never abandoned the mimetic view of writing first outlined in his letter to Schnitzler, always maintaining that art is a mirror of life (F188).

[22] Hans Leybold, *Die Aktion*, 5 (1915): 74.

[23] Eckhardt Köhn, "Stenograph des Wiener Lebens. Großstadterfahrung im Werk Peter Altenbergs," *Sprachkunst* 17 (1986): 25

contained in Zola's definition. For Altenberg lays equal stress on the objective need for art to reproduce nature, but everything he does is nonetheless "vu à travers un tempérament." Without the theoretical underpinning of Holz and Schlaf's work in the late 1880s, Leybold believes Altenberg's work would have been technically inconceivable, yet the force of "vu à travers un tempérament" can be felt behind the choice of title for his first book. In *Wie ich es sehe* Altenberg might well have had Zola's maxim in mind when he has the Revolutionary, after acclaiming Anton Chekhov, whose works had yet to appear in German translation, give his own view of art: life must "sich mit Geist und Seele durchtränken wie ein Schwamm" [soak up mind and soul like a sponge]. Then it will emerge greater, fuller, and more vital. That, he claims, is art (WS 112).

Nietzsche, who according to Thomas Mann found a genuine exponent in Altenberg (AB 71–72), equally points out in *Jenseits von Gut und Böse* that despite the attempt to record sensory experience in an objective fashion, we often end up with a fabrication. Towards the end of his life, Altenberg acknowledged the refracted nature of his observations, but believed that the objective reproduction of what is perceived merely demands "ein gewisser Mut" [a certain courage: NF 92]. Never one to hide his light under a bushel, Altenberg implies that he indeed possesses this courage. When Albert the revolutionary exclaims that the world is rich and beautiful, an omniscient narrator corrects this erroneous appraisal of reality. What is beautiful is Albert's inner world: "Denn die Welt um ihn herum war armselig und alltäglich" [For the world around him was poor and mundane: WS 65]. This diagnosis of everyday reality parallels that of Hofmannsthal's aesthetically deluded merchant's son in *Das Märchen der 672. Nacht*, a work contemporaneous with *Wie ich es sehe*. Faced with reality, Altenberg, a merchant's son himself, prefers poetry, the "Märchen des Lebens," to life itself.

On other occasions Altenberg is less of an aesthete and more of a social realist. Whereas in "Kunst" he calls for the direct reproduction of sensory impressions, once again referring to the eye as the "Rothschildbesitz des Menschen," in *Nachfechsung* his practical aestheticization of reality is spelled out with particular lucidity. In "Das Erlebnis" a narrator called Peter recounts a touching scene which highlights the pathos of individual relationships within the horrors of war. Sitting in his favourite Graben Café at 7 a.m., he has just witnessed a touching scene between an officer and his beautiful lover. After they had breakfasted, the officer had removed the spoon from her saucer, kissed it and placed it in his pocket. It strikes the interlocutor as odd that it is precisely the poet who is so often party to such scenes, whereupon Peter replies: "Ich erlebe sie, weil ich sie mir erdichte!" [I experience them because I fabricate them: NF 61].

Although it is a fabrication, the poet will not accept the charge of deception, drawing a line between the fabrication of the anecdote ["erdichten"] and the accusation of simply making it up ["erfinden"]. Many officers in a similar situation would wish to take precisely such leave of their lover, but are ashamed of their own romanticism and the softness of their hearts. The function of the poet — and here the didacticism is much clearer than in *Wie ich es sehe* and other early works — is to lend a helping hand, to instruct people in their lives through fiction purporting to be reality (NF 61). As he declares in "Individualität," deep inside every human being there lies a poet (P 156). Altenberg demands of the reader a willingness to join in the act of artistic creation, for a function of his extravagant use of silence, indicated by the punctuation marks - - - at the end of so many statements, is precisely an invitation to fill in the gaps, to finish off the work of the writer in an individual way and ultimately to become a poet.

The reality of *Wie ich es sehe*, and the other early works, is to a considerable degree a poetic reality, in which the poet is ready to interpret seemingly simple events and give them a piquancy often hidden from the participants in his *Skizzen*. (This was the term Altenberg originally gave to many prose poems before switching to *Studien* in later revisions of *Wie ich es sehe*.) We will frequently note, along with much dialogue, the poet's tendency to read added significance into the stuff of his narration. Hence the constant reporting of thoughts and feelings formulated by the author on behalf of figures who, in keeping with their often humble station in life, are not considered capable of consciously formulating such notions. At the end of "Blumen-Corso," which contains more urban realism than most of Altenberg's early writing, the street-sweeper who picks up a flower which has fallen from a decorated float is seen from the idealized perspective of the writer. His daughter declares with unsentimental realism that the flower stinks, whereas the street-sweeper is elevated in the poet's imagination above his station in life to the point where he too makes poetry out of everyday life. The street-sweeper might have replied, so the narrator claims, that such are the flowers which bloom on the asphalt of the city, though he modestly says nothing. Not content with this silence, the omniscient poet-narrator at the close of the piece reports the thoughts of the street-sweeper, and thereby reveals the extent to which this man of the people is lacking in poetic response. In this instance, at least, reality is preferred to poetry, for with striking bathos the man simply thinks the obvious: the flower is left over from the procession:

> Sein Töchterchen sagt: "Pfui, sie stinkt - -". Der Gassenkehrer hätte antworten können: "Das sind die Blumen, die auf dem Asphalt einer Grossstadt blühen - - -!" Aber er sagte das nicht. Dazu war er zu bescheiden - - -. Er dachte: "Es ist vom Blumencorso - - -!" (WS 214–215)

> [His little daughter says: "Pfui, it stinks - -." The street-sweeper could have answered: "Those are the flowers which bloom on the asphalt of a city - - - !" But he didn't say that. He was too humble - - -. He thought: "It's from the flower parade".]

With its mix of direct and reported speech and thought "Blumen-Corso" may serve as a typical example of *Wie ich es sehe* as a whole. It is intensely visual, but it is almost equally noteworthy for its sensitivity to sound. Writing about Anton Webern on the occasion of the composer's fiftieth birthday in 1934, David Joseph Bach remarked that all of Webern's work could be seen as the aural equivalent of Peter Altenberg's *Wie ich es sehe*, a sort of "Wie ich es höre" [How I hear it].[24] A close reading suggests that this would be almost as suitable a title as that chosen by the author for his literary début.

In "Blumen-Corso" the reader is aware that the stimulus for the poet's observations is as much aural and oral as visual. A striking feature of this tightly-structured prose-poem is the effect of apparently random street sounds woven collage-fashion into the fabric of the text. A pale shop-girl who works in a business producing artificial flowers carries white roses to a carriage standing outside in the early-morning street, awaiting its decoration for the forthcoming parade. Almost imperceptibly, Altenberg shifts from presentation of visual perceptions (the girl carrying flowers,) via olfactory experience (the artificial blooms smell like old muslin clothes) to the sounds of the street criers and the half-heard snippets of conversations culled from passers-by:

> Blumencorso - - - für Nachmittag 4 Uhr! Logen-Sitze 5 Kronen! Es soll Geld unter die Leute kommen, Tausende verdienen indirekt, hat man eine Idee? Es geht herunter bis zum - - -. Niemand kann es ausdenken. (WS 213)

> [Flower parade - - - for 4 p.m.! Stand seats 5 crowns! People will get money, thousands earn indirectly, can you imagine that? It goes right down to - - -. Nobody can imagine it.]

Altenberg's love of restaurants, cafés, variety theatres and late-night bars as settings for his work may well be related to their potential for aural as much as visual stimuli.[25] This is especially obvious in "Der Trommler Belín," inspired by a performing drummer at Vienna's Ronacher night-club. Here Altenberg simply gives himself up to some joyous sound-painting, not unlike Liliencron's evocation of the military band in his celebrated poem "Die Musik kommt." Like Kraus, Altenberg thought highly of Liliencron, and contributed to a celebration of his work in 1903:[26]

> Die Schlacht singt ihr Lied, jauchzt, kreischt, brüllt, stöhnt, athmet aus - - - -. Pause. Plötzlich beginnt ein furchtbarer Wirbel - - - - Rrrrátaplan rrráta rrráta rrráta rrratatatái tá tá tá tá - - - trrrrrrrrá! (WS 78)

> [The battle sings its song, rejoices, screeches, bawls, groans, breathes out - - - - -. Pause. Suddenly there begins a terrible turmoil - - - - Rrrrátaplan rrráta rrráta rrráta rrratatatá tá tá tá tá - - - trrrrrrrrá!]

Altenberg's joyful reaction to physical stimuli is summed up perfectly when he exclaims in *Was der Tag mir zuträgt*: "Leben, ich verneige mich vor Dir! Zwei Augen, zwei Ohren besitze ich, ich Kaiser!" [Life, I bow be-

[24] David Josef Bach, *Anton Webern zum 50. Geburtstag*, (Vienna: Verlag der IGNM [Sektion Österreich], 1934). Cited in Friedrich Wildgans, *Anton Webern*, (London: Calder and Boyars, 1966), 178.

[25] Köhn, "Stenograph," 33.

[26] Fritz Böckel, *Detlev von Liliencron im Urteil zeitgenössischer Dichter*, (Berlin: Schuster und Loeffler, 1904), 15.

fore you! Two eyes, two ears have I, emperor that I am!: WT 128]. Compared with Spitzer's Viennese perambulations, a specific local model for his
work, Altenberg's stance is much less that of the *flâneur*, far more that of the
watcher and listener. In his pioneering study, Friedell laid particular stress on
his friend's role as someone who wrote simultaneously with his experiences
like a stenographer of life taking down dictation.[27]

Altenberg reacted with particular sensitivity to the nuances of the spoken
word: indeed, he seems from the outset to have been almost over-aware of
the impossibility of the written word catching the rich under- and overtones
of speech. Friedell sees this as the reason underlying an unmistakable visual
feature of Altenberg's texts: the plethora of punctuation marks, used in
seemingly profligate abandon. They are, thinks Friedell, nothing more than
the attempt to impart to the deadness of the printed word the liveliness of
spoken speech.[28]

At the same time, the way speech acts so often trail off into a row of enigmatic dashes, exclamation and question marks can be seen as Altenberg's
recognition of the impossibility of any language, written or spoken, to fully
express the complexities of lived or thought experience. In this he not only
mirrored the "cult of silence" in contemporary French writing, he also continued a topos in German literature which would expand into the general crisis of language so prevalent in Vienna during the final days of Hapsburg rule.

Wie ich es sehe

Künstler sein heißt, Wecker sein, Wachrufer, Muezzin, auf den Minaret-
thürmen über den flachen Dörfern der schlummernden Menschenseele[29]

[Being an artist means arousing people, calling them awake, a muezzin atop
the minarets above the flat villages of the slumbering human soul]

When Altenberg presented his first book to public scrutiny, even he was
probably unaware of its originality. A work superficially in the tradition of
Spitzer's Viennese saunters, *Wie ich es sehe* was in reality more indebted to
Huysmans's confrontation with the prose poems of Mallarmé and Baudelaire. Not without reason did Altenberg enquire of S. Fischer in a letter of
June 1896 how his work could be made better known in Paris.[30] At the time
of its initial appearance, however, Altenberg made no acknowledgment of his

---

[27] Friedell, *Ecce Poeta*, 164.

[28] Ibid., 165–166.

[29] Inscription by Altenberg in a first edition of *Wie ich es sehe*. Private collection of Heinz and
Viktoria Lunzer, Vienna. This section is adapted from Andrew Barker, "'Die weiseste Ökonomie
bei tiefster Fülle.' — Peter Altenberg's *Wie ich es sehe*," *Studies in Nineteenth Century Austrian
Literature*, ed. Brian O. Murdoch and Mark G. Ward, (Glasgow: Scottish Papers in Germanic
Studies, 1983), 77–101.

[30] *Peter Altenberg: Leben und Werk in Texten und Bildern*, ed. Hans Christian Kosler, (Munich:
Matthes and Seitz, 1981), 119.

book's place in the lineage of the French *poème en prose*, preferring to preface it with an unattributed quotation from Alfred de Musset. Like the letter to Schnitzler, this acknowledged the essentially small-scale nature of his writing. At the same time it also emphasized an awareness of his ability to maximise its potential:

> Mon verre n'est pas grand - - - - Mais je bois dans mon verre.[31]
>
> [My glass is not large - - - - But I drink from my glass.]

It should also be noted that the *Wie ich es sehe* of 1896 was considerably different from the book which at its last printing in 1928 had reached twenty editions. By 1904, when *Wie ich es sehe* assumed its final guise, the original 246 pages had grown to 332. By the second edition in 1898, two significant changes had occurred. Most obvious was the appearance of a photograph of the author opposite the title page, a most unusual practice for Fischer Verlag books (or for that matter for any work of fiction) and drawing attention to the importance which publisher and author alike attached to the congruence of writer and work.[32] A further visual aid in the second edition was a caricature of Altenberg by Hans Schließmann, placed at the end of the book.

The creation of "Peter Altenberg" was now complete, and in future only *Ashantee*, *Pròdròmòs* and *Märchen des Lebens* would lack a photographic representation of the author. Together with a table of contents, not present in the first edition, came also a preface. This is not, however, in German, but French, and purports to be a quotation from page 264 of J.-K. Huysmans's novel *A rebours*. In fact it is adapted by Altenberg from Huysmans — the names of Baudelaire and Mallarmé, present in the original, are omitted — and gives the Duc d'Esseintes's views on the prose poem. Of all forms of poetry, this was his favorite because it represents the dry juice, the osmazome of literature, its essential oil. Garrulousness is reduced to sober silence, the sea of prose condensed into a droplet of poetry. The programmatic nature of Altenberg's quotation is at once relativized, however, by the self-deprecating irony of "Un mot de monsieur P.A. sur monsieur P.A." who, having had the good fortune of being neither a lyric poet, nor a novelist nor a philosopher, had made a unique literary combination out of three talents he did not possess.

---

[31] In the second edition the initials A. de M appear at the end, but in its final form, from 1905 onwards, this motto is dropped altogether. It is itself an adaptation of: "je hais comme la mort l'état plagiaire; Mon verre n'est pas grand mais je bois dans mon verre." (Alfred de Musset, *La coupe et les lèvres*, Dédicace à M. A. Tattet, 1832.)

[32] The various photographic frontispieces are republished in Barker and Lensing, *Rezept*, 148–149. W. B. Spinnen thinks these images are an attempt by the publisher to help readers orientate themselves, providing an extra-literary counterbalance to the problematic "I" present even in the book's title. (WBS, "Die Seele in der Kritik. Zur zeitgenössischen Rezeption Peter Altenbergs," M.A. diss., Münster, 1983, 154.) He contends that the frontispiece portraits strengthen the perception of Altenberg's work as the experiential outpourings of an eccentric and are thus antiliterary (157.) See also Peter de Mendelssohn, *S. Fischer und sein Verlag*, (Frankfurt: Fischer, 1970), 732.

Another important French antecedent was Maurice Maeterlinck, an author frequently referred to by Altenberg. He approves especially of Maeterlinck's emphasis on the spiritual advancement of mankind: both of them, he claims, want the soul to gain ground, seeing in this the source of further human development (P 27). Technically too, Maeterlinck's influence can be felt, for the rows of dots he employs to signify unspoken thought are very reminiscent of Altenberg's use of multiple dashes. In both authors it is here that the *dialogue du second degrée* is located. This particular technique, a "sort of conversation of souls alongside and beyond the audible dialogue,"[33] was a favourite device of Maeterlinck's and appealed also to Hofmannsthal, who both translated and imitated him. Further examples of the way in which Altenberg may well have responded to Maeterlinck's lead are the static nature of many sketches, reminiscent of the *tragédie immobile*, and the "cult of silence."[34]

By prefacing the new edition of *Wie ich es sehe* with a quotation from an "authority" like Huysmans, Altenberg hoped to persuade readers that his sketches were more than simply "impressions" of life in *fin de siècle* Vienna, transmitting the view of Peter Altenberg in the guises of the "Revolutionär", the "Dichter", Albert Königsberg and P.A. They must also be seen in the context of a genre in which form plays a crucial role. By "quoting" Huysmans, Altenberg further tries to guide the aesthetic responses of his readership away from the narrowly Austrian sphere of reference which his pieces might suggest, and into a wider European tradition. He felt that his works demanded a fundamentally different approach to the act of reading than that required when looking at a piece by Spitzer. However, it is also possible Altenberg felt the need to preface his work in order to overcome incomprehension on the part of his literary peers in Young Vienna. The most obvious instance was Hofmannsthal, who floundered to describe the impact this new work clearly had made upon him:

> Das ist ein neues Buch, eine Art von Buch. Ich weiß nicht recht, von welcher Art dieses Buch ist.

> [This is a new book, a sort of book. I don't quite know what sort of book this is: AB 145]

Besides attempting to guide the reader and to correct inappropriate critical responses — particularly incomprehensible on the part of Hofmannsthal, given his level of involvement with French literature — Altenberg undertook other changes in the format of *Wie ich es sehe*. The contentious "Familienleben" was dropped, and other pieces were added, either to pre-existing cycles or as independent items. What is clear from examining the first two editions in particular is the strong sense of architecture governing the work's structure. With successive editions, however, further items were added, until

---

[33] Jens Malte Fischer, *Fin de Siècle. Kommentar zu einer Epoche*, (Munich: Winkler, 1978), 161.

[34] Ibid., 161–162.

the original 68 had been fleshed out to 119, an inflation caused chiefly by incorporating large chunks of *Ashantee* in the fourth edition of 1904.

Such apparently ad hoc accretions undoubtedly distort the formal coherence which the first two editions, but especially the first, had demonstrated. Only towards the end of the first edition, in the final seventeen items from "Wie ein Bild" to "Das Leiden," does the impression arise of a disparate collection of mood pictures. Most items are grouped into three tightly-composed and carefully arranged *Skizzen-Reihen* [sequences of sketches]. Within these cycles Altenberg develops themes which will remain central to his work for the next two decades: the fate of women in contemporary society, the life of the child (usually female) the supreme role of nature as artist, the need for a "New Man" if human kind is to develop its full evolutionary potential, and the importance of adopting a diet very different from that consumed by the majority of bourgeois Austrians.

Altenberg never surpassed the creative consistency of *Wie ich es sehe*, and it is to the "See-Ufer" cycle, which opens the collection, that I shall devote the most detailed examination. This cycle reveals that, in his early work at least, Altenberg could achieve formal coherence not merely within individual sketches, the majority of which are prose poems, but also over a more extended span.[35] Set in an unnamed Salzkammergut resort readily identifiable as Gmunden am Traunsee, which Altenberg often visited, "See-Ufer" is largely devoted to the lives, loves, and fantasies of girls and women aged between nine and thirty-five. Thereafter, Altenberg shows scant interest, for he considers their physical beauty to have faded, a beauty of central importance for the spiritual regeneration of men. Altenberg may not be sexist, but he is certainly ageist. In "See-Ufer," however, insofar as males impinge at all, they are always observed in the context of female influence, and at times domination.

Altenberg also shows himself a keen observer of fashion — he was later to design jewelry — and for historians of fashion his descriptions can provide quite detailed information. The faded sepia photographs from the camera's early days emerge in full color; for these vignettes are based upon real women, not the stereotypes of *fin de siècle* art, the nymph in the woodland pool or the sensuously voracious Salomé-figure. One of Altenberg's achievements was to see ordinary women for what they were. At a time when they were still excluded from many areas of society, he gives them pride of place. Separated from their menfolk at work in the hot, summery city, these often isolated women, abandoned in the resort, demonstrate how peripheral their lives are. They may benefit from the financial rewards of a burgeoning economy, but play no active role in it. In their lake-side existence they are sus-

---

[35] Burkhard Spinnen objects to this interpretation as an example of the "temptation of the reader to read the sequence, *contrary* to its conception, as a traditional narrative unit." (*Schriftbilder. Studien zu einer Geschichte emblematischer Prosa*, [Münster, Aschendorff 1991], 129). As we have no knowledge of what Altenberg had in mind when he wrote "See-Ufer," I am not sure how this reading can be "*gegen* ihre Konzeption." Nor do I understand how formal coherence is necessarily a feature only of traditional narration.

pended between the metropolis and the countryside, between the dry land and the water, between society and nature.[36]

Altenberg's female figures challenge conventional wisdom, but the apparent security in which so many lead their compartmentalized lives is revealed as suspect. As the season progresses, as the days grow shorter and the lake stormier, so the very social order upon which the lives of the women in "See-Ufer" are based is questioned. Setting the sequence in a holiday resort might make it appear peripheral to the major concerns of society at large, but just as Joseph Roth was to show in *Radetzkymarsch*, it was precisely at the extremities, both geographical and social, of the Hapsburg Empire that fissures in its fabric were initially most clearly perceived.

The lasting impression is of a society on the brink, far removed from Zweig's nostalgic evocation of "the golden age of security."[37] Indeed, the final study of "See-Ufer" is set not in the idyllic lakeland of Upper Austria, but back in Vienna's Grillparzerstraße, peopled not primarily by the middle and upper classes but by an army of workers. It may be significant that this street, named after nineteenth-century Austria's most problematic writer, is sandwiched between the University and the City Hall, both apparent bastions of the established social order in which, however, ominous cracks were starting to appear in the 1890s.

The opening four studies in "See-Ufer" are designated simply by reference to the ages of the girls and women who appear in them: "Neun und Elf," "Zwölf," "Neunzehn," "Siebzehn bis Dreißig." It is high summer, yet in three of these four items there are references to the presence of autumn and the abandonment of the resort. In "Zwölf," which alone contains no specific reference to autumn, the relationship between the passage of the seasons and the inescapable aging process in women is nevertheless implied in the interaction between the insouciantly vital fisher-girl and the morally scrupulous gentlewoman who watches her. Compassion, warmth and feeling are on the side of the older woman, yet Altenberg makes plain his view that such "higher feelings" are only developed at a price. Somewhat cynically, the narrator sketches the origins of ethical awareness which, he contends, grows only on the grave of shattered dreams and dead hopes (WS 7). The older woman's face is pale and weather-beaten, she will provide no more joy, warmth or light for anyone, which is why she has sympathy for the plight of the dying fishes. The twelve-year old girl, however, with her dark blond hair and gazelle-like legs, kills the fish without compunction. She is an early example of the "child-woman" who so fascinated Egon Schiele two decades later. The narrator acknowledges her cruelty, but she also embodies a spontaneous beauty to be fostered regardless of ethical considerations. She is to be encouraged because her spontaneity will soon be destroyed by the dictates of society and the process of maturation. Altenberg claimed never to have

---

[36] Gisela Wysocki, *Peter Altenberg: Bilder und Geschichten des befreiten Lebens*, (Munich: Hanser, 1979), 81.

[37] Stefan Zweig, *Die Welt von gestern: Erinnerungen eines Europäers*, (Stockholm: Bermann-Fischer, 1947).

read a word of Nietzsche, but in pieces like "Zwölf" we realize the aptness of Thomas Mann's assessment of Altenberg as one of those who along with the novelist himself, his brother Heinrich, the poets Dehmel and George and the critic Alfred Kerr, are the true critics and fragmentary elucidators of Nietzsche (AB 72).

The following study, "Neunzehn," is dominated by an awareness of the transience of both the long summer days and of youthful romance. Yet even in the midst of her courtship by a besotted young man, the nineteen-year old girl displays a disturbing lack of vitality, of spontaneous pleasure in her youthful beauty. She has received a card from her paramour, apostrophizing her as the ideal of human beauty, and she can admire objectively the impact of her nakedness as she looks in the mirror. All this amounts to, however, is that for a fleeting second she ceases to feel bored (WS 9). The study concludes with her traveling back by train to the autumn and winter in a state of shivering boredom (WS 9).

The pessimism of "See-Ufer" is extended in "Siebzehn bis Dreißig" to encompass the relationship between the social classes. Pointedly linking motifs from piece to piece, Altenberg shows in "See-Ufer" how young women of various ages and social backgrounds are joined together in a way transcending social divides. The exploited cashier of "Siebzehn bis Dreißig" has the same gazelle-like legs as the girl in "Zwölf", her unclothed beauty establishes a link between her and the strangely lifeless girl in "Neunzehn." The narrator speculates that the cashier will be seduced by a count or a prince, working as she does in the capital's leading hair salon. In fact she marries the proprietor of a café who dies within a year, leaving her alone with a child to rear. For all the desperation of the girl's plight, the writing nevertheless manages to retain a touch of suggestive levity:

> Sie heiratete einen Cafétier, der in einem Jahre zu Grunde ging. Sie war gebaut wie eine Gazelle. Seide und Sammt erhöhten nicht ihre Schönheit -
> - am schönsten war sie wahrscheinlich nackt. Der Cafétier ging zu Grunde.
> (WS 10)

> [She married the owner of a café who perished within a year. She was built like a gazelle. Silk and satin did not enhance her beauty - - she was probably most beautiful when naked. The café owner perished.]

The mood of the study changes, however, as the narrator outlines the inevitable course of her life. Idle speculation as to who might seduce this sweet young thing is replaced by the hard, unforgiving account of her future lot. He recalls a friend who had contracted typhus, a rich bachelor living in a lakeside villa. When visiting him he discovers a resigned young woman with silky yellow hair making ice compresses, her hands red raw from the icy water. After his recovery the friend had simply passed the woman on to another rich young man. That was in the summer. Later, in the autumn, as a sense of longing came over him, he wrote asking her to come back to him. One October evening the narrator saw them both, and as he greeted her, the girl looked at him with a gaze which said: "Das Leben liegt hinter mir, das Leben - -! Weisst Du das?!" [my life is behind me, my life is - -! Do you know that?!: WS 11].

Such exploitation of an attractive working-class girl by a rich young bachelor is like Schnitzler at his most mordant, reminding us that *Wie ich es sehe* is contemporaneous with the composition of *Reigen* and *Liebelei*. Women are conventionally most desirable between seventeen and thirty, but if they belong to a certain social class, Altenberg sees them at the mercy of predatory men who may abandon them at will. Conveying a starkly prosaic message, "Siebzehn bis Dreißig" is a prose poem whose construction resembles a set of musical variations. The narrator's opening words are repeated virtually verbatim after recounting the fate of the blond cashier. Now, however, the young girl at the till has brown wavy hair. Like her predecessor, she also challenges the narrator with a "triumphal stare of youth" which declares, like that of the blond girl: "Ich sage Dir, das Leben liegt vor mir, das Leben - - -! Weisst Du das?!" [I'm telling you, life lies before me, life - - -! Do you know that?!: WS 12]. Once more the narrator speculates that a count or a prince will seduce her, whereupon the narration breaks off and the variations remain fragmentary, subsequent development being pointless. The implication is that in the round dance of existence the brunette will suffer an identical fate to that of her predecessor, cheated by men and by "life" alike. The overt social criticism shows that whatever Altenberg may later have said about the title of his book, it is feasible to relate it not merely to the author's perception and reproduction of reality, but also to his stance vis à vis society: "Wie ich es sehe . . . ", "The way I see things . . . ".

The sequence depicting younger women is interrupted after "Siebzehn bis Dreißig." Whereas this ends with the narrator's speculations upon the lasciviousness of the aristocratic male, the next sketch, "Die Natur," has at its center an aristocratic woman. Ignorant of life's deeper currents, she is almost comically unaware of youthful sexuality. As she rows along the lake at nightfall, everything she encounters is moribund. A dying poet lies in his villa, in another a dying marriage is on the point of collapse. Further on lives a duchess who has lost a son she never possessed in the first place. Lulled by the beauty of nature and the peace of evening, the lady floats obliviously past these signs of decay. Appearances are never more deceptive than when nature presents an idyllic front. The task of the writer, however, is both to portray things "on the surface" and to reveal the reality behind appearances which otherwise would slip past unheeded in the playground of the rich. In "Siebzehn bis Dreißig" a pillar of the Establishment made life a trial for an underling, here the superficially unruffled surface of polite society conceals not just dissension, decay and isolation, but above all ignorance of reality. The only things to blossom and grow are children, young love and nature. But children grow up, love grows stale and the very calm of nature, as of society, is deceptive.

Not only does the narrator repeatedly emphasize summer's imminent decline, but in "P.A. und T.K." balmy days collapse into more typical Salzkammergut weather. In this, the longest study so far, we hear repeatedly the lashing rain and the thud of waves against the shore. Despite employing a third person narrator, Altenberg is at the center of the sketch, projecting for the first, but by no means the last time, his persona as a narrative figure and enabling an apparently more objective insight into the feminine psyche. As Stefan Zweig noted in 1901, the "soul of woman is for Altenberg the most intimate and sensitive of instruments, whose nervous vibrations he listens to with deep devotion, just as he honours woman's body as a gospel, whose sanctity can never be violated."[38]

The sympathy "P.A." feels for young women is boundless, and in "P.A. und T.K." he is appalled by the strains society subjects them to. How, he wonders, can a girl be happy and enjoy herself unless she is beautiful? How can she be happy, unless she feels attractive? For three whole summers P.A. has been fascinated by the beautiful, virtually flawless Theresa K. Yet even she moves with only the "tired grace" (WS 14) which so often characterizes the *décadence* of the late nineteenth century. Dancing a number called "Sir Roger," she loses her footing, and as she tumbles, all her existential fears reveal themselves. Her features assume the pained expression of a madonna, she questions her place in the order of things, wondering where she belongs and what, apart from giving pleasure, she was created for (WS 15). In her relationship with a shadowy young man of poetic temperament she realizes enough of her femininity to achieve a not altogether convincing transformation into a "Weib-Königin" [Woman-Queen], but the narrator places her small triumph against the backdrop of inclement weather and his gloomy view that life, an essentially destructive force, was passing her by (WS 18).

As the cycle advances, Altenberg's pessimism comes to embrace his whole society. As mercilessly as in *Frau Beathe und ihr Sohn*, Schnitzler's study of a Salzkammergut resort (1913) the atmosphere of genteel recreation and civilised discourse is revealed as a facade. Women present an alluring picture to the eye, but they are exploited, uncertain of themselves and their function, and quintessentially lonely, thanks to the rigid segregation both of the sexes and the classes. This lakeside community also lacks a firm male presence: "No age," which follows "P.A. und T.K.," is the first sketch with a dominant male figure. Carrying over a motif from the previous sketch, Altenberg shows him dancing the fashionable "Sir Roger" which Teresa K. enjoyed. Although "No Age" may indicate Altenberg's perception of the constancy of the masculine principle as opposed to the aging process in women highlighted throughout the cycle, this male is an ambivalent figure. He dances like a clown, and his masculinity is not heightened but rather dampened and repressed by the proximity of the beautiful woman (WS 20). Paradoxically, but perhaps also more conventionally, the man displays a noble physique, with muscles of steel, as if on well-oiled hinges, powered by wit and grace. In the words of a pale-faced girl with a "sacred" face, he is a "real man," (Altenberg uses English here), the best the resort has to offer. Rather

---

[38] *Das junge Wien: Österreichische Literatur- und Kunstkritik 1887–1902*, vol. 2, ed. Gotthart Wunberg, (Tübingen: Niemeyer, 1976), 1156.

pointedly, he is not an Austrian but comes from the New World, his name is "mister Bigloff" and he is married with three angelic children. The sketch ends with the girl's sigh of longing: "Ah, missis Bigloff - - -!" (WS 21)

Women's fundamental isolation is nowhere better illustrated than in "Fünfundzwanzig," resuming the sequence designated merely by the ages of the mostly nameless women featured in them. Here the woman is again predictably beautiful, exquisitely dressed and well-placed — her child has a nanny — but also frighteningly alone. Men cast admiring glances, they sit nearby but never beside her. Nothing alleviates the loneliness of a young mother with (we must assume) an absentee husband, a woman stranded in a world of half-meetings, wordless glances, empty conversations in the endless round of socializing beside the lake.

"Fünfunddreißig" presents a similar family unit of mother and daughter ten years on, although for once the husband is present and the outward picture is one of conjugal contentment. However, the poet is not prepared to let this impression prevail and imbues the woman with a fantasy life shared only by himself. It is a life of longing which implores the poet to spirit her away from the bounds of family life and off with him into the profoundly mysterious ocean of life (WS 25). Despite the title of his book, Altenberg here proves unwilling to record what he sees. The objective evidence bespeaks married bliss, but to record this would go against his deeper perception of the life he is at pains to portray in "See-Ufer." He wishes to show that even where, unusually, the apparent embodiment of bourgeois satisfaction is at hand, the woman still remains dissatisfied with her lot. Nothing, Altenberg declares, is simply as it appears to be on the surface of life. Just as the lake itself conceals hidden depths, displayed only when whipped up by wind and storm, so too do the lives of the lake-dwellers.

Thus far "See-Ufer" has presented a steadily unfolding picture of women's sad and unfulfilled isolation as they age, a process viewed against the background of a society ever ready to exploit or neglect them, be it as lover, mother or wife. An acute awareness of a society riven by class and sexual stereotyping is indicated. The dominant motifs of isolation, class-division and exploitation are drawn together in "Roman am Lande," a culmination of the first half of the cycle which is also a preparation for subsequent sketches in its growing sympathy for certain aspects of male as well as female existence.

"Roman am Lande" must be the shortest "novel" in the German language: thirty lines long, 165 words in its revised version. Yet in the best traditions of the nineteenth-century novel, it holds a mirror up to society, albeit a boudoir mirror rather than one reflecting the world at large. Although the theme of a poor boy's unrequited love for a rich woman brings this "concentrate of a novel" close to the best traditions of the pot-boiler, it has a poignancy which lifts it above *Trivialliteratur*. There is pathos in the lad's genuine and unrequited love, and in his willingness to endure four years of exploitation — the job, the food and the boss are all bad — merely to be near his "Linden Princess," unattainable behind the walls of her villa set in its

parkland dotted with limes. He must remain content with his longing, and
the memory of a fleeting contact during which she gave him cigarettes. Like
a cavalier he kissed her hand, but this merely reinforced the social gulf:
"Dann schaut er wieder aus 'vom Söller des Lebens' und sieht den weiten
endlosen Weg - - -." [Then he looks out from 'life's balcony' and sees the
distant endless path - - -.: WS 27].

"Roman am Lande" exudes a timeless quality, suggesting the immutability of society and its divisions, but in "Sanct Wolfgang," at the very center
of the cycle, Altenberg is at pains to contrast the lime-scented breezes of the
"novel" with the here and now of modern technology, represented by the
narrow-gauge Schafberg railway. Wafted on the breeze come not the scents
of lime trees but clouds of dark smoke. The smells of nature have been replaced by a stink such as mythical creatures leave behind them. In this central
study, Altenberg moves away from the resort for the first time, creating a cae-
sura in the flow of studies set at the lakeside.

The omnipresence of technology is an inescapable theme of late nineteenth-century writing, and specific mention of the then recently-constructed
Schafbergbahn permits Altenberg to further underline the actuality of his
writing. To this day the same little engines struggle up the mountain, maintaining a tangible link with Altenberg's era. Opened in 1893, the cog railway
now seems part of the landscape and forms an integral part of the area's
charm. When Altenberg was writing, however, the newly-laid track was still
an open scar on the fragile landscape and represented a further division for
the poet, a division which will loom large in the whole work: the gulf between mankind and the natural world.[39] The woman who takes the train
cannot enjoy the view from the summit although the panorama is at its most
splendid. On the other hand, the girl who has remained below, watching the
ascent of the "squat little monster" is not alienated from the natural world
(WS 28).

Exactly half way through "See-Ufer" Altenberg has placed the cycle unmistakably into the context of the relentless mechanisation taking place in the
1890s. This process is apparently far removed from the superficially timeless
idyll of the resort, but it determines the material success of those who escape
there for the summer. From now on the autumnal mood constantly hinted
at in the opening half of the cycle, will predominate. With it the themes of
personal isolation and above all of social division and incipient conflict will be
ever more strongly drawn, a reminder that there is no escape from the realities and conflicts of the day. Hofmannsthal's assertion that Altenberg's work
is concerned only with trivia (AB 151) and lacks historical awareness (AB
158) could not be further from the truth.

Positioned on either side of "Sanct Wolfgang," with its theme of the al-
ienation of man from nature through technology, are two studies, "Roman
am Lande" and "Assarow und Madame Oyasouki". Both portray the specific

---

[39] For an alternate reading see Burckhard Spinnen, *Schriftbilder. Studien zu einer Geschichte emblematischer Kurzprosa*, (Münster: Aschendorff, 1991), 115–116.

division of man from woman. Whereas in the "novel" the man is separated by the chasm of class from the woman of his dreams, in "Assarow und Madame Oyasouki" Assarow falls victim to the femme fatale, a rare instance in *Wie ich es sehe* where Altenberg depicts a sexual stereotype of *fin de siècle* literature. The open bias of Altenberg's sympathies in the first nine studies is redressed here in a text which projects woman not as a victim, but a destroyer.

The depiction of life rejected and crushed heralds the rapidly approaching end of the "season." In the subsequent study "Spätsommernachmittag," the boy-meets-girl scenario is muted by the girl's uncertainty as to the manifestations of her sexuality: she can only attract, she cannot not make lasting attachments. The bad weather prevents the development of their relationship along the customary woodland paths, the days are now short and the gales blow through the chestnut trees (WS 32). In an eerie finale the girl's brother plays a Chopin étude, the wind howls outside, and the couple dance slowly and soundlessly (WS 33). Although moved by the beauty of the music, the young man can only express himself in the most conventional terms.

Communication difficulties between the sexes are even more apparent in "Landparthie," where the autumnal turn of the season, nature's cold and darkness are stressed. Presented with a bouquet, a girl can react only with cold clumsiness to the most traditional of compliments. She complains that flowers always wilt when she gets them and sticks the bouquet into her brown silk waistband (WS 33). Conversation is always strained, requests are ignored, communication is at best tenuous. The inadequacies of language to convey feeling, reflected constantly in Altenberg's punctuation technique, and the resort to coded utterances rather than direct statement, contribute to a sensation of tension and unease, heightened by the hostility of nature, the girl's lack of grace and the not-so-young man's vain attempt to stanch the flow of the years (WS 35).

The shortest study in "See-Ufer," nine lines in all, is "Flirt," yet within this restricted space Altenberg conveys all the superficiality of relationships within the resort, the faithlessness of men, the loneliness of woman fulfilling one of the many rôles demanded of her:

> Sie trug ein Kleid von der mattgrünen Farbe der Diamant-Käfer und gab einem Cavalier Rosen-blätter zu essen, welche sie abzupfte. "Ambrosia" - - - sagte der Cavalier. Später sass sie immer allein. Ihr mattgrünes Kleid schimmerte wie Phosphor. Sie zupfte langsam Rosenblätter ab, gab sie niemandem zu essen. Eine Träne fiel auf ihr Kleid. Aber Niemand sagte "Nektar!" (WS 37)[40]

> [She wore a matt green dress the color of the stag-beetle and gave a cavalier rose-petals to eat, which she plucked off. "Ambrosia - - -" said the cavalier. Later she always sat by herself. Her matt green dress shimmered like phos-

[40] In *Peter Altenberg. Expedition in den Alltag. Gesammelte Skizzen 1895–1898*, ed. Werner J. Schweiger, (Vienna and Frankfurt: Löcker and Fischer, 1987), 35, the last line reads simply "Nektar!"

phorus. She slowly plucked off the rose petals, but gave them to nobody to eat. A tear fell on her dress. But nobody said nectar!]

After reading such a piece we may be tempted to conclude that what the Revolutionary says about Chekhov in "Der Besuch" applies equally to Altenberg's own achievement in *Wie ich es sehe* as a whole:

Mit Wenigem Viel sagen, das ist es! Die weiseste Ökonomie bei tiefster Fülle, das ist auch beim Künstler Alles - - wie beim Menschen. (WS 112)

[To say much with little means, that's it! Wisest economy with the profoundest plenitude, that is everything for the artist too - - as it is for people.]

"Fleiss," just twenty-three lines long, again shows communication all but absent as a young poet repeatedly walks past a woman knitting doggedly like a latter-day Norn (WS 38). Behind both "Flirt" and "Fleiss" there is a relativisation of accepted behavioural concepts: amorous dalliance is not romantic, it merely masks sadness and loneliness. At the opposite end of the moral scale from flirtation, hard work is ironically portrayed as a mindless time-filler with no end-product. "Friede," just seventeen lines long, completes this small group of ironic commentaries on their titles. Here a girl perceives the illusory nature of the peaceful times she lives in, but prefers to pretend that her insight has no validity:

" . . . Aber es giebt Störer, in der Ferne, am Horizonte. Was werden sie machen aus uns?! Wir werden wahrscheinlich den Sommer nicht mehr geniessen können wie die Grille und wie die See-Schwäne." . . . Und sie genoss den Sommer wie die Grille und wie die See-Schwäne - - -! (WS 39)

[" . . . But there are storm-clouds in the distance, on the horizon. What will they do with us?! Probably we will no longer be able to enjoy the summer like the grasshopper and the swans on the lake." . . . And she enjoyed the summer like the grasshopper and the swans on the lake - - -!]

The peace is thus felt to be threatened, the times are disturbed, and as the cycle progresses the distant disturbances on the horizon draw ever nearer, becoming more tangible as Altenberg foresees the end of a society which, cocooned by wealth and privilege, can still permit itself long warm weeks beside the lake, forgetful of the state of the nation as a whole.

The trivial cynicism of human relationships is well illustrated in "Wie es geht," where the readiness of the actress and the writer to indulge in a sexual adventure with no concern beyond that of the moment anticipates a similar scene in Schnitzler's *Reigen*. The theme of the theatre broached here is further developed in "Fromont," which in turn, by introducing members of the aristocracy, prepares for "Es geht zu Ende," one of the more apocalyptic passages in Austrian letters at the close of the nineteenth century. In "Fromont" the standing of the aristocracy is already questioned: seeing a young Austrian countess from the Ebner-Eschenbach family during a visit to the theatre, a young man and woman discuss the nature of nobility. The man presents a romantic view with which the woman initially agrees before presenting a cooler and more objective assessment of how the upper crust acquires its bearing: charm may well be nothing other than "matter impregnated with soul," but could it not also be the result of the gym teacher and the dancing instructor? (WS 40).

As soon as aristocracy loses its mystique, its power base is threatened, a development accurately reflected in *Wie ich es sehe*. "Es geht zu Ende" envisages the imminent demise not just of the "Saison," but of the Establishment as a whole. The weather is properly autumnal and superficially beautiful as a duke and his son drive along in their open carriage. Everywhere, however, there are signs of death and decay. Despite the sun there is a "Keller-Kälte" [cellar-cold: WS 41] in the shade, the smell of fresh damp earth seems linked to the little sun-drenched cemetery they drive past, their feet kept warm by the skin of a dead tiger. As they enter the estate through the cast iron gates, the birch trees shiver and the crows call. In menacing tones Altenberg now apostrophizes the ruling order:

> Hochadel und Villenbesitzer! Ihr sitzt noch in den Gärten in der Herbstsonne und fahrt auf den Landstrassen in den Equipagen - - -! Ihr dürft noch die goldenen Lichter der letzten Herbsttage trinken, Ihr, die Georginen und die Krähen - - - kraa! (WS 42–43)

> [High aristocracy and owners of villas! Still you sit in your gardens in the autumn sum and travel the high roads in your carriages - - -! Still you may drink the golden light of the last days of autumn, you, the asters and the crows - - - caw!]

Writing in the German Democratic Republic in the 1950s, Uwe Johnson was scornful of Altenberg's unrevolutionary "Revolutionär," who represents the author's position in later sections of *Wie ich es sehe*. In "Es geht zu Ende," however, there can be little doubt about the radical stance of the narrative voice. Gone is Altenberg the "master of suggestion."[41] Rather, he confirms Friedell's view of an "an ethically reformatory personality of an almost religious character" (AB 12). Perhaps Altenberg alone among his contemporaries in Vienna, protected by his reputation for eccentricity, could have made this prophecy of doom twenty years before the end of the Hapsburg hegemony. It is in such a passage that Friedell's words have the smack of truth: that Altenberg is a seer in the double sense of the word: someone who sees things as they are as well as seeing into the future (AB 14).

In "Herbstabend," the penultimate sketch of the cycle, Altenberg enlarges upon the mood of "Es geht zu Ende," describing the shuttered hotel and the avenue with its falling leaves and departed guests. He calls out after his vanished cast of characters: the young lady, the smitten young man, the "Greek," Margueritta and Rositta, Herr von Bergmann with his bandy little legs, the young fisher-girl, the American, the Russian woman: where are they now? The answer is simple: the autumn has blown them away like the yellow

---

[41] Wunberg, *Das junge Wien*, 608.

leaves in the park (WS 43). Lakeside society, a cross-section not merely of the Austrian Establishment but of the well-to-do world as a whole, has as little permanence as the leaves on the trees. Its sense of security is a delusion, its demise imminent. The sense of *fin de siècle*, of resigned acceptance that things are drawing to a close, is pervasive. Increasingly as the cycle progresses, it appears to bear out Max Nordau's assertion that

> One epoch of history is unmistakably in its decline, and another is announcing its approach. There is a sound of rending in every tradition, and it is as though the morrow would not link itself with to-day. Things as they are totter and plunge, and they are suffered to reel and fall, because man is weary, and there is no faith that it is worth an effort to uphold them."[42]

Nevertheless, Nordau contends that "the great majority of the middle and lower classes is naturally not *fin de siècle*,"[43] but possessed of its own vitality, a view Altenberg seems to share at least in part in "At Home," the final sketch of the "See-Ufer" cycle.

In this richly ironic study, whose tone is ultimately humorous rather than apocalyptic, Altenberg takes his readers back to an apartment in the Grillparzerstraße in Vienna, back to a world where the cracks in the fabric of society, so evident in the resort, can still be papered over. A regiment of painters and decorators, wearing overalls the same color as the dress uniforms in Franz Joseph's army, is refurbishing the house, but the pampered Fräulein Margarethe remains sublimely unaware of the proletariat whose very existence has hitherto hardly been acknowledged in *Wie ich es sehe*. The alienated servants are dominant in the household, but she knows nothing of this:

> Die Dienstboten! Hasserfüllt verlassen sie im Frühjahr die Stadt und ziehen mit stupider Hoffnung in die Wälder, in die Berge - - -. So verlassen sie hasserfüllt im Herbst das elende Land und ziehen mit stupider Hoffnung in den Stadtkerker ein -. (WS 44)

> [The servants! Filled with hatred they depart the city in the spring and full of stupid hope they make for the forests, for the mountains - - -. Then in the autumn they depart the miserable country and full of stupid hope return to the prison of the city -.]

Spending their lives in a shuttle between the prison of the city and the miserable countryside, they nevertheless represent for the author the survivors in the coming cataclysm: when everything has collapsed into ruins and ashes, the little light brown clouds from the servants' coffee will still curl up peacefully out of the debris of the house (WS 44). Fully aware of the forward march of Social Democracy in the 1890s, Altenberg apparently portrays, not without tongue in cheek, a world in which the conflict has already begun. Fräulein Margarethe, however, simply gives herself up to the pleasure of eating a ripe pear, celebrating a quiet, refined orgy of the taste buds (WS 45).

---

[42] Max Nordau, *Degeneration*, (London: Heinemann, 1895), 5–6.
[43] Ibid., 7.

She is patently a product of Nordau's "caste in decay," yet in the end the sketch shies away from anything remotely revolutionary. The regiment of painters is marshalled not by a revolutionary leader, but by the lady of the house, who has donned a red silk headscarf and turned into a general with a red silk helmet. The battlefield is not that of a proletarian revolution, but the apartment in need of decoration. Triumphant at the end of "See-Ufer" is not a new order, but a matriarchy and a younger generation with little thought for the future:

> Der Abend senkte den Frieden über das Schlachtfeld. Der siegreiche Feldherr nimmt das rothseidene Kopftuch ab und die Lagerfeuer der Lampen und Kerzen erglänzen durch die stille Nacht - - -. Das Fräulein träumte: "Adieu Sommer - - -!" (WS 46)[44]

> [The evening brought peace to the battlefield. The victorious general removes the red silk headscarf and the camp fires of lamps and candles glow through the still night - - -.The young lady dreamt: "Adieu, summer - - -!"]

Although the last sketch in the cycle plays down the vision which had inspired "Es geht zu Ende," in the course of "See-Ufer" Altenberg nevertheless portrays his society with a measure of critical insight and a sense for future developments rarely encountered in the works of his Young Vienna contemporaries. Beyond that, however, the cycle also demonstrates that Altenberg is far more than a naive eccentric who somehow chanced to produce impressionistic trifles in a haphazard and unstructured way.

One of the earliest critical responses to *Wie ich es sehe* was, unsurprisingly, that of Hermann Bahr. Writing in *Die Zeit* on 2 May 1896, his positive review set the tone for many to follow, indeed, echoes of this review are still heard today.[45] The review anticipated and may have even stimulated, Altenberg's preface to subsequent editions by pointing out that these sketches were frequently prose poems.[46] In fact, it could even have been Bahr who was instrumental in drawing Altenberg's attention to Huysmans in the first instance. In the influential *Studien zur Kritik der Moderne* (1894) Bahr refers specifically to *A rebours*, quoting (in German) a passage which would surely have appealed to Altenberg. The extract reflects the book's documentary truthfulness, its attention to detail and realism, coupled with its desire to plumb the depths of the soul without ascribing every secret to mental illness.[47]

There seems little doubt that when, a few months later, Hofmannsthal came to review *Wie ich es sehe* in the Berlin journal *Die Zukunft* (5 September 1896) he used Bahr's earlier review as a prop. Privately, Hofmannsthal had expressed less than total enthusiasm for *Wie ich es sehe* in a letter to Beer-

---

[44] I acknowledge Burkhard Spinnen's correction of my earlier misreading of this passage, (*Schriftbilder*, 129.)

[45] Wysocki, *Peter Altenberg*, 7.

[46] Wunberg, *Das junge Wien*, 588.

[47] Hermann Bahr, *Studien zur Kritik der Moderne*, (Berlin: Fischer, 1894), 23.

Hofmann soon after its publication: it compared poorly with other books in his library such as poems by Goethe and Pindar and the stories of Maupassant.[48] By September, however, he was trying, with some success, to overcome his initial antipathy. For once, though, the young Hofmannsthal was at a loss for words, as the hapless opening of his review indicates. Having provided some random examples of the range of "little stories" in the work, Hofmannsthal falters again when he says that Altenberg's pieces are easier to summarize than to describe, therefore he will simply quote in full the sketch "Musik" (WS 59). The lengthy review finally gets into its stride when seizing upon the key point in Bahr's earlier appraisal, namely, that *Wie ich es sehe* has "its own tone through and through."[49] Although Hofmannsthal says the "little stories" have "their own tone" (AB 147), he finds that the collection is "all too in love with life" (AB 147). On the other hand, these same pieces are too "sweet" for the reviewer's taste. Throughout his review Hofmannsthal fails to note the darker shades in Altenberg's writing. How else could he note that Altenberg writes without historical awareness, or that the book has such a clear conscience although it is quite unconcerned with things of importance?

The uncertainty in Hofmannsthal's response to *Wie ich es sehe* most openly expresses itself in his simultaneous rejection of its closeness to life and his perception of it as "a completely romantic work." He echoes Bahr in appraising the book as essentially Viennese rather than German, paradoxically giving it some credit for its social realism. Moreover, by declaring that the book was certain to please, Hofmannsthal at least showed himself a knowing judge of the reading public of the day. Furthermore, despite reservations about both book and author, Hofmannsthal nevertheless discerns behind the work the secret word "Kultur." The condescending tone of much of this essentially well-meaning review has, however, loomed large in shaping subsequent attitudes to Altenberg's work, masking the high regard in which he was held by his contemporaries.

Ashantee: the "People from Paradise"

Incredible as it may seem today, in the summer of 1896 a touring exhibition of Ashanti people was mounted in Vienna's Prater Zoo to entertain the curious natives of the Austrian-Hungarian metropolis. Having already been on show in Budapest, the Ashanti, in whose homeland a savage war was then raging, would spend many months in Vienna supposedly recreating African village life before proceeding to the next station on their long journey home in October 1897.

Although masquerading as an educational exercise, the prime purpose of this exhibition must have been to provide profit for the organizers, who may

[48] *Hugo von Hofmannsthal, Richard Beer-Hofmann: Briefwechsel*, ed. Eugene Weber, (Frankfurt: Fischer, 1972), 59.
[49] Wunberg, *Das junge Wien*, 588.

have had in mind such models as Buffalo Bill Cody's hugely successful Wild West Show which had first toured Europe in 1889–90.[50] There can be little doubt either that many visitors to the exhibition were drawn less out of anthropological curiosity than by the prurient desire to observe and mingle with "naked savages." The proximity of German ethnological research to soft pornography is well documented in the pseudo-scientific studies of the time which mingle "scientific" data about skull sizes and skeletal development of the various races with photographs of naked men and women in frequently erotic poses.[51] It is evident, too, that the physical and sexual allure of the Ashanti women was a key factor in seizing Altenberg's imagination. So moved indeed was he by the Ashanti exhibition that he made it the kernel of his next book, entitled simply *Ashantee*, a further collection of prose miniatures published in Berlin in spring 1897.

Altenberg's love of the natural and unspoiled and his capacity for spontaneous enthusiasm were attributes of his work and poetic persona which particularly appealed to the nineteen-year-old Martin Buber. His first publication, written in Polish in 1897, was an essay devoted to Viennese literature of the 1890s, and arose from contact with the new literature of Vienna during his first year at Vienna University. He devotes an entire section to Altenberg, rated alongside Bahr, Schnitzler and Hofmannsthal as one of the outstanding figures of Young Vienna.[52] Altenberg's bohemian lifestyle did nothing to diminish his status in Buber's eyes:

> His 'qualité mâitresse,' the quality that makes him great and powerful, is love, a bottomless and boundless love for the entire world, for beings living and dead, for children playing, for fresh roses, for melancholy animals, and for setting suns. Whatever he sees he endows with his love; it is as if he pours radiance from his soul on to all phenomena, and then, when they sparkle with his light, he beholds them with pleasure. Such a love is a feeling that Bahr and Hofmannsthal do not and cannot have.[53]

This love undoubtedly infuses *Ashantee*, which appeared in a special series costing only two Marks, its cover adorned with a photograph of the bare-breasted girls who so captured Altenberg's admiration and imagination. During their stay he could not see enough of what he felt was a healthier, more natural life than that on offer in the metropolis. He had been on the point of leaving Vienna to spend the summer in the Alps when the Ashanti arrived, but he unpacked his cases on the spot, and thereafter spent all the

---

[50] Andrew Barker, "'Unforgettable People from Paradise!': Peter Altenberg and the Ashanti visit to Vienna of 1896–7," *Research in African Literatures* 22, no. 2 (1991): 57–70: see also Ian Foster, "Altenberg's African Spectacle: *Ashantee* in context," *Theatre and Performance in Austria. From Mozart to Jellinek*, ed. Ritchie Robertson and Edward Timms, (Edinburgh: Edinburgh University Press, 1993), 39–60.

[51] For example C. H. Stratz, *Naturgeschichte des Menschen*, (Stuttgart: Ferdinand Enke, 1904).

[52] William M. Johnston, "Martin Buber's literary début: 'On Viennese Literature' (1897)," *The Germanic Quarterly* 47, no. 4 (1974): 559.

[53] Ibid., 563.

day and half the night with his new-found friends who promptly dubbed him "Sir Peter."[54] Max Graf recalls how he and Altenberg spent many romantic nights at the zoo where Altenberg admired the young black beauties Bibi Akolé, Tioko, Monambô Akoschia, just as he admired Marguerite, Rositta, Evelyn and Dorothea, whose acquaintance he had made at the lakeside in Gmunden or on the Semmering. In Graf's recollection Altenberg lived in a world in which girls and women were both the singer and the song.[55]

Not just the poet, but Moriz Englander too became besotted with the Ashanti, inspiring the quip that the father was suffering from an inherited illness passed down from his son. It was, however, precisely this sort of cynical, implicitly racist humour that Altenberg wished to counter in *Ashantee*. Thus when a small boy makes derogatory comments about the Ashanti drummers, saying "It's what they call music - - -" (A 8), his tutor rebukes him at once for opening up an abyss between black and white. What, asks the tutor, does the boy mean by "they"? Does he use the word because stupid people look down on blacks and treat them like exotic animals simply because their epidermis contains dark pigmentation? (A 9).

In the popular imagination of the Viennese, Altenberg's open infatuation with young black women simply confirmed his reputation as someone with views and behavior too eccentric to be taken seriously. Writing to Schnitzler on 22 May 1897, soon after *Ashantee* was published, Beer-Hofmann recalls contemptuously what he considers the unpleasantly farcical performance Altenberg put on when visiting the village. Unbidden by Beer-Hofmann, Altenberg had accompanied him around the exhibition, going into a trance at the sight of one of the black people. With an obvious sense of disgust, Beer-Hofmann tells how Altenberg

> waits for some chance passer-by (— of course he's only seen there during afternoon visiting hours —) to jerk him out of his entrancement. At the same time he's blind to the real attraction of these dark people. He's incapable of telling the truth.[56]

Altenberg's posturing as described here introduces a jarring note to his personal relationship with the Ashanti. A letter to S. Fischer shortly before publication of *Ashantee* also brings into question the extent of Altenberg's own freedom from conventional racial prejudice. Discussing the book's dedicatees, and where to situate the dedication, Altenberg notes that he cannot and will not dedicate a whole work to these black girls, especially as individual items in the book are dedicated to other prominent ladies.[57] In the end,

---

[54] *Das Junge Wien. Österreichische Literatur- und Kunstkritik 1888–1902*, vol. 2, ed. Gotthart Wunberg, (Tübingen: Niemeyer, 1976), 824.

[55] Max Graf, *Jede Stunde war erfüllt*, (Vienna and Frankfurt; Forum, n. d.) 150.

[56] Richard Beer-Hofmann papers, State University of New York, Binghamton. The correspondence between the two has been published as *Briefwechsel 1891–1931: Arthur Schnitzler und Richard Beer-Hofmann*, ed. Konstanze Fliedl, (Vienna: Europa Verlag, 1992).

[57] *Jugend in Wien. Literatur um 1900*, ed. Ludwig Greve and Werner Volke, (Marbach: Deutsche Schillergesellschaft, 1987), 306.

the opening seventy-two pages, devoted solely to the Ashanti exhibition, bear the dedication to his black [girl]friends, the unforgettable "Paradise-People" Akólé, Akóshia, Tioko, Djôjô, Nãh-Badûh. The remainder of *Ashantee* returns to the Viennese ambience familiar from *Wie ich es sehe*.

Time and again Altenberg's correspondence with S. Fischer[58] reveals the attention he paid to the production of his work. Far from his bundling off sketches and then forgetting about them, Altenberg's letter of 15 March 1897, for example, demonstrates a real concern for detail as well as a certain dissatisfaction with Fischer's performance — he had already sent off three revisions of the opening sequence alone. An undated letter from around the same period shows the gap between an author who assumes that changes here and there at the proofs stage would be of little consequence, and a publisher who viewed things rather differently. Starting to flex his muscles, Altenberg is even confident enough to take a sideswipe at Moritz Heimann, Fischer's Cheflektor and a key figure in the success of the company, and hence of German modernist literature as a whole.[59] Fischer's reply has not survived.

Whatever Altenberg's qualms about the book's dedication, there is little evidence of racist attitudes in the texts. Contemporary critics and other writers were mostly enthusiastic, although Rudolf Steiner was unconvinced of the book's sincerity.[60] Hermann Bahr, who if anything disgusted Beer-Hofmann even more than Altenberg did, responded to *Ashantee* just a few day's after Beer-Hofmann's letter to Schnitzler, and it is almost as if he had in mind a riposte to Beer-Hofmann. Writing in *Die Zeit* on 5 June 1897, Bahr declares that if he envies anyone, then it is Altenberg. He would more than welcome such success — to be at the same time the darling of the cognoscenti and detested by cold rationalists. Altenberg, however, simply goes his own blissful way, laughing at the stupid horde of "clever people" who, because they cannot understand him, have to loathe him.[61] In the *Wiener Rundschau* of 1 June 1897 Max Messer is just as enthusiastic as Bahr, finishing his review with the ringing declaration that Altenberg is a "poet and prophet of future humanity."[62] In old age Max Brod recalled how as a young man he had found aid and comfort in *Ashantee*.[63]

History soon revealed Messer's prediction as wildly optimistic, but today's readers will recognise how besides providing the "passive pedophile" with instant objects for his enthusiasm, the Ashanti girls also provided him with extra ammunition for the *Kulturkritik* which distinguishes his early

[58] *Peter Altenberg. Leben und Werk in Texten und Bildern*, ed. Hans Christian Kosler, (Munich: Matthes and Seitz, 1981), 123–126.

[59] SPK, 1–1427.

[60] Rudolf Steiner, "Ein Wiener Dichter," *Gesammelte Aufsätze zur Literatur 1884–1902*, (Dornach: Rudolf Steiner-Verlag, 1971), 185–190.

[61] Wunberg, *Das junge Wien*, 726.

[62] Ibid., 725.

[63] Josef Fraenkel, *The Jews of Austria*, (London: Valentine and Mitchell, 1967), 242.

writing. Altenberg, an early Austrian adherent to the view that black is beautiful, confronts the racial prejudices of the Viennese head-on in *Ashantee*.[64] Not only thematically, but technically too, Altenberg proves himself a progressive writer, as when employing a favorite aural collage technique to record the reactions of visitors to the show:

> "Das soll die schönste sein" sagen die Besucher, "eine beauté ihrer Heimath. Wo liegt dieses Aschanti?! Nun, für eine Negerin - - -. Stolz ist sie, wirklich unsympathisch. Was glaubt sie eigentlich, dieses Mohrl?!" (A 38)

> ["They reckon she's the best-looking one," the visitors say, "a belle back home. Where is this place Ashanti?! Well, for a Negress - - -. She's haughty, really not nice. Who does she think she is, this piccaninny?!"]

Presumably this was the sort of writing which led a critic of 1898 to claim that Altenberg had demonstrated in *Ashantee* how far western civilization and humanity were from being synonymous.[65] Altenberg was famed for the optical nature of his writing, but equally for the ethical qualities he perceived in the act of seeing. Not only did he find the Ashanti visually appealing, he made efforts to get to know them as people, anticipating later anthropological studies when recording Ashanti attitudes to issues such as adultery, corporal punishment, dowries, and rights of succession. That the Ashanti themselves, far from being just naively charming *Naturkinder*, were aware of the level of their exploitation is something Altenberg records with moving simplicity. His new friends complain how they are forced to go around virtually naked, with women not even permitted to wear a headscarf lest they be taken for "ladies." Their job is to portray African savages:

> Ganz närrisch ist es. In Afrika könnten wir so nicht sein. Alle würden lachen. Wie "men of the bush", ja, diese. In solchen Hütten wohnt niemand. Für dogs ist es bei uns, gbé. Quite foolish. (A 14)

> [It's completely stupid. We couldn't be like this in Africa. Everyone would laugh. Like 'men of the bush', yes, those people. Nobody lives in huts like these. Here we live like dogs, gbé. Quite foolish.]

Notable for its vehement criticism of white civilization *Ashantee* also demonstrates Altenberg's readiness to challenge accepted literary genres. Although a work of fiction, *Ashantee* opens with a purported reproduction of the entry on the "Aschanti" from *Meyer's Conversations-Lexikon* of 1897.[66] The opening sketch "Der Hofmeister" leads the reader into the world of the African "natives" via the visit of a girl named Fortunatina in the company of her personal tutor. Before arriving at the human exhibits, tutor and girl visit a series of caged animals, coming at length to the lioness, the last stop before the Ashanti village itself. The tutor, falling into a mild trance before the cage,

---

[64] Hilde Spiel, *Vienna's Golden Autumn 1866–1938*, (London: Weidenfeld and Nicolson, 1987), 118–119.

[65] Kosler, *Peter Altenberg*, 80–81.

[66] Foster, "Altenberg's African Spectacle," 47–48.

imagines an unwritten ballad with the title "Fortunatina und die Löwin - - -".[67] Leaving behind the privileged world of the Viennese bourgeoisie, the texts subsequent to "Der Hofmeister," considered by Alfred Kerr a quintessential example of Altenberg's art,[68] then enter into the world of these human exhibits from the dark continent, as perceived and recorded through the eyes of Peter Altenberg.

Although Beer-Hofmann well appreciated how Altenberg's aestheticization of reality meant he was unable to distinguish between fact and fantasy, today's reader of *Ashantee* is immediately struck by Altenberg's empathy with and appreciation of African culture. Particularly striking are his attempts to reproduce the acoustic palate of the Ashanti "village." In the prose poem "Akolé's Gesang, Akolé's süsses Lied" a terrible storm is raging in the zoological garden, ruffling the feathers of the geese and littering the surface of the pond with leaves and twigs. Squatting beside the pond, Akolé sings her sweet song:

andelaína andelaína andelaína gbomolééééé - -
andelaína gbomolé.
andelaína Akkraūma, andelaína gbomolé
andelaína andelaína - - -.
andelaína hé oblation, andelaína gbomolé
andelaína andelaína andelaína gbomolé.
andelaína A k k r a-lédé andelaína hé oblaíno,
andelaína andelaína - - -
andelaína V i e n n a-lédé andelaína bobandôôô - -
andelaína andelaína andelaína bobandôôô [. . .]
andelaína andelaína - - - - - -. (A 39)

At other points Altenberg endeavors to reproduce not only the sounds of the Ashanti language, which he made some effort to acquire, but also the syncopated rhythms of the Ashanti dances (A 8). In "The School" (the original title is in English,) he provides a glossary of words in both English and the African language before asking what can only be regarded as a rhetorical question: "Which language is the more beautiful?" (A 17). Many items mix together elements of Otshi, English and German (and often French as well) producing bewildering aural effects unique in their day and seemingly anticipating the avant-garde sound experiments of the modern Viennese poet Ernst Jandl.

<hr>

[67] It is precisely this moment in the text, when the tutor "feels' a piece of literature as yet unwritten, which provides the stimulus for what is probably the earliest extant text by the Viennese novelist Heimito von Doderer (1866–1966). See Wendelin Schmidt-Dengler, "Das Ende am Anfang. Zu unbekannten Texten Doderers aus der Frühzeit," *Internationales Symposion Heimito von Doderer. Ergebnisse,* (Vienna: Niederösterreich-Gesellschaft für Kunst und Kultur, 1986), 107–108. See also Heimito von Doderer, *Die sibirische Klarheit: Texte aus der Gefangenschaft,* ed. Wendelin Schmidt-Dengler and Martin Loew-Cadonna, (Munich: Biederstein, 1991), 87–97.

[68] Alfred Kerr, "Dem toten Peter Altenberg," *Die neue Rundschau* 30, no. 3 (1919): 331.

Equally astonishing are Altenberg's own communications in English. After the departure of the villagers he wrote a disconsolate letter to Monambô, who would then read it out to Nabadû. It was to Nabadû in particular that Altenberg had lost his heart, and in a letter to S. Fischer he revealed that some of the royalties from *Wie ich es sehe* had been spent on clothes for her.[69] In his "Brief aus Wien. (An die Negerin Monambô)" Altenberg's English makes no concessions to usage or spelling conventions, but reproduces his own idiosyncratic poetic idiom:

My dear Monambô:

> As I only know one single word in Odschi, "misumo" (I love you), which may be enough for the simple happieness in life, but too little for the sad days, so I cannot talk with Nabadû and you must be so kind, dear Monambô, to read to her my stupid letter, which is a bit of my stupid heart. Dear Monambô, the first day when Nabadû came from the Ashan-tee-village in Buda-Pesth to Vienna, I was in the Arena. Nabadû came in. Nabadû sat down quite near to me. She leaned her head on my shoulder, put her hand on my knee. So we stopped sitting and I was like in a drunk-enness of happieness. Never before had I seen her. And she leaned her head on my shoulder! The same evening she sat before her hut and sung sad things of Afrika. When I went up to her, she did'nt keep silence like all the others, like birds in a wood. But she sung and sung, as if no stranger would have been near her. And so it was! That was the last day of my happyness, dear Monambô. Beginning from this day she was quite altered. Like a stranger she got towards me. I always remember this magic first day, when Nabadû arrived from Buda-Pesth, quite a stranger to me and leaned her head on my shoulder!
>
> Oh dear Monambô, do not laugh - -.
>
> Like a sickness remains this evening in me, when Nabadû behaved as if I had been a brother or a home, like Akkra or the whole of Afrika. Why did she put her head on my shoulder?! It makes a heart sick, when it is for one evening full of happieness and for all the others full of sorrow.
>
> I suppose, the reason of all this will be the joung "Blackman" Noë Salomon Dowoonnah.
>
> Say to Nabadû, that, when she returns to Akkrâ, a white man will for ever remain sick after this one evening, when Nabadû leaned her head on his shoulder like on the shoulder of a friend - - - - -!!
>
> Dear Monambô, do not laugh - - -.
>
> Jours
> Peter (A 46–47)

The literary persona of Altenberg himself plays a central rôle in the majority of the sketches devoted to the Ashanti, mediating between the cultures in a manner which, though never condescending, never attempts either to conceal his erotic responses to the Ashanti girls. While swooning over Nabadû, however, the neurasthenic poet was also writing to Ännie

---

[69] *Peter Altenberg Almanach. Lese-Heft des Löcker Verlags*, (Vienna: Löcker 1987), 11.

Holitscher, complaining of his unbearable physical suffering. On 11 August 1896 he tells her that despite his woes his beloved little black friend transports him to worlds where there is no suffering, just spiritual delight. If only he could keep her beside him, buy her, and give her an unconventional education![70] By thus admitting his desire to possess Nabadû, Altenberg of course succumbs to the very values he set out to counter in his book. Otherwise, the letter provides a delightful pen-picture of life in the village, concluding with an expression of contempt for the inability and unwillingness of Western civilization to give the Ashanti their due.[71]

Despite the obstacles of class, color and society, Altenberg demonstrates in *Ashantee* how none of these impediments will stop him from expressing the language of his soul. The conscious exoticism of the book can nevertheless be regarded as typical of much *fin de siècle* art, as is also the frequent stylization of the Ashanti into unsullied children of nature, a living contrast with and reproach to the decadence of the Hapsburg metropolis. Sander Gilman, however, notes that "the stereotype of the pre-pubescent female and that of the Black merge in Altenberg's fantasy producing a figure quite typical of the fin-de-siècle. In Karl Kraus . . . this false sentimentality is lacking."[72]

Though not unfounded, Gilman's objection fails to take due account of that ethically-motivated *Reform-Kultur* with roots going back to Ruskin, Morris and Nietzsche which informs Altenberg's responses to African culture. Ten years after *Ashantee*, Kraus discussed the black-white dichotomy with reference to the double standards of the German bourgeoisie, contrasting their sexual prurience at the merest hint of a sexual relationship with blacks to the blatantly commercialized marriage advertisements in the private columns of the bourgeois-liberal press.[73] In Kraus's case, however, the critique is further complicated by the anti-Semitic slant of his attack on the "business mentality" as a whole which reduces human relationships to trading relationships.

Whilst Altenberg's book is the most extended artistic consequence of the Ashanti visit to Vienna, he was not the only Austrian writer who responded to their plight as they were shipped around Europe in the name of profit through popular entertainment. Writing in Paris shortly after the turn of the century, Rilke expressed his dejection after a hesitant visit to an Ashanti settlement which had been erected in the Jardin d'Acclimation. His poem "Die Aschanti" betrays that unlike Altenberg, he has been granted

> Keine Vision von fremden Ländern
> kein Gefühl von braunen Frauen, die
> tanzen aus den fallenden Gewändern.

---

[70] Kosler, *Peter Altenberg*, 164.

[71] Ibid., 165.

[72] Sander L. Gilman, *On Blackness without Blacks: Essays on the Image of the Black in Germany*, (Boston: G. K. Hall, 1982), 149.

[73] Karl Kraus, "Die weiße Kultur oder Warum in die Ferne schweifen?," *Die chinesische Mauer*, (Frankfurt: Fischer, 1967), 97–100.

Keine wilde fremde Melodie,
Keine Lieder, die vom Blute stammten,
und kein Blut, das aus den Tiefen schrie.[74]

[No vision of foreign lands
No feeling of brown women, who
dance out of falling garments.

No wild foreign melody.
No songs which came from the blood,
and no blood crying from the depths.]

Far from being fascinated by what he sees, Rilke is frightened even to look. The exotic eroticism of the Ashanti girls which fired Altenberg is quite lacking here. The imaginative empathy which Altenberg felt is denied the timid Rilke, for whom there are no Gauguinesque visions of dusky maidens whose languid movements barely conceal hidden fires. He prefers caged animals to caged people and has eyes only for the way the Ashanti have been corrupted by exposure to new and strange things which they do not understand. Whereas Altenberg uses the exploitation of the Ashanti as the basis for a critique of late nineteenth century mores, Rilke, typically, shies away from the social overtones of his material. A reference in the final stanza to caged animals is reminiscent of Rilke's poem "Der Panther," where the poet enters into the spirit of the captive beast. Might this too be an echo of a line in *Ashantee* where the tutor in "Der Hofmeister" states that there is nothing shameful about imaginative empathy with animals? (A 7)

That Rilke knew *Ashantee* may come as no surprise, given the poet's obsession with the act of seeing, which is the basis for all of Altenberg's writing too. Moreover, when Stefan Zweig pointed out in February 1901 that Altenberg's work was slowly freezing into predictability,[75] he was merely echoing fears Rilke had expressed three years earlier in a lecture delivered in Prague on 5 March 1898 entitled "Moderne Lyrik."[76] Also in that year Rilke's first volume of verse *Advent* had been published by Friesenhahn in Leipzig. The poem "Seelenstille" was dedicated to Altenberg.[77] In his lecture Rilke declared Altenberg one of the two most important lyric voices in Vienna. In fact, on the basis of just *Wie ich es sehe* and *Ashantee*, Rilke devotes more space to Altenberg than to Hofmannsthal. Particularly impressed by Altenberg's sense of form, Rilke regards him as "the first proclaimer of modern Vienna"[78] and believes that in Altenberg the city has suddenly found its

---

[74] Rainer Maria Rilke, *Werke in drei Bänden*, vol. 1, *Gedicht-Zyklen*, (Frankfurt: Insel, 1966), 150–151.

[75] Wunberg, *Das junge Wien*, 1156.

[76] Rainer Maria Rilke, *Sämtliche Werke*, vol. 5, *Worpswede, Rodin, Aufsätze*, (Frankfurt: Insel, 1965), 385.

[77] Rainer Maria Rilke, *Sämtliche Werke*, vol. 3, *Jugendgedichte*, (Frankfurt: Insel, 1959), 437.

[78] Rilke, *Worpswede*, 388.

own voice. This generous response is all the more remarkable because of Rilke's openly expressed dislike of the prose poem form which Altenberg had made his own.[79] Rilke's insight into the potential problems facing Altenberg is openly stated: he believes Altenberg must find a new form if he wishes to remain honest and avoid repetition.[80] Altenberg could not, and did not wish to change. Indeed, it was this very immutability which added to his stature, at least among his contemporaries, for in their eyes he remained a *Dichter*, a poet, and never became a *Schriftsteller*, that is a mere wordsmith.

Altenberg's interest in the Ashanti did not fade with the publication of his book. When they eventually departed from Vienna at the end of October 1897 he them paid a final tribute in the *Wiener Allgemeine Zeitung*. This piece, not reprinted in Altenberg's lifetime, was entitled simply "Abschied der Aschanti."[81] The Ashanti village, he decided, had been an oasis of romanticism where the Viennese, like characters in Ibsen's *The Wild Duck*, had been enabled to become "poets of their own selves," rediscovering poetic aspects of themselves customarily repressed by the "saving lie." To mix with these honest, noble and dignified black people had been like medicine for the overladen, overfed, yet undernourished souls of the Viennese. In a most revealing comment, however, Altenberg once again shows his preference for poetic fantasy over mundane reality, even making us question whether he had fully understood the implications of those texts which unmasked the exploitation of the Ashanti by their managers:

> Man kann es sagen, niemals störten sie unsere romantische Phantasie, welche sie zu "Paradies-Menschen" umdichtete.

> [One can say they never disturbed our romantic fantasy, which through poetry transformed them into "paradise people."]

Yet Altenberg the aesthete soon gives way to the *fin-de-siècle* poet, yearning for a fresh input into a tired continent. The Ashanti, so Altenberg believes, could have been a "regeneration cure" for the old and tired European cultural soul. However, all that the soul of European culture can do is look pityingly upon those whose sympathies stray so far from the mainstream as to find inspiration and recuperation in African culture.

Altenberg did not forget the Ashanti when they departed from Vienna, nor did his contemporaries forget his response to them. This emerges from Oskar Kokoschka's reminiscences composed almost four decades later.[82] Writing in Vienna in March 1934, Kokoschka noted how from one day to the next the Ashanti village in the Prater had confirmed Altenberg's natural

---

[79] Ibid., 391.

[80] Ibid., 387.

[81] *Wiener Allgemeine Zeitung* 5898, (1897): 2. Reprinted in *Juni. Magazin für Kultur und Politik* 3, no. 4 (1989): 29–30.

[82] Leo A. Lensing, "Scribbling squids and the Giant Octopus: Oskar Kokoschka's Unpublished Portrait of Peter Altenberg," *Turn-of-the-century Vienna and its legacy. Essays in Honor of Donald G. Daviau*, ed. Jeffrey B. Berlin, Jorun B. Johns, Richard H. Lawson, (Vienna: Edition Atelier, 1993), 193–220.

philosophy of life, namely that primitive man is preferable to polite society. That was also why "society scribblers and ink-squirters" failed to understand Altenberg and considered him a fool. Kokoschka goes on to recall how in 1909, at the instigation of Adolf Loos, he had come to paint his celebrated portrait of Altenberg, which he later described as being that of an outraged octopus.[83] The reasons for the poet's ire were some provocative comments passed about his commercial activities, though these amounted to no more than hawking little strings of glass beads, fashioned after the patterns once taught him by Ashanti friends. Their very simplicity, however, was inherently provocative in a society given to opulent consumption, and as Kokoschka further noted, they marked a blatant aesthetic contrast to the European taste for jewelry in "phony styles made from genuine or fake gold."

A year before Kokoschka painted his portrait, Altenberg had returned in print to the Ashanti visit of a dozen years earlier, publishing "Abschiedsbrief eines Aschanti-Mädchens von Wien" (ML 110), while in summer 1910 history repeated itself on the occasion of the International Hunting Exhibition in Vienna, when another African village was imported to the Prater. This time, however, it was an Abyssinian rather than an Ashanti village, but Altenberg's reactions remained undimmed by the passage of time, as an inscribed photograph of an Abyssinian girl's head indicates:

> Katidja - - - 1910, im Abyssinierdorfe
> Nâh-Badûh - - - 1896, im Ashanteedorfe.
> *Unterdessen* ein Greis geworden - - -.
> Aber die *Begeisterung* ist *geblieben*; wie
> eh und je - - -. Peter Altenberg[84]

> [Katidja - - -1910, in the Abyssinian village
> Nâh-Badûh - - -1896, in the Ashanti village
> *in the meantime* grown old and grey - - -.
> But the *ecstasy* has *remained*; for
> ever and a day - - -. Peter Altenberg]

Ashantee was the first of Altenberg's books to go out of print, but the Ashanti material itself soon re-emerged, incorporated into the revised version of *Wie ich es sehe* in 1904. The fate of the book is perhaps best shown in a 1902 lithograph by Bertha Czegka depicting a rather mournful Peter Altenberg, cup in hand, entertaining a clothed but barefooted black girl not in the Ashanti village, but rather at his habitual table in the coffee-shop.[85] (Kirschner's *Literatur-Kalender* for 1897, and for many years thereafter, gives Altenberg's address simply as: Café Central, Vienna). With his left foot he ap-

[83] Andrew Barker, "Peter Altenberg," *The Dictionary of Literary Biography*, vol. 81, *Austrian Fiction Writers 1875–1913*, ed. James Hardin and Donald G. Daviau, (Detroit: Bruccoli Clark Layman, 1989), 9.

[84] Hans Bisanz, *Mein äußerstes Ideal: Altenbergs Photosammlung von geliebten Frauen, Freunden und Orten*, (Vienna and Munich: Christian Brandstätter, 1987), 70.

[85] Barker, "Unforgettable People," 69.

pears to be stroking the ankle of the smiling girl who noticeably fails to return the enquiring gaze of the poet. Clad in an off-the-shoulder garment whose material and style are remarkably similar to that worn by a girl on the dust-jacket of *Ashantee*, she displays her rapid adaptation to Viennese bourgeois culture both in her delicately cocked fingers as she stirs a steaming glass of hot chocolate and in the cigarette she is holding in the other hand. The artlessness of Altenberg's Ashanti girls has become transformed into knowing artifice.

Czegka's drawing could hardly stand in greater contrast to the message Altenberg had tried to convey through his writing. Seizing upon Altenberg's all too well-known mania for courting young women, she blithely overlooks the whole thrust of the work which inspired her drawing. Her picture is as good an example as any for Altenberg's reception in Vienna, where fascination with Altenberg the character constantly dulled the perception of Altenberg the ártist. His enthusiasm for the Ashanti had simply become a standard feature of the mythology others built up around him, a distorted counter to the spiritual and social renewal he hoped to effect through the twin media of his artistic persona and his works.

Femmes fatales and the flight to Munich

Fired by the success of *Wie ich es sehe* and *Ashantee*, Altenberg was briefly tempted into the mainstream culture of Vienna as theater critic of the *Extrapost*, a paper of no particular distinction. Given the histrionic nature of the Altenberg persona, which lent it added appeal in a city obsessed with the stage, it is no surprise he felt an affinity with the theater. Unsurprisingly too, given his predilection for small forms, it was the cabaret and variety halls which claimed the lion's share of his affection and attention.

The credit for drawing Altenberg in to the world of the stage goes to Max Graf, music critic of the *Extrapost*, who suggested him when asked by the editor to nominate a theater critic. Altenberg gladly accepted the invitation, and took to carrying a large pair of opera glasses around his neck as a signal of his professional status, for which he earned a modest twenty gulden per month.[86] He took up his post late in 1898, opening with a review of Schnitzler's *Das Vermächtnis* on 30 November. He relinquished the job in July 1899, at a time of emotional crisis, with notices of Hauptmann's *Das Friedensfest* and Tolstoy's *Die Macht der Finsternis*. All told, Altenberg reviewed twenty-four plays in seventeen separate notices, but his assessments differ markedly from conventional theater notices. Unlike the pseudoscholarly reviews of the Viennese feuilleton tradition, Altenberg was concerned to capture the mood of a work, or the nuances of a performer, rather than provide an analytically evaluative comment on the production.

Altenberg also used his position as a theater critic to settle a score with Hofmannsthal, who had dared suggest the author of *Wie ich es sehe* was no

[86] Max Graf, *Jede Stunde war erfüllt*, (Vienna and Frankfurt: Forum, n. d.), 151.

genius. Hofmannsthal had made his authorial début at the Burgtheater on 18 March 1899 with the double bill *Der Abenteuerer und die Sängerin* and *Die Hochzeit der Sobeide,* but the plays were not well received. Altenberg dismissed the former with the words "Arme Schauspieler, armes Pubklikum, armer Dichter!" [pity the actors, pity the audience, pity the poet!][87] In the opening number of his new journal *Die Fackel,* Kraus was equally acerbic, writing off *Der Abenteuerer* as "ein Tändeln mit Degen und Mantel" [cloak-and-dagger nonsense].[88]

Altenberg's relationship with Hofmannsthal developed neither warmth nor depth. Hofmannsthal was convinced Altenberg had little time for him, and his own feelings for Altenberg were at best muted. Given the nature of Hofmannsthal's relationship with Kraus, who lampooned him at every opportunity, he cannot have expected much from Altenberg's review of his *Elektra,* first printed in *Die Fackel* in 1903, and reprinted in *Pròdròmòs* (P 117). This, however, is one of Altenberg's most interesting essays in theater criticism, eschewing the *ad hominem* remarks of his earlier review of Hofmannsthal's dramas. He even wrote to the author praising the piece, as Bahr, who must have been shown the letter, reports in his diary for 29 November 1903.[89] Altenberg, however, was impressed less by the artistic qualities of *Elektra* than with its concern with justice. In the same letter the critic and essayist Paul Goldmann is apparently berated for his feuilleton on the work, Altenberg concluding that a Jew can simply never understand such matters. Bahr can only shake his head and wonder what is going on inside Altenberg.[90] We do not know how Hofmannsthal reacted to Altenberg's pained relationship with Judaism, but he would have recognized the passage in *Pròdròmòs* where Altenberg's views mirror those in the "Chandos Brief" (1902) regarding the need to overcome the body-soul dichotomy and start thinking with the heart:

> Er besass das *rechtzeitige,* das *vorzeitige* Mitleid, das *Präventiv-Mitleid,* jenes *allein* wertvolle *Gefühl,* das sich bereits mit dem Denken vermählt hat, das *Herz-Gehirn,* das *Gehirn-Herz!* (P 187)

> [He possessed the *timely,* the *premature* sympathy, the *preventative-sympathy,* that *sole* valuable *feeling,* which is already wedded to thought, the *heart-brain,* the *brain-heart.*]

It speaks for Hofmannsthal's charity that when Alfred Kerr launched a financial appeal for Altenberg in 1904, he went out of his way to try and solicit support, writing to Wladimir Schujlow that disagreeable as Altenberg was he

---

[87] Robert Werba, "Ein Außenseiter der Theaterkritik. Peter Altenberg und das Wiener Theaterjahr 1898–99," *Maske und Kothurn,* 20 (1974): 181.

[88] Karl Kraus, *Die Fackel,* 1 (1899): 26.

[89] Hermann Bahr, *Prophet der Moderne. Tagebücher 1888–1904,* ed. Reinhard Farkas, (Vienna: Böhlau, 1987), 157.

[90] Ibid.

still felt sorry for him.[91] Hofmannsthal's efforts were much appreciated, as emerges from a letter Altenberg sent to S. Fischer on 27 February 1905. Hofmannsthal himself had recently received a letter of thanks in which Altenberg accused his close friends of letting him starve. Hofmannsthal requested Fischer to inform him how much he sent Altenberg each month so that he might feel at ease with himself. With the letter he once again remitted 360 crowns for a man he barely knew and who he was sure could not abide him.

Altenberg's overriding feeling towards Hofmannsthal may well have been one of envy. In a letter also to S. Fischer, written in the winter of 1908 after correcting the proofs of *Märchen des Lebens*, Altenberg relates how he had just been to a toboggan party on the Semmering where he saw Hofmannsthal (*sic*) and the dancer Grete Lang-Wiesenthal go waving past him. He admits to Fischer his feeling that "Diese es besser verstanden haben, dem grausamen Leben Stand zu halten als ich total Verkommener!" [these people had a better understanding of how to face up to life's cruelty than I in my completely abased state!][92] And it is in *Märchen des Lebens* itself that Altenberg cattily reproduces a conversation he has purportedly overheard concerning himself and Hofmannsthal:

> "Und ich halte den Altenberg dennoch für einen Dichter - - -."
> "Er ist nur ein Momentphotograph, aber freilich ein geschickter - - -."
> "Und wohin rangieren Sie den Hugo von Hofmannsthal?!"
> "In einem Kurparke" (ML³ 34)

> ["Nevertheless I reckon that Altenberg is a real poet."
> "He's merely an instant photographer, although admittedly a skilled one - - -."
> "And where would you place Hugo von Hofmannsthal?!"
> "In the garden of a health spa"]

Altenberg's stint as a theater critic of the *Extrapost* was short-lived, but his attendance at *Zaza*, by Pierre Berton and Charles Simon, performed at the Deutsches Volkstheater on 18 February 1899, marked the start of a relationship with profound consequences not so much for himself as for Karl Kraus. In his review of this long-forgotten drama, Altenberg first mentions Annie Kalmar, a beautiful, consumptive actress who was to die in a Hamburg sanatorium on 2 May 1901, aged only twenty-three. Her part in *Zaza* was small, but Altenberg wrote that Kalmar was the only thing in the whole evening which was genuinely artistic and perfect.[93] We must assume, however, that this singling out of Kalmar was more than a spontaneous reaction to her talent. On 2 February 1901 he had sent the influential critic Franz Servaes a

---

[91] *Ria Schmujlow-Claasen und Hugo von Hofmannsthal: Briefe, Aufsätze, Dokumente*, ed. Claudia Abrecht, (Marbach: Deutsche Schillergesellschaft, 1982), 107.

[92] Samuel Fischer and Hedwig Fischer, *Briefwechsel mit Autoren*, ed. Dierk Rodenwald and Corinna Fiedler, (Frankfurt: Fischer, 1989), 393.

[93] Werba, "Ein Außenseiter der Theaterkritik," 176.

studio portrait of the actress taken, by the Viennese photographer R. Kriz-wanek with an inscription betraying his enthusiasm for "gentle kind Annie Kalmar, who freely dispenses beauty and grace to all as the sun does light!"[94] Two years previously, after her performance alongside the great Alexander Girardi in Alexandre Bisson's French farce *Der Schlafwagen-Kontrollor*, Kraus had written equally appreciatively of Kalmar in *Die Fackel*.[95]

Although Kalmar wrote thanking Kraus for his kind words, he did not get to know her until the summer of 1900; thereafter a very deep relation-ship developed, to the exclusion of Altenberg, whose feelings for her re-mained strong. With absolute regularity he worshipped women sexually involved with his friends, and he habitually lost out. In the coming years these defeats would strain many relationships, including that with Kraus (e.g. over Lina Loos). However, in the erotic triangle between Altenberg, Kraus and Kalmar, shared grief at her death obviated further complications. More-over, Altenberg was also infatuated at this time with the enigmatic Annie R., whom Großmann mentions in his memoirs, and with Emma Rudolf, better known as Ea von Allesch. Rudolf, however, preferred Alfred Polgar.

After Kalmar's death it was Altenberg, and not Kraus himself who pub-lished an elegy entitled "Wie Genies sterben" in *Die Fackel* of June 1901.[96] Altenberg's evocation of the dead woman, in his view a victim of the de-structive forces of Viennese society, ranges her firmly in the sequence of fe-male figures who give his third book *Was der Tag mir zuträgt* its particular flavor. In an undated letter to the actress he expresses sentiments which form a recurring motif in that collection:

> Die Schönheit der Frau allein ist das Mysterium Gottes, vermittelst welchem diese Welt "Männer-Seele" groß, tief, reich, sanft, edel, selbstlos, göttlich wird. Die "schöne" Frau ist die vom Schöpfer in die Welt gesetzte Weckerin der Welt-Kräfte des Mannes.[97]

> [The beauty of woman alone is God's mystery, through which this world "man's soul" becomes great, deep, rich, gentle, noble, selfless, divine. The "beautiful" woman is placed on earth by the creator to awaken the world-powers of the man.]

In *Was der Tag mir zuträgt* Altenberg repeatedly articulates his notion of the aesthetic genius of the female as opposed to the intellectual genius of the male. These are fundamentally different to each other in kind, purportedly of equal value, but predicated on sexual difference. In "Wie Genies sterben" Altenberg formulates a notion, echoed in Kraus's conception of the relation-ship between the sexes, which is usually placed in the context of Kraus's re-ception of Weininger's *Geschlecht und Charakter*. This work, however, with its antithetical juxtaposition of the male with the female, was not published

---

[94] SPK.

[95] Karl Kraus, *Die Fackel*, 2 (1899): 29.

[96] Karl Kraus, *Die Fackel*, 81 (1901): 18–21. Kraus did, however, edit Altenberg's text.

[97] WSB 136.249.

until May 1903, and Weininger would not have permitted the word genius to appear in the context of anything female.

In other areas of sexual politics too, Kraus and Altenberg took closely similar positions. Both contend that woman's aesthetic function frees her from the demands of bourgeois sexual morality, and both take a dim view of male sexual lust and its associated desire for possession. In reality, Kraus took the theory more liberally than his friend, which could occasion furious tirades from Altenberg.[98]

In a letter postmarked 9 May 1901, just a week after Annie's death, Altenberg wrote to his grieving friend, assuring him how he grieved alongside him for the sweetest, most inspired and most childlike woman on earth.[99] Similar locutions reappear in "Wie Genies sterben," though the letter's suggestion of their own complicity in her death is absent from Altenberg's assault upon the Viennese society which had "extinguished the light of grace and sweet humanity." He thus writes a "Grabschrift und Anklageschrift" [epitaph and indictment] at a time when Kraus's health had collapsed under the strain of his loss. With the publication of "Wie Genies sterben," *Die Fackel* assumed an altogether different tenor: Altenberg's epitaph to the dead woman proved to be of nothing less than "programmatic significance" for the journal.[100] No longer would its chief concern be with institutional corruption; instead it launched ever more concerted attacks upon Viennese bourgeois morality and its organized mouthpiece, the liberal press. In short, it became *Die Fackel* as we think of it today.

The roots of this change are personal and grounded in Kraus's experience of Annie's death. She had believed herself on the road to recovery until a Viennese paper informed her she was dying; after her death, press reports claimed she had traded her body in return for jewelry from her lovers. Kraus supported legal action by her family and even published details of her modest finances in *Die Fackel*. So stricken was he that no issues appeared for the next three months. Neither Altenberg nor Kraus forgot Annie Kalmar: writing in 1909, when his own mental equilibrium was severely threatened, Altenberg sent Kraus a long, reproachful letter reminding him not only of what she had meant to them both, but also of the significance of "Wie Genies sterben" for Kraus's whole future development: she had been nothing less than his *"seelische Errettung"* [*spiritual deliverance*].[101] His brief love for Kalmar may

---

[98] See Barker and Lensing, *Rezept*, 265.

[99] Barker and Lensing, *Rezept*, 225.

[100] Susanne Rode, *Alban Berg und Karl Kraus. Zur geistigen Biographie des Komponisten der "Lulu"*, (Frankfurt: Lang 1988), 22.

[101] Barker and Lensing, *Rezept*. 241:

> Die Lüge des Lebens nahm später, *wie stets*, auch von *unseren Herzen* Besitz; aber daß wir *diese Gipfel* einst erklimmen konnten, *zeugt* für uns!!! [. . .] Du erbatest von mir einen Nachruf der Theuren, Unvergesslichen. Und in einer bangen Morgenstunde schrieb ich ihn hin. Du erklärtest es damals für Deine *seelische Errettung*. [. . .] Heil Annie Kalmar! Da "fanden wir uns," da "verstanden wir uns ganz"! Es war das *"lebende Ideal"* unserer *Träume*.

be seen as the matrix upon which he based much of his subsequent under-standing of the relationship between the sexes.[102]

When Helga Malmberg returned to her Hamburg home late in 1909, sick and exhausted from caring for Altenberg, Kraus requested that she seek out Annie's grave in the Ohlsdorf cemetery and lay flowers there. The inscription on the grave, with its echoes of "Wie Genies sterben," is by Altenberg.[103] In February 1911 Kraus published the poem "Widmung des Wortes,"[104] inspired by her death nearly a decade previously, while Altenberg provided an earlier memorial to her in the opening number of his short-lived journal *Kunst* in 1903. This piece he entitled "Ideale Grabschrift," and accompanied it with her photograph. It was then republished (without the photograph) in the fourth edition of *Wie ich es sehe* in 1904 as "Annie Kalmar" (WS 284). As late as 1915 "Wie Genies sterben" was republished in *Nachfechsung* (NF 252), and when Kraus finally brought out his Altenberg anthology in 1932, he included both pieces in it.

Although the impact of Altenberg's first two books had established his presence Viennese letters, success brought little peace of mind. His emotional life was dominated not just by Annie R. and Annie Kalmar, but from 1898 onwards by Emma Rudolf, a *femme fatale* with a list of lovers just as distinguished as Lou Andreas Salomé or Alma Mahler. Born Emma Täubele in the working-class district of Ottakring in 1875, she was the type of woman to whom Altenberg felt most drawn: boyishly slender, wide-eyed and with an elegant gait. In short, a *femme enfant*. Eventually she became a successful fashion journalist, her marriage in 1894 to the Leipzig bookseller Theodor Rudolf having meant little to her. Altenberg was an early conquest, along with Polgar, who also vied for her affections in the summer of 1899. Polgar was the victor, but only a partial one, for Emma lived with him in a menage à trois, along with an English pianist named Skeene. Nevertheless it is possible, as Malmberg suggests, that Emma remained the most important woman in Altenberg's life.[105]

> [Later on life's mendacity, *as always*, took hold of *our hearts* too; but that we once were able to ascend *this pinnacle* speaks on our *behalf*!!! [...] You requested of me a memorial to the dear and unforgettable one. And in an anxious morning hour I wrote it down. You said then it was your *spiritual deliverance* [...] Heil Annie Kalmar! There "we found each other," there "we understood each other totally"! It was the "*living ideal*" of our *dreams*.]

[102] Edward Timms, *Karl Kraus. Apocalyptic Satirist. Culture and Catastrophe in Habsburg Vienna*, (New Haven and London: Yale University Press, 1986), 72–73.

[103] Helga Malmberg, *Widerhall des Herzens. Ein Peter Altenberg-Buch*, (Munich: Langen and Müller, 1961), 222–223.

[104] Timms, *Karl Kraus*, 259–260.

[105] A photograph of Emma Rudolf, "Peter Altenbergs große Liebe," is published in Malmberg, *Widerhall*, 224. Rudolf's list of lovers included Rilke, who in 1916 wrote her a poem which he inscribed on the title page of the third edition of his *Neue Gedichte*. In that same year she married Johann von Allesch, and it is as Ea, friend of Musil and Canetti and lover of Hermann Broch that she is perhaps better known today. Altenberg's published references to her are oblique (e.g. the use of her initials,) but she was probably the model both for Elizabeth in Broch's *Pasenow* and for

Altenberg's expressed his love for Emma in a deluge of inscribed picture postcards. More than thirty cards addressed to and inspired by Emma — whom he often called Nadjeshda — have survived, but it is not clear how many were actually delivered. She is constantly apostrophized, but the cards bear no postal address or stamp. Apparently Emma presented Altenberg with twenty-six pictures of herself, which he then inscribed as verbal and visual icons. When she requested their return he extravagantly pleaded to be allowed to keep them for the sake of his "willfully *tortured soul.*" To be deprived of kissing her "beloved Beethoven-brow" was torture for his poor nerves.[106] If Altenberg's love was not reciprocated, which seems fairly certain, these cards may have served to sublimate his frustration at the lack of direct communication with the beloved.

Of exceptional interest is the series of black and white postcards depicting winter scenes whose inscriptions reveal the depths of the poet's melancholy. They are perfect examples of the fusion of photography and poetic text, a technique which Altenberg pioneered but for which he long received no recognition.[107] Forming a sort of Schubertian "Winterreise" minus music, they are also fine examples of the impact of oriental art upon the imagination of the European *fin de siècle*, being clearly reminiscent of Japanese nature paintings with their inscribed haiku.

Although Altenberg may even have avoided the physical reciprocation of his feelings lest sexual reality impair his idealized view of the *Frauenseele*, the strength of his feelings for Emma should not be underestimated. His sexuality was simply not conventional. The correspondence with Emma makes abundantly clear that in the summer of 1899 he was living at an intolerable level of emotional intensity. On 18 July, the day after his last review appeared in the *Extrapost*, he inscribed a coloured postcard depicting a spray of mixed carnations. Writing at 4 a.m., he speaks of his indescribable love for the "blessed" Emma and of his own state of unspeakable perturbation and longing.[108] A week later, on 25 July, he inscribed a further card depicting carnations with the words: "Emma Rudolf, Deine Schönheit forderte als Opfer nicht allein die Seele eines Maschin-Ingenieurs, sondern das Herz eines Dichters!" [Emma Rudolf, your beauty demanded as a victim not merely the soul of a machine engineer but the heart of a poet!]. On the reverse he delivers a melodramatic address again not so much to his beloved as to himself. The self-apostrophization reveals the writer's mental anguish:

> Auch diesen Morgen, auch diesen grauenvollen Morgen überstand
> Dein armes Herz, Peter Altenberg! Zum erstenmale im Leben besiegtest

---

Alpha, the main figure in Musil's *Vinzenz oder die Freundin bedeutender Männer*. See Elisabeth Albertsen, "Ea oder die Freundin bedeutender Männer. Porträt einer Wiener Kaffeehaus-Muse," *Musil Forum* 5, no. 2 (1979): 138–139.

[106] Elisabeth Albertsen, "Ea oder die Freundin bedeutender Männer," *Musil-Forum* 5, no. 1 (1979): 31.

[107] GSE. The card "Bach im Winter" is reproduced in Barker & Lensing, *Rezept*, 120.

[108] GSE

Du Deinen armen kranken Leib, rafftest Dich auf aus tiefstem Schlafe, eiltest hin, die Geliebteste noch zu sehen vor ihrer Abreise. Eine Stunde lang standest Du, standest Du, Peter Altenberg! Später erfuhrst Du, daß sie und er in einer Ecke des Restaurants die Abschiedsstunde verbracht hatten. Gelbe Rosen, die ich brachte, erbleichet über das Schicksal Peter Altenbergs!!!

Ich *liebe* Dich, Emma Rudolf - - -.[109]

[Peter Altenberg, your poor heart managed to survive even this morning, even this appalling morning! For the first time in your life you conquered your poor sick body, wrested yourself from the deepest sleep, hurried along to see the beloved before her departure. A whole hour you stood you there, stood you there, Peter Altenberg! Later you learnt that she and he had spent their parting moments in the corner of the restaurant. Yellow roses, which I brought, pale before the fate of Peter Altenberg!!!

I *love* you, Emma Rudolf - - -.]

A postcard portraying the Martyrdom of Sodoma reads simply "Wer krönt, wer erlöst *mich*?!? PA" [Who crowns, who redeems *me*?!? PA]. Something had to give, especially in view of Emma's strengthening relationship with Polgar. One card, dated Gmunden, 2. 9. 99, needs little elaboration. It shows the Traun waterfalls but bears no intensely felt dedication. Indeed, there is no text at all, it is merely signed, one signature on each side of the picture, Peter Altenberg and Alfred Polgar.

It seems probable that the failure of this infatuated relationship with Emma was the prime cause of Altenberg leaving Vienna for Munich in the autumn of 1899. This is suggested in the memoirs of several Munich writers, who recall Altenberg's sojourn in the Bavarian capital which lasted, with intervals back in Vienna, until early May 1901. He would thus not only have escaped the influence of Emma Rudolf, but would also have been spared the intensity of Kraus's involvement with Annie Kalmar. Whether his return to Vienna was in any way prompted by her death is not known. He was already in Munich on 9 October 1899 as a despairing postcard to Otto Erich Hartleben reveals; Hartleben then passed it on to Frau Fischer in Berlin.[110] In the same month Altenberg wrote to his brother, wondering when he might return to Vienna, a city which he now feared. As usual, the question of money loomed large, especially as he was still paying rent for an unused room. Almost as an afterthought he adds that he must return to the city to complete his third book, and for that he needs total solitude.

Altenberg's first stay in Munich was probably quite short, unlike that of 1900–1901 which was to last some five months in all. In 1899 his reputation went in advance of him, and on arrival he was treated as a cult figure. Max Halbe, who already knew Altenberg from Vienna and regarded him as the

[109] GSE
[110] GSE

essence of an *Asphaltliterat*,[111] recalls him exploding like a meteor on to literary life of Munich: the "Archipoeta der Boheme" [The arch-poet of la Bohème] had arrived.[112] Writing a couple of decades after this visit Halbe felt at a loss to explain to his post-war audience the almost fetishistic Munich Altenberg cult.[113] The Viennese writer held court in the Café Stefanie, the Munich equivalent of Berlin's Café Größenwahn, accepting as no more than his due the adoration of his followers.[114] He came into contact with many of the writers and artists then resident in Munich, and as usual found other men's wives attractive, especially Max Halbe's. Dated 6–7 February 1901 are three sketches which Altenberg inscribed in Luise Halbe's guest book with a dedication to her wondrous beauty and "Berges- und Waldnatur" [mountain and forest nature.][115] At the Halbes' Altenberg also met Otto Erich Hartleben: two antipodes, who understood not a word the other said but got on famously.[116] The same goes for Altenberg's relationship with Eduard von Keyserling, whose story "Nicky" (1918) portrays an artist whose obsession with pureed vegetables is very reminiscent of Altenberg. Korfiz Holm saw Altenberg and Keyserling respectively as the enthusiast and the sceptic, each unhappily in love with life and for precisely that reason enjoying every good hour and providing joy for others.[117]

A more extended literary memorial to Altenberg in Munich is found in Jakob Wassermann's novel *Die Geschichte der jungen Renate Fuchs*, first published in 1900. Wassermann had met Altenberg on a visit to Vienna in 1898, and his impact upon the characterization of the Jewish eccentric Christian Süssenguth, who lives in Munich, is instantly recognizable. His reddish moustache drooping in a deep semi-circle, Süssenguth writes letters to children, is in love with every girl, preaches the unthinkable and hangs around disreputable bars with disreputable women. He conceives of himself as the saviour of women and girls, wishing to save them from the clutches of men, whose fault it is that so many women come to grief. According to Altenberg-

---

[111] Max Halbe, *Jahrhundertwende. Erinnerungen an eine Epoche*, (Munich: Albert Langen and Georg Müller, 1976), 211.

[112] Ibid.

[113] Halbe, *Jahrhundertwende*, 213.

[114] Hofmannsthal's friends kept him informed about Altenberg's progress in Munich. On 16 December 1899 Ria Schujlow-Claasen tells of going to hear a Miss Rabitow read from Altenberg's works and meeting him there. Schujlow-Claasen had earlier reviewed *Ashantee*, but her once favorable response had changed. (RS-C, "Die neuentdeckte Frau [Peter Altenberg Ashantee]," *Das Magazin für Litteratur* 42, [1897]: 1274–79.) She agrees with Hofmannsthal that both Altenberg and his writing make an unpleasant impression: *Ria Schmujlow-Claasen und Hugo von Hofmannsthal: Briefe, Aufsätze, Dokumente*, ed. Claudia Abrecht, (Marbach: Deutsche Schillergesellschaft, 1982), 52.

[115] "Entwicklung," "Die Frau," "Baum in Prater." Manuscripts in SPK.

[116] Halbe, *Jahrhundertwende*, 214.

[117] Korfiz Holm, *ich klein geschrieben. Heitere Erlebnisse eines Verlegers*, (Munich: Langen, 1932), 174.

Süssenguth, however, woman has an "asbestos soul" which "remains un-
scathed in the fire of life."[118]

Altenberg's presence in the Bavarian capital may also conceivably have
had an impact upon the portrayal of Detlev Spinell in Thomas Mann's *Tristan*, a work begun in Munich early in 1901. Critics have noted Mann's penchant for drawing upon real-life prototypes for both milieu and characters,
but besides Altenberg they also moot Arthur Holitzscher (1869–1941)
author of the novel *Fin de siècle*, as a possible model for Spinell. Altenberg is
seen, like Spinell, as embodying typical features of the *fin de siècle* literary
aesthete, and given his high opinion of Altenberg's first book, it may be significant that the very words "Wie ich es sehe" appear in Mann's text. The
femme enfant embodied in Gabriele Klöterjahn figures especially prominently in *Wie ich es sehe*. What Jost Hermand sees as "the uncanny bond
between the poet and the misunderstood female soul"[119] in *Tristan* is equally
a feature of Altenberg's work, as is also the poet's "outrage at the abuse of
woman's delicate being" as noted by Wolfdietrich Rasch.[120] However, in
their anxiety to find yet further parallels between Spinell and Altenberg these
critics go beyond anything warranted by the facts. To observe that Altenberg
and Spinell both spent time in sanatoria is to forget that Spinell's problem
was ostensibly a physical one, whereas Altenberg's was more spiritual. Cru-
cially, Altenberg's institutionalization did not begin until 1910, whereas
Mann published *Tristan* in 1903.[121]

Thomas Mann contributed a warmly understanding essay to *Das Altenbergbuch* — he completed it on 28 August 1921 — but his diary for 1919
shows him mired in anti-Semitic loathing for everything Altenberg represented. He claims that "Herr Peter" is his born enemy just like the Jews
Theodor Lessing and Alfred Kerr. People of Altenberg's type have no sense
of conservative values and are not competent to judge his work. He has now
put Altenberg's teachings behind him.[122] The labyrinths of Mann's art were
probably not to Altenberg's taste either, if one of Max Oppenheimer's anecdotes is anything to judge by:

> *Der Festtag.*
> "Peter, gestern ist die 50. Auflage der 'Buddenbrooks' erschienen."
> "Öder Schurke! Und das ist mein Sonntag!"
>
> [*Celebration Day*
> "Peter, the 50th impression of 'Buddenbrooks' came out yesterday."

---

[118] Jakob Wassermann, *Die Geschichte der jungen Renate Fuchs*, (Berlin: Fischer, 1910), 19.

[119] Ulrich Dittmann, *Erläuterungen und Dokumente. Thomas Mann "Tristan,"* (Stuttgart: Reclam, 1983), 52.

[120] Ibid., 52.

[121] Ibid.

[122] Thomas Mann, *Tagebücher 1918–1921*, ed. Peter de Mendelssohn, (Frankfurt: Fischer, 1979), 55–56.

"Miserable wretch! That's the end of my Sunday!"][123]

A long letter to Großmann, written in Munich on 25 October 1899, reveals much about Altenberg's relationships with Judaism, alcohol and literature, and indicates how desperate he had been when he deserted Vienna. The move to Munich represented the last attempt of a "verhältnismäßig günstig organisierte Natur" [relatively well organized nature] to pull itself together. He needs rest and solitude, and pays tribute to his brother Georg, whose economic support guarantees his freedom. For his sake, and that of S. Fischer, he feels he must rein in his self-destructive urges and work on himself. Writers like Halbe, Hartleben, Viktor Bamberger and Karl Hauer are:

> eigentlich nichts anderes als christlich-germanisch verbummelte Saufbrüder und Burschenschaftler. Sie erhalten sich naiv durch Saufen, sind der letzte Gegensatz zu Schnitzler, Salten, Beer-Hofmann, Loris!
> Sie trinken sich frei, ledig!
> Denn alle Freundschaft erblüht dieser Quelle. Man ist naturgemäß mißtrauisch gegen einen, der nicht saufen kann! Hält ihn für einen spintisierenden Juden! Ich gewann alle Sympathien durch meine Spatenbräu-Verehrung![124]

> [are actually nothing but boozy Christian-Germanic wasters and fraternity men. They stay naive by boozing, they are the very opposite of Schnitzler, Salten, Beer-Hofmann, Loris!
> They drink themselves foot-loose and fancy-free!
> For all friendship blossoms from this source. One is naturally mistrustful of someone who cannot drink! You consider him a crazy Jew! I won everybody's sympathy through my veneration of Spatenbräu!]

A further letter to Großmann was dated 20 November 1899 and indicated that the move from Vienna had not had the intended effect. Altenberg did not regret going to Munich, however, for the previous summer had been destroyed by a "geliebte Circe und Menschenfresserin Ogre" [beloved Circe, man-eater and ogre.][125] It was only fear of Emma Rudolf which was now keeping Altenberg away from Vienna.

It is not known exactly when Altenberg finally returned to Vienna from this first sojourn, but from the memoirs of Korfiz Holm it transpires he had returned to Munich by the end of 1900, by which time *Was der Tag mir zuträgt* had come out.[126] Holm writes that he got to know Altenberg on New Year's Eve 1900 and crossed the threshold of the twentieth century

---

[123] Max Oppenheimer, "P. A. Text und Zeichnung," *Berliner Tagblatt* 286, 19 June 1927. This anecdote was probably amongst those recited by Oppenheimer at the Cabaret Voltaire in Zürich in 1916. See Barker and Lensing, *Rezept*, 125–126; 340–342.

[124] Hedwig Prohaska, "Peter Altenberg. Versuch einer Monographie," Dr.phil diss., Vienna, 1947, 215.

[125] Ibid., 220.

[126] The document "Erhöhung," dedicated to Ida Lang reveals he was still in Munich in January 1900. WSB 149.790.

with him.[127] There must be doubt about Holm's memory, however, for he also claims that the venue of their meeting was the pioneering cabaret Elf Scharfrichter, which did not open until 13 April 1901.[128]

Deeply disaffected by life in Vienna, Altenberg remained in Munich until May 1901. He found "everything nicer in Munich"[129] — especially the women — and for almost half a year it seemed he might settle there.[130] He lived at the Hotel Stachus, claiming that nowhere else could he get the undisturbed peace necessary to his well-being. This greatly amused his friends, for the hotel stood on one of Munich's busiest corners. He remained in Munich during Fasching, striking up a strange but revealing relationship with a plain-looking girl from North Germany which Holm assumes was purely platonic. Contrary to fashion she wore her hair cropped short, had herself addressed as a man and using a male pseudonym wrote works that nobody would print. This "wunderliche Zweigespann" [strange duo] turned up at a Fasching party in the Café Luitpold, but when in the small hours the girl wanted to be accompanied home, she was understandably displeased when Altenberg simply said adieu, adding:

> Weib, warum habe ich deine Seele befreit, wenn du nicht einmal allein durch das Lokal gehen kannst![131]

> [Woman, why have I liberated your soul if you cannot even walk alone through the pub!]

With this their odd relationship was at an end.

On what was to be Altenberg's last evening in Munich, Keyserling and Altenberg joined Holm and his wife at a restaurant table, where the talk came round to Vienna. Keyserling sang the praises of the city and of Altenberg's "Viennese style",[132] but he took this as an insult, shouting "Und Kitsch ist Trumpf! . . . Ich hasse Wien und geh in meinem Leben nicht mehr hin!" [And Kitsch is trumps! . . . I hate Vienna and am never going there again in my life!] On leaving the restaurant the Holms invited Keyserling and Altenberg to supper the next evening, an invitation which was gladly accepted. In the afternoon, however, a telegram arrived from Altenberg, who by now was in Salzburg, regretting his inability to take supper in Schwabing that evening. According to Keyserling, Altenberg's mannerliness had prevented him from declining the invitation on the spot, the reason being shame at his bad table manners. Accordingly he fled from Munich, sending postcards from various parts of Austria, culminating in one from Vienna. That was the last Holm ever heard from him. On 9 May 1901 Altenberg

---

[127] Holm, *ich klein geschrieben*, 167.

[128] Harold B. Segel, *Turn-of-the-century cabaret: Paris, Barcelona, Berlin, Munich, Vienna, Cracow, Moscow, St. Petersburg, Zürich,* (New York: Columbia University Press, 1987), 149.

[129] Holm, *ich klein geschrieben*, 169.

[130] Ibid., 171.

[131] Ibid., 173.

[132] Ibid., 176.

wrote Kraus his condolences at the death of Annie Kalmar, five days later
Frank Wedekind received a postcard from Altenberg asking when the Munich Überbrettl cabaret was coming to Vienna. The card confirms that, for
the moment, he was reconciled to the city he had denounced just a few days
previously: "Unerhört schön ist's in Wien" [It's incredibly beautiful in Vi-
enna].[133]

Was der Tag mir zuträgt:
Wagner, Women and bouillon-cubes

Regarded by Rudolf Kassner as "Dichtung im reinen und neuen Sinne"
[poetry in the pure and modern sense] and by a modern critic as Altenberg's
least original book,[134] *Was der Tag mir zuträgt* was published at the end of
1900, in the wake of its author's thwarted passion for Emma Rudolf. Despite
the subtitle *Fünfundfünfzig neue Studien*, not everything in the new work
was original, several items having previously appeared in newspapers and literary journals. *Was der Tag mir zuträgt* also incorporated material from
Ashantee, which then went out of print. The material trawled from the previous book was not, however, the central section depicting the Ashanti themselves — this reappeared in the fourth edition of *Wie ich es sehe* (1904) — but
other aspects of Altenberg's *Kulturkritik* such as his humorous appraisal of
the widespread Wagner-cult in Vienna.

Altenberg was devoted to Wagner, perhaps responding to those qualities
which had led to Nietzsche's assessment of Wagner as a miniaturist. However, rather than eulogize Wagner, Altenberg chose to satirize the bourgeois
manifestations of the cult followers. Hence he highlighted the difference
between the lofty ideals he and fellow artists perceived in the music dramas,
and the commonplace reactions of the Viennese middle class. In "Fliegender
Holländer," one of several texts named directly after Wagnerian operas, the
role of woman as man's redeemer, a central theme in *Was der Tag mir
zuträgt*, is appropriately reflected in a Senta-figure. She, however, is a middle-class wife, her husband is seen only in his underwear, and for her redemption lies in chocolate-filled dainties. In "Tristan und Isolde," Altenberg
reproduces a familial constellation similar to that in "Familienleben" in *Wie
ich es sehe*, presenting once more the figure of the revolutionary Albert in su-
percilious conflict with the philistines. Albert is no more spared the narrator's
irony than is his family, with Wagner's "herrliche Maid" Isolde, the object of
Albert-Tristan's attentions, turning out to be Hedwig the maidservant.

[133] The card is dated Wien 13 Mai 1901-München 14 Mai 1901. Städtische Bibliothek, Munich,
156–63. Further postcards from this time suggest an amicable relationship between Altenberg and
Wedekind. This contradicts Friedell's "Gespräch über Wedekind" in which Altenberg calls
Wedekind the "Antichrist" (AB 419)

[134] Rudolf Kassner, "Peter Altenberg: 'Was der Tag mir zuträgt,'" *Wiener Rundschau* 5, no. 3
(1901): 75; Burkhard Spinnen, *Schriftbilder. Studien zu einer Geschichte emblematischer
Kurzprosa*, (Münster: Aschendorff, 1991), 158–159.

"Walküre" (WT 235), the third Wagnerian title in *Was der Tag mir zuträgt*, is set in the Vienna opera itself and relates events during a performance featuring Pauline Dönges as Sieglinde and Sophie Sedelmayr as Brünnhilde. No male singer is mentioned, nor is the conductor, though it could well have been Gustav Mahler.[135] An unnamed woman forms the focus of "Walküre," which counterpoints some inaccurate quotations from Wagner's text with her own reactions to the unfolding music drama.[136] Intently following events with her own libretto, the woman prays to her "God" Richard Wagner, while her husband brings her coffee-creams in the interval. Particularly interesting in "Walküre," which again revolves around the centrality of women in the evolution of men to a new state of perfection, is the way Altenberg appropriates Wagner's text as the basis for his own linguistic variations. Wagner's female characters thus end up speaking the words of Peter Altenberg, as if the poet saw in himself an extension of the composer.[137]

Although more concerned with visual art than music, Altenberg's next book *Pròdròmòs* continued the allusions to Wagner broached in *Was der Tag mir zuträgt*. Sometimes the references seem personally inspired: if, after attending a performance of *Götterdämmerung* with one's beloved, one then makes love at 1 a.m., this is no longer a sexual encounter:

> Es war gar kein Unterschied mit dem heiligen Opernhause. Sie sagte sanft: "Es ist die Fortseztung - - -." (P 90)

> [There was no difference from the sacred opera house. She said softly: "It is the continuation - - -."]

More significant is Wagner's promotion to supreme artist whose music encompassed every conceivable spiritual experience:

> Er hat unser Herz und alle seine Emotionen bereits in Musik umgesetzt! (P 50)

> [He has already set our heart and all its emotions to music.]

Wagner of course perceived himself, and was perceived by others, as a *Reformkünstler* par excellence, and his example, along with that of Nietzsche, was clearly of major significance for Altenberg. Seriously as he took the composer, however, Altenberg could not resist using his example to

---

[135] Altenberg became indirectly linked with Mahler in 1903 through his association with the Wiener Ansorge-Verein, founded to honor the German pianist and composer Conrad Ansorge (1862–1930). See: Heinz Lunzer, "Karl Kraus und der 'Akademische Verband für Literatur und Musik in Wien', *Karl Kraus, Ästhetik und Kritik: Beiträge des Kraus Symposions Poznan*, ed. Stefan H. Kaszynski and Sigurd Paul Scheichl, (Munich: Edition Text + Kritik, 1989), 142.

[136] Raymond S. Furness, *Wagner and Literature*, (Manchester: Manchester University Press, 1982), 116.

[137] The role of Richard Wagner in their cultural critiques of Vienna is common to both Altenberg and Loos. Loos's most celebrated confrontation was with Alfred Roller's *Tristan* production of 1903. See: Kurt Blaukopf, *Gustav Mahler*, trans. Inge Goodwin, (London: Allen Lane, 1973), 174; *Traum und Wirklichkeit. Wien 1870–1970*, (Vienna: Eigenverlag der Mussen der Stadt Wien, 1985), 161.

apparently comic effect, as when he makes dietary claims for Wagner's heroes. Yet is this any more preposterous than Freud's psychoanalysis of Hamlet?:

> Schwarzes Fleisch erzeugt Schwarz-Alben, weisses Fleisch Licht-Alben. Siegfried, Poulard-essend, Hagen, Rindfleisch, Wildpret-essend! (P 95)

> [Dark meat produces black demons, white meat airy spirits. Siegfried, chicken-eating, Hagen eating beef and game!]

Interesting though Altenberg's confrontation with Viennese cultural life in *Was der Tag mir zuträgt* is — in "Luci-fer, Licht-Bringer" (WT 319) he affectionately satirizes himself as well as the self-regarding aesthetes who so enraged Kraus — it is as the most sustained expression of Altenberg's *Frauenkult*, his quasi-medieval veneration for women, that the work has most often attracted comment. Although it is here that Altenberg most consistently presents himself as the last of the troubadours, *Was der Tag mir zuträgt* also appears to demonstrate his success in surmounting his frustration over Emma Rudolf. That his real-life feelings, in contrast with those projected by the artistic persona, frequently tended towards misogyny, surfaces in relatively few places. Yet as early as 1897, when preparing *Ashantee*, Altenberg made careful editorial decisions in the light of the idealized view of femininity he wished to project. Thus the cycle of sketches entitled "Hausball," later included in *Was der Tag mir zuträgt*, is not identical with that first published in the journal *Liebelei* in March 1896, whose proprietor Baron Brockdorff appears barely disguised as Baron B. in "Luci-fer, Licht-Bringer." In "Mylitta" we read:

> Strindberg hat recht. Das Weib saugt uns geistig aus, lebt quasi von uns, wie die Leimmistel von der Birke - - -.[138]

> [Strindberg is correct. Woman sucks us dry spiritually, lives quasi on us like mistletoe on a birch tree - - -.]

This passage has also been edited out of *Was der Tag mir zuträgt*. In later collections, Altenberg came to speak ever more positively of Strindberg's misogyny, whereas earlier Ibsen was invariably the Scandinavian most frequently, and approvingly, referred to.[139]

Just as *Wie ich es sehe* was followed quickly by a second edition clarifying in a new foreword what was only implicit in the first edition, so too a second edition of *Was der Tag mir zuträgt* (1902,) now expanded from fifty-five to sixty-five "new" studies, contains an explicatory text. In "Selbstanzeige" the author makes clear beyond doubt how he wishes his work to be received. Its chief addressees are girls and women, with whom he claims a special relationship: "Denn siehe, ich bin nur Euer *tönend* gewordenes *stummes* Herz sel-

---

[138] *Peter Altenberg. Expedition in den Alltag. Gesammelte Skizzen 1895–1898*, ed. Werner J. Schweiger, (Vienna and Frankfurt: Löcker and Fischer, 1987), 325.

[139] Strindberg, like Altenberg, was also a voluminous letter-writer given to bracing personal invective frequently anti-Semitic in tone.

ber!" [For behold, I am merely your *mute* heart itself which now gives forth *sound*: WT 1]. With men, on the other hand, the author fails utterly to identify himself. They are "perfide Pactirer mit dem Leben" [perfidious wheeler-dealers with life: WT 2] whose only hope of redemption is through women, a notion treated ironically in "Fliegender Holländer." In Altenberg's *Frauenkult*, however, for all its contempt for the contemporary bourgeois male, we still do not find feminism in a modern guise. For woman's ultimate function is not regarded as the fulfillment of her own potential, but rather seen in respect of the otherwise doomed male. Women will thus redeem men who, in their new-found, woman-given perfection, will then redeem women: "Deine *Vollkommenheit* ist ihre *Erlösung*!" [Your *perfection* is their *salvation*: WT 2]. It is, however, through the artist that women will become whole: quite typically, Altenberg speaks through the voice of a woman:

> So ersehnen wir den Künstler und seine Phantasie, damit wir *seien*! In seiner *Seele* werden wir zur Frau geboren! (WT 51)

> [Thus we long for the artist and his imagination, that we may *be*! In his *soul* we are born as woman!]

In *Pròdròmŏs* Altenberg expresses more concisely even than in *Was der Tag mir zuträgt* a philosophy where women's ultimate function is to facilitate men's perfection. Once more adopting a female voice, he writes:

> Kraft und Freudigkeiten will ich ihm bringen, dass er an seiner Mission arbeiten könne, die Welt zu erlösen von ihren Lügenhaftigkeiten! . . . Der Schöpfer dachte sich in genialer Weise mich als *Mittel* aus, den Mann durch mich zu Seinem Ebenbilde zu erhöhen! (P 140)

> [Power and delights will I bring him, that he might work at his mission, to redeem the world from its mendacities! . . . In an inspired way the Creator devised me as a *means* of raising men to His likeness.]

The symbiotic relationship between poet and woman is a major theme of *Was der Tag mir zuträgt*, but it is not the sole manifestation of his fascination with the other sex. The "P.A." persona is simply not consistent. On the one hand Altenberg encourages reform of the way bourgeois society treats women, on the other, he supports views more readily associated with the society he wishes to reform. Hence alongside a sympathetic awareness of a woman's needs, feelings and aspirations, there is also Peter Altenberg, citizen of Vienna 1900, hotbed of anti-feminism and anti-Semitism. In "Ein Wiener" (WT 290) Altenberg commends Karl Lueger, the anti-Semitic mayor of Vienna; in "Tulpen" he first gives vent to his misogyny then tries, without success, to gild the lily with something he hopes might pass for grim humour: "*Reality* - - woman! *Reality* destroys" (WT 66). The difference between tulips and women is that you can twist the head off a tulip without being sent to jail. If such sentiments are unacceptable today, the idealization of young women and adolescent girls, with their uniformly exquisite limbs, eyes, and hair, can be equally hard to stomach. Only the rather startling references to such aspects of their corporality as the fragrance of their mouth juices and the odour of their armpits redeems many of these women from a relationship with flesh-and-blood reality as tenuous as the art nouveau icons with which they might understandably be compared.

Altenberg's unabashed obsession with boyish young women also marks a move away from the stereotyped femme fatale of the *fin de siècle*, reflecting "a common concern with the adolescent body in Europe around 1900."[140] It might also be thought to indicate a homoerotic component in his psychological constitution, but only rarely did he confront the issue of homosexuality. The unpublished and undated manuscript "Päderastie" shows him sharing the same intellectual climate as Kraus, whose generally liberal stance on this issue was well known. As Edward Timms notes:

> Kraus's basic attitude was that of an advocate of reform. He argues for a more liberal attitude towards sex and for specific changes in the law. There should be a clear separation of spheres between "Sittlichkeit" and "Kriminalität" — sexual morality and criminal justice. Sexual behaviour (he argues) belongs to the private sphere. Every person is entitled to privacy in the pursuit of sexual satisfaction.[141]

Kraus's campaign had opened in the September 1902 issue of *Die Fackel* with the essay "Sittlichkeit und Criminalität."[142] In "Päderastie" Altenberg similarly pleads tolerance for those to whom such feelings come as naturally as heterosexual men's feelings for women, though he remains quite conventional in his condemnation of male prostitution and homosexual abuse of minors.[143] His tolerance of lesbianism was especially marked, confirmed by his close relationship with Smaragda Berg, sister of Alban Berg, and by the erotic texts he wrote on lesbian themes. These texts, which mirrored Klimt's many drawings of Sapphic couples, remained unpublished until the 1980s,[144] and contrast starkly with a text published in the early years of the war in which Altenberg displays the most routinely predictable homophobia (NF 16).

Altenberg's relationship with Adolf Loos, which flowered at the same time as that with Kraus, is marked not only by the convergence of their artistic views, culminating in their abortive co-editorship of the journal *Kunst*, but also in the convergence of their sexual interests. This included a shared response to adolescent girls which led eventually to Loos facing legal proceedings. Recently, critics have seen Loos's obsessive dislike of ornamentation as related to his fear of mature female sexuality.[145] At a more manifest

---

[140] Patrick Werkner, *Egon Schiele. Art, sexuality and Viennese modernism*, (Palo Alto: Society for the Promotion of Science and Scholarship, 1994), 61.

[141] Edward Timms, *Karl Kraus. Apocalyptic Satirist. Culture and Catastrophe in Habsburg Vienna*, (New Haven and London: Yale University Press, 1986), 63.

[142] Karl Kraus, *Die Fackel*, 115 (1902): 1–24.

[143] WSB 160.468.

[144] *Peter Altenberg. Leben und Werk in Texten und Bildern*, ed. Hans Christian Kosler, (Munich: Matthes & Seitz 1981), 75–76.

[145] Werkner, *Schiele*, 64–65.

level, Altenberg relates in "La Zarina" (WT 216) how he and Loos came across the actress Lina Obertimpfler, later to become the first Frau Loos and to remain an object of Altenberg's admiration long after the marriage had foundered. Even then, however, the relationship would resume its familiar triangular pattern when a constant rival for her attention emerged in the figure of another of Altenberg's close friends, Egon Friedell.[146] Lina, according to F. T. Csokor the most beautiful woman in Vienna,[147] married Loos on 21 July 1902 in Eisgrub in Loos's native Moravia. Altenberg was to have been the best man, but when the time came was nowhere to be found, having overslept in Vienna. This was plainly no accident, and conflict over women remained a major source of the problems which arose between Altenberg and Loos. Loos's marriage to Lina was to prove a short one, with Loos himself accepting responsibility for the breakdown of their relationship.[148]

Because he made no secret of his rage and frustration, Altenberg's propensity for being on the losing side of a triangular relationship often led to public humiliation. This contributed greatly to his friends' amusement, and led in no small measure to a widespread opinion of Altenberg as a supreme fool which culminated in Felix Mitterer's screen play Der Narr von Wien (1982). That Altenberg subconsciously engineered these sexual defeats seems more than likely: his real love was reserved for adolescent girls, untouched, he felt, either by lust or by bourgeois ambition. Clearly he was no Freudian,[149] and Freud was no admirer of Altenberg, for whom the adolescent girl remains the essence of unspoiled physical and mental purity (F 249).

Altenberg's reactions to women were thus far more complex than a schematic perception permits. Far from being an antipode to Weininger, in a sense he even exemplifies Otto Weininger's contentious conception of sexuality, where the shorthand symbols of M and W are employed to designate the male and female principles which all people share in differing proportions. Like Wilhelm Fließ, Weininger believed in a universal bisexuality, yet in looking at Altenberg critics have adopted a similar antithetical stance to that adopted by Weininger only in his crudest moments. Thus Peter Altenberg is equated with gynolatry, Otto Weininger with misogyny. Yet just as Weininger was by no means always as schematic in his thought as is often suggested, so Altenberg does not merely equal gynolatry. "A" also has more than a touch of "W" in him.

Important though it was in determining the public perception of his iconography of women, Was der Tag mir zuträgt is also where Altenberg, though by not without irony, analyses his artistic aims and methods. Here

---

[146] Burkhardt Rukschcio and Roland Schachl, Adolf Loos: Leben und Werk, (Salzburg and Vienna: Residenz, 1987), 75–76; Du silberne Dame Du. Briefe von und an Lina Loos, ed. Franz Theodor Csokor and Leopoldine Ruther, (Vienna and Hamburg: Zsolnay, 1966), 16.

[147] Csokor, Lina Loos, 7.

[148] Rukschcio and Schachl, Adolf Loos, 92, reproduces photographs of Altenberg, Loos, Lina Loos and Heinz Lang on the Semmering, circa 1902–3.

[149] Minutes of the Vienna Psychoanalytical Society, 2 (1908–09), trsl. H. Nurnberg, (New York: International Universities Press Inc., 1967), 386–392.

too, in a so-called "Selbstbiographie," he tries to define his persona for his audience. The book is generously dedicated to his brother Georg Engländer, for just as Kraus could only pursue his life's work because of a steady income from the family firm, so Altenberg relied upon his brother's business efforts to provide a healthy financial lifeline. (Altenberg's income at this time was 240 crowns per month, equal to the salary of a middle-ranking official.)[150] When *Was der Tag mir zuträgt* was published, Altenberg was living with Georg Engländer at 3 Währingerstraße in the ninth district of Vienna, but he left in 1902 to lodge in the seedy Hotel London at 17 Wallnerstraße, a stone's throw from the Café Central.

Helga Malmberg has left a detailed account of Altenberg's tiny room, the cheapest he could find, high up on the fourth floor with an enchanting view over the roof-tops of Vienna. She writes graphically of the foetid air, the narrow stairs and corridors of the hotel, whose main business was providing short-stay bedrooms for courting couples. The neat order of Altenberg's hideout, its walls coated with images of the women he most admired, was in marked contrast to the tattiness of the Hotel London in general. This picture gallery was probably the closest he ever came to claiming a woman as his "own."[151] It represented the semi-public exhibition of a collecting mania most conspicuous in the thousands of picture postcards he had started gathering in 1897 (LA 269).

In "Selbstbiographie," a reworking of material published previously in 1899 and translated that same year into French, Altenberg disposes quickly of his bourgeois antecedents with a witty tribute to his father's tolerance and the ironization of himself as someone who had studied law without becoming a lawyer, medicine without become a doctor, the book-trade without becoming a book dealer, who had been a lover but never married and a poet without producing literature. Indeed, in the "Selbstanzeige," which was inserted into the second and subsequent editions of the work, he goes even further, claiming "Ich bin kein Dichter, kein Künstler" [I am no poet, no artist: WT 3]. Unabashed, he then delivers an analysis of his poetic method which all later commentators have relied upon when assessing Altenberg's relationship with his craft.

Altenberg insists that his work represents essence rather than excrescence, and by using the deliberately anti-poetic image of the "Rind im Liebig-Tiegel" [ox in the bouillon-cube][152] Altenberg further underlines his affinity with Adolf Loos's crusade to reduce architecture to basic principles. Yet precisely as Altenberg's relationship with Loos deepened, he continued his friendships with the "Secessionists" for whom Loos had little but contempt. Indeed, it was in 1902 that Altenberg produced his own catalogue for the

---

[150] Rukschcio and Schachl, *Adolf Loos*, 76.

[151] Emil Szittya remarks: "Es war in ihm ein krankhaftes Auflehnen gegen die Männlichkeit. Und wie über jeden Mann, der nie eine Frau besaß, können die Frauen nur Schönes von ihm erzählen" ("Fuer Karl Kraus ueber Peter Altenberg," *Ausgedachte Dichterschicksale*, [Paris: Les Ecrivains Réunis, 1928], 84–85.)

[152] Hilde Spiel, *Vienna's Golden Autumn*, (London: Weidenfeld and Nicolson, 1987), 118.

twelfth Secession exhibition which he contains important statements about the relationship of his own aesthetic to photography.

In the image of the bouillon cube Altenberg links the disparate worlds of aesthetics and dietetics in that arresting combination which will dominate much of his work from *Pròdrŏmŏs* onwards. This analogy has frequently been remarked upon, but what is less well appreciated is the linguistic influence of the Liebig company's marketing strategies. Contemporary advertising for their meat extract uses formulations remarkably close to Altenberg's while at the same time associating the product with the world of art. This was done via a series of inscribed picture postcards which form an arresting parallel to Altenberg's own procedures.

One of Liebig's cards illustrates Act 3, scene 2 of Meyerbeer's opera *Der Prophet*, when prayers are offered up prior to the "Sturm auf Münster"; alongside this scene from grand opera, portrayed in the best nineteenth century mock-medieval manner, there is a bottle of Liebig's meat extract. It is an incongruous juxtaposition, but might have particularly appealed to Altenberg, who increasingly saw himself as the prophet of a new healthiness, propagated through his own art. On the reverse of the postcard, which is personalised by a large facsimile of Liebig's own signature, the slogans are reminiscent not only of Altenberg's locutions but also of his predilection for bold typography. In language strikingly reminiscent of Altenberg's, consumers are told that Liebig's product:

> ist wegen seiner *außerordentlich leichten Verdaulichkeit* und seines *hohen Nährwerthes* ein *vorzügliches Nahrungs- und Kräftigungsmittel* für *Schwache, Blutarme* und *Kranke*, namentlich auch für *Magenleidende*.[153]
>
> [is thanks to its *extraordinary ease of digestion* and its *high nutritional value* an *exceptional source of nourishment and strength* for the *weak, anaemic and sick*, and also for those with *stomach disorders*.]

The cumulative effect of Liebig's advertising upon Altenberg's style is most pronounced in *Pròdrŏmŏs*, which came out four years after *Was der Tag mir zuträgt*, and which for long sections reads like advertizing copy for a health-food agency. Less than five years separate *Pròdrŏmŏs* from *Was der Tag mir zuträgt*, but in that time Altenberg had suffered a series of personal and professional blows from which he never fully recovered. These setbacks not only exacerbated the deterioration in his mental and physical health, they also highlighted the ever widening chasm between what Altenberg preached in public and what he did in private. Although it would be unfair to accuse Altenberg of hypocrisy, it is tempting to see in him someone who, in Heine's memorable phrase, preached water to the world but drank wine at home.[154] The years of long, slow decline had begun.

---

[153] See Burkhard Spinnen, "Idyllen in der Warenwelt. Peter Altenberg's *Pròdrŏmŏs* und die Sprache der Werbung," *Zeitschrift für Literaturwissenschaft und Linguistik* 22, nos. 87–88 (1992): 133–150. Spinnen does not refer to these advertising texts.

[154] Heinrich Heine, *Deutschland ein Wintermärchen*, (Stuttgart: Reclam, 1977), 8.

Kunst and other catastrophes

Whatever fame his first three books may have brought him, Altenberg remained insecure and unfulfilled. His hypochondria never waned, his financial anxiety was unallayed by his private income from the family firm. Professionally, too, he fell victim to his success when an "S. Altenberg" cashed in on his name to publish *Aus Liebe und andere Novellen* (1902) with Pierson in Dresden. Luckily, however, the real Altenberg, concerned for both his pocket and his reputation, was able to summon Kraus to his aid in *Die Fackel.*[155] Where some tried to exploit his name for quick profit, others who had happily used him as a model turned against him, Richard von Schaukal, for example, parading his new-found independence by priggishly attacking Altenberg's use of German.[156]

Assailed on all sides by outrageous fortune, Altenberg saw a God-sent opportunity for personal and aesthetic fulfillment when two strangers offered him the editorship of a new journal to be entitled *Kunst.*[157] Though famed for fecklessness, Altenberg seized his chance and in the autumn of 1903 the opulent *Kunst: Halbmonatschrift für Kunst und alles andere* appeared with his name on the title page. To the outside world it signaled his entrance into the mainstream of artistic life, but the notion of Altenberg organizing a regular publication was difficult for some to take seriously. Otto Falckenberg declared in the Munich periodical *Freistatt* that Altenberg as editor must have come as a shock to the Viennese, likening it to taking an exotic bloom from the greenhouse and putting it for sale in a greengrocer's shop.[158]

From the outset all was not well with the new magazine, for *Kunst* comprised only half of the product, whilst "alles andere" turned out to be something altogether different, a supplement written and produced by Adolf Loos with the provocative title *Das Andere: Ein Blatt zur Einführung Abendländischer Kultur in Österreich.* [The Other: A Journal for the introduction of Western Culture in Austria].[159] Frantic letters reveal that Altenberg far from welcomed Loos's "cooperation" on the journal, over which he had developed strongly proprietorial feelings. Why the managing editors Friedrich Krauss and Arthur Brehmer provided him with a co-editor can only be guessed at, but given Altenberg's reputation they had probably developed cold feet.

---

[155] Karl Kraus, *Die Fackel,* 114 (1902): 8–11; 116 (1902): 20–21.

[156] Richard von Schaukal, *Um die Jahrhundertwende,* (Munich and Vienna: Langen and Müller, 1965), 118.

[157] DLA

[158] Otto Falckenberg, "Peter Altenberg, der Redakteur," *Freistatt* 5, no. 45 (1903): 891.

[159] A further section of the journal was devoted to monographs on specific artists, the opening number featuring Alfons Canciani; over the coming months the selected artists were Vlaho Bukovac, Ernst Wagner, Tysa Kleen, Anton Schöner, Ivan Mestrović and the photographer N. Perscheid.

A series of vituperative letters confirms how betrayed Altenberg felt by Loos's unwelcome arrival. He accuses Loos of secretly offering the publishers money in order to win control of "his" journal, and when this ploy failed, he claims Loos bribed the publishers into founding a competing journal to rob him of overall control. He alleges Loos had perfidiously undermined him by arranging for lucrative ads to be placed in the magazine. Outraged, he complains to Kraus: "Oh Karl - - -. Ich bin kein Inseraten-Agent, ich bin ein Dichter!" [Oh Karl - - -. I am no advertising agent, I am a poet!][160] In reality, the numerous and prominent notices in *Das Andere* were published gratis because Loos believed the products were models for the regeneration of Austrian life at the interface of culture and commerce.

Another letter to Loos, written more in sadness than anger, suggests that their cooperation foundered on something as mundane as a power struggle, with Loos withdrawing his support. Textual evidence from the first volume indicates that although Altenberg felt Loos was motivated by envy and resentment, philosophical differences may have been the real source of the difficulties. Altenberg attempts to stress their communal interests, but also gives unmistakable indications of paranoia:

> Einen Peter Altenberg als *Dichter* verehren und als *Menschen* nicht unterstützen, ist eine *Gemeinheit*! Du bist ärger, schmählicher als alle Anderen. Du stellst Dich von vornherein feindselig gegen mein Blatt, das kein anderes Verbrechen hat als Peter Altenberg zu seinem Redacteur zu ernennen statt Adolf Loos.[161]

> [To revere a Peter Altenberg as a poet and not support him as a *human being* is a *dirty trick*! You are worse, more shameful than all the others. From the outset you have been hostile to my journal, whose only crime has been to name Peter Altenberg as editor instead of Adolf Loos.]

What had made Loos even contemplate collaboration with his unstable friend was perhaps the example of Kraus, whose four-year old journal *Die Fackel* had proved so successful. Moreover, both Altenberg and Loos had money worries. Loos, recently married, was earning only 2,000 crowns per annum but spending vast amounts on his young wife and new home; Altenberg was constantly pumping Kraus for cash, so they doubtless hoped to reap a financial reward as well as having the chance of controlling a periodical to be shaped in their own image. However, unlike Kraus, neither Loos nor Altenberg possessed much financial acumen. Loos admitted his "moralische Schwäche in Geldsachen" [moral weakness in financial matters],[162] and neither he nor Altenberg had anything like the economic muscle of Kraus's family firm behind him. Whatever cooperation there was lasted just long enough to bring out the first volume of *Kunst*. The second contained a sup-

[160] Barker and Lensing, *Rezept*, 231.

[161] WSB 137.024.

[162] *Du silberne Dame Du. Briefe von und an Lina Loos,* ed. Franz Theodor Csokor and Leopoldine Ruther, (Vienna and Hamburg: Zsolnay, 1966), 32.

plement entitled *Das Andere*, but it was not by Loos; the second, and last, of Loos's *Das Andere* appeared on 15 October 1903, but independently of *Kunst*.

That Altenberg and Loos had important ideas in common is beyond dispute. Altenberg's plea for "essence" in art is paralleled by Loos's distaste for the meaningless decoration he perceived to be all around him in the art world of Vienna, dominated as it was by the *Jugendstil* ideas of the Secession. Their cooperation on *Kunst* would, therefore, have been a public manifestation of a shared outlook. The first number carried Altenberg's name as sole editor, but *Das Andere* is so different from *Kunst* that Loos already appears to be dissociating himself from the venture. It may be that Altenberg had produced something all too reminiscent of Secessionist art. Certainly, in the essay "Kunst" prefacing the début number, Altenberg seems in two minds about the guiding philosophy of the journal. An anthem to the Kodak camera reflects a quasi-Naturalist aesthetic common to Loos and Kraus, but a ringing declaration to aestheticize life may have struck Loos as all too like a motto from the Secession:

> Die Kunst ist die Kunst, das Leben ist das Leben, aber das Leben künstlerisch zu leben, ist die Lebenskunst. (WS 294)

> [Art is art, life is life, but to lead life artistically is the art of life.]

Visually, too, the evidence of collaboration is not especially marked. In *Das Andere* Loos eschews the pastel shade of Altenberg's section, printed in brown ink on parchment in double columns. His layout has black ink on white satin paper in single columns.

With the essay "Kunst" Altenberg again provided his audience with a programmatic text. In the second edition of *Wie ich es sehe* the selective translation from Huysmans' *A rebours* had provided a quasi-theoretical contextualisation for his prose poems, in *Was der Tag mir zuträgt* "Selbstbiographie" performs a similar function. Now an essay bearing the same title as the journal fulfils that role. Not only the introduction of a "program" but even the journal's motto, "natura artis magister," shows Altenberg's proximity to certain aspects of literary Naturalism. He attached considerable significance to "Kunst," reprinting it in the revamped version of *Wie ich es sehe* (1904,) his next publication after the collapse of *Kunst*. There it is positioned as the final item of *Wie ich es sehe* proper (WS 293), directly before a new section filled with bleeding chunks carved from the deleted *Ashantee*. In its final form, *Wie ich es sehe* therefore opens and closes with sections reminiscent of literary manifestos.

The motto of *Kunst*, blazoned across its title page, points to the journal's advocacy of nature's supremacy over art and the inferiority of artifice. Glossing this motto with the phrase "die größte Künstlerin von allem ist die Natur" [the greatest artist of all is nature], Altenberg declares that nature's treasures can be gleaned effortlessly by the use of a Kodak camera "in einer wirklich menschlich-zärtlichen Hand" [in a really delicate human hand]. The photographic evidence is provided by two images of the hand of Risa Horn, a woman known to both Kraus and Schnitzler.

In his mostly critical review of *Kunst*, Otto Falckenberg welcomes Altenberg's commitment to the unjustly neglected medium of photography: representations of a beautiful female hand make for a promising start, apart from what the critic considers the poor technical quality of their reproduction. This contrasts with the reception given these photographs in Ottokar Tann-Bergler's review in the *Neues Wiener Journal*.[163] He also discusses Horn's hands, but whereas Falckenberg is dissatisfied with the reproduction quality, Tann-Bergler first faults her manicure. He damns *Kunst* with mock praise, his perception more colored by his view of Altenberg than by the merits of the publication. The basis for Tann-Bergler's facetious rejection of the photos may have, however, a deeper reason than the standard Viennese view of Altenberg as a buffoon; it could be that Altenberg's apparent rejection of a social taboo touched a raw nerve:

> To be honest, we are especially curious to learn which parts of the body of the divinely endowed Mrs. Risa H., who is scheduled for publication in installments, are destined to be exposed for adoration next.

If indeed Altenberg did intend the photograph of the hand to be a metonym of nudity, as Tann-Berger hints,[164] he gives no indication of it. In yet another outraged letter to Kraus he asks what he thinks about the insolent attack in the *Wiener Journal* in which Herr Tann-Bergler takes the opportunity to drag the entire enterprise through the mud. Altenberg claims to be unconcerned by the critic's cheap humour, what bothers him is his shameless remarks about Risa Horn, "a living work of art" who had been kind enough to turn over her noble hands to him for photographic reproduction. He had informed her that it was her artistic responsibility to do so.[165]

Whatever hopes Altenberg and Loos initially had harbored for the journal, its demise was swift. From March 1904 onwards Altenberg's name disappeared from the title page, though his contributions continued; by November 1904 *Kunst* had effectively lost its identity. Also in March 1904 *Das Andere* went, replaced with a photography section edited by Friedrich Krauss entitled "Der Gummidruck. Blätter zur Förderung der modernen Kunstphotographie" [The Gum Print. Papers for the Promotion of Modern Art Photography]. This development was inspired by Hermann Clemens Kosel, an important Viennese photographer known to have undertaken commissions from Altenberg for pictures of women in various states of un-

---

[163] "'Kunst.' Eine Wiener Offenbarung," *Neues Wiener Journal*, 19 September 1903. See Leo A. Lensing, "Peter Altenberg's fabricated photographs. Literature and photography in fin-de-siècle Vienna," *Vienna 1900: from Altenberg to Wittgenstein*, ed. Edward Timms and Ritchie Robertson, (Edinburgh: Edinburgh University Press, 1990), 65–66.

[164] Lensing, "Fabricated photographs," 66. The translation is taken from this pioneering study.

[165] Ibid., 65–66.

dress.[166] Given the journal's emphasis on the visual arts, it was not inappropriate that photography should loom ever larger in its contents.

As to the literary side of *Kunst*, apart from some verse by Ilke Maria Unger (AB 303), everything in the opening volume is from Altenberg's pen. Thereafter, during its short life, Altenberg would introduce work by the poet Hugo Salus, of whom he thought highly (AB 233–234), Roda Roda, Richard von Schaukal, Gustav Falke, Ferdinand Pagin, Paul Busson, Paul Scherbart, and George Bernhard Shaw. It is surely a measure of Altenberg's artistic self-confidence at this time that he felt secure enough to print a parody of his own work by Josef Hafner entitled "Wie er es sieht" in the February 1904 number. In this same volume, however, the last to show his name as editor on the title page, he also includes "Individualität," which tries to direct the way the book which inspired Hafner's parody should be read: "Es muß heißen 'Wie ich es SEHE'!" [It has to be called 'How I SEE it']

The reasons why *Kunst* failed are easily found. The annual subscription rate of ten crowns was high, though commensurate with a sophisticated production standard. With its large format and high quality paper, *Kunst* aimed for the top end of a market already well provided with similar publications. In the double issue 10–11 (November 1904) the managing editor Krauss blamed its failure on maladministration and the unwillingness of the Austrian publishing industry to back such ventures properly. Be that as it may, its collapse could not have come at a worse time for Altenberg, whose family firm, controlled by Georg Engländer, went bankrupt in October 1904, denying him his only regular source of income. Asked by a friend when the next number of *Kunst* would appear, he replied: "Nie! Man hat mir mein Kind gemordet!" [Never! They've murdered my baby!][167]

A position reviewing cabaret and variety shows for the *Wiener Allgemeine Zeitung* from the autumn of 1905 until 1909 eventually provided Altenberg with a fixed one hundred crowns per month, hardly enough to survive on, and for the rest of his days he became obsessed with persuading all and sundry to provide him with a guaranteed monthly hand-out ("Rente".) In September 1905, inspired perhaps by the work of the *Wiener Werkstätte*, with whose director Fritz Wärndorfer he was on good terms, Altenberg patented his "P.A. Kollier," necklaces made of semi-precious stones and turned wood (ML 97). In order to sell them personally in the bars and cafés of Vienna he then acquired a hawker's license, made out in his original name of Richard Engländer. The irony cannot have been lost on someone so desperate to shed the trappings of his Jewish mercantile heritage.

In his complex relationship with Loos and Kraus, Altenberg formed the third link of what Kraus called the "besserer Dreibund" [superior triple alliance]. He shared many of their thoughts on literature, art and fashion, but

---

[166] Ibid., 49.

[167] Arthur Werner, "Redakteur Peter Altenberg," *Der österreichische Zeitungshändler. Presse und Vertrieb in Österreich* 10, no. 4 (1967): 19. A request for Kraus to give him a monthly hand-out of twenty Crowns came to naught, as he reflected bitterly to Bessie Bruce, comparing this with Kraus's munificent treatment of the "whore" Irma Karczewska (Unpublished letter, DLA.)

was never cowed into meekly following a party line. Hence he retained his friendship with Gustav Klimt, despite Kraus's loathing of the artist, devoting a piece to him in the December 1903 issue of *Kunst*. In it Altenberg even quoted Kraus's pun on his admiration for the painter: "Mit einem Wort, er KLIMMT zur Höhe!" [In a word, he's Klim[t]bing to the top!].[168] Similarly, Altenberg stayed friends with the architect Josef Hoffmann, with whom Loos was at daggers drawn. Altenberg also failed to share Loos's infatuation with things American, but this did not stop Loos from wishing to dedicate the interior of his "American Bar" on the Kärntner Straße to Altenberg. Loos humorously and pointedly acknowledged their difference of opinion when he made a photomontage of the bar with Gustav Jagerspacher's large caricature portrait of Altenberg as its visual focus.[169]

Despite the *Kunst* debacle, the downturn in Altenberg's relationship with Loos did not last long. By Christmas 1905, despite a passion for Loos's new lover, the English dancer Bessie Bruce, Altenberg sent Loos an effusive letter claiming that there was an absolutely truthful and completely natural accord between them.[170] This affinity, expressed in a critique of decoration as unethical, emerges in "Der Trattnerhof" where Altenberg bemoans the forthcoming demolition of the "aristokratisch-einfache, zweckmäßig gegliederte alte Bau" [aristocratically simple, functionally proportioned old building], to be replaced by one coated in "schreckliche Unnötigkeiten" [appalling superfluities] (NA 155). The Trattnerhof building was important to Altenberg because the composer Hugo Wolf, whom he revered, had lodged there, along with Hermann Bahr and a law student named Edmund Lang, the husband of Marie Lang, the female emancipationist who in 1900 helped set up the first Viennese women's club in the Trattnerhof. The Langs were friendly with both Altenberg and Loos, who had received the commission to design the interior of the Frauenklub. Altenberg reacts with horror at the impending destruction of the "old, simple, noble Trattnerhof" for something where "Künsteleien ihre schändlichen Orgien feiern" [artificialities celebrate their shameful orgies]:

> Die Menschen suchen Ornamente, Verschnörkelungen, *Zieraten* (ein ekelerregendes Wort), weil sie zu ihren eigenen, in sie von Gott gelegten *Paradieseseinfachheiten* noch nicht vorgedrungen sind! (NA 155–156)[171]
>
> [People seek ornaments, embellishments, *decorations* (a nauseating word) because they have not yet progressed to their own divinely implanted *heavenly simplicities!*]

[168] Peter Altenberg, " Gustav Klimt," *Kunst* 3 (1903): VII. See Barker and Lensing, *Rezept*, 97–103.

[169] *Adolf Loos: Theory and Works*, (Milan: Idea Books Edizioni, 1982), 117. The photomontage is preserved at the Photo Gerlach archive in Vienna.

[170] *Für Adolf Loos: Gästebuch des Hauses am Michaelerplatz. Festschrift zum 60. Geburtstag*, ed. Burkhardt Rukschcio, (Vienna: Löcker, 1985), 7. See also AB 161–162, 349–350.

[171] See Josephine N. M. Simpson, *Peter Altenberg: A neglected writer of the Viennese "Jahrhundertwende,"* (Frankfurt: Peter Lang, 1987), 197.

The affinities here with Loos's philosophy and practice are unmistakable, and must be read in the context of the wider debate in Vienna at that time which focused on Loos's radical design for the Goldmann and Salatsch building on the Michaelerplatz. In the furor surrounding this building, one of seminal importance in the development of modernist architecture, Altenberg stood firmly by his friend, inscribing the visitors' book on 11 March 1914:

> Es gibt nur "*Zweckmäßigkeit*"!
> Alles andere ist *Schwindel!*
> Sei es nun ein Hut oder
> ein Haus! . . .[172]

> [*"Getting to the point"* is all!
> Everything else is *fraud!*
> Be it a hat or
> a house! . . .]

Probably from this time too comes the sketch "Plauderei," unpublished in Altenberg's lifetime, which alludes rather more ironically to the Michaelerplatz building and its architect without mentioning Loos by name. Altenberg remarks that some of those wandering about freely are as deranged as people locked up in the Steinhof asylum. Referring to "someone" who is convinced that God created the world *exclusively* so that he might put up buildings devoid of ornament, Altenberg adds that he too is in favour of buildings without ornament, for ornamentation cannot add to human happiness. Even more, though, Altenberg favours houses with comfortable, cheap and self-contained rooms. And for all he cares the walls outside can be covered in caryatids! The exterior of a building may be an elevating sight, but he is more impressed by gracious, light-footed gait of an unknown girl. And for that one doesn't have to pay for any architects' fees or for their disgraceful megalomania. Art is something to be overcome by "Natürlichkeit" [naturalness], by "Zweckmäßigkeit" [getting to the point]. In that he agrees with the modern "*Schreihälsen*" [loud-mouths]: "Kunst ist nicht, künstlich zu sein!" [Art is not about being artificial!] (N 14–15).

For Altenberg, as for Loos, beauty is a function of utility:

> "Die Schönheit eines Sessels *kann* nur darin bestehen, daß Du *bequem* auf demselben sitzst!"
> "Wenn er mir aber *abgesehen* davon *dennoch* gefällt?!"
> "Dann bist Du ein ausgewachsener Schmock!" (VI 96)

> ["The beauty of a chair can *only* come from it being *comfortable* to sit on!"
> "But what if I like it *apart* from that?!"
> "Then you're an overgrown idiot!"]

---

[172] Rukschcio, *Gästebuch*, 74.

A photograph taken of Altenberg and Loos together at the very end of Altenberg's life, with Loos looking down paternally at the writer, is inscribed by Altenberg with the words: "Architekt Adolf Loos und Peter Altenberg! 1918 Zwei, die sich 'hinweg-setzen'. Über Das, was *bisher* unrichtig war!" [Architect Adolf Loos and Peter Altenberg! 1918 Two, who 'went beyond'. Went beyond what had *previously* been incorrect!: NE 66].[173] Ten years after Altenberg's death, a sour postscript was added to their relationship when Loos was found guilty of committing acts of indecency with minors. Alfred Polgar suggests the charge was brought not least because of Loos's long association with Peter Altenberg.[174]

Because Altenberg lived his artist's life publicly, and without discretion, he was an object of constant fascination even for artists who approved neither of his work nor his persona. At no time was this more marked than in 1904, when the twin catastrophes of *Kunst*'s failure and Georg Engländer's bankruptcy placed Peter Altenberg's mental and pecuniary plight at the very centre of gossip in Viennese literary circles. To mark his forty-fifth birthday on 9 March 1904 a group of friends gathered with Altenberg to discuss a possible financial appeal on his behalf, and in his diary for 30 September 1904, Hofmannsthal (who was unlikely to have been there) gives an account of the meeting, Altenberg slumped in a chair, head in hands, muttering how he was a beggar who wished to die in peace.[175] At this point Lina Loos, exclaiming that her love for Altenberg outstripped everyone else's, said nothing could be more beautiful than for him to expire in a corner, covered only with a thin blanket. Not wishing to be taken quite so literally, Altenberg responded with alacrity:

> Dumme Gans . . . verfluchte Gans! ich will nicht sterben! ich will leben! ich will ein warmes Zimmer und einen Gasofen, einen amerikanischen Schaukelstuhl, eine Rente, Orange Jam, Kraftsuppe, Filets mignon; ich will leben![176]

> [Stupid fool . . . accursed fool! I don't want to die! I want to live! I want a warm room and a gas stove, an American rocking chair, an allowance, marmalade, beef tea, filets mignon; I want to live!]

Details of this grotesquely comic episode, embellished in the retelling by the time Hofmannsthal recorded it, were noted down by Bahr in his diary for 3 August 1904. Bahr had heard about it from the actress Tini Senders, who knew Altenberg well, and he discussed the matter with Schnitzler, who had long been toying with the idea of writing a play about Altenberg and what Schnitzler considered his unacceptable laxity with words. In his diary

---

[173] For further illustration of Altenberg's relationship with Loos see F 61, 123, 137, 223, VI 245.

[174] Alfred Polgar, *Kleine Schriften*, vol. 1, ed. Marcel Reich Ranicki and Ulrich Weinzierl, (Reinbek bei Hamburg: Rowohlt, 1982), 380–381.

[175] Hugo von Hofmannsthal, *Gesammelte Werke in Einzelausgaben. Aufzeichnungen*, ed. Herbert Steiner, (Frankfurt: Fischer, 1959). 135–136.

[176] Ibid.

for 7 August 1904 Schnitzler noted that the incident would provide a "kostbare Scene" [precious scene] for the planned drama.[177] In the Senders-Bahr version Lina declared that nobody was to help Peter Altenberg. He should be left to die alone and in misery, for it would be so touchingly beautiful. To which Altenberg responded rather less colourfully than in Hofmannsthal's version, telling them they were crazy. He did not want to be touching, he wanted to be healthy and alive![178]

The financial appeal apparently came to nothing (AB 96), unlike one launched in Berlin by S. Fischer and Alfred Kerr, whose personal acquaintance with Altenberg amounted to a single meeting in Vienna in June 1898.[179] Composed by Kerr, the appeal went out as a round-robin in the name of Jean Paul, like Altenberg a writer renowned both for his consumption of alcohol and his appeal to female readers. From his grave in Bayreuth, Jean Paul requests help from the living for his successor Peter Altenberg, "ein Meister unter den Deutschen" [a master amongst Germans]. The first to respond was Gerhart Hauptmann, who pledged 200 marks, followed by Max Liebermann with 100 Marks. S. Fischer donated 300 marks, Kerr 100 marks before the appeal was passed on to Walther Rathenau, who also gave 100 marks. In all 44 people responded, among them Paul Cassirer, Fritz Mauthner, Richard Strauss and Thomas Mann. Hugo von Hofmannsthal had his donation of 200 marks transmitted by Otto Brahm, in Brahm's name. In all, the donations totalled 2606.50 marks.[180]

Touched by the appeal, which had been organised without his knowledge, Altenberg wrote to Kerr, thanking him effusively for his help in these times of "seelischer Bedrückungen und unermeßicher körperlicher Leiden" [spiritual depression and immeasurable physical suffering: AB 95]. Four years later, with money worries as acute as ever, Altenberg turned to Kerr again after an appeal he had organised himself proved ineffective. Writing on 27 September 1908, he requested Kerr place an announcement in every German newspaper to the effect:

> Ich sammle für eine Ehrengabe zum 50. Geburtstage Peter Altenbergs, 9. März 1909! Alfred Kerr, Berlin. (AB 97)

> [I am making up a collection in honor of the 50th birthday of Peter Altenberg on 9 March 1909! Alfred Kerr, Berlin.]

Small wonder Altenberg concluded a subsequent resumé of his life with the observation that he had turned into a "Schnorrer" [beggar: S 36].

While Altenberg's behavior early in 1904 had struck Schnitzler as the basis for an effective scene in a drama first mooted in 1901, the play only assumed shape after a catastrophe in the summer of 1904. This was the suicide

---

[177] Arthur Schnitzler, *Tagebuch 1903–1908*, (Vienna: Akademie der Wissenschaften, 1991), 83.

[178] Hermann Bahr, *Prophet der Moderne: Tagebücher 1888–1904*, ed. Reinhard Farkas, (Vienna, Cologne and Graz: Böhlau, 1987), 197.

[179] Arthur Schnitzler, *Tagebuch 1893–1902*, (Vienna: Akademie der Wissenschaften, 1989), 286.

[180] The S. Fischer Verlag Papers, Lilly Library, Indiana University, Bloomington Indiana.

of the nineteen-year-old Heinz Lang, eldest son of Altenberg's friends Edmund and Marie Lang.[181] Although teenage suicide was distressingly prevalent in Vienna, the death of Heinz Lang nevertheless triggered off more shock waves than usual.

In his diary for 30 September Hofmannsthal followed his account of Altenberg's angry response to Lina Loos (whom he referred to as Frau X) with a summary of her love affair with the "fifteen-year-old grammar-school boy Y., an unusually gifted and passionate young man."[182] The relationship had begun in summer 1903, when Loos, many years his wife's senior, was away from Vienna. An affair of great intensity between an eighteen and a twenty year old, it remained a secret only from Loos, who regarded the mature and gifted Lang as a close friend.[183] At the end of July 1904, his school studies now complete, Lang went to England on holiday as he did every year. Having arranged for Lina to join him at the beginning of September, he then confessed everything to her husband. In the meantime, Loos had discovered a bundle of letters to Lina and realized he had been cuckolded in the very bedroom whose photograph he had paraded in the pages of *Kunst* as "Das Schlafzimmer für meine Frau" [The bedroom for my wife].[184]

When confronted by her husband, Lina admitted adultery but claimed the affair was over and that her desire to visit England, which had already raised Loos's suspicions, had evaporated. From Zürich both wrote to Lang, who in desperation wrote to Altenberg for advice. Altenberg, whose own state of mind was not good, replied in a manner both flippant and cynical:

> Was Sie tun *sollten?* Sich erschießen. Was Sie tun *werden?* Weiterleben. Weil Sie ebenso feig sind wie ich, so feig wie die ganze Generation, innerlich ausgehöhlt, ein Lügner wie ich. Deshalb werden Sie weiterleben und später einmal vielleicht der dritte oder vierte Liebhaber der Frau werden.[185]

> [What you *ought* to do? Shoot yourself. What you *will* do? Carry on living. Because you're just as cowardly as me, as cowardly as the entire generation, hollow inside, a liar like me. That's why you'll carry on living and later on become perhaps the lady's third or fourth lover.]

Shortly after Heinz Lang had received Altenberg's letter, the *Neue Freie Presse* of 28 August 1904 reported the boy's suicide. The *Kidderminster Times* noted he had been found with a revolver shot through his body.[186]

---

[181] The Langs had two other children, Erwin, the artist husband of the dancer Grete Wiesenthal and friend of Heimito von Doderer, and Lilith who appears as "Mädchen Li" in Kokoschka's *Die träumenden Knaben*.

[182] Hofmannsthal, *Aufzeichmungen*, 135.

[183] Rukschcio and Schachl, *Adolf Loos*, 92, reproduces photographs of Altenberg, Loos, Lina Loos and Heinz Lang on the Semmering, circa 1902–3.

[184] Dietmar Grieser, *Eine Liebe in Wien*, (St. Pölten and Vienna: Niederösterreichisches Pressehaus, 1989), 46–58.

[185] Ibid., 55–56.

[186] Ibid., 56.

The facts of this miserable case show that Hofmannsthal's streamlined retelling of the story must be treated with caution. Having received Lina's letter, Hofmannsthal claimed that Lang, distraught and helpless, ran with the letter in his hand to Altenberg, whom he revered. Whereupon he went home and shot himself.[187] Nevertheless, even if Altenberg's intervention were less direct than suggested here, his complicity remains disturbing. For Schnitzler it became the central incident in his unfinished Altenberg play *Das Wort*, whose first version was written in the summer of 1906. In contrast, not only Altenberg but also Adolf and Lina Loos, whose marriage was now over, kept silent about the matter. Lina set sail for America on 7 January 1905 to resume her acting career, but returned to Vienna only five months later. Altenberg continued adoring her from a distance. Always the loser in an eternal triangle, he now found that Egon Friedell had become emotionally dependent upon Lina. Meanwhile, Altenberg was now lost in a hopeless passion for Bessie Bruce, the new woman in Loos's life.

The action of Schnitzler's play, where Altenberg appears as the impecunious writer Anastasius Treuenhof, mirrors the scenario sketched out by Hofmannsthal in his diary. Like Hofmannsthal, Schnitzler was troubled by the question of individual responsibility, not just for one's actions, but also for one's words. For language triggers deeds. When Lina Loos, taking him at his word, told Altenberg to go off and die, his reactions showed his wish for death to be no more than histrionic posturing. Altenberg cannot have meant what he said, and assumed Heinz Lang would react with the same degree of latitude to the meaning of words. That he did not was proof to Schnitzler not just of the power of the word, but also of the particular responsibility which writers above all others must exercise in their use of language.

Schnitzler's portrayal of Altenberg-Treuenhof, who also figures in the story "Der tote Gabriel," written in September 1906, is of course part of his wider concern with the role and function of Jewish literati in Vienna, many of whom he detested for their glibness, superficial intellectualism and vicious feuding. The figures of Gleissner and Rapp, who appear both in the novel *Der Weg ins Freie* and in *Das Wort*, are based directly on Polgar and Großmann, described by Schnitzler in his diary on 2 June 1898 as Altenberg's "widerliche Jünger" [revolting disciples].[188]

Schnitzler's exasperation with Altenberg's verbal irresponsibility was not confined to his horror at Heinz Lang's suicide. Olga Schnitzler tells how during a conversation with Altenberg her husband pointed out that he had just contradicted something said five minutes earlier, whereupon Altenberg retorted that he was "ein kranker nervöser Mensch — mich darf man nicht so festnageln!" [a sick man with bad nerves — You can't pin me down like

---

[187] Hofmannsthal, *Aufzeichnungen*, 135–136.

[188] Arthur Schnitzler, *Das Wort. Tragikomödie in fünf Akten*, ed. Kurt Bergel, (Frankfurt: Fischer, 1966), 12.

that!] To which Schnitzler responded: "Dann könnten wir ebenso gut bellen!" [Then we might as well bark!] [189]

Schnitzler worked on *Das Wort* virtually until his death, producing a last version in 1927. He was, however, unable to complete it to his satisfaction because of a profound ambivalence towards Altenberg, appreciating his talent and never forgetting his own role in promoting his career. On 21 November 1907 he noted in his diary that he had read with great pleasure Altenberg's new book *Märchen des Lebens*. He now realized why his Altenberg drama was unsuccessful: because of his sympathy for Altenberg. The contradictions in Altenberg's character were proving simply too great for Schnitzler to portray him convincingly in a single dramatic figure.[190] The real Peter Altenberg was a genuinely creative writer who also manifested many of the traits of the Jewish literary dilettantes in the Café Central for whom Schnitzler, himself a Jew, had only contempt. The Altenberg who emerges in the figure of Treuenhof, far from being portrayed too sympathetically, reproduces all the negative features of Altenberg as Schnitzler saw him — his neurotic hypochondria, his self obsession and verbal irresponsibility — but none of the features which would make credible his status as a genius worthy of financial appeals, whose word had been sufficient to drive a healthy and privileged young man to suicide.

Unlike Schnitzler, the popular dramatist Karl Rößler had little difficulty catching the essence of a sympathetic Altenberg in his light-hearted comedy *Das Lebensfest*, published by Fischer in 1906. Rößler knew Altenberg quite well,[191] and in English exile wrote a fond memoir of him in the London-based *Die Zeitung* in 1944.[192] Set in a Bavarian mountain village near Munich, *Das Lebensfest* features the artist Albert Roderich, a Viennese domiciled in Berlin, and his dealings with an artist colony. Probably based on material which Rößler recalled from Altenberg's stay in Munich, Roderich is Altenberg down to the last letter: fond of drink, short of money, subject to instant changes of mind and towering rages which subside as quickly as they arise. His appearance mirrors that of Altenberg too, the stage directions indicating a man with an incipient bald patch, pale face and mustache clipped English-style who has contrived to dress in a peculiar fashion. His garb consists of a green Boer's hat, sloppy shirt with a large tie, a bright velvet jacket and trousers with gaiters.[193] Roderich's mode of discourse is that of Altenberg himself:

> Der höchste Zweck des Weibes ist — einem Mann, der zugrundegegangen oder irgendwie verkommen ist, das Leben zu retten. (36)
> Die alten Griechen sind Schuster an Tragik gegen die Tragödien, die ich erlebe. (62)

[189] Olga Schnitzler, *Spiegelbild der Freundschaft*, (Salzburg: Residenz, 1962), 37.

[190] Bergel, *Das Wort*, 25–26.

[191] They consorted together during Altenberg's Munich sojourn. See Kurt Martens, *Schonungslose Lebenschronik 1870–1900*, (Vienna, Berlin, Leipzig and Munich: Rikola, 1921), 247–248.

[192] Carl Rossler [*sic*], "Peter Altenberg," *Die Zeitung*, 14 January 1944, 7–8.

[193] Karl Rößler, *Das Lebensfest*, (Berlin: Fischer, 1906), 13.

Ich muß in eine Heilanstalt. Nur eine sanfte Milchkur kann mir helfen!
(84)

[The highest purpose of woman is — to save the life of a man who has
gone to pieces or somehow gone to the dogs.
Compared with the tragedies I have experienced the Ancient Greeks
could only cobble theirs together.
I must go into a nursing home. Only a delicate milk diet can help me!]

The play is an enjoyable, well-crafted romp, whose ending is an Altenberg dream come true: Roderich marries an attractive young woman with a
rich father. In words reminiscent of the real Altenberg, Roderich concludes
that one must be the "Bismarck seines eigenen Schicksales" [Bismarck of
one's own fate: 86]. His reward is a girl with the "Genialität eines Frühling-
swindes" [genius of a spring breeze: 86] in whom he has found "das ganze
zwanzigste Jahrhundert" [the entire twentieth century: 87]. For Rößler at
least, Altenberg remained an unproblematic figure, untainted by domestic
tragedy.

4: New Directions, Old Habits

Pròdrŏmŏs: Poetry and Hygiene

In his diary for 17 November 1905 Hermann Bahr recorded reading Altenberg's new book *Pròdrŏmŏs*, noting appreciatively how the author had retained his youth because he still believed in life: artists do not age, for they are constantly being astonished.[1] Yet contrary to the impression the book made on Bahr, the period of its composition was one when its author often (though not for the first time) felt close to death. Typically, despite his close ties to Bahr's arch-enemy Kraus, Altenberg had felt no qualms about sending a copy of *Pròdrŏmŏs* to Bahr. This contained a long dedication to "Lieber Hermann Bahr" which claimed that for the first time since books had been written, hygiene and poetry were peacefully conjoined in a single volume.[2]

Poetry and hygiene are not obvious bedfellows, but from *Wie ich es sehe* onwards Altenberg had been building up to a work uniting these twin obsessions. In his review of *Wie ich es sehe* Hofmannsthal might have been anticipating *Pròdrŏmŏs* when he noted a discourses on the arts of bathing and sleeping, sections on getting a good complexion, getting hot and keeping cool, healthy and unhealthy tiredness, drinking soup and eating fish. According to Hofmannsthal, these were no mere dry tracts, but miniature poems, like the antique fragments of the earliest doctors and natural history teachers (AB 150). That said, *Pròdrŏmŏs* is also a manifestation of *Reformkultur* around 1900, when Victorianism gave way to *Wandervögel*, youth movements and nudism. For Albert Ehrenstein, who always regarded Altenberg as the Jew which Altenberg himself preferred to deny, *Pròdrŏmŏs* is a book which reformed and modernized the Mosaic dietary laws, preaching a "gospel of digestibility."[3] A more recent critic finds at the root of Altenberg's obsessions Nietzsche's claims that all prejudices come from the intestines, and that the decline of the Germans was directly linked with their

---

[1] Hermann Bahr, *Tagebuch*, (Berlin: Paul Cassirer, 1909), 66.

[2] The full text is reproduced in: Dieter Messner, "Die Hermann-Bahr-Stiftung in Salzburg," *Hermann Bahr Symposion: Der Herr aus Linz*, (Linz: LIVA, 1987), 188. In the *Wiener Camera-Almanach* for 1907 Altenberg again showed his regard for Bahr by attaching a fulsome text to H. Rosen's portrait of Bahr.

[3] Albert Ehrenstein, "Peter Altenberg," *Juden in der deutschen Literatur*, ed. Gustav Krojanker, (Berlin: Welt Verlag, 1922), 194.

unwholesome diet. Altenberg, like Nietzsche, believed that the salvation of humanity was more a question of nutrition than theology.[4]

Judged simply by its appearance, *Pròdròmòs* marks a departure from the norm for Altenberg. Instead of prose poems and sketches, the reader encounters a profusion of aphorisms, aperçus and bons mots. The extent to which *Pròdròmòs* has since been neglected would not have surprised Altenberg, for he predicted it. However, the neglect can be gauged when a specialist such as William Johnston, writing about the aphorism in *fin-de-siècle* Vienna, makes no mention of the work, though aware of Altenberg's role in Viennese *Kleinkunst* as a whole.[5] Viktor Žmegač, however, has little doubt of the significance of *Pròdròmòs*, accounting it the most personal as well as rhetorically the most compelling Austrian contribution to *Reformkultur* at the turn of the century.[6]

Although it lies at the heart of the Austrian tradition, the aphorism has been widely neglected, largely because literary taxonomists have such trouble defining it. Along with Kraus and Canetti, Altenberg is the subject of Stefan Kaszyński's survey of the genre in modern times. As other potential subjects Kaszyński lists Grillparzer, Stifter, Schnitzler, Hofmannsthal, Musil, Kafka and Doderer, and he might equally have mentioned Altenberg's friend and mentor Egon Friedell. Altenberg's aphorisms, Kaszyński believes, are characterized by an ironic linguistic distancing which the author never surpassed in his other works.[7] Altenberg himself modestly comments in the course of his book that

> Ein Aphorismus ist etwas, was dem *Schreibenden* einen Essay als Kommentar erspart, dem *Lesenden* jedoch infolgedessen aufs höchste schockiert. (P 129)

> [An aphorism is something which spares the writer an essay by way of commentary, but in consequence is deeply shocking to the reader]

In his intense confrontation with Altenberg's work, Uwe Johnson examined Altenberg's definition of the aphorism, only to find it, and his aphorisms in general, wanting: if the aphorisms of Larochefoucauld or Lichtenberg were shocking it was because of their unavoidable reference to reality, which the reader was forced to confront because of their concise and aggressive form. According to Johnson, Altenberg's "Splitter" [splinters]

---

[4] Josephine M. N. Simpson, *Peter Altenberg: A neglected writer of the Viennese Jahrhundertwende*, (Frankfurt: Peter Lang, 1987), 277–78.

[5] William M. Johnston, "The Vienna school of aphorists 1880–1930. Reflections on a neglected genre," *The turn of the century. German literature and art 1890–1915*, ed. Gerald Chapple and Hans H. Schulte, (Bonn: Bouvier, 1981), 275–290.

[6] Viktor Žmegač, "Zum literarischen Begriff der Jahrhundertwende (um 1900)," *Deutsche Literatur der Jahrhundertwende*, ed. V. Z., (Königstein im Taunus: Athenäum, 1981), XXXII.

[7] Stefan Kaszyński, "Überlegungen zum österreichischen Aphorimus im 20. Jahrhundert," *Literatur und Sprache im Österreich der Zwischenkriegszeit*, ed. Walter Weiß and Eduard Beutner, (Stuttgart: Hans-Dieter Heinz, 1985), 8.

shocked because their claim to be binding were excessive and they failed because they were overly didactic.[8]

Despite the shift from prose poems and sketches to aphorisms, some fundamental tenets from earlier books are nevertheless carried over into *Pròdrŏmŏs*: the desire for condensation, the wish to *épater le bourgeois*, and a quasi-naturalistic aesthetic shared with Kraus and Loos. In "Nippes" (P 149) a story of such brevity as to be little more than an aphorism, a young woman buys first of all a Tiffany vase (a quintessential art nouveau object) then a mounted specimen of an exotically-coloured Brazilian beetle. She places both objects in glass display case, with the label:

> *Natura*
> *Artis*
> *Magistra* (P 149)

From its very first page *Pròdrŏmŏs* is, however, an intensely self-conscious work. Through the title alone — Greek for forerunner, signpost or antechamber — Altenberg claims guru status, but unlike most gurus he remembers the yawning gulf between intention and realization (P 7).

In *Pròdrŏmŏs* the author is manifestly aware of his success in establishing the Altenberg persona in contemporary Viennese consciousness, but in the wake of the public appeal on his behalf he also deals with the more problematic aspects of what it meant to be Peter Altenberg.[9] The author is mindful of the discrepancies between what he preached and what he did; thus *Pròdrŏmŏs* is not only the most sustained expression of Altenberg's reformative notions, it comments on aspects of his persona for which he was now as well known as for his writings, and which openly contradict his philosophy of life. Hence he writes about his alcoholism, his attitude to the *Frauenfrage* and his increasing depressions. But far from belittling them, he regards them as something positive and strength-giving:

> Melancholie ist, den Abstand seines Seins von seinen eigenen möglichen erreichbaren Idealen spüren! Wehe dem, der diese Melancholien nicht hätte! Vorzeitig seine Ruhe finden, seinen Frieden finden, heisst die Sedan-Kapitulation seiner selbst unterzeichnen! (P 86)

> [Melancholy is sensing the distance of one's being from its own possible, attainable ideals! Woe betide him who never knew such melancholy! To find premature contentment and peace is to sign one's own surrender at Sedan!]

The gulf between intention and performance, articulated so clearly in *Pròdrŏmŏs*, stimulated the flow of anecdotes — many of them classic Jewish jokes — which as much as anything defeated Altenberg's entirely serious intentions. By today's standards, concern for fresh air, decent food and sound

---

[8] Uwe Johnson, *"Wo ist der Erzähler auffindbar? Gutachten für Verlage 1956–1958,"* ed. Bernd Neumann, (Frankfurt: Suhrkamp, 1992), 95.

[9] For details of the 1904 collection see the S. Fischer Verlag Papers, Lilly Library, Indiana University, Bloomington Indiana.

sleep is both sensible and healthy, but in the hothouse of Viennese intellectualism it was simply the spur for jest. Friedell relates with gusto the story about
Altenberg's claim to sleep with the window open on even the coldest of
nights:

> Peter Altenberg said: "Well, I am the only modern person who is really
> hardened, I sleep with my window wide open even on the coldest night!"
> To which I countered: "But that doesn't seem quite right. Last night I
> went past your place and all the windows were shut tight."
> "Well", said Peter Altenberg, "was yesterday the coldest night?!?" (AB
> 419–420)

So conscious was Altenberg of the discrepancy between his ideals and the
personal realisation of them, that with resigned irony he condemned his
book to popular failure before it had even been received by the public:

> Das jüngste Buch von Peter Altenberg bereitete seinen zahlreichen
> Verehrern und Verehrerinnen eine arge Enttäuschung. Man erwartete sich
> von seinem engumgrenzten Talente nicht viel. Aber mehr oder weniger
> richtige Aphorismen zur Lebensführung?!?
> Wozu haben wir unsere Ärzte und Hygeniker?!?
> Ein Dichter sollte uns überraschen. Nun, überrascht hat er
> uns! (P 14)

> [Peter Altenberg's latest book was a sore disappointment to his numer-
> ous admirers of both sexes. Not much was expected of his narrowly-defined
> talent. But more or less correct aphorisms on life-style?
> Why do we have our doctors and hygienists?!?
> A poet should surprise us. Well, surprised us he certainly
> has!]

An ironic third-person voice laments Altenberg's unctuous tone which often
wrecks any pleasure in his grains of truth (P 20), whereas a first-person voice
exclaims that although others may have expressed his ideas better or more
clearly, it remains necessary to form a phalanx against stupidity. For:

> Die Wahrheit muss, in welcher Form immer, Vorstösse machen, immer
> und immer. Eine "lächerliche Figur" werden dabei, ist das geringste
> Märtyrertum. (P 63)

> [Truth must, in whatever form, make advances, always, always. To become
> a "ludicrous figure" in the process is no great martyrdom.]

Altenberg was correct in predicting that *Pròdrŏmŏs* would not find universal favour. The Freudian apostate Wilhelm Stekel's review was doubtful
about the book's medicinal qualities, though not surprisingly it received an
entirely positive review in the gymnastics magazine *Monatsschrift für Turnwesen*. However, only Otto Stoessl's review recognizes the astonishing linguistic diversity of *Pròdrŏmŏs*, with its experimental mixture of advertising
and marketing jargon alongside medical and hygienic discourse and passages
of lyrical prose; it was a poeticisation of material seemingly inimical to poetry

and even romanticized the metabolism.[10] Although accepting advertisements for *Pròdrŏmŏs* in *Die Fackel*, Kraus doubted the quality of the work,[11] which may well have prompted his growing criticism of Altenberg for accepting without discrimination everything life dished up before him.[12]

Another doubter was Carl Sternheim. Writing to his wife, he says he cannot share her enthusiasm for the book; it might contain helpful hints for women and children, but Frau Sternheim should be sparing in her enthusiasm. He enjoins her to say nothing about *Pròdrŏmŏs*, for he has already had enough of the book and fails to understand what she find so beautiful in it. He does not like Altenberg at all: at times he's astonishing, but he is inconsistent. Wedekind is preferable and what he says about health is also more important than Altenberg.[13]

In *Pròdrŏmŏs* Altenberg leads with his chin, knowing the book will merely confirm his reputation as a clown, an inebriate preaching healthy sobriety, a failed medical student pontificating on dietary reforms and the treatment of the alimentary canal. With great thoroughness he lays out a complete life-program, yet against the evidence of the text denies that there is any system to it:

> "Bringen Sie doch Ihre Erkenntnisse in ein *System*," sagte ein Wohlwollender zu mir.
>
> Erkenntnisse in ein System bringen ist, einige wenige lebensfähige Wahrheiten in einem toten Meer von Lüge ertränken wollen! (P 127)

> ["Put some *system* into your insights," a well-wisher said to me.
>
> Putting insights into a system is like drowning a few viable truths in a dead sea of lies.]

Displaying an almost Anglo-Saxon aversion to systematization, Altenberg is convinced of the empirical correctness of his reform program. Reading through *Pròdrŏmŏs* makes increasingly plain, however, that only at the most superficial level is there no system present. His method is kaleidoscopic, yet for all the apparent randomness in the presentation, examination reveals that the texts discuss and summarize a vision present already in *Wie ich es sehe*. *Pròdrŏmŏs* effectively spells out the ideas and obsessions which had guided Peter Altenberg's development as both writer and persona. The tone is often serious and exhortatory, only occasionally ironic and humorous. Sometimes the humour is, at least to a modern reader, unconscious. Containing less pre-

---

[10] W. B. Spinnen, "Die Seele in der Kritik. Zur zeitgenössischen Rezeption Peter Altenbergs, Diss., Münster 1983, 65. See also Burkhard Spinnen "Idyllen in der Warenwelt. Peter Altenberg's *Pròdrŏmŏs* und die Sprache der Werbung," *Zeitschrift für Literaturwissenschaft und Linguistik* 22, nos. 87–88 (1992): 133–150.

[11] Karl Kraus, *Die Fackel*, 213 (1906): 24.

[12] Ibid., 274 (1909): 2. See W. B. Spinnen, "Die Seele in der Kritik," M.A. diss., Munster, 1984, 101

[13] Carl Sternheim, *Briefwechsel mit Thea Sternheim, Dorothea und Klaus Sternheim*, ed. Wolfgang Wendler, (Darmstadt: Luchterhand, 1988), 349, 350–351.

viously-published work than Altenberg's earlier volumes, *Pròdròmõs* points forward — as the title suggests — not merely to a vision of a future humanity, but also more mundanely to Altenberg's future writing praxis, where the aphoristic and openly didactic would increasingly marginalize the expression of his ideas in poetic prose.

Barely noted until now has been the extent to which *Pròdròmõs* points forward to some central tenets in the emerging literary mode of expressionism, in particular the notion of the "New Man." Thus Altenberg's work was featured in the early readings of the Neuer Club, founded in Berlin by Kurt Hiller in 1908, and at the heart of the early expressionist movement. A leading light in the Club, Erwin Loewenson, regarded *Pròdròmõs* as a practical expression of the "New Man" who knows how to live better, more easily and more freely than previously.[14] Kurt Pinthus, editor of the great collection of expressionist poetry *Menschheitsdämmerung*, was in no doubt whatsoever about Altenberg's significance for expressionism. He called him "Unser aller Onkel, der gute Lebens-Reform-Peter A." [the uncle of us all, the good old reformer Peter A.][15] In the work's dietary stance and in Altenberg's general desire to reform humanity through a more elemental simplicity, the early expressionists also found a practical expression of their reaction against decadence. This, certainly was how Loewenson regarded *Pròdròmõs*.[16] As Hermann Bahr remarked in his diary, Altenberg's program was certainly no quirk: it accorded strongly with the "Sehnsucht" [longing] of the entire generation. They all suffered because their bodies did not follow their will.[17]

However, not every expressionist shared this positive view of Altenberg. Writing to Charlotte Krohn at the beginning of 1911, Georg Heym advised her not to read those "idiots" George, Rilke, Altenberg. They were all sick and belonged in a hospital where they could perform a Saint Vitus' Dance on the crutches of their verses.[18] Precisely at this time, as Heym may perhaps have known, Altenberg was undergoing treatment in sanatoria for his schizoid, alcoholic condition. Other expressionists reacted more charitably, with Loewenson suggesting a charity matinee on behalf of the sick writer. Ferdinand Hardekopf declined an invitation to appear, but engineered a performance by Gertrude Barrison, "the best and most charming A[ltenberg]-recitor in Europe."[19] The ensuing event was memorably captured in a prose sketch

---

[14] *Die Schriften des Neuen Clubs 1908–1914*, vol. 1, ed. Richard Sheppard, (Hildesheim: Gerstenbergverlag, 1980), 495.

[15] *März* 7, no. 19 (1913): 213.

[16] *Die Schriften des Neuen Clubs, 1908–1914*, vol. 2, ed. Richard Sheppard, (Hildesheim: Gerstenbergverlag, 1983), 476.

[17] Hermann Bahr, *Tagebuch*, 67.

[18] *Georg Heym. Dokumente zu seinem Leben und Werk*, ed. Karl Ludwig Schneider and Gerhardt Burckhardt, (Munich: Heinrich Ellermann, 1968), 507.

[19] *Die Schriften des Neuen Clubs*, vol. 1, 239.

by Alfred Döblin.[20] Moreover, if confirmation were needed that Heym's disparaging comments about Altenberg were atypical of the expressionists' regard for him, Herwarth Walden was only too happy to publish his work in the revolutionary new journal *Der Sturm*. Writing in 1919 Musil noted the close proximity of the expressionists and the impressionists, who also followed the stimulus of the instant:

> Aber was ist mit Impressionismus gemeint? Die Skizzen Altenbergs? Man könnte sie Impressionen nennen, aber ebensogut kleine Reflexionen und je älter er wird, tritt das rezeptive Element hinter das reflexive züruck.[21]

> [But what is meant by impressionism? Altenberg's sketches? One could call them impressions, but also just as easily little reflections and the older he gets, the more the receptive element retreats behind the reflexive.]

In a similar vein, the Austrian critic Eduard Castle may have had *Pròdrŏmŏs* in mind in 1929 when he summed up Altenberg as a literary phenomenon standing between impressionism and expressionism.[22]

Notions present *ab ovo* from the start of Altenberg's career are made explicit in *Pròdrŏmŏs*. Notions outlined in the earlier collections in a more overtly literary fashion, for instance concerning prepubescent women, are now stated with utter clarity:

> Künstler, Dichter, ahnet ihr noch nicht, dass das "werdende Weib" euch näher stehe als das "gewordene"?! ... In welcher Freiheit hingegen, losgelöst vom Zwecke, ganz in Grazie und Zartheit schwebend, steht das Kind-Weib vor dir, Künstler. (P 53)

> [Artists, poets, do you not yet realize that the "nascent woman" stands closer to you than the "mature" one?! ... Yet with what freedom, detached from its goal, floating in total grace and delicacy, stands before you, artist, the femme-enfant.]

Sex is merely a "procreation business," hence pre-adolescent girls are preferable:

> Die Welt der "Fertigen" ist nützlich!!
> Die Welt der Unfertigen jedoch ist schön!! (P 54)

> [The world of the "mature" is useful!!
> The world of the "immature," however, is beautiful!!]

Not only is there the same mixture of feminism and misogyny as before, but even a whiff of public anti-Semitism:

> "Begeisterung ist das Nervenmaterial Gottes! Es fehlt den Juden!"

> [Enthusiasm is God's nervous tissue! Jews don't have it!: P 102].

[20] Alfred Döblin, "Gertrude Barrison (Oktober 1911)," *Kleine Schriften I. Ausgewählte Werke in Einzelbänden*, ed. Anthony W. Riley, (Olten and Freiburg: Walter, 1982), 108.

[21] Robert Musil, "Expressionismus. 1919," *Expressionismus. Der Kampf um eine literarische Bewegung*, ed. Paul Raabe, (Munich: dtv, 1965), 160–61.

[22] Eduard Castle, "Peter Altenberg," *Radio Wien* 5, (1929): 229–30.

Summing up the sexual ambivalence apparent in the first three collections, *Pròdròmòs* culminates not in aphoristic form, but in a fictitious extract "Aus dem Tagebuch eines süssen Mädels in Wien," a feminine voice asking quizzically "Hat er uns gern, hat er uns nicht gern?!?" [Does he like us, does he not?!?: P 204]. Weininger is also a recognizable point of reference in *Pròdròmòs*, the more so as *Geschlecht und Charakter* had by now been published to widespread debate in Vienna. Expressed far more concisely even than in *Was der Tag mir zuträgt* is a philosophy which regards woman's highest function as to be the facilitators of men's perfection (P 140).

As well as responding positively to Weininger, Altenberg seemed ready also to challenge Freudian notions which were very much in the Viennese air. Surprisingly perhaps for a writer central to the Viennese debates about sexuality, Altenberg contends that the spiritual alone can provide what is essential to the human nervous system:

> Das *Sexuelle* kann nur die letzte unentrinnbare Auslösung ungeheurer aufgesammelter seelischer Lebens-Spannkräfte sein! (P 24)

> [The *sexual* can only be the final inescapable release of enormous stored spiritual vital tensions!]

He further contends that for cultured people there are no *sexual* inevitabilities, merely *spiritual* ones (P 36). Such statements have, of course, to be read in the context of Altenberg's general concern for the soul, the subjective and imaginative, the empathetic and spiritual in the face of modern "progress."

In a letter to Karl Bleibtreu, written after reading his essay "Was ist Kunst," Altenberg says the only justification for the artist's existence is to expand the awareness of the soul.[23] Typical of the contradictions in Altenberg's formulations, however, is his choice of a mechanical image, the antithesis of soul, when summing up his views in such formulations as "Die Seele allein ist der Motor dieser zarten Lebensmaschine 'moderner Mensch'!" [The soul alone is the motor of this delicate life-machine 'modern man'!: P 64]. Altenberg's many analogies between the human body and a machine not only reflect the age's ambiguous reactions to technology, they also form a further link with the aesthetic functionalism he shared with Adolf Loos. Apparently at the opposite end of the spectrum from the fascination with technology, Altenberg's view of the soul accords also with ideas he assimilated when reading Maeterlinck's *Le trésor des humbles* in the 1890s and to which he pays tribute in *Pròdròmòs*. Speaking of himself in the third person, he says that Maeterlinck and Altenberg both want the soul to gain ground, seeing in this the source of future development (P 27).

Echoing Weininger, Altenberg believes that woman in her sexual, as opposed to her spiritual, mode is devoid of a soul and governed by her appetites. Even the intimacies of the menstrual cycle concern him because it is a "weakening of the organism" (P 28). On the other hand, spiritual, that is

---

[23] Nachlaß Bleibtreu, SPK.

non-sexual, love is "der genialste Akkumulator und Regenerator" [the most inspired accumulator and regenerator: P 40]. This vitalism also belongs to the intellectual climate from which expressionism arose, although the tone of Altenberg's discourse on women is notable for its pseudo-scientific terminology (*Organismus, Akkumulator, Regenerator*). At other times he strikes a cosier note, contending that the effect of a woman should be like a cup of tea. (P 153)

Although Altenberg denies there is any system in *Pròdrŏmŏs*, recurring themes, indeed idées fixes, are quickly established in the reader's mind, such as the importance of easily digested foods, of laxatives, physical suppleness and a detestation of obesity which today seems like a perilous encouragement of anorexia nervosa: only the human skeleton is beautiful. The flesh must be renounced as rapidly as possible:

> Heilige Magerkeit, getreueste Beschützerin unserer Beweglichkeiten! Werde das Ziel kommender Generationen! (P 116)

> [Sacred leanness, truest defender of our mobility! May you become the goal of future generations!]

Further obsessions are alcohol and its abuse, fresh air, proper sleep, healthy dress modes — here Hermann Bahr and Gustav Klimt seem to be role models — and the Kafka-like analogies between food and art, culminating in the cry that:

> *Ästhetik* ist *Diätetik*! *Schön* ist, was *gesund* ist! Alles andere ist teuflische Irrlehre! (P 128)

> [*aesthetics* are *dietetics*! *Health* is *beauty*! Everything else is diabolical heresy!]

Overall, Altenberg conceives of his book in a way which transcends the narrowly aesthetic, claiming it to be "ein erster Versuch einer *physiologischen Romantik*" [an initial experiment in *physiological romanticism*: P 110]. The word romantic applies perhaps chiefly to an awareness of the discrepancy between the ideal and reality, not least where Peter Altenberg himself was concerned. At other times, however, Altenberg can seem truculent and frivolous in his own defence, imploring those who have problems with his forms and the meagerness of his repertoire at least to extract what strikes them as plausible.

Romantic in a trivial sense is Altenberg's desire to see marriage as a state existing outside of normal societal conditions, a desire perhaps induced in defiance of what he saw all around him and reflecting a personal life which never brought the contentment of a settled relationship. Thus, in self-reference to a *Skizzen-Reihe* in *Wie ich es sehe* entitled "Zwei, die nicht zusammenkamen" (WS 67),[24] he eulogizes Elizabeth and Robert Browning,

---

[24] This text appears only in editions 1–3.

finding at least in their relationship an example of the fairy-tale nature of existence — two, who came together:

> Zwei, die, im Weltenraume einzig für einander bestimmt - - - sich fanden!
> Dies, dies allein ist das Wesen der Ehe, wie Gott es sich erträumt hat in
> seinen romantischen Weltenplänen! (P 152)

> [Two, who, alone in the entire universe destined for each other, found
> themselves! This, this alone is the the nature of marriage as God dreamed
> of it in his romantic plans for the world!]

Such kitsch explains why Kraus grew to judge Altenberg as a writer who
casually offered a pearl one day and the day after ceremonially offered the
shell.[25] "Fünf Kreuzer-Tanz" (P 196), however, a sketch about the trial of a
man set free after gratuitously killing his lover, shows Altenberg's proximity
to causes dear to Kraus.

In general, however, *Pròdròmòs* seems profoundly anti-illusionist in its
conviction that fulfilment can indeed be found in contingent reality: talking
about naturalism and romanticism, Altenberg records his realisation that the
blaue Blume of the Romantics can be found growing on real fields: the ability
to trace the ideal in the real, that alone, so Altenberg contends, is what it
really means to be a romantic (P 123). This catches the essence of Altenberg's aesthetic thinking, and shows why, despite much that is typical of his
place and age, he cannot be lumped together with neo-romantic writers like
George and Hofmannsthal. Indicative of Altenberg's desire to locate poetry
in reality, rather than decry everyday reality as unsuitable subjects for poetry,
are panegyrics to toothbrushes and toothpaste, to a special sort of nib, and
even matchsticks, toothpicks and sleep-inducing earplugs.

To today's readership *Pròdròmòs* will seem very "green" in its emphasis
on healthy living, clean air, and good working conditions. It is also surprisingly modern in some of its ecological observations, for instance on the felling of the Brazilian rainforest. Sometimes it is simply eccentric, as in its
vitalist obsession with the accumulation of "Lebens-Energieen" [vital energies: P 13]. Disarmingly — but *Pròdròmòs* is a disarming work — Altenberg
anticipates our reactions when he admits that many things in this little book
bear the character of superficial dilettantism (P 15). Essentially modern —
although we may note en passant how "modern" the Romantics proper
were in this respect — is the book's awareness of its status as a text, and of
the problematic nature of the authorship of that text as the expression of a
fabricated persona. Hence *Pròdròmòs* concludes with the feminine voice of
the Wiener Mädel exclaiming that Peter Altenberg only exists on the written
page (P 204).

Because *Pròdròmòs* is such a self-aware text, it comes as little surprise to
find in it provocative statements about the relationship between art and
technology, and especially between painting and photography. Although
Altenberg himself was a frequent subject for painters as well as photogra-

---

[25] Karl Kraus, *Die Fackel*, 274 (1909): 2.

phers, in portraiture at least he appears to have believed that the lens had rendered the brush redundant. Hence his comments on the twelfth Secession exhibition of 1902 and a fondness for Fjaestad's landscapes, but also his unwavering admiration for Klimt, who despite his obsession with the female form always remained a landscape painter. Equally clear is Altenberg's view of the artist, and specifically the painter, as one whose aesthetic means ultimately have a moral and didactic end: bringing non-artists to a state of perception in which, thanks to the modern miracle of photography, they too can now go on to become artists in the widest sense of the term (P 41–42).[26]

Altenberg is equally positive about the role of the movie camera, predicting there would soon be theaters specifically designed for cinematographic performances. Where movies are concerned, his thoughts on the superseding of the artist go much further than in his views on still photography. The mediating role of the artist is now not just as a teacher, but takes on a negative connotation insofar as any mediation is also a potential falsification. He thus espouses at the outset of his discussion a naive naturalism which even Zola, himself an accomplished photographer, ultimately did not support. These musings may not amount to a finished aesthetic; nevertheless they afford insight into the challenge to tradition posed by developments in optical technology at the beginning of the twentieth century. Altenberg contends that to experience nature at first hand, unfalsified by the artist, will be the mark of future development. No longer shall we get to know Brazil and the felling of the jungle through reports, fantastic tales and paintings, but directly and with all the poetry and horror of nature itself:

> Wir sind endlich reif geworden für die *Darbietungen* der Natur auf direktem Wege! *Zola* war das *erste Genie*, das das *erkannt hat*! Dass die Menschheit *reif* geworden ist für die *künstlerische Kraft der Natur selbst, vita ipsa.* (P 50)

> [We have finally grown mature enough for direct *presentations* of nature! *Zola* was the *first genius* to *recognize* that! That humanity is *mature* enough for *artistic power of nature itself, vita ipsa.*]

Altenberg clearly does not envisage cinema itself as an art form. With the advent of cinema, traditional art has revealed itself not as the master of life but merely as its apprentice. Now, with moving pictures, the individual can experience the beauties of the world "*aus erster Hand*, erfasst von diesen Künstlern 'Auge', 'Ohr', 'Herz', 'Gehirn'"! [*at first hand*, grasped by these artists we call 'eye', 'ear', 'heart' and 'brain'!: P 51]. The subjectivity inherent in such modes of perception, to say nothing of the manipulation of the camera by the person holding it, appear not to have entered Altenberg's mind in his rush of enthusiasm for the new medium. Before long, he would be as much a devotee of actresses on the silver screen as he was of them on the boards of the traditional theater.

---

[26] For a detailed examination of Altenberg's relationship with painting see Barker and Lensing, *Rezept*, 87–121.

For more than a hundred pages, readers of *Pròdrŏmŏs* move in a kaleido-scopic world of aphorisms and laconic assertions. Therefore it comes as a surprise suddenly to be led back into the world of prose poems so character-istic of earlier works. Only in the most tenuous way has the reader been pre-pared for this change, by an oblique reference to the "Extrakt-Theorie." For the remainder of the book, some seventy-odd pages, Altenberg sets a pattern to become recognizable throughout all the subsequent collections: a medley of prose poems, short essays, revues, quasi-feuilletons such as "Die Maus," (P 162) and aphorisms.

The more extended pieces in *Pròdrŏmŏs* are often of high quality, gloss-ing themes already presented earlier in aphoristic form. Frequently the gloss is both ironic and satirical, thus "Konditorei im Seestädtchen" is a typical "extract" from polite society life as observed by the poet. The text presents a cast of characters well-known since *Wie ich es sehe* — a thirteen-year-old girl who has "wunderbar edle Beine" [wonderfully noble legs], a young count-ess, a mature aristocratic lady and of course the poet — in an ambience at some odds with the culinary ideals of the rest of *Pròdrŏmŏs*. To make matters worse, the poet makes a slender adolescent girl a present of "zehn Nuss-Crême-Kugeln in Malagatrauben eingebettet" [ten nut-cream balls bedded in malaga grapes: P 146].

Despite such whimsy, this sketch raises serious issues regarding women's relationships with their own bodies, and the extent to which their sexuality is commercialized both in the theatre and in the photographic world. As might be expected from an avid collector of pin-ups, Altenberg makes a spirited defense of nude photography — perfection has no need to hide itself, only imperfection does — but the piece as a whole is whimsical rather than ten-dentious, ending with the mature lady flouncing out of the cake-shop, the young countess enquiring where she can get herself photographed naked, and the young girl suffering stomach pains after over-consumption of good-ies.

Because of its apparent haphazardness, *Pròdrŏmŏs* has been dismissed as Altenberg's most careless creation,[27] pretentious pseudo-science to be dis-missed out of hand. Yet we should not overlook the despairing idealism which motivated it, made more touching because Altenberg knew he was doomed not to be taken seriously. Individual insights may not bear much scrutiny, but his overall belief in the relationship between mind and body is in line with much modern thinking, while the mixture of naïvety and wis-dom is something which makes him valuable today.

---

[27] Camillo Schaefer, *Peter Altenberg. Ein biographischer Essay*, (Vienna: Freibord, 1980), 93.

Cabaret and Commemoration:
Märchen des Lebens; Die Auswahl aus meinen Büchern; Bilderbögen des kleinen Lebens

It could hardly escape notice that the health and fitness manual *Pròdròmŏs* coincided with the visible deterioration of its author. Dogged by mental instability since early manhood, as he freely admitted in a begging letter to the Schiller Foundation in Weimar in 1905,[28] his condition was scarcely helped by obsessions with money and other men's women. Events had taken a severe turn for the worse by 27 January 1906 when barely a month after receiving Altenberg's Christmas letter protesting eternal friendship, Adolf Loos wrote to his estranged wife Lina expressing fear for his life. He and Altenberg had not met for months because Loos's relationship with the twenty-year old English dancer Bessie Bruce was not merely reducing Altenberg to tears, but far worse: Altenberg, so Loos claimed, was threatening to shoot him.[29]

To the consumptive Bessie, whose German never rose above the fractured, Altenberg poured out his heart in picturesque pseudo-English, thus continuing a tradition launched with his letter to Nah-Baduh in *Ashantee*:

> The beauty of all the world is imprimed in your beloved and adorated front, Bessie, in your fearing and melancholic sweet eyes, Bessie! I love your eyes fanatically - - -.
> The heart of a mother is coming in my heart as I saw your eyes, Bessie! Now you are at London, and I am crying and sick here. *You sweered me, to wright!*
> God, only God sees me and He knows what my soul had to bear - - -. Bessie, I wish to die for you, Most beloved, adorated Bessie, - - - I can not wright more.
> Yours. Yours.
> Peter Altenberg
> swimming in tears. (AB 345–46)

In his diary for 14 April 1906, Schnitzler mentions that when talking to him at a café in the Graben Altenberg had confessed to contemplating suicide: he had been severely ill for the past twenty years, and what he needed was not admirers but financial supporters.[30] Salvation of a kind, however, was at hand in the shape of a patrician young woman from Hamburg, Helga Malmberg, who had come to Vienna to study art history in 1905. Aged only eighteen on her arrival in the Austrian capital, she worked first in the Galerie Miethke, Vienna's most important commercial gallery, before going to work for Fritz Wärndorfer at the Wiener Werkstätte. She met Altenberg through a colleague at the gallery, situated in the Dorotheergasse, just off the Graben,

---

[28] The S. Fischer Verlag Papers, Lilly Library, Indiana University, Bloomington Indiana.

[29] *Du silberne Dame Du. Briefe von und an Lina Loos*, ed. Franz Theodor Csokor and Leopoldine Ruther, (Vienna and Hamburg: Zsolnay, 1966), 34.

[30] Arthur Schnitzler, *Tagebuch 1903–1908*, (Vienna: Akademie der Wissenschaften, 1991), 196.

and today the site of Vienna's Jewish Museum. Her initial dislike of the poet eventually yielded to an awareness of his uniqueness, their relationship quickly deepened, and by the summer of 1906 she was the mainstay of his life.

Despite having to endure the moody, childish and debilitating side of his personality, there emerges from Malmberg's chronologically confused memoirs, written in old age, a picture of Altenberg infinitely more appealing than that evoked by Schnitzler in *Das Wort*. She is not blind to his faults, but her work emphasizes his extraordinary ability to captivate people of all ages and backgrounds. In an age of hierarchical social relationships, Altenberg's respect for the shop-girls, chambermaids, waiters and cabbies, treated with scant regard by most bourgeois Viennese, was as unusual and impressive as his regard for black people. Malmberg's account of his delight at the African village exhibition in the Prater in 1910, and in particular with the young dancing girl Katidja, forms a revealing coda to *Ashantee*.[31] Plagued by alcoholism, paranoia and insomnia to the point where treatment in an institution became the only answer, Altenberg could still empathize with people of a very different culture. Success in curing a sick black child with a surreptitious dose of laxative pills merely heightened his pleasure. As Polgar remarked, it was Altenberg's achievement to talk about a laxative as though it were a declaration of love.[32]

It is ironic, and recognizably Viennese, that while Altenberg vociferously celebrated the naturalness of African tribal life in "Abschiedsbrief eines Aschanti-Mädchens von Wien" (ML 110), he took scant notice of the various cultures on his own doorstep. Yet as Adolf Loos had noted in an essay of 1903, virtually on Vienna's doorstep one could meet people who were more foreign to most Viennese than people living thousands of miles away across the ocean.[33] When on a rare occasion Altenberg does respond to this world, as in the sketch "Die Slowakei" (B 8), written during a trip to Slovakia in April 1908,[34] his pleasure in the folk costume of the thirteen-year-old Víctora Kírínovic contrasts markedly with the attitude of Loos, for whom the cultivation of traditional dress was an example of how rural people were denied contact with the privileges and benefits of modern civilisation: "national costume is the symbol of resignation," wrote Loos in 1903.[35] On the other hand, in his seminal essay "Ornament und Verbrechen," written, like "Die Slowakei" in 1908, Loos specifically mentions the ornamentation of the Slovakian peasant girl as something he could tolerate because it is the only way

---

[31] Hans Bisanz, *Mein äußerstes Ideal: Altenbergs Photosammlung von geliebten Frauen, Freunden und Orten*, (Vienna and Munich: Christian Brandstätter, 1987), 70.

[32] Alfred Polgar, *Kleine Schriften*, vol. 4, ed. Marcel Reich-Ranicki and Ulrich Weinzierl, (Reinbek bei Hamburg: Rowohlt, 1984), 14.

[33] Erich Kaessmayer, "Adolf Loos und die Volkskunde," *Adolf Loos*, ed. Burkhardt Rukschcio, (Vienna: Graphische Sammlung Albertina, 1989), 282–283.

[34] In the Galerie St. Etienne there is a postcard to Georg Engländer sent from Preßburg [Bratislava], dated 25 April 1908.

[35] Kaessmayer, "Loos und die Volkskunde," 284.

in which she can reach the "höhepunkte ihres daseins" [high spots of her existence.][36]

This formulation sounds very Altenbergian, and it is tempting to speculate that Loos and Altenberg may have undertaken the trip to Slovakia together, especially as there is an apparent allusion to Loos in "Die Slovakei." In his essay of 1903 Loos contends that as soon as the steam threshing machine arrives the peasant will be liberated and that folk dress will go to the theatrical costume agency where it belongs.[37] In "Die Slovakei," Altenberg's thoughts on Víctora's future development from adolescent into the village beauty, displaying her still-costumed charms at local dances, are triggered by the appearance of "das schwarze Gespenst 'Dampfpflug'" [the black ghost 'steam plough': B 9].

Helga Malmberg is coy about the physical nature of her relationship with Altenberg; she was not his type sexually,[38] and there is no evidence that he ever focused his manic passion on her. In a letter he admits with total lack of tact that he has a "spiritual" accord with her because he is sufficiently old and she is not sufficiently pretty for him (AB 247).[39] Malmberg's book and Altenberg's letters confirm that theirs was a partnership of minds in which physical attraction played a modest part, an assessment only strengthened when we read of her declaring to the poet that she had become his "Heilige Fraue," an antiquated term normally referring to the Virgin (AB 249). Altenberg endlessly repeats his gratitude to and dependence upon the "darling of his dying soul" (AB 250), pleading in a letter of 8 September 1908 that she remain loyal to him because he is old and sick and surrounded by malicious, uncomprehending people. She alone provides him with the proof of who he is: she is the sole instance where his theories about the female soul and the female organism have actually turned into something practical and viable. He and Helga are "ultimate forms of organization in today's culture," they have left others far behind, and her love is "die Liebe zur wirklichen *Verkörperlichung* von etwas *Seelisch-Geistigem* im Menschen! Das ist der *Fortschritt!*" [love of the real embodiment of something *spiritual and intellectual* in man! That is *progress*!: AB 258].

In the context of such exalted diction, Altenberg's remorse at what he terms many an act of brutality on his part may appear of scant significance (AB 249), but a scurrilous letter from Karl Kraus to Herwarth Walden in Berlin, dated 27 September 1909, suggests a sado-masochistic streak in their relationship which Malmberg was at pains to conceal in her memoirs. Kraus recounts Altenberg sitting with Helga at an outdoor café in the Graben

---

[36] Ibid., 292

[37] Ibid., 284.

[38] Helga Malmberg, *Widerhall des Herzens. Ein Peter Altenberg-Buch*, (Munich: Langen and Müller 1961), 171.

[39] The ten letters to "Anita M." in *Das Altenbergbuch* are, in fact, letters to Helga Malmberg. A letter from Malmberg to Friedell in 1920 in the Austrian National Library explains her apparent absence from *Das Altenbergbuch*. A large number of letters to Malmberg are now housed in the WKA.

when Oskar Kokoschka walked past and greeted them. Altenberg then got up and quickly returned with Helga to the Hotel London. There he beat her up, telling her that as she had set eyes on the devil, he was now driving him out of her. Kraus concludes laconically that poor Helga had probably failed to notice the devil but was grateful for the blows.[40] A disturbing letter from Altenberg to Kraus seems to confirm that Malmberg's memoirs painted a picture that was prettier than the reality had been. He boasts that he conquered Helga with blows, like the trainer with his polar bear, forcing her to hand over to him every penny she possessed.[41]

Malmberg made no moves to conceal that during the course of their long relationship, which finally ended in 1911, Altenberg was repeatedly wracked by unreciprocated passion for other women, including an unabated obsession with Emma Rudolf. Malmberg denies that such passions ever made her jealous,[42] but in the latter part of 1909 she returned to Hamburg, unable to cope with the strength of Altenberg's feelings for Ilna Ewers, wife of the writer Hans Heinz Ewers. This "desertion" led to a sad and bitter parting,[43] and in the sketch "Treuebruch" Altenberg refers to the loss of his "freundschaftlichste Freundin" [friendliest lady friend] without ever mentioning Helga by name. Direct quotations by Altenberg's friends about the matter are barely disguised through the use of their initials — discretion in print was never Altenberg's strong suit — and in the final paragraph he imputes, preposterously and revealingly, thoughts to the lady who had "deserted" him:

> Es gibt doch nur ihn, ihn! Aber leider konnte er nicht allen Ansprüchen genügen, die das Leben von einem sogenannten "ganzen Mann" erfordert. Ich werde ihn jedenfalls nie vergessen - - -. Dafür werden vor allem alle die anderen sorgen! (B 114)

> [There is only him, him! But alas he could not satisfy all the claims which life makes upon the so-called "whole man." At all events I shall never forget him - - -. All the others will take care of that!]

That this smug assurance was not unwarranted is evinced by the desperate telegram Malmberg sent from Hamburg on 5 November 1909 to Alban Berg's sister Smaragda, with whom Altenberg was at the time miserably besotted:

> ich hoffte sie wuerden unsern geliebten dichter erretten nun sehe ich dass sie ihn nur zu grunde richten tiefst verzweifelt helga.[44]

> [i hoped you would save our beloved poet now i see that you are only destroying him in deep desperation helga.]

---

[40] *Sturm*-Archiv, SPK.

[41] Camillo Schaefer, "Peter Altenberg," *Literatur und Kritik*, 96–97 (1975): 426.

[42] Malmberg, *Widerhall*, 171.

[43] Ibid., 207.

[44] WSB 204.562.

Malmberg did not forget Altenberg, answering his call and that of Georg Engländer to return to Vienna to nurse the poet through his coming years of treatment in sanatoriums and mental asylums. Her devotion even prompted Altenberg to compose the comically pompous "Dokument" dated 8 February 1910 in which he bequeathed her his fortune should he become "old, sick, forgotten, left in the lurch by villains *for whatever reasons,* without a job, etc. etc. etc."[45] This unaccustomed largesse failed to survive their final parting, for the words "the sum which I leave to my friend Helga Malmberg" were heavily scored out in red pencil at some later date.

Malmberg's memoirs are occasionally self-serving, but there can be no question that the relationship caused her both mental and physical anguish; over the years she endured several bouts of ill-health, one of which cost her the job with Wärndorfer and the Wiener Werkstätte. She recalls a warning from Wärndorfer about her close relationship with Altenberg, whose art he valued but about whose personal infirmities he was in no doubt. Her reply to Wärndorfer, as recalled in old age, probably encapsulates why a romantic young woman should have put up with Altenberg for so long: she believed he was of sufficient value to warrant protection. He was sick and abandoned by everyone and needed someone who would stick by him. Above all she felt confidence in him and believed that she walked more safely on his arm than on that of a wealthy middle-class husband who would not perhaps understand and comprehend her.[46]

Malmberg's gossipy cameos illuminate not just Altenberg, but the whole ambience of the Wiener Werkstätte, and in particular Fritz Wärndorfer, who was instrumental in founding the Cabaret Fledermaus. Earlier he had been closely involved in setting up the Cabaret Nachtlicht, the Viennese offshoot of Die elf Scharfrichter in Munich. In a programmatic text of 1905 entitled "Peter Altenberg, der Begründer der 'Nachtlichter'," Altenberg declares that cabaret is art theater in miniature, it is the art of making the same impact on a small scale as the major things in the theater (B 164). Cabaret artists such as Yvette Guilbert, Marya Delvard and Egon Friedell appeal to him because they are similar talents to his own: all of them could make everything out of nothing. That Altenberg became deeply involved in cabaret is not surprising, for its sequences of short sketches, songs and dances were very much the theatrical equivalent of his own books. Indeed, he links cabaret quite specifically with his own writing, citing once more his "extract theory" of art and digestion:

> You can write a 200-page novel and it is excellent. You can say the same on three pages, and it is just as excellent. The whole saves time. Today there are many otherwise decent people who don't have the time to read 200 pages. These people you give three pages in extract form!
>
> Nowadays many people can no longer manage a 10-course dinner. These you simply give Sanatogen, Somatose: why should they make the

---

[45] GSE

[46] Malmberg, *Widerhall,* 180.

effort of digesting 200 pages - - - you give them three pages which fulfil the
same purpose! That is the position of "cabaret" vis-a-vis "theatre." (B 164)

At this period cabaret and variety notices for the *Wiener Allgemeine Zeitung*
were Altenberg's sole source of regular income, but being often in poor
shape he did not always attend the performances in person. Helga Malmberg
would go in his place and on the basis of her récit he would then compose
his pieces.

The first Viennese cabaret had been Felix Salten's ephemeral Jung-
Wiener Theater zum lieben Augustin at the Theater an der Wien, modelled
after the Berlin Überbrettl and the Die elf Scharfrichter in Munich. The first
performance took place on 16 November 1901, but even the presence of
Frank Wedekind could not redeem the venture, which collapsed after just
one week.[47] Vienna was not to see cabaret again for over four years, when the
Künstler-Cabaret Nachtlicht opened in the Ballhausgasse in January 1906.
Centred on the talents of the Frenchman Marc Henry, formerly of the Die
elf Scharfrichter, his wife the chanteuse Marya Delvard, and the musician
Hannes Ruch, the "Cabaret Nachtlicht" immediately became the favored
meeting point of the Viennese avant-garde.

Its program booklets were illustrated by the military painter and cabaret
singer Carl Hollitzer, who frequently featured caricatures of his friend Altenberg. The inaugural number depicts a felt-hatted, raglan-coated Altenberg,
cane in hand, looking on askance, whilst the program for September-
October 1906 contains a series of Altenberg vignettes, as well as an illustration of him standing on the outer edge of the ring at the "Cirkus Henry."
Hoop in hand, he stands transfixed by the baleful gaze of the black-gowned
ringmistress Marya Delvard, who points her whip at him.[48] Hollitzer's companion Gertrude Barrison, one of the celebrated Five Sisters Barrison, recited
Altenberg and danced in a Biedermeier costume.[49] Might this have been the
inspiration for Robert Musil's short story "P.A. und die Tänzerin"?[50]

Whereas Thomas Mann, Arthur Schnitzler and Jakob Wassermann had
distilled various aspects of Altenberg's complex persona in their creation of
more or less fictitious characters, Musil imported Altenberg into his story
undisguised. Its very title is reminiscent of the way Altenberg operates, constantly turning the reader's attention upon himself both through the content
and titles of his sketches. Altenberg's fondness for dancers was well know and
in Musil's undated story the narrator attends a bizarre cabaret act in which an
attractive girl alternately dances and reads extracts from Altenberg's works.

---

[47] Harold B. Segel, *Turn-of-the-century cabaret*, (New York: Columbia University Press, 1987),
184; *Jugend in Wien. Literatur um 1900*, ed. Ludwig Greve and Werner Volke, (Marbach:
Deutsche Schillergesellschaft, 1987), 383–84.

[48] *Das Altenbergbuch* reproduces some of the vignettes, now individually entitled. See also Werner
J. Schweiger, "Peter Altenberg als Varietékritiker," *Parnaß*, no. 2 (1982): 26.

[49] Greve and Volke, *Jugend in Wien*, 383. Barrison also recited Altenberg in Berlin in 1907.

[50] Robert Musil, "P.A. und die Tänzerin," *Gesammelte Werke*, vol. 7, ed. Adolf Frisé, (Reinbek bei
Hamburg: Suhrkamp, 1978), 711–715.

She dances well, but reads excruciatingly. Based as it doubtless was on real life, this story seems to confirm the fears that Altenberg had expressed when writing to Stefan Großmann from Munich on 20 November 1899. There he had remarked, apropos of a recital of his work in Munich, that his sketches did not work when read aloud.[51]

In Musil's story the girl's dancing induces the narrator to think back over his past life, and as she maladroitly reads Altenberg, his earlier, inchoate thoughts on the poet also return. There ensues an acutely sympathetic assessment of Altenberg's art and personality, introduced by the statement that Altenberg was a great writer and culminating in his transmogrification into a Christ-figure with horn-rimmed pince-nez, a description which brings to mind the portrait photograph of Altenberg that appears both in *Die Auswahl aus meinen Werken* and *Bilderbögen des kleinen Lebens*. The incidence in Musil's story of the unusual adjective "bilderbogenhaft" may indeed indicate that it was written sometime after the appearance of *Bilderbögen des kleinen Lebens*.[52] Whatever its exact dating, there can be no doubt that the story, which Musil never published, betokens esteem for Altenberg. Its tone is also strangely elegiac, similar to that of Erich Mühsam's review of *Die Auswahl aus meinen Büchern*, as though Altenberg were no longer a living writer.[53]

Although Musil considered Altenberg the best writer of the *fin-de-siècle*, his judgment of him is at times equivocal. He continued reading him, but asks: "When reading P.A.: is he a great writer? Feeling: mostly no, sometimes yes."[54] Altenberg had become problematic for Musil because reading sketches was far more exhausting than reading novels, although the opposite might be expected. Musil then asks himself whether reading Baudelaire's prose poems is exhausting, and the answer is again yes, for "you cannot read poems one after the other."[55] It is not without irony that Musil's problematic regard for prose poems and sketches, shared with Rilke, failed to prevent him publishing his own collection in 1935, the *Nachlaß zu Lebzeiten*. It is doubly ironic that Altenberg's brevity, which he himself considered his prime merit in an age when time stress prevented people reading, should have become a hindrance for one of his most sensitive readers.

---

[51] Hedwig Prohaska, "Peter Altenberg. Versuch einer Monographie," Dr. Phil diss., Vienna 1948, 220. Döblin might well have attended something similar, for in 1911 he reports on Gertrud Barrison's Altenberg recital in Berlin. *Kleine Schriften*, vol. 1, ed. Anthony W. Riley, (Olten and Freiburg: Walter, 1982), 108. Reprinted in Barker and Lensing, *Rezept*, 289.

[52] Adolf Frisé posits the Musil story in 1908. Schaukal's review of *Märchen des Lebens* in 1908 already refers to the title of *Bilderbögen des kleinen Lebens*, which probably came out later on in that year.

[53] Erich Mühsam, *Ausgewählte Werke*, vol. 2, *Publizistik. Unpolitische Erinnerungen*, ed. by Christlieb Hirte, (Berlin: Volk und Welt, 1978), 51–53.

[54] Robert Musil, *Gesammelte Werke*, vol. 7, ed. Adolf Frisé, (Reinbek bei Hamburg: Suhrkamp, 1978), 842. See also Robert Musil, *Tagebücher*, vol. 2, 896.

[55] Musil, *Gesammelte Werke*, vol. 7, 842.

Writing to an American editor in 1938, Musil gladly acknowledged the influence *Wie ich es sehe* had had on him,[56] but three years previously he had been less open when writing to Simon Menzel at the Humanitas Verlag in Zürich. Humanitas was about to bring out the *Nachlaß zu Lebzeiten*, and it was this factor which probably induced Musil to score out the section in his draft letter which acknowledged how indebted his work was to Altenberg and his successor Polgar. Writing to his publisher, Musil presumably thought better of drawing attention to something which might have detracted from the book's apparent originality.[57] Approaching the relationship between Altenberg and Musil not from Musil's specific comments about the Viennese poet, but rather from striking parallels between *Der Mann ohne Eigenschaften* and Altenberg's "Selbstbiographie," an eminent Musil scholar has suggested that Altenberg's autobiographical essay may plausibly be regarded as the prototype for the *Der Mann ohne Eigenschaften* both in its essayistic stance and in its theory of the individual.[58]

Else Lasker-Schüler, in some respects a female Altenberg, recalls his presence in the Cabaret Nachtlicht, where Marya Delvard, looking like "a recently awakened Klimt flower" sang Wedekind's bleary-eyed boulevard songs with "the shyness of a child."[59] It was in the Cabaret Nachtlicht too that Erich Mühsam met Kraus and Altenberg when engaged to recite his satirical verses in March and April 1906.[60] Although Kraus had directed a one-act play at the cabaret, he fell out with Henry and Delvard after a critical notice in *Die Fackel* of 19 April regarding Delvard's Wedekind performances.[61] On 30 April Mühsam, Friedell and Kraus were enjoying a drink at the Casino de Paris when Altenberg, Henry and Delvard came and sat at a different table. Altenberg was apparently already angry with Kraus because of a perceived slight,[62] but Henry could not contain himself, and launched an assault which left the satirist unconscious. At the end Mühsam lay in a corner with a dislocated finger, a broken pince-nez and a shredded contract. Altenberg wandered around sighing between the deserted upturned tables, drinking up the champagne dregs of friend and foe and telling everyone that he was in

---

[56] Robert Musil, *Briefe*, vol. 1, ed. Adolf Frisé and Murray G. Hall, (Reinbek bei Hamburg: Suhrkamp, 1981), 837.

[57] Musil, *Briefe*, 677.

[58] Joseph Strutz, "Der Mann ohne Konzessionen. Essayismus als poetisches Prinzip bei Altenberg und Musil," *Robert Musil. Essayismus und Ironie*, ed. Gudrun Brokoph-Mauch, (Tübingen: Francke, 1992), 143.

[59] Else Lasker-Schüler, "Kabarett Nachtlicht— Wien," *Prosa und Gedichte*, (Munich: Kosel, 1963), 195. First published in *Gesichte. Essays und andere Geschichten*, (Leipzig: Kurt Wolff, 1913). The volume contained individual essays on Kraus, Loos and Kokoschka, but not Altenberg.

[60] Mühsam, *Ausgewählte Werke*, 572, 575–76.

[61] Karl Kraus, *Die Fackel*, 201 (1906): 26–28. Mühsam (571) considered her the best interpreter of Wedekind after Wedekind himself and his brother Donald

[62] Erich Mühsam, *In meiner Posaune muß ein Sandkorn sein. Briefe 1900–1934*, ed. Gerd W. Jungblut, (Vaduz: Topos, 1984), 60.

despair.[63] Marc Henry was sentenced to a month's imprisonment, Marya Delvard was fined 300 crowns, the appeal court later reducing these sentences to 600 crowns and 150 crowns respectively. Altenberg and Kraus remained friends.[64]

Altenberg's genuine and fervent attachment to the Cabaret Nachtlicht is further evident from a letter Franz Blei sent Karl Kraus from Munich on 15 May 1906 to commiserate over the Henry affair:

> Good old P.A. is crazy. He tells everybody in Vienna that I'm a criminal, rogue, trickster etc. because one night I told Henry and Delvard that any variety hall was superior to this stupid Cabaret Nachtlicht, the reason being that a variety hall is what it wants to be and this cabaret wants to be something different from what it is: soloists' night of a small male voice choir.[65]

The Cabaret Nachtlicht, continuing Vienna's fitful attempts to establish a viable cabaret tradition, failed to last beyond 1906, but in the autumn of 1907 Marc Henry took charge of the new Cabaret Fledermaus on the corner of the Kärntnerstraße and the Johannesgasse. It was very much a creation of the Wiener Werkstätte, and in particular Fritz Wärndorfer, who may well have founded the Fledermaus as a vehicle for Peter Altenberg.[66] Looking back in 1928 at the birth of the Cabaret Fledermaus, Egon Friedell remembered how Wärndorf possessed two things which hardly ever coexist in one person: wealth and taste. As a result, the cabaret's black and white auditorium was an intimate and tasteful gem. Accustomed to getting red plush and gilded plaster for their money, the audience went wild, and the opening evening turned into an enormous scandal.[67]

Altenberg's centrality to the venture, as well as the black and white interior, obviously made an impact on Richard Beer-Hofmann who, in a note to Schnitzler enclosed a caricature of Altenberg along with the depiction of a bat, one of whose wings bears the black and white checks of the cabaret's auditorium.[68] In the Cabaret Fledermaus the desire of the Wiener Werkstätte to create a *Gesamtkunstwerk* came near to realisation;[69] every aspect was designed down to the last detail, with special care lavished on the sanitary arrangements, much to Karl Kraus's amusement. Even a special booklet was published to accompany the opening of the cabaret, explaining its mission "to create a place fit to serve a true *culture of entertainment* through the uni-

---

[63] Mühsam, *Ausgewählte Werke*, vol. 2, 576–77.

[64] Mühsam, *Briefe*, 79.

[65] Greve and Volke, *Jugend in Wien*, 384.

[66] Peter Vergo, *Art in Vienna 1898–1918. Klimt, Kokoschka and their comtemporaries*, (London: Phaidon 1981), 148.

[67] *Das Friedell-Lesebuch*, ed. Heribert Illig, (Munich: Beck, 1988), 32. Translated in Eduard F. Sekler, *Josef Hoffmann: The architectural work. Monograph and catalogue of works*, (Princeton N.J.: Princeton University Press, 1985), 113.

[68] Richard Beer-Hofmann Nachlaß, State University of New York, Binghamton.

[69] Werner J. Schweiger, *Der junge Kokoschka. Leben und Werk 1904–1914*, (Vienna and Munich: Christian Brandstätter, 1983), 39–46.

fied and organic treatment of all pertinent artistic and hygienic elements."[70]
Other critics were more taken with the bar, its specially imported American
barman and myriad of mosaic tiles. Only Friedell sounded a note of warning:
"Hopefully the program will in time match the artistic level of the interior."[71]

The new cabaret was inaugurated on 19 October with Lina Loos reciting
Altenberg's "Prolog," in which he attempted to define the purpose of the
venture. That he was also talking about himself and the needs of his own existence goes without saying:

> Everyday things make me sick and tired. Concerts, theaters, over-rich fare
> on narrow seats in smoky auditoriums! . . . But our greatest care is how to
> pass a carefree day! For the specter of boredom forever threatens us. The
> ability to banish it is tantamount to being cultured! So I dream of a room
> where freedom reigns, alongside comfort, art and culture! Will it arise?!? It's
> there in my dreams![72]

Lina also recited Altenberg's "Kabarettlied" (ML 124) on the opening
night, but *Das getupfte Ei*, the planned fairy-tale lantern-slide entertainment
by Oskar Kokoschka, was not ready and had to wait until 28 October for its
first performance.

A further Altenberg item on the opening night was his "Maske der
Frau," dated September 1907, and dedicated to the cabaret's architect Josef
Hoffmann. In this tableau, designed by Carl Otto Czeschka, three women
designated variously as "The Dancer," "The Philosopher," "The Poetess,"
"La femme du monde" etc., each exquisitely dressed in a costume from the
Wiener Werkstätte, took fleetingly to the tiny stage and declaimed a few
words of often considerable obscurity before disappearing again. The chorus
concluded:

> Seht ihr in uns nur ein wüstes *Farbengetändel*?!?
> Wir können's nicht hindern - -
> Ist's mit *Geschmack* gemacht, lebt es auch *ohne* Idee![73]

> [Do you see in us merely a superficial *riot of colour*?!?
> We cannot prevent that - -
> If it's done with *taste*, it doesn't *need* ideas to live!]

Malmberg recalls that Altenberg considered "Maske der Frau" to be the
summit of intellectual pretentiousness, designed to mock the artistic preten-
sions of the snobs.[74]

---

[70] Sekler, *Hoffmann*, 112

[71] *Die Schaubühne* 3, no. 45 (1907): 454–55.

[72] Greve and Volke, *Jugend in Wien*, 384. A different translation can be found in Segel, *Cabaret*, 203.

[73] Peter Altenberg, *Die Auswahl aus meinen Büchern*, Berlin, Fischer 1908, 384. Also translated in Segel, *Cabaret*, 205.

[74] Malmberg, *Widerhall*, 77.

The masque was not a great success, nor according to Malmberg was *Das getupfte Ei*, unlike the Goethe sketch by Polgar and Friedell, first performed in January 1908, and eventually given over three hundred times. In this burlesque, Goethe presents himself as an examination candidate in his own works, only to fail abysmally. Friedell claimed that the best episodes in this marvellous lampoon of academics were from Polgar's pen; Polgar claimed they were by Friedell. In his review for the *Wiener Allgemeine Zeitung* on 4 January 1908 Altenberg wrote: "it is absolute rubbish and moreover it's by me from A to Z."[75]

Thanks to his review work for the *Wiener Allgemeine Zeitung* Altenberg managed to be both the cabaret's in-house writer and also its first chronicler. He was also the first regular cabaret and variety critic in the German-speaking lands, and remained virtually unique, as Kurt Tucholsky lamented.[76] The possibility of conflicting interests presumably troubled neither Altenberg nor the newspaper. In the edition of 22 October 1907 he both reviewed the decor of the new building and composed an accolade to Gertrude Barrison's performance on the début night: thanks to her, the room had become a temple of dance, for never before had Vienna seen dancing of such charm; dancing which was tragic, serious, cultured and melancholy, but also joyful, childishly astonished and sweet.[77] However, even this would soon be eclipsed when the Wiesenthal sisters made their debut in January 1908. From then on they would inspire some of Altenberg's most ardent and hymnlike praise.[78] On the opening night Marya Delvard again sang Wedekind, as she had done in Munich and in the Cabaret Nachtlicht, which may have accounted for Kraus's antipathy to the Cabaret Fledermaus. Kokoschka's acid comments to his friend Erwin Lang suggest that the passage of time had withered Delvard, whom he describes as "the old stork" still singing the same old songs about killing babies ["Kindsmordlieder"].[79]

Altenberg did not only write for and about the Cabaret Fledermaus, however, he was also the subject of one of its most popular entertainments: Egon Friedell's Altenberg anecdotes. Writing under the pseudonym Karl Albrecht, Felix Salten depicts the scene in the Fledermaus at the end of his laudatio for Altenberg's fiftieth birthday:

> In the Cabaret Fledermaus Dr. Egon Friedell tells Altenberg-anecdotes. No matter how often he begins with the words "it has fallen to me to play the

[75] Egon Friedell, "Wie 'Goethe' entstand," *Die Bühne* 9, no. 320 (1932): 24–25.

[76] Kurt Tucholsky, *Gesammelte Werke*, vol 1, ed. Mary Gerold-Tucholsky and Fritz J. Raddatz, (Reinbek bei Hamburg: Rowohlt, 1960), 1008.

[77] Werner J. Schweiger, *Wiener Werkstätte. Kunst und Handwerk 1903–1932*, (Vienna: Christian Brandstätter, 1982), 139, 148; "Kabarett Fledermaus," *Wiener Allgemeine Zeitung* 28, no. 8873 (1907): 4–5. See also: *Tanz im 20. Jahrhundert in Wien*, (Vienna: Österreichisches Theatermuseum, 1979).

[78] Greve and Volke, *Jugend in Wien*, 386: "Die Schwestern Wiesenthal, Tänzerinnen," *Wiener Allgemeine Zeitung* 29, 8940 (1908): 3.

[79] Schweiger, *Der junge Kokoschka*, 42.

same role in the life of the poet Altenberg as Eckermann did in that of Goethe," the audience roars, believing Altenberg has now been suitably mocked. For them it's already a joke when Dr. Friedell says "the poet Altenberg." For they believe you cannot seriously call him a poet. They also roar at the anecdotes, having no idea how brilliantly invented they are. The storm of jollity Dr. Friedell always whips up with his Altenberg anecdotes is to a certain extent a false, a misleading jollity. For the people do not understand how the entire value of these excellent little tales consists solely in the way the moving and unique figure of Altenberg comes to life in them, that through them Altenberg's being is illuminated by a clear and unusually psychological humor and is sometimes transfigured.[80]

In February 1908 Marc Henry resigned the directorship of the Fledermaus, after which a steady decline set in. Altenberg nevertheless retained his links with the cabaret, though it was not an untroubled relationship. A long and ferocious diatribe against Josef Hoffmann, dated 17 July 1908, accuses Hoffmann and Wärndorfer of dropping him in favour of Friedell and Polgar, though he claims to have expected such treatment all along. The letter comes to a climax with a typical verbal assault:

> nach der ersten Probe der "Masken" wußte ich *innerlich*, daß man mich *in einem* Jahre fallen lassen würde!!! Ich bin "*ein Dichter*"! Und die Herde hat *keinerlei Sympatie für mich*! Wehe denen, die mich darum aber *verdammen* oder *bestrafen* wollen! Wehe, wehe ihnen, denn sie sind "Verräther" und "*Judasse*"!

> [after the first rehearsal of "Masks" I knew *inside* that they would drop me within a year!!! I am "*a poet*"! And the common herd has *no sympathy for me*! Woe betide them who want to *damn* me or *punish* me for it! Woe, woe to them, for they are "traitors" and "*Judases*"!]

Altenberg then resumes his attack on Hoffmann, telling him that he can stand being humiliated and insulted by anyone but him. Having finally and defiantly signed off, Altenberg then added in a postscript that he loved and revered Hoffmann.[81]

Altenberg must have quickly made his peace with Hoffmann and Wärndorfer, for the Cabaret Fledermaus issued a special brochure for his fiftieth birthday. It was illustrated by Berthold Löffler, the graphic artist largely responsible for the decor in the cabaret. They also put on an Altenberg matinee to mark the occasion.[82] On the appearance of *Bilderbögen des kleinen Lebens* Altenberg sent Hoffmann an inscribed copy with a dedicatory verse indicating the close understanding between the two men:

> "*Abrechnung*.
> - - - - - und dann gedenke ich Derer,

---

[80] The essay was subsequently reprinted in Felix Salten, *Das österreichische Antlitz*, (Berlin: Fischer, 1910), 99–113.

[81] WSB 151.356.

[82] *Wiener Allgemeine Zeitung*, 9291 (1909): 2; 9295 (1909): 3.

die milde mit mir waren, weil
sie mir *für einiges Licht* meine *Dun-
kelheiten* verziehen haben - - -."[83]

[" *Reckoning.*
- - - - - and then I think of those,
who were gentle with me, because
they have forgiven me my *dark side* because
I shed some light - - -."]

Hoffmann's Cabaret Fledermaus would survive until 1913, after which it was turned in to a strip-joint called Femina.

It is a signal of Altenberg's ironic defiance in the face of his decline that the book appearing at the end of 1907 should have been called *Märchen des Lebens*. A far less aphoristic and evangelical work than *Pròdrŏmŏs*, Altenberg made no attempt in it to resurrect the formal, cyclical integration of the early work. Instead, dietary concerns are ranged alongside warmed-up cabaret notices and nostalgic evocations of the pre-Altenbergian days as the means to recapture life's magic. In his daily round, constant money worries now rendered him less able than before to seek refuge from the stresses of city life in the countryside, and this proved particularly trying during the summer months, when friends and drinking companions left Vienna en masse for the Semmering and the Salzkammergut. For Altenberg, his visits to the woods and mountains were now increasingly journeys of the imagination to recall the past.

In his review of *Märchen des Lebens* Max Brod, who had taken the book to cheer up a friend in hospital, commended it for its healthy atmosphere and evocation of the days of a happy childhood.[84] By the time Altenberg brought out the third, revised and enlarged version in 1911, he too had endured long spells of hospitalization in an attempt to cure alcoholism and depression. With conscious and sometimes bitter irony, a book evoking life's magic, written in the face of despair and disillusion, now ends with the cycles "Krankheit" and "Sanatorium I." (that is, Inzersdorf.)

In this new coda, Altenberg revives the earlier practice of linking texts in thematic cycles, but gone are the scenes from childhood, the visits to variety shows, cabaret and circus where, for a few short hours, fantasy could reign. Already disturbed by treatment first in the Sulz hydropathic clinic near Mödling, then in the Vienna Fango clinic, where patients were subjected to mud baths and mineral water cures, Altenberg found that in Inzersdorf the fairy-tales had turned to nightmares. In frighteningly intense sketches the author excoriates himself for the abnegation of everything he had preached in *Pròdrŏmŏs*. Assuming the role of the *poète maudit*, he declares that the

---

[83] Sekler, *Hoffmann*, 486–487.

[84] Max Brod, "Peter Altenberg: 'Märchen des Lebens'," *Die Gegenwart* 37, no. 74 (1908): 350. Reprinted in Barker and Lensing, *Rezept*, 284.

artist in him was divine, but the human being was Satan's slave, too weak to live out his own poetry and his own thought:

> Ich predigte die reine Frauenseele und liebte Huren - - -.
> Ich predigte den Schlaf, und lebte in der Nacht! (ML 217)

> [I preached the purity of the female soul and loved whores - - -
> I preached sleep and lived through the night!]

The final item in both versions of *Märchen des Lebens* is a belated preface, in the manner of Strindberg: the "Nachträgliche Vorrede." In it the author contends that fairy tales should be released from the realm of childhood to which adults have banished them. The sober adult should search out the romanticism of the day and the hour in the cold light of everyday life, and then we would all become poets in our own right. As so often in earlier texts, Altenberg provides readers and critics with an unambiguous statement of his poetic credo: everything is special if it is experienced as something special, and we are all capable of creating literature (ML 240).

This splendidly democratic view of literature and life proved particularly appealing to the Novalis expert Friedell, who in his essay on Altenberg's fiftieth birthday declared somewhat hyperbolically that one day the words "Märchen des Lebens" would be as famous a poetic watchword as the '*blaue Blume*' of the romantics (B 217). Altenberg's faith in life's inherent poetry would be put to increasingly severe test, and it says much for his commitment to the notion that, in the midst of his depiction of sanatorium life, he repeatedly unearthed snippets of existence to rekindle his belief in life's magic, be it in the adolescent Anna Konrad who stole his heart, or in the bourgeoning romance between Alban Berg and Helene Nahowski on their visits to Inzersdorf.

Reviewing *Märchen des Lebens*, Max Brod commented that Altenberg's style had become an integral component of contemporary culture. In an enthusiastic albeit belated review of November 1908, Richard Schaukal, who had only turned to Altenberg when confined to his sickbed and bored to tears by Balzac and Mallarmé, refined the verdict on Altenberg's style that he had reached in 1900: Altenberg's German fails to measure up to the strict demands of good style, he is extremely careless, sloppy, and slovenly: but he writes excellently. Schaukal was just as positive as Brod in his overall response to *Märchen des Lebens*, but with one reservation. Unlike Friedell, he disliked the title, which he thought "papiern" [bookish]. We do not know how Altenberg reacted to this quibble, but the final line of Schaukal's review may possibly have provided him with the title of *Neues Altes*. "Vielen, vielen Dank, lieber Peter Altenberg für dein neues altes Buch." [Many, many thanks, dear Peter Altenberg for your new old book.][85]

Such friendly reviews presumably confirmed Altenberg's own perception of his quasi-classic status, evinced by the publication of the anthology *Die*

---

[85] Richard Schaukal, *Fremden-Blatt*, 319 (1908): 17.

Auswahl aus meinen Büchern hard on the heels of *Märchen des Lebens* in November 1908. At the same time as preparing the anthology, for which he had received an advance of 500 marks from S. Fischer (NF 209), he was also planning an edition of his letters which, had it appeared, would have further emphasized his status within the bourgeois literary tradition. When Erich Mühsam reviewed *Die Auswahl aus meinen Büchern*, he nevertheless emphasised, as one would expect from him, the anti-bourgeois nature of both Altenberg's persona and his literary achievement: his work is the antithesis of those writers who deliver "entertaining conversation topics for gentlemen's evenings."[86] Moreover, while Mühsam is alert to the paradox of Altenberg's fame and his coexistent neglect in Vienna, he is far from blind to his weaknesses: it is clear, he asserts, that in the course of its intensive preoccupation with the banal, many things slip into Altenberg's work which are themselves banal. That does nothing to alter the value of what Altenberg's work is all about: a trailblazing way of seeing things anew.[87] What worries Mühsam is the impression such an anthology imparts of an author at the end of the road, given that the quality of Altenberg's recent work, especially in Jacobsohn's influential Berlin periodical *Die Schaubühne*, encourages expectations of a further important book. Ending with an exhortation to go out and buy *all* of Altenberg's earlier books, the review greatly cheered the beleaguered poet who, according to Mühsam, carried it around constantly with him.[88]

After it became obvious that a fiftieth birthday was a milestone with considerable publicity and pecuniary potential, Altenberg did his utmost to correct the fiction of his short biography in *Was der Tag mir zuträgt*, where vanity had led him to lop three years off his real age. As friends and admirers rallied round to ensure that 9 March 1909 was celebrated in style, *Bilderbögen des kleinen Lebens*, the new collection which Mühsam had looked forward to, not only delivered the proof of his continuing ability to write memorable short prose, it concluded with a long essay by Friedell celebrating the anniversary. The book's motto, quoting Goethe — "Es gibt nichts *Unbedeutendes* in der Welt. Es kommt nur auf die *Anschauungsweise* an" [There is nothing *insignificant* in the world. It all depends upon the *way you look at it*] — places its philosophy firmly in line with *Märchen des Lebens*, confirming what had long been obvious to Schaukal among many others:

> His books show no development. Nor are they a sequence. One day he simply became himself. Since then he has written himself. And so — let us hope — he will keep painting these attractive broadsheets of life for a long time to come, a fitting title for his ... book, better at any rate than the bookish *Märchen des Lebens*.[89]

---

[86] Mühsam, *Ausgewählte Werke*, vol. 2, 575.

[87] Ibid., 52.

[88] Ibid., 575.

[89] Schaukal, 17.

Judging by its the prominent place in the Altenberg anthology he compiled in the late 1920s, Kraus also held *Bilderbögen des kleinen Lebens* in high regard. As the anthology was intended for the S. Fischer Verlag, it is conceivable that Kraus highlighted *Bilderbögen* as an irritant to Fischer, this being Altenberg's only work not to appear with them. Nor was Kraus's admiration for this book merely posthumous and provocative; in February 1910, when Altenberg's depressive illness was already very advanced, he published a short poem by Ludwig Ullmann in homage to Altenberg's continuing ability to discover the poetry in mundane existence.[90] A few years later, and using anything but the "mild words" Ullmann attributed to his work, Altenberg requested Kraus to annihilate the "Juden-Köter" [Jewish cur] Ullmann, calling down God's wrath upon "der *Nährer*, der *organische* des philosophischen *Antisemitismus*!!!" [the *organic nourisher* of philosophical *anti-Semitism*!!!][91]

The stock-taking, initiated by Altenberg with his own anthology and the proposed volume of letters, was to have been reinforced by a study commissioned from Friedell by the Fischer Verlag to mark Altenberg's fiftieth birthday. As Fischer still believed that Altenberg was born in 1862, *Ecce Poeta* did not appear until 1912, when it turned out to be really two books in one: a modern cultural history and the other an extended tribute to a friend, expanding material first adumbrated in *Bilderbögen des kleinen Lebens*. With its obvious allusions to Nietzsche, *Ecce Poeta* is Friedell's tribute to what he considered Altenberg's representative status as "Ur-poet,"[92] but it failed to satisfy Fischer, who may have been expecting more of a promotional effort. Writing around 1935, Friedell noted laconically in a letter to Hanns Sassmann that although Fischer had commissioned the work, in the end he did his best to sabotage it.[93]

Altenberg's ability to bridge the cultural divides in Vienna was nowhere more evident than in the celebrations surrounding his fiftieth birthday. In addition to the Cabaret Fledermaus celebrations, Kraus published one of his most acute essays in *Die Fackel*, later reproduced in *Die chinesiche Mauer*,[94] and at the same time one of Kraus's bitterest foes, Felix Salten, published his own encomium to Altenberg in *Die neue Rundschau*, albeit under the pseudonym Karl Albrecht. In their estimation of Peter Altenberg at least, the enemies were at one. For Kraus and for Salten, Altenberg is cherishable because he is genuine in a world full of falseness; both find the pregnancy of his short forms preferable to garrulous length, both cavil at his neglect in Vi-

---

[90] Karl Kraus, *Die Fackel*, 296–297 (1910): 39.

[91] Barker and Lensing, *Rezept* 259. I am informed by Dr. Heinz Lunzer that Ullmann was in fact a gentile.

[92] *Egon Friedell. Abschaffung des Genies. Essays bis 1918*, ed. Heribert Illig, (Vienna and Munich: Löcker 1982), 160.

[93] Ibid., 283.

[94] Karl Kraus, *Die Fackel*, 274 (1909): 1–5.

enna, where he was famous only as an object of derision. Where they diverge is in the tone of their writing.

Where Salten is expansive and anecdotal, warm and relentlessly positive, Kraus is ever the cerebral critic, not hesitating to admit that Altenberg's reactive talent stretches neither to discrimination nor to consistency. Altenberg himself offered a disarming variant upon Kraus's analysis when replying in 1911 to a critic in the *Berliner Lokalanzeiger*, who denied he had any talent whatsoever: Altenberg claimed that his books contained many pretty little pieces, but that the reader had to know how to sort them out from the rubbish.[95] For Kraus, Altenberg's lack of judgment is something organic, and no more than the inevitable consequence of his eternal vivacity.[96] Kraus believes Altenberg is "ein Seher, wenn er sieht, aber er ist bloß ein Rufer, wenn er ein Seher ist" [a seer when he sees, but merely a loudmouth when he's being a seer].[97] This judgment prefigures Uwe Johnson's, who concluded that Altenberg's work contains many remarkable features to which we can still respond today access today, but only in those which in which he is not overtly didactic. Johnson further maintains that Altenberg's work is at its best when it is not simply poetic, but "true." Again like Kraus, Johnson contends that Altenberg's objective truth is unintentional and comes by chance.[98]

A belated birthday present of a sort arrived in October 1909 when, thanks to Loos's patronage, Kokoschka achieved his ambition of painting a portrait of Altenberg, whom he considered one of the most physically graceful people he had ever met.[99] Unable to arrange a sitting during the day, when Altenberg slept, Kokoschka had to catch his likeness during an evening session at the Löwenbräu restaurant in the Teinfaltstraße. Kokoschka records in his essay *cum* lecture "Der Wiener und der Künstler" (1934) how, as he was sketching him, Altenberg's original good humor turned to fury as his friends made fun of his penchant for black women.[100] Kokoschka confirms that Altenberg's circle not only expected these outbursts, but even sought to provoke them, little realizing how truly disturbed he was. Edith Hoffmann writes that:

> the spectacle reminded Kokoschka of a cuttle-fish he had seen in an aquarium where, for the payment of a trifle, one was allowed to tease the creature and make it eject the black fluid. He saw at first an entreaty for peace, then

---

[95] *Peter Altenberg. Leben und Werk in Texten und Bildern*, ed. Hans Christian Kosler, (Munich: Matthes and Seitz, 1981), 140.

[96] Karl Kraus, *Die Fackel*, 274 (1909): 5.

[97] Ibid., 3.

[98] Uwe Johnson, *"Wo ist der Erzähler auffindbar?" Gutachten für Verlage 1956–1958*, ed. Bernd Neumann, (Frankfurt: Suhrkamp, 1992), 109–110.

[99] Edith Hoffmann, *Kokoschka. Life and Work*, (London: Faber and Faber, 1947), 93.

[100] Leo A. Lensing, "Scribbling Squids and the Giant Octopus: Oskar Kokoschka's Unpublished Portrait of Peter Altenberg," *Turn-of-the-century Vienna and its legacy. Essays in Honor of Donald G. Daviau*, ed. Jeffrey B. Berlin, Jorun B. Johns, Richard H. Lawson, (Vienna: Edition Atelier, 1993), 193–219.

anger, finally rage in the victim's eyes. And so he painted Altenberg, his small hands lifted, half imploringly, half in defence, his eyes protruding, his moustache hanging down sadly, his neck collarless in accordance with his principles ("Only waiters, who are condemned to it by society, wear stiff collars!") . . . The portrait, which expressed Kokoschka's whole sympathy, is one of his best works.[101]

Writing a quarter of a century afterwards, Kokoschka claimed that the miserly Altenberg was so delighted with the painting that he even bought him a packet of cigarettes.[102] This may be poetic license, although in a letter of 3–4 February 1910 to Herwarth Walden Kraus reports Altenberg telling Loos that Kokoschka was the greatest artistic genius who had ever lived.[103] In reality it could be that the psychological truth of the painting was all too painful to the ailing Altenberg, who on 6 February entered the Vienna Fango clinic for treatment of his alcoholism. As Leo Lensing has observed, Altenberg was accustomed to manipulating his image when being photographed, but with Kokoschka, no such control was possible. What emerges from the black aureole framing his agitated features "suggests a state of psychological chaos that might be understood as the visual expression of 'geistige Umnachtung', mental derangement or benightment."[104] The painter Max Oppenheimer (Mopp) who himself produced a portrait of Altenberg in 1910, concluded: "He hated painting. He loved photography."[105] Kokoschka's portrait helps us understand why.[106]

Unlike Kokoschka, Mopp had been a regular at the Löwenbräu *Stammtisch* for several years when he painted Altenberg's portrait. His likeness of Altenberg is far less demonic than Kokoschka's, but this and several other portraits seemed similar enough to Kokoschka's work to bring charges of plagiarism.[107] Writing just before the outbreak of the second World War, Oppenheimer, who was a genuinely gifted painter, recalled how his picture came into being. This recollection too is somewhat reminiscent of Kokoschka:

> He refused energetically to come to my studio. "This atmosphere bores me! It is contrary to me, as I am contrary to it!" So I painted his picture in his atmosphere - - in the Café! . . . My martyrdom lasted for several settings. When the picture was finished Peter Altenberg said: "So, I shall now

---

[101] Hoffmann, *Kokoschka* 93–94.

[102] For Altenberg's complex responses to the portrait see Lensing, "Scribbling squids," 205–207.

[103] Ibid. 206.

[104] Ibid., 208.

[105] Max Oppenheimer, *Berliner Tagblatt* 286, 19 June 1927.

[106] Kokoschka's interest in mentally unbalanced sitters can be gauged from his portrait of Ludwig Ritter von Janikowski, painted on 14 October 1909 when the sitter was a patient in the Steinhof asylum.

[107] Schweiger, *Der junge Kokoschka*, 202–208.

write my name in my characteristic hand on the wide oak frame so that this rubbish gains some value!"[108]

In 1910–11 Mopp, who was Jewish, composed an astonishing descent from the cross depicting Altenberg, Kraus and Heinrich Mann grieving beside the body of the naked Christ, and in 1914 his profile drawing of Altenberg provided the frontispiece to an edition of Pfemfert's *Die Aktion*.[109]

Kokoschka's portrait was exhibited at Walden's great Kokoschka exhibition at the Salon Cassirer in Berlin in June 1910, then at the Vienna Hagenbund in February 1911, where the anti-Semitic critic of the Vienna *Reichspost* gratuitously reacted to Altenberg's likeness by describing him as the "Ahasverus of modern soul poetry."[110] Following the Hagenbund show came an exhibition in Karlsbad in July 1911, organized by Walter Serner. He describes the scornful laughter of the customs officials on opening the container out of which the Altenberg picture emerged first, one of them whispering in his ear: "Are these pictures finished?"[111]

Altenberg belatedly revealed his reactions to the Hagenbund exhibition in December 1911 when he published the sketch "Authentisch" in the satirical magazine *Simplicissimus*. His views on the painter and his paintings simply kept step with all the other negative critics: the artist had calculatingly adopted the genuine insanity of van Gogh in the furtherance of his career, his works were "die nackten und die angezogenen Devastationen" [devastations naked and clothed: N 12]. Although Kokoschka is mentioned neither by name nor by the initials O. K. which had become as well known as Altenberg's own, Altenberg may have felt that he had gone too far in this all too recognizable attack on Kokoschka's integrity, for "Authentisch" was not reprinted in Altenberg's lifetime.

As Lensing has plausibly suggested, this public condemnation of Kokoschka's work must also be seen in the context of Altenberg's own mental deterioration by late 1911. The portrait:

> failed to provide a unified representation of the poetic personality and perhaps even suggested a destabilized psyche, which could explain Altenberg's focus in "Authentisch" on the problematic relationship between insanity and artistic creation . . . he cannot help but see himself included in their "naked and clothed devastations" and therefore essentially avoids a literary confrontation with these disturbing images."[112]

Moreover, Altenberg had in fact been grappling with Kokoschka since the autumn of 1909. In the unpublished letter to Walden of 27 September 1909, Kraus describes Altenberg's physical abuse of Helga Malmberg, relat-

---

[108] Max Oppenheimer, *Menschen finden ihren Maler*, (Zürich: Oprecht, 1938), 12.

[109] *Die Aktion* 7, (1914); See Patrick Werkner, *Physis und Psyche. Der österreichische Frühexpressionismus*, (Vienna and Munich: Herold, 1986), 260–262.

[110] Schweiger, *Der junge Kokoschka*, 187.

[111] Ibid., 197–198.

[112] Lensing, "Scribbling squids,", 210.

ing this violence to his having seen the "devil" Kokoschka. In a letter four days previous Kraus had remarked to Walden how jealous Altenberg would be when he heard that Kokoschka intended to paint Kraus first. In an unpublished text, marked "Inzersdorf 1910" in Kraus's hand, Altenberg composed a quasi-satirical "lecture" in which he railed against a perceived Kraus-Loos-Kokoschka clique, all of which indicates the disturbed state of Altenberg's mind and his capacity for envy which turned so easily into paranoia.[113] A furious letter to Loos in 1911, complaining about Kraus, is signed off with this spirited envoi: "Dein Dir wohlgeneigter, keiner Clique angehörender, unbotmäßiger, Niemand im Arsch leckender PA" [Your devoted, unruly PA, who belongs to no clique and kisses nobody's arse].[114]

When Kokoschka's path again crossed Altenberg's at the Semmering in the summer of 1912, the resultant text "Der Maler" (S 141) again failed to mention the painter by name. Not until four years later, recalling perhaps his own experience as a sitter for Kokoschka, did Altenberg remark that the art of portraiture is to make the image as plausible to a stranger as the reality of the face is to a relative or loved one. On this score Kokoschka, he concludes, fails miserably: "Oh, oh, oh, O.K.!" (NF 304). Yet as Lensing observes, Altenberg's command of English was amply good enough for this final sigh also to be construed as "a reluctant concession to his genius."[115]

For all his subsequent admiration for Egon Schiele's work,[116] Altenberg's taste probably never progressed beyond Klimt, whose work for him had real substance as well as technique:

> Unsere modernen Genies in Musik und Malerei (Gustav Klimt ausgenommen) sind lauter Leute, die viel *können* und wenig *sind*! (NF 276)

> [Our modern geniuses in music and painting (except for Gustav Klimt) are all people who can *do* a lot, but *are* little!]

A print of Klimt's lost picture of Schubert, described by Bahr as the most beautiful painting ever executed by an Austrian,[117] hung in pride of place over Altenberg's bed, and of the 54 rooms and 968 objects exhibited at the great 1908 "Kunstschau" in Vienna, Altenberg singled out for his attention "Room 22, the Gustav Klimt-Cathedral of modern art" (B 115). Klimt's approbation was evidently important, as the inscription which Altenberg wrote in Klimt's copy of *Bilderbögen des kleinen Lebens* reveals:

> Liebster Gustav Klimt, ich werde mich sehr freuen, wenn Deine Künstlerseele in diesem Buche irgendetwas finden wird, was Dir aus dem Herzen

---

[113] WSB 160.488.

[114] DLA, 89.95.88–1.

[115] Lensing, "Scribbling squids,", 211.

[116] For the relationship between Altenberg and Schiele see Patrick Werkner, "The Child-Woman and Hysteria: Images of the Female Body in the Art of Schiele, in Viennese Modernism, and Today," *Egon Schiele. Art, Sexuality, and Viennese Modernism*, ed. Patrick Werkner, (Palo Alto: Society for the promotion of science and scholarship, 1994), 50–78.

[117] Hermann Bahr, *Secession*, (Vienna; Wiener Verlag, 1900), 122–123.

gesprochen wäre. Dein Peter Altenberg. Wir haben nur Brüder, Schwestern, und Feinde! P.A.[118]

[Dearest Gustav Klimt, I will be delighted if your artist's soul finds something in this book which speaks from your own heart. Your Peter Altenberg. We have only brothers, sisters, and enemies! P.A.]

On the eve of his fiftieth birthday, it was with Klimt, not Kraus or Loos, that Altenberg went carousing.[119] On the day itself he found time to write to "dearest, dearest Gustav Klimt" telling him that even if he knew nothing of his work apart from his two farmhouse gardens, the portrait of Margaretha Stonborough-Wittgenstein and The Three Ages of Man, he would still have to show him the deepest lifelong reverence. The little quarrels they had had now and again were always due to Altenberg's nervous dissipation and had never been Klimt's fault.[120]

---

[118] Christian M. Nebehay, *Gustav Klimt: Zeichnungen und Dokumentation*, (Vienna: Galerie Christian Nebehay, 1968), 52.

[119] Wolfgang G. Fischer, *Gustav Klimt and Emilie Flöge. An artist and his muse*, (London: Lund Humphries, 1992), 137. Other members of the party were Josef Hoffmann, Franz Blei, Max Halbe.

[120] Nebehay, *Klimt*, 424.

5: Madness and Confinement

Neues Altes: Something old, something new

Gratifying as his birthday celebrations were, they could not alleviate Altenberg's condition, in which chronic alcoholism masked deeper psychological disturbances. It was, however, for the treatment of his drinking that Altenberg spent time first in the Sulz clinic at Mödling, and then at the Vienna Fango clinic, which specialized in water cures. At the behest of both the poet himself and of Georg Engländer, who had assumed responsibility for his brother's treatment, Helga Malmberg returned from Hamburg early in 1910 to look after her increasingly demented friend as he endured first the "Fango-torture-chamber" and then, more ominously, the private mental institution "Siberia-Inzersdorf."[1]

Confinement in a mental hospital cannot have surprised Altenberg, who had already anticipated events in "Sanatorien für Nervenkranke" where mental illness is characterized in terms typical of his obsession with money. Nervous disorders are like any other bankruptcy: you have paid out more than you took in, hence the natural deficit (B 23). The suggested remedies recapitulate the *Pròdròmòs* life-plan which Altenberg had already conspicuously failed to observe: proper sleep, fresh air, and easily digested foods, prescribed by the "chief cook," the neurologist. The best remedy of all would be a happy love affair, but this is even harder to obtain than peace, quiet and proper food.

Schnitzler tersely recorded Altenberg's pitiful state when he visited him in the Fango clinic on 30 March 1910. There he found him crumpled up in bed, tearful, grey-bearded, complaining of terrible pain, and accompanied by a "moderately pretty young girl" from Hamburg. According to the doctor, there was nothing organically the matter with Altenberg apart from the effects of too much alcohol.[2] Helga Malmberg, his moderately pretty companion, was not the happy love of Altenberg's fantasies, but she played the role of unpaid secretary, nursemaid, and protector until an emergency appendectomy brought an end to their relationship in the late summer of 1911. By this time even Altenberg's close friends were shrugging him off with a sigh and a quip, but the series of often accusatory letters Malmberg wrote to Kraus between May 1910 and April 1913 shows that she at least understood the extent of the crisis. After it became obvious nothing could be

---

[1] Helga Malmberg, *Wiederhall des Herzens. Ein Peter Altenberg-Buch*, (Munich: Langen and Müller), 1961, 272–273.

[2] Arthur Schnitzler, *Tagebuch 1909–1912*, (Vienna: Akademie der Wissenschaften, 1981), 137.

done for him in the detoxification clinic, Altenberg entered Dr. Emil Fries's Inzersdorf sanatorium on 10 May 1910; Vienna may have long thought him crazy, but it still hit the headlines when the medical profession finally concurred with popular opinion. Although preparations for the English King Edward VII's funeral vied with Altenberg's madness for pride of place, on 17 May 1910 the *Neues Wiener Journal* led its daily news section with the headline that Peter Altenberg was now in the asylum.[3]

Malmberg's letters to Kraus are dominated by concern for Altenberg's plight, by his financial obsessions, which were further exacerbated by the need to pay the sanatorium bills, and by her distress at the lack of commitment of so-called friends at this nadir of his life. In the only study concentrating on the clinical aspects of Altenberg's condition, however, Springer concludes that Altenberg's personal tragedy lay in his particular ability to so stylize his depressive hypochondria that even good friends never guessed the depth of his suffering.[4] In the ironic, posthumously published sketch "Geselligkeit," evidence emerges of how greatly Altenberg was aware not only of being the creator of his own persona, but also its victim:

> Diese schreckliche falsche Komödie "P. A." muß aufhören . . . Jahrelang war ich euer dummer Sklave, nein, euer Diener, euer Hanswurst. Ich wünsche nun, ich verlange meine Ruhe. (N 75)

> [This terrible false comedy "P.A." must stop . . . For years I was your stupid slave, no, your servant, your Tom Fool. I now wish, I demand my peace]

Malmberg's first extant letter to Kraus, which predates Altenberg's admission to Inzersdorf by a week,[5] sets the tone for many to follow. The satirical journal *Simplicissimus*, to which Altenberg had contributed since 1897, had been paying fifty crowns per month, but was understandably loath to continue unless provided with suitable material. Unsurprisingly, however, all he now wrote about, when he could write at all, was his depression. Malmberg therefore sought Kraus's help with the publishers to persuade them to keep paying up when nothing was coming in. Whether Kraus supported this bid for subvention is not known. His financial help for Altenberg was nevertheless real, albeit on a lesser scale than that provided for another deranged friend, Ludwig von Janikowski, who was interned in the same state mental asylum at Steinhof to which Altenberg would be committed in December 1912.

The day after Malmberg's letter of 2 May, Kraus announced in a notice prefacing *Die Fackel* that the profits from his next public reading on 3 June would go partly to Altenberg, as had those from the reading of 3 May at the

---

[3] *Peter Altenberg. Leben und Werk in Texten und Bildern*, ed. Hans Christian Kosler, (Munich: Matthes and Seitz 1981), 171.

[4] A. Springer, "Peter Altenberg. Eine pathographische Skizze," *Wiener Zeitschrift für Suchtforschung* 1, no. 4 (1977–78): 46.

[5] The letters are in the Wiener Stadt- und Landesbibliothek.

Akademischer Verband für Literatur und Musik.[6] A week after Altenberg's committal to Inzersdorf, Malmberg again wrote to Kraus, this time providing a precise analysis of what was wrong with their friend. They could no longer stay in the Fango clinic because Altenberg's illness had increasingly assumed "a neurasthenic and hypochondriac character," and a fresh set of doctors had confirmed that his disorder was primarily nervous, with alcohol playing a lesser role than originally thought.[7] A letter from Altenberg to Kraus from this time adopts a quite different tone from Malmberg's coolly sober report. In it he attacks his friends — primarily Kraus and Loos — but his major theme, as ever, is money: he is suffering immeasurable physical and spiritual agonies, and they could relieve things for him a little. For God's sake, he implores Kraus, will they not guarantee him the 100 crowns he gets from the "Sechsuhr-Blatt"[Six o' Clock News]?[8]

Five days after Kraus's reading of 3 June, which included "Heine und die Folgen," his attack on the greatest nineteenth century German-Jewish writer, Malmberg again contacted Kraus by letter, offering him the sketch "Der einsame Park" (ML^3 219) and suggesting a further public appeal for cash via the pages of Kraus's journal.[9] Although the sketch deals with Inzersdorf, the publication of "Der einsame Park" was particularly important to Malmberg as a counterbalance to lurid press reports about the extent of Altenberg's madness. However, for some at least, Altenberg's mental illness was merely an amusing extension of his customary role as the buffoon of German letters. The Berlin magazine Die lustigen Blätter even published sneering verse dedicated to "Peter the Great."[10] Such poor taste occasioned a staunch defense of Altenberg from Walther Heymann in Walden's Der Sturm, which was later to publish articles written by Altenberg during the course of his illness.[11]

The appeal in Die Fackel had to wait until 22 September, after Malmberg had personally approached Kraus on Altenberg's behalf. Her letters to Kraus are cool and correct, her displeasure at his failure to visit Altenberg tempered by the need for his assistance. On 12 July she enclosed a copy of an appeal she had already sent to twenty-eight prominent figures in the art world (including Bahr, Hofmannsthal, Schnitzler, Kainz, Reinhardt, Dehmel, Hauptmann) after consulting with Moritz Szeps, editor of the Neues Wiener Tagblatt. She asked Kraus's permission to add his name to the appeal which came out on 14 August as a leading feature in newspapers across the German-speaking world and which enjoyed considerable success.

In the meantime Altenberg had been discharged from Inzersdorf and returned to his room on the fifth floor of the Hotel London. His condition

---

[6] Karl Kraus, Die Fackel, 301–302 (1910).

[7] Springer, "Eine pathologische Skizze", 45; Arthur Schnitzler, Tagebuch 1913–1916, (Vienna: Akademie der Wissenschaften, 1983), 32.

[8] Andrew Barker and Leo A. Lensing, Rezept die Welt zu sehen, (Vienna: Braumüller, 1995), 245.

[9] Karl Kraus, Die Fackel, 305–306 (1910): 22–25.

[10] Barker and Lensing, Rezept, 288.

[11] Ibid., 288.

was, however, far from satisfactory, as Malmberg informed Kraus in a begging letter of 17 August. Having compelled her to go out and seek work, Altenberg found himself once more alone, the upshot being "deepest melancholy and hypochondria." Claiming he was unable to take food, he then wrecked his stomach by living on coffee, Sanatogen and ten bottles of beer a day. Reduced to a meal a day, Malmberg was at her wit's end as Altenberg's thrift assumed manic proportions. She told Kraus she was absolutely desperate, the more so as everything could be so good, given that Sunday's appeal had already raised five hundred crowns. She believed that the rapid change from a completely secluded life to all the distractions of the city — bars, variety theatres, pubs, staying up late and so on — had brought upon this change in her friend's condition.

Despite the obvious financial success of the public appeal, the combined forces of Malmberg, Loos und Kraus could not persuade Altenberg it was in his best interest to leave the summer heat of the city and go to the Semmering. He would promise only to go for a month in October when off-season price reductions had begun. Kraus's own work on Altenberg's behalf came to fruition when an appeal was published in *Die Fackel* on 22 September 1910, signed by a host of prominent figures, many of whom would normally have dreaded seeing their name appear in that publication: Richard Dehmel, Alexander Girardi, Ludwig Thoma, Hermann Hesse, Alfred Kerr, Gabriele Reuter, Hugo von Hofmannsthal, Richard Schaukal, Egon Friedell, Hermann Bahr, Josef Hoffmann, C.O. Czeschka, Emil Orlik, Wilhelm Sternberg, Max Reinhardt and S. Fischer.

At the same time, efforts on Altenberg's behalf were also being made in Berlin. On 26 September Gertrude Barrison gave an Altenberg reading at Herwarth Walden's Verein für Kunst, the proceedings of which would go to Altenberg.[12] Like the previous newspaper appeal, the considerable financial gain from Kraus's plea made little impact upon the dedicatee's mental well-being. On 18 November a despairing Malmberg wrote yet again to Kraus with the news that Altenberg's condition was appalling and made still worse by fear he had forfeited Kraus's friendship and that people were trying to poison him: she concludes that his condition was such as to preclude a normal sanatorium. By the beginning of December, he was back inside Inzersdorf.

Karl Kraus may have been one of the most feared figures of his age, but this did little to dampen Malmberg's ire in her letter of 8 January 1911, expressing disgust at the neglect of her friend by Kraus and others. Malmberg failed to comprehend that even compassion has its limits. Writing her memoirs half a century after the events, she preferred to remember Kraus as a man who had never disappointed her, and as a man who had loved and understood Altenberg as well as cherishing his art. Early in 1911 she saw things differently. She claimed that apart from Loos not one of Altenberg's so-called "best friends," Kraus and Friedell included, had been near him or even

[12] Alfred Döblin, *Kleine Schriften*, vol. 1, ed. Anthony W. Riley, (Olten and Freiburg im Breisgau: Walter, 1982), 108.

contacted him for five weeks. As long as he was healthy people had laughed at his jokes, but now, when he was so in need of friendship, people had written him off as insane. She anticipates Kraus's objections to her accusations — that he himself had many worries, had to work nineteen hours a day, had no time for reflection, that such "concern" had no place in Bohemian circles and that she was making these unjust accusations against him because of her "hysterical love" for Peter. But all this, she retorts, was no excuse from someone who can never have been a real friend to Altenberg. She ends by expressing her respect and admiration for Kraus as a humorist and as editor of the *Fackel*, but as a person, as a friend to a poor and valuable friend, she had come to despise him just as much as most of the others.

Altenberg was still in Inzersdorf on 11 April 1911 when he received a visit from Loos and Kraus, who failed to persuade him to leave his bed. The next day Malmberg wrote to Kraus that Loos should not have even attempted to get him to rise, for he was suffering from a form of psychosis. The solution to Altenberg's psychosomatic lameness was for her to push him around in a wheel chair, though on 22 May he was well enough to attend Gustav Mahler's funeral at the Grinzing cemetery, located at the other end of Vienna from Inzersdorf. What Altenberg required for recovery was neither psychiatric treatment nor Malmberg's companionship, but an intense emotional experience, even though the always unsuitable and unattainable objects of his desire led inevitably to further depression. In "Krankenlager," published in *Neues Altes* soon after his release from Inzersdorf in September 1911, Altenberg poked fun at his own posturing while making clear how he saw his means of salvation:

> Ich lag wieder einmal im Sterben. Einer sandte mir daher Kalbsfußgelee in Glasdose, statt mir seine junge, schöne Geliebte zu senden, die mich unbedingt eher hätte erretten können als Kalbshaxen! (NA 41)

> [I was on my deathbed again. Therefore someone sent me calf's foot jelly in a glass jar instead of his beautiful young lover who could definitely have saved me!]

In the summer of 1911, however, he was at last able to focus his pent-up emotional energy after making the acquaintance of the thirteen-year-old Anna Konrad while on a short, alcohol-free furlough from the sanatorium in the company of Helga Malmberg. She recounts extensively and resentfully how Altenberg lost himself in instant ecstasy over the poor cobbler's daughter whose mother had died, leaving her to bring up a brood of younger siblings. Malmberg especially disliked the way Anna so quickly learnt to exploit the sick poet's vulnerable passion. Altenberg published several texts about Anna in *Neues Altes*, but some of the most revealing records of his obsession only appeared posthumously in Polgar's edition, *Der Nachlaß*. In "An die Dreizehnjährige" he admits that his feelings for her amount virtually to mental sickness in themselves (N 7), while in the significantly titled "Fetischismus" he tells how he keeps under his pillow, unused, a handkerchief he had once used to wipe the rain off Anna's face. It has become a

"Heiligtum" [sacred object: N 9]. Even her spittle becomes the object of his adoration; to put into his mouth a cigarette she has briefly held in hers brings him bliss (N 8). Altenberg's predilection for girls' saliva is also revealed in "Brombeeren," a text in which it emerges that the Wiener Werkstätte had presented him with a silver chain and bird pendant to give to his "vergötterte Dreizehnjährige" [idolised thirteen-year-old] on her name-day (N 10).

Their relationship met its inevitable end when Altenberg was confronted by Anna's father, who was incensed by the gift of an expensive silver watch to his daughter. Taking back the watch, Altenberg threw it to the ground and crushed it under his heel. He knew full well that relationships with adolescent girls could only end in recrimination and rancor; what was important was that once again he had a target for his libido. Thus his condition improved precisely at the time he was once more embroiled in a hopeless passion, and early in September he received his discharge from Inzersdorf. By the end of the month he was back at the Semmering.

Although Malmberg detested Inzersdorf, doubly so as Altenberg's obsession with Anna flourished, she attended devotedly to his daily needs until rushed off to the Franz Josef's Hospital in Vienna for an emergency appendectomy late in the summer of 1911.[13] The ensuing break, when concern for her own well-being took precedence, had a profound effect, breaking the quasi-magical grip Altenberg had hitherto held over her. She convalesced in Gmunden am Traunsee, a town close to Altenberg's heart, and it was there that she accepted that their intimate days were over. Returning to Vienna she went to live with the family of Genia Schwarzwald, the celebrated educationalist, in their apartment designed by Adolf Loos at 68 Josefstädter Straße. She had one final, unpleasant meeting with Altenberg before returning home to Hamburg in January 1912. Her correspondence with Kraus continued over the coming months when she went to train as a horticulturalist in Sweden, but the name of Peter Altenberg is now no longer central: Malmberg seems indeed to have been flirting with Kraus.

One of Altenberg's last acts before leaving Inzersdorf was to compose a passionate letter to Anna Konrad on 8 September, full of foreboding that things were coming to an end (NA 198), and one of the first things he did upon going to the Semmering later that month was to write her an ecstatic love letter (NA 190). Financially cushioned by the successful appeals, Altenberg would stay well away from the temptations of Vienna until the middle of 1912, living in an annex of the Hotel Panhans. Surrounded by the peaceful forests and high hills of the Semmering, he found time not only to prepare the third, revised edition of *Märchen des Lebens*, expanded to reflect his experiences in Inzersdorf, but also to assemble *Neues Altes*, which appeared late in 1911. One of the more astonishing features of Altenberg's illness was undoubtedly his ability to write during the blackest of times, spurred on no doubt by the knowledge that should his contributions to

[13] The reverberations of Altenberg's relationship with Anna Konrad could still be felt in the 1960s, after Helga Malmberg published her version of events. See Camillo Schaefer, *Peter Altenberg, oder, Die Geburt der modernen Seele*, (Vienna: Amalthea, 1992), 133–136.

journals such as *Die Schaubühne* and *Simplicissimus* dry up, so too would a regular source of income.

What little scholarly comment *Neues Altes* has attracted has been mostly negative, as critics have perhaps projected on to the texts their awareness of Altenberg's depression at the time of its appearance.[14] Writing to Kraus on 7 December 1911 even the author himself derided his new work:

> Was kostet eine Annoncirung meines soeben bei S. Fischer, Berlin, erschienenen epochalen Schmarrn's "*Neues Altes*"?!?
> Was kostet die *Nicht*-Besprechung von Seite *eines Deiner Apostelchen*, vulgo *Scheißdreck-Leute*?!?
> Dein Dich verehrender (was ist mit fixer Monatsrente?!)
> Peter Altenberg[15]

> [What does an announcement cost for my epoch-making nonsense *Neues Altes* which has just appeared with S. Fischer in Berlin?!? What does a *non*-review cost by one of *your little apostles*, vulgo *shitbags*?
> Yours in reverence (how about a fixed monthly allowance?!)
> Peter Altenberg]

Regarding form and content, the 108 items in *Neues Altes* mark no progress on *Märchen des Lebens* or *Bilderbögen des kleinen Lebens*, providing as the book's title suggests a similar pot pourri of sketches, aperçus, cabaret and variety reviews and autobiographical vignettes. In his research for the *Gesammelte Werke*, Werner J. Schweiger traced the often bewildering array of sources for the new book, which does indeed provide something old and something new. "So sollte es immer sein" (NA 83) first appeared as far back as the February 1904 edition of *Kunst*, other material first saw light of day in *Die Fackel*, the Munich periodical *März*, the Berlin journals *Pan* and *Der Sturm*, while no fewer than fifty-seven items came out originally in Jacobsohn's *Die Schaubühne*; a further major source was the *Wiener Allgemeine Zeitung*.

Although the provenance of much of *Neues Altes* may be a source of bewilderment for the modern editor, to read the book reveals that the driving force behind much of the collection was Altenberg's dual relationship with Helga Malmberg and Anna Konrad, his old and new loves. The title page is led by its dedication to Anna Konrad and bears a triple motto. The first is Goethe's famous remark to Eckermann that men of genius experience puberty repeatedly whereas other people are only young once. The second motto is Altenberg's own riposte to Goethe, praising those fortunate enough to need to be young only once. The others, that is to say men of genius, Altenberg himself doubtless included, are accursed, tortured by "eternal inner intoxication." The final motto is taken from Baudelaire, like Altenberg a

---

[14] Ibid.

[15] Barker and Lensing, *Rezept*, 248.

member of that "diseased club" who "lack the natural balance that other people have":[16]

> J'ai de mes tourments multiplié les causes - - -
> d'innombrables liens vont de mon âme aux choses!

Making the dedicatee of *Neues Altes* a thirteen-year-old girl for whom he had a passing obsession rather than the woman who had sacrificed herself for him for years was a callous act, doubtless fueled by resentment at Malmberg's "desertion" of him. It is barely redeemed by the first item, which comprises a series of dedications he had inscribed in various of his books, beginning with one to "Fräulein H. M." (NA 13). Such generosity is, however, offset by a host of other glowing dedications, all of them to women, including a "Frau M. B. in Aachen" as well as Gertrude Barrison, Else Wiesenthal and "Frau E. R." (Emma Rudolf).

The second item in *Neues Altes*, "Wesen der Freundschaft," might have been calculated to upset Helga Malmberg. Altenberg begins by stating that he knows of only two people who are well-disposed towards him: his brother and "A. R." (probably the actress Anka Rakaric) (NA 17). Malmberg is evidently the unnamed subject of the patronizing fourth item, the poem "Bekenntnis," with its recurring refrain of "You gave me all - - - and I gave you nothing!" (NA 20). This verse was composed after Malmberg had left Altenberg; since she fell ill "der magische Schein der Selbstaufopferung" [the magical glow of self-sacrifice] has been extinguished; the poem ends with the unspeakably patronising lines:

> Du gabst mir alles - - - und ich gab dir nichts!
> Und dennoch traure ich verzweifelt am Sarge deiner
> armen Seele - - -. Denn, glaube mir, sie starb! (NA 20)

> [You gave me all - - - and I gave you nothing!
> And yet I grieve despairingly at the coffin of your
> poor soul - - -. For, believe me, it died!]

Malmberg may well have recognized in the seventh item "Konzert" the figure of Helene Nahowski-Berg, "schön und prächtig, gelb und golden" [lovely and splendid, yellow and golden: NA 25], whom Altenberg adored from afar, and she will have had no difficulty at all in recognizing her in the poem "H. N.," where Altenberg writes that her voice "replaces for him the music of the world." The poem ends with a preposterous warning to Helene:

> Entfern dich nicht! Denn wenn du mich verläßt,
> erlischt für Dich dein eigener Zauber - -
> und eine Welt ersteht, die dich brutal geniessen will! (NA 45)

---

[16] Australian painter and heroin addict Brett Whiteley, quoted by Janet McKenzie in her obituary, *The Guardian*, 18 June 1992, 35.

> [Do not go away! For if you leave me
> your whole magic will be extinguished - -
> and a world will arise which wishes to brutally enjoy you!]

What the Alban and Helene Berg made of such stuff is anybody's guess, but it did not prevent the composer from using *Neues Altes* as the source for his opus 4, the so-called *Altenberg Lieder.*

Altenberg must have known that Helga Malmberg would be upset by this material, which in the narrow world of Viennese culture could only serve to make her devotion to Altenberg seem still more ludicrous. It can have been no coincidence, then, that the next item is the poem "Helga," in which Altenberg presumably tries to make amends for the earlier material. Although he apostrophizes her as his guiding star, it is doubtful whether he will have succeeded with writing like this:

> Hilf mir, Helga - - -!
> Alle anderen Frauen
> nehmen und plündern die Seele, den Leib, die
> Kraft des Gehirnes - - -!
> Du allein *spendest* und *spendest* und *spendest!*
> Kaum bist du fort, *umdüstert* sich alles - - -.
> Die bösen Geister nehmen mich in Besitz - - -.
> Guter Geist, Helga, ich entbehre dich,
> wie ein krankes Kind seine Baba - - -.
> Gütige Kinderfrau, Helga,
> ich gebe dir *diesen* Ehrentitel,
> Statt dieses schnöden, inhaltslosen Titels: Geliebte! (NA 46)

> [Help me, Helga - - -!
> All other women
> take and plunder the soul, the body, the
> power of the brain - - -!
> You alone *gave* and *gave* and *gave!*
> Hardly are you away, and everything *goes dark* - - -.
> The evil spirits take possession of me - - -.
> Good spirit, Helga, I miss you
> as a sick child does his nana - - -.
> Kind nurse, Helga,
> I give you *this* honorary title,
> Instead of that base, empty title: Lover!]

As late as 1916 Altenberg recalled again the "treachery" of Helga Malmberg, unfavorably comparing her attitude with that of Anna Konrad. Presumably he intended the title "Verrat" to refer to Malmberg, who remained unnamed, but it is not difficult to read the piece as Altenberg's mean-spirited betrayal of her, given all that she had undoubtedly sacrificed for him. He claims contemptuously that she was more interested in her romantic dreams than in caring for him. His suffering was medicine for her romantic soul. She should never have fled from the bourgeois world in the first place. With extraordinary cruelty he then exclaims:

> Heil Anna Konrad! Du *pflegtest* mich *nicht*, doch an meinen Träumen von dir *gesundete* ich! (NF 93)
>
> [Heil Anna Konrad! You did not *care for me*, but I *recovered* thanks to my dreams about you!]

What Altenberg really needed was not a lover at all, but a mother. In "Vöslau" (NA 101) he compares the town with the days of his youth, the main difference being that his "wunderschöne Mama" is no more. In "Der Tod" (NA 131) he toys unconvincingly with the idea of suicide, driven to despair by unrequited love for an unspecified woman whose sleep must not be disturbed by the news of his death, even though she is the cause of it. Helga Malmberg crosses his mind, but the prospect of her grief does not concern him; Altenberg's association of himself with Christ is perhaps in questionable taste:

> Nach Hamburg wird die Kunde später dringen, und H. M. ist gewappnet mit Ergebenheiten!
> In ihrer Religion sind Kreuzigungen vorhergesehen, und sie wird leben aus innern Kräften, durch Leid erhöht, betaut, befrüchtet! (NA 131)
>
> [Later the news will get through to Hamburg and H. M. is forearmed with submissiveness! In her religion crucifixions are foreseen and she will live on her inner strength, elevated by suffering, bedewed, stimulated!]

The picture of the poet which emerges from *Neues Altes* is ugly, and must have given Helga Malmberg pain. In "Wie ich gesundet bin," he concludes that he is not cured at all, and never will be, and goes through the list of people at the Inzersdorf sanatorium who provided him with succor, but her name is absent (NA 141). It is not insignificant, therefore, that in her memoirs Malmberg chose to reproduce a facsimile of the otherwise unpublished dedication Altenberg wrote in her copy of *Neues Altes*. There he seems to accept her remonstrations with some humility; fifty years after the end of their relationship, Malmberg felt the need to put certain matters straight. In the dedication Altenberg accepts she was correct in reminding him of her crucial role when he was at such a low ebb. Acknowledging that she had done all she could for him, Altenberg thanks and blesses her. The dedication is signed and dated Semmering, 27 January 1912.[17]

For the publication of *Neues Altes* Altenberg had returned to the Fischer Verlag, who showed their appreciation by printing the sketch "Rückkehr vom Lande" twice (NA 39, 183). There is further evidence of shoddy production in the overlap between *Neues Altes* and the revised *Märchen des Lebens*, with some sketches appearing in both books, though sometimes with a

---

[17] Malmberg, *Widerhall*, 272–273.

changed title.[18] As in other collections, Altenberg again provides readers of *Neues Altes* with quasi-programmatic declarations, one such being in "Beschäftigung," where he states:

> Ich erfinde nichts, daher bin ich kein Schriftsteller und kein Dichter. Das Leben trägt mir alles zu, ich habe nichts dabei zu verrichten, als das Zugetragene nicht zu verfälschen . . . (NA 203)

> [I invent nothing, therefore I am not a writer and not a poet. Life brings everything to me, I have nothing to do except not falsify it . . .]

In "Übers Schreiben," although he is concerned specifically with letter-writing Altenberg comments upon the importance of hearing the "voice" of the writer, underlining the significance he attaches to reproducing the nuances of spoken language rather than the punctilious observation of grammatical rules. The obviously "spoken" impression which so many of Altenberg's texts convey, often at the expense of correctness, was particularly important in Uwe Johnson's reception of Altenberg in the 1950s. Johnson responded enthusiastically to the many texts laid out in conversation or dialogue form, even claiming that Altenberg had "no relationship with the written word."[19] Johnson's editor regards this as a determining parallel between the two writers, accounting for Johnson's attraction to Altenberg. For like Altenberg's work, so too Johnson's *Mutmaßungen über Jakob* represents the writing down in dictation form of the dialogic voices which an intensively inventive writer hears in his head.[20]

Return to Paradise?: *"Semmering 1912"*

The many months Altenberg spent at his "childhood paradise" (NA 197) formed the nucleus for *"Semmering 1912"*. This work is akin to *Neues Altes* in that the core of the work is the fevered response to a young girl, the eleven-year-old hotelier's daughter Klara Panhans, who rapidly and seamlessly replaced the humble Anna Konrad as the focus of his emotional delirium. They met when Altenberg moved from Inzersdorf to the Hotel Panhans, a grandiose edifice erected when the railway transformed Semmering's rural isolation into a playground for wealthy Viennese indulging a modish penchant for fresh air.

Though cushioned by money from the appeals, Altenberg could only afford an attic in an annex to the hotel, whose exuberantly headed notepaper proclaimed it as the summer residence of Reichskanzler Fürst Bülow. Although Anna Konrad still aroused his enthusiasm at the end of September 1911, her days were now numbered. In "Ende" Altenberg refers to but does not name Klara Panhans, stating with extraordinary precision that from 17

---

[18] For details see Schaefer, *Peter Altenberg. Ein biographischer Essay*, 133.

[19] Uwe Johnson, *"Wo ist der Erzähler auffindbar?" Gutachten für Verlage 1956–1958*, ed. Bernd Neumann, (Frankfurt: Suhrkamp, 1992), 98.

[20] Ibid., 186–187.

September 1911 until 19 October 1912 she was "a little saint" (S 104). We also learn here about the cessation of their "relationship" in one of the bleakest texts Altenberg ever composed. It recounts unsparingly how the little saint had been informed by a society lady that Altenberg was a hopeless alcoholic with a history of mental illness:

> sie schämte sich seitdem seiner Verehrung - - -. Die Liebe eines besoffenen Tollhäuslers?! Pfui Teufel! Da wollte er ihr das ersparen, und mied sie von nun an.[21]

> [thereafter she was ashamed of his veneration - - -. The love of a drunk from the madhouse?! No way! He wanted to spare her that und avoided her from now on.]

Within two months of the ending of "one of his loveliest, deepest life poems" (S 104), Altenberg was committed to the Steinhof asylum in Vienna, ostensibly for dipsomania. In reality, he had once more been consumed by passion for a pre-adolescent girl. On 6 January 1912, for example, he had inscribed a photograph of Klara in terms ecstatic even by his standards. She represents the dream of his sick nights, his fate, his joy, his inspiration, his destiny. Her gaze is the gaze of the madonna, angelically pure, transfigured and unearthly. Her voice is unspeakably gentle, melodious like the magic of bells.[22] Once the "relationship" had ended, Altenberg wrote to S. Fischer requesting that after his imminent death his collected works be published under the title "Wie ich es sehe (Märchen des Lebens)," with all proceeds going to Klara.[23]

Other unpublished texts from January 1912, composed on Hotel Panhans paper, reveal a different aspect of Altenberg's sexuality. Written in French, the five erotic poems entitled "Amour moderne" express delight in oral sex with a lover whose "corps de marbre" [marble body] will be brought to life by "la chaleur qui me *tue*." [the heat which is killing me]. Though one poem suggests that Altenberg receives sexual favours from his "adorée fillette," they generally reveal a desire to please rather than be pleased, and a Schiele-like delight in female auto-eroticism where the male has become superfluous:

> Et moi, sur mes genoux,
> à côté de vous,
> j'étais *superflu*; et *quandmême*,
> quand on aime,
> on jouit du *bonheur d'autrui*!
> *Mon* bonheur à moi ne m'est

---

[21] Other published texts about Klara Panhans are "Ende" (S 104); "Herbstlied" (S 116); "22 August" (S 124); "Klara" (S 184, 187); "Berghotel-Terrasse, Semmering" (S 185); "Ein Regentag" (S 195).

[22] GSE. See also NE 47–48.

[23] DLA 73.239

rien - - -
ton bonheur seul est le *mien!*[24]

[And me, on my knees
at your side,
I was *superfluous,* yet *all the same,*
when one is in love
one enjoys the *happiness of the other!*
To me my own pleasure is
nothing - - -
your happiness alone is *mine!*]

This direction is followed further in a text written in German on 13 January entitled "Lesbische Liebe."[25] Other texts written this same day concern themselves with prostitutes and orgasms both male and female.[26]

Although Altenberg's response to Klara Panhans forms the emotional core of *"Semmering 1912"*, the first version of the book also reflects, more than any other single collection, delight in the natural world and the changing seasons. A memoir composed in January 1919 by the Jewish Socialist writer and Holocaust victim Else Feldmann recollects her four months convalescence on the Semmering, during which every day was spent in Altenberg's company. It was a source of great enrichment, for he taught her to appreciate nature in all its aspects. Through him, she says, she learned to appreciate the trees, the snow, the sun, the moon, the mountains and the forest.[27]

In *"Semmering 1912"* the natural world is implicitly contrasted with the well-heeled socialites who flock to the Semmering to recharge their batteries but whose assumptions remain unassailed and unchanged. It is the least urban of Altenberg's works, its photographic frontispiece depicting the poet in his Raglan coat and Scottish bonnet (homespun by peasants)[28] walking stick in hand, posing on a snowy slope against the wooded backdrop of the winter hills. The picture itself makes a statement about Altenberg's relationship with nature, challenging assumptions that Altenberg is a metropolitan writer with little real feeling for the natural world. It proclaims a new and healthy Peter Altenberg, one perhaps even in accord with the message of *Pròdromos*.

The final shape of *"Semmering 1912"* may have benefited from Kraus's helping hand, for a letter of 24 January 1913 from the Steinhof asylum reveals the author's concern for his latest work and his relief that the first proofs are in Kraus's faithful hands. Although he tells Kraus to correct whatever he considers totally wrong, Altenberg believes the book is complete in his sense

[24] GSE

[25] Kosler, *Peter Altenberg,* 76.

[26] WSB 203.716.

[27] Ilse Pollak, "Über Else Feldmann," *Literatur und Kritik,* 279 (1993): 193–194.

[28] DLA, 89.95.88–1.

of the word.[29] Upon its appearance in the spring of 1913, Kraus included various items both in his journal and in his readings. Ulrik Brendel (a pseudonym for Leopold Liegler) reported that Kraus was equally successful in finding both the comic and the lyrical elements in the work of this "von Gott autorisierte Übersetzung des Menschen in die Sprache" [divinely authorized translation of the human into language.][30]

Altenberg's gratitude to Kraus was made public when the Innsbruck periodical *Der Brenner* published his passionate defense of the satirist as part of its response to the pillorying of Kraus in the journal *Zeit im Bild*.[31] He was equally indebted to S. Fischer, as emerges from an accusatory letter to Kraus, dispatched from the Venice Lido on 2 June 1913. Complaining that during his six months illness none of his friends had inquired either of him or his brother how they would meet the bill, he revealed the generosity of the publisher whom Kraus could not abide:

Nobody knew that *3 weeks before* my collapse S. Fischer had given me 1000 marks for the luxury edition of "Wie ich es sehe" and 1000 marks for the 1st impression of "Semmering 1912." That has now *gone* on the illness - - - . Other people, who have not written my *9* books, *undergone* and *suffered* the things I have, have been bought *bookshops* in *capital cities*!!![32]

Paul Stefan, co-editor of *Der Ruf* and author of the first Kokoschka monograph, reacted effusively to *"Semmering 1912"* in his review for the *Neue Zürcher Zeitung*, claiming that Altenberg's illness had brought him to a point of new maturity in work more beautiful and more gripping than any he had previously produced. Illness, Stefan claims, had made Altenberg's work less anecdotal, and returned him to the world of nature which had initially shaped him. Hence Stefan is at pains to challenge the already entrenched notion that Altenberg's work shows no signs of development: in the mind and in truth, he claims, there is no earthly space. The universe resides in the notion of the smallest being.[33]

For Kurt Pinthus, *"Semmering 1912"* represents an encyclopedia of all Altenberg's previous experiences: up in the mountains he discovered spring, winter, forests, meadows, beautiful women and very well-groomed children of noble birth.[34] Oskar Maurus Fontana, like Stefan, notes Altenberg's move away from the anecdotal as he ascends into a realm of the purest and most intimate poetry. He also elaborates the comparison between Altenberg and

[29] Kosler, *Peter Altenberg*, 126; Barker and Lensing, *Rezept*, 251.

[30] Karl Kraus, *Die Fackel*, 372–373 (1913): 20. See Ulrik Brendel, "Theater, Kunst und Musik," *Die Wage*, 16 (1913): 393–394.

[31] Ludwig v. Ficker, *Briefwechsel 1909–1914*, (Salzburg: Otto Müller, 1986), 154. Altenberg's sketch "Die Güte" was published in *Der Brenner*, 3 (1913): 794, but not subsequently republished.

[32] Barker and Lensing, *Rezept*, 254.

[33] Ibid., 290.

[34] Kurt Pinthus, "Peter Altenberg, "*Semmering 1912*"," *Beiblatt der Zeitschrift für Bücherfreunde*, 5, no. 2 (1913): 71–72.

Jean Paul, mooted by Alfred Kerr at the time of Altenberg's first major public crisis in 1904. He notes that Altenberg had rarely written verse, but like Jean Paul his prose is full of verse; both are among the greatest lyric poets in the language.[35] For a prosaic modern scientist, however, *"Semmering 1912"* is best understood merely as an expression of sensitivity after a detoxification course.[36]

Unusually, there is no programmatic statement in *"Semmering 1912"*, which Altenberg partly assembled from texts previously published in *Simplicissimus* and the *Wiener Allgemeine Zeitung* as well as the revolutionary new expressionist periodical from Berlin, *Der Sturm*. Many texts, however, were freshly minted for the new book. The autobiographical "So wurde ich," widely regarded as a key document, demonstrates how at an advanced stage in his career Altenberg was now taking stock (S 36). Another low-key, albeit truculent, assessment of his literary value emerges in "Plauderei" where Altenberg concludes that his talent was meagre, but his capacity to feel was great. Most people have no talent and no feeling (S 153).

A particularly noticeable feature of *"Semmering 1912"* compared with *Märchen des Lebens, Bilderbögen des kleinen Lebens* and *Neues Altes,* is the increased tendency to very short texts and to the aphorisms (*Splitter*) which would dominate all Altenberg's later collections. More than *Neues Altes,* *"Semmering 1912"* is thus the fulcrum between Altenberg's earlier work, with its strong social and lyric impulses, and the later, kaleidoscopically diffuse work.

"Semmering 1912", like all of Altenberg's collections, is the published reflection of its author's thoughts, feelings and experiences. Alongside his literary output, Altenberg was also an avid collector of picture postcards and photographs, many of which he inscribed with texts in his unique idiom. As Hans Bisanz and Leo Lensing have observed, these form something akin to a "second oeuvre."[37] Nowhere is this more the case, however, than in the collection of 259 cards and photographs also entitled "Semmering 1912." This album is nothing less than the visual recapitulation of the first edition of the book of the same title.[38] It is obsessed with natural images, page upon page depicting the natural world around the Semmering, especially in winter. Equally dominant are the numerous images of Klara Panhans herself, as well as many photographs of churches with inscribed references to Klara's saintly nature. Perhaps most striking of all is a page consisting of four copies of a detail from a painting of St. Clare, each image furnished with a textual exhortation that Klara, his "little saint," be kept pure. Other images, however,

---

[35] Oskar Maurus Fontana, "Peter Altenberg auf dem Semmering," *Der Merker*, 4 (1913): 959–960.

[36] Springer, "Eine pathologische Skizze," 45.

[37] Hans Bisanz, *Mein äußerstes Ideal: Altenbergs Photosammlung von geliebten Frauen, Freunden und Orten,* (Vienna and Munich: Christian Brandstätter, 1987); Barker and Lensing, *Rezept,* 133–167.

[38] Internal evidence within the album, acquired by the Wiener Stadt- und Landesbibliothek in 1994, suggests that it was assembled as late as 1916.

such as a disturbing head and torso shot of the naked 14-year old Albine Ruprich, her gaze brimming with reproach, betoken a side of Altenberg's sexuality which is far from wholesome.

The album exhibits many snapshots of both the author himself, in clothes similar to those worn in the photograph forming the frontispiece of the published *"Semmering 1912"*, and also personages mentioned in the course of the work. The final series of postcards and photographs retraces the trip he made to the Dolomites in August 1912, as recounted in the latter pages of the original version of *"Semmering 1912"*. Besides representing a fascinating example of parallel modes of creativity, the existence of the album "Semmering 1912" is a striking confirmation of Altenberg's continuing concern with a text even after publication. Thus the experiences at the Semmering are recorded in no fewer than three forms: the book *"Semmering 1912"* in its first guise, in its revised and expanded form, and in the photograph album which has only now, over eight decades after its compilation, become available for scrutiny. Interestingly, however, the photograph album, which was probably compiled in 1916, prefers not to recap the final items of the revised text. These refer to Altenberg's experiences in Venice following his release from the Steinhof asylum in April 1913.

Although he was geographically isolated from the temptations of the capital while at the Semmering, Altenberg still came into steady contact with Vienna's citizens. As Paul Stefan noted, to avoid Viennese society it was also necessary to avoid the Semmering,[39] now within easy reach of the capital thanks to Carl von Ghega's miraculous Semmering railway. Unsurprisingly, public knowledge that Altenberg was now resident at a haunt of the leisured rich had a negative impact upon the poet's incessant fund-raising activities on his own behalf. This in turn triggered financial panic, thereby vitiating the therapeutic intentions behind his stay there. In a letter of 11 January 1912 he tells a "dear venerated lady friend" that he is tortured by insomnia, caused by the withdrawal of financial support by patrons who reckon that only millionaires can afford the Hotel Panhans: despite his sickness, reputation and achievements, people seem to expect him to vegetate in some workers' encampment in Ottakring and kick the bucket like an old dog ["in einem Ottakringer Massenquartier vegetire und krepire wie ein alter Hund."][40] With some percipience, he adds that the Semmering is his earthly paradise and that leaving it can only mean suicide or madness. Writing to an unnamed actress (possibly Lina Loos) on 15 February 1912, he thanks her for the fifty crowns from a matinee performance, forwarded by Egon Friedell. His condition has not, however, been improved by her generosity, for as his physical woes increased his mood grew gloomier by the day.[41] On 18 May 1912 he sent out a reminder to a Dr. Günsberg for his monthly allowance of twenty crowns,

---

[39] Paul Stefan, "Der Semmering und Peter Altenberg," *Neue Zürcher Zeitung*, 1 June 1913. An extract is reprinted in Barker and Lensing, *Rezept*, 290.

[40] LBI.

[41] LBI.

bemoaning that others too were callously abandoning him up on the peaceful but pricey Semmering. Thus at the age of fifty-three, and devastated by depression, he was now having to make do with 480 instead of 600 crowns.[42] This, and numerous similar documents, account for the heartfelt conclusion to "So wurde ich," for Peter Altenberg had indeed become a *Schnorrer*.

Without mentioning the artist by name, Altenberg records in "Der Maler" (S 141) Kokoschka's visit to the Semmering in July 1912 and how he came to paint a portrait of the six-year-old Sonja Dungyersky. This picture does not appear to have survived, unlike the photograph depicting Kokoschka, Friedell and Altenberg seated at a table on the terrace of the Hotel Panhans.[43] Briefly separated from Alma Mahler, with whom he was in the throes of an affair climaxing in the magnificent dual portrait "Die Windsbraut" (1913–14,) Kokoschka wrote to her on 20 July from the Hotel Panhans, remarking how very unhappy people on the Semmering made him. Included in the list were Altenberg, Friedell and Kokoschka's more than generous patron Adolf Loos, who had been so bold as to ask a small favor of the artist. What made Kokoschka especially unhappy was having to earn some money painting a Hungarian brat whose entourage disgusted him.[44] The name of Sonja Dungyersky, the child in question, crops up on several occasions in *"Semmering 1912"*, but always in the glowing terms Altenberg reserved for female children. There are also several photographs of her in the album "Semmering 1912." According to Altenberg, the painter received 500 crowns for the portrait, but Kokoschka was deeply unimpressed by Altenberg's "Tartar Queen."

In "Der Maler," however, the poetic imagination pushes inconvenient facts aside, and Altenberg's painter cannot be equated with the real Kokoschka as expressed in the letter to Alma (hence perhaps Altenberg's unusual coyness about his identity.) The painter's praise for his sitter, which is backed up by his offer to paint Sonja free of charge, is expressed in Altenberg's own exalted poetic idiom; painter and writer are united over a subject the non-artistic world, represented here by "die Damen," finds unappealing. Whereas these ladies also find Sonja "much less nice, more self-willed, less gentle than most of the other delightful children," Altenberg's painter can only echo the poet's words. Thus Sonja is no longer the Hungarian brat of Kokoschka's letter to Alma, rather a "Tatarenkönigin, Wildkatze, Besiegerin" [Tartar queen, wild-cat, victor: S 141]. The mothers of obedient, well-brought up children blanch at the artist's language, but the next day they write offering him a fortune to paint their offspring. At first he refuses, then he relents, painting them in all their douce, conformist respectability. The narrator concludes the sketch with an expression of contempt: yes, they were "*sanfte*

[42] LBI.

[43] Oskar Kokoschka, *Briefe*, vol. I, *1905–1919*, ed. Olda Kokoschka and Heinz Spielmann, (Düsseldorf: Claassen, 1984), 256–257.

[44] Ibid., 54.

Kälber von dummen Kühen, richtig porträtiert!" [*gentle calves from stupid cows,* properly portrayed!] And each little calf cost 2,000 crowns at the cheapest estimate (S 142). Here, at least, Altenberg is in full agreement with the suffering Kokoschka, who complained to Alma about these examples of a breath-taking materialistic outlook.[45] Although the boundary between reality and invention is unclear in "Der Maler," there seems no reason to doubt that Kokoschka did indeed finish a picture of Sonja. One wonders what has become of this and the other portraits Kokoschka executed during his unhappy visit to the Hotel Panhans in the summer of 1912.

"*Semmering 1912*" also records the impressions of Altenberg's three week motoring holiday to the South Tyrol and Italy in August 1912, undertaken in the company of his friend and patron, the millionaire banker Dr. Ernst von Lieben, along with Lieben's teenage female companion Lióschka. Altenberg fails to mention either of them in the travel sketches which trace his journey from Klagenfurt through the Dolomites to Bozen-Bolzano via Seeboden am Millstätter See, Toblach-Dobbiaco, Tre Croci — visited by Kokoschka and Alma Mahler exactly one year later and captured in a superb landscape — Lago di Misurina and the Falzarego Pass.[46]

In "Dokument," composed sometime after moving into his final quarters in the Graben Hotel in autumn 1913, Altenberg wrote a record of his experiences with Lieben and the girl. These dated back to his psychosomatic lameness in Inzersdorf, when Lieben had brought along the young Polish girl to be "inspected" by Altenberg. Depending on Altenberg's judgment, Lieben, who presumably was linked to Altenberg not merely through admiration of his work — Lieben paid him 60 crowns per month — but also through shared sexual preferences, would decide whether or not he would "take, look after, and save her." He describes how the thin pale girl came in and was probably horrified at the sight of this pig in his bed:

"Nimm sie!" sagte das Schwein, das zu inneren Thränen gerührt war durch den Anblick dieser *Äußersten Vollkommenheit auf Erden.* Und der Millionär *nahm* sie und *behielt* sie.

["Take her! ", the pig said, moved to silent tears at the sight of this *total earthly perfection.* And the millionaire *took* her, and *kept* her.][47]

The following August a telegram from Lieben invited him to fulfil a dream by sharing their holiday to the Dolomites. There he would live "like an old, sick prince," but by the third day Lióschka had grown jealous of her protector's "neue Geliebte" [new girl friend] (!) When a couple of days later Al-

---

[45] Oskar Kokoschka, *Briefe,* 54.

[46] Altenberg wrote Georg Engländer a card from the Millstätter See (GSE) a further card was sent from Lago di Misurina on 10 August 1912. On 11 August he was in Toblach. Texts commemorating this trip are: "Bergesewelt" (S 15); "Bozen" (S 16); "Frühstück in Klagenfurt" (S 21); "Dolomiten" (S 39); "Ewige Erinnerungen" (S 117); "Falzarego-Pass-Höhe" (S 178).

[47] LBI; The text was published for the first time in Barker and Lensing, *Rezept,* 41.

tenberg fell off a horse, her joy was complete.[48] Thereafter, the "Dokument" makes no mention of the holiday.

Although the Dolomite items in *"Semmering 1912"* refer neither to Lieben nor his young companion, she is mentioned in "Fahrt" (S 163) when Altenberg recalls how Lieben and Lióschka drove him down to Wiener Neustadt on a fresh July morning at the considerable speed of 70 kph. Having been dropped off in the town, Altenberg bought postcards of mountain flowers before going to the railway hotel for a restorative nap, assisted by ten bottles of Pilsner (S 164).[49] So much for attending Dr. Hansy's alcohol clinic, which was supposedly part of his "cure" at the Semmering!

Altenberg and Lióschka would be together once again during his convalescence in Venice after discharge from Steinhof, and a photograph shows them standing on the beach at the Lido, Altenberg in bathing costume and cap, the alluring Lióschka in a black shift with her arm around his shoulder. The caption, in Altenberg's hand, merely states "Peter und Lióschka."[50] By this time, Lieben had grown jealous of Altenberg's feelings for her. It is tempting to speculate that intimate details of their triangular relationship form the subject of letters between Altenberg and Lieben now kept in the Jewish National Library in Jerusalem, permission to inspect which has been twice refused the author.[51] In the revised version of *"Semmering 1912"* Lióschka Maliniéwich is listed as one of the book's nine female dedicatees and she is the subject of further sketches in *Fechsung*.[52]

When tracing Altenberg's biography during the years of his illness, the Dolomite venture of August 1912 should not be confused with a week's motoring holiday to the Dolomites at the invitation of the actress Frau Vallière, undertaken soon after arriving in Venice in May 1913. This Venetian interlude of some five months was only commemorated in the revised version of *"Semmering 1912"* which came out late in 1913. After his holiday with Lieben and Lióschka, Altenberg returned to his attic room in the Hotel London, whereafter his condition rapidly deteriorated. Fueled by financial

---

[48] In the album "Semmering 1912," the final item is a snapshot showing Altenberg, Lieben and Lióschka, all on horseback. The inscription on the rear refers to the fall, in which the poet broke a rib.

[49] Both the car, a magnificent open tourer, and the postcards can be seen in the album "Semmering 1912."

[50] Barker and Lensing, *Rezept*, 43.

[51] Altenberg also mentions Lióschka in a letter to Lotte Franzos of 2 February 1912, shortly after the composition of "Amour moderne." (WSB 115.778) Might she have been his "fillette adorée"? This assumption may be strengthened by the postcard of the Vienna South station in the album "Semmering 1912," which Altenberg sent to himself after a brief trip back to Vienna in August 1912 during which he had clearly indulged in sexual activity.

[52] The other dedicatees are: Lilly Steiner; Grete Engländer; Kamilla von Nagy; Ilci Honus; Cäcilia Brandstätter; Friede Frank; Mitzi Thumb; Frau Machlup. Shortly after Altenberg's death, Cäcilia Brandstätter, who lived in a fashionable Ringstraße apartment, wrote a letter of condolence to Egon Friedell. A doctored version appeared in *Das Altenbergbuch* as the touchingly illiterate letter of a Viennese prostitute "Fini D.," mourning the death of "dear Herr Peter"! (Österreichische Nationalbibliothek, Handschriftensammlung, 1127–39–1.)

fears, his drinking ran out of control, sleep became even more erratic, and his paranoia returned.

On 16 November 1912 Schnitzler wrote to Bahr about a recently received letter in which Altenberg complained that many regular donors had withdrawn support. Altenberg had not only asked Schnitzler for aid, he had also asked him to tout for other patrons, mentioning Bahr by name. It emerges from Schnitzler's letter that another rescue operation was being mounted, that Hofmannsthal was once again willing to give Altenberg of his charity and that S. Fischer was prepared to coordinate the action.[53] By 10 December Altenberg's condition had grown so acute that the most drastic measures yet had to be taken. Instead of returning him to the private Inzersdorf clinic, Georg Engländer now had him assigned to the Villa Austria in the Steinhof asylum in Vienna's 14th District, best-known today for its Otto Wagner church. Engländer had clearly acted in desperation, with his brother's best interests at heart, but Altenberg never forgot what he considered an act of betrayal.

Writing in 1918 to his patron Dr. Emil Franzos — he was the lawyer husband of Lotte Franzos, an early subject and supporter of Kokoschka's — Altenberg expressed his terror that Georg Engländer would again take steps to have him locked up out of misunderstood brotherly love.[54] In another beseeching letter he told Franzos how insomnia was placing him at the terrible gates of Steinhof,[55] while in a letter of 13 December 1918 to Lotte Franzos he claimed that putting him in a sanatorium would be not just a case of murder, but an assassination. The people who would do such a thing he describes as criminal idiots who have not the faintest inkling of his pathologically eccentric constitution.[56]

For Schnitzler, Altenberg's problem was rooted in sustained alcohol abuse which had developed into dipsomania. In Inzersdorf he had bribed warders to obtain liquor, and his sojourn on the Semmering, despite attendance at Dr. Hansy's clinic, hardly removed him from alcoholic temptation. His admiration for Hansy's wife Resa may well have made him willing to attend the clinic, along with a lively interest in their young daughter Grete whom he apostrophized in a letter to her mother as being both Dante's Beatrice and Petrarch's Laura.[57] In another letter to Frau Hansy from Steinhof five months after his banishment from the "mountain paradise Semmering," Altenberg complains of becoming a vegetable, leading a life which is destroying him. Reminding her of outstanding payments on the monthly thirty crowns *Rente*, he concluded by blaming her husband's rejection of him for his present predicament. Something had clearly happened between

[53] *The letters of Arthur Schnitzler to Hermann Bahr*, ed. Donald G. Daviau, (Chapel Hill: University of North Carolina Press, 1978), 109–112.

[54] WSB 115.770.

[55] WSB 115.761.

[56] WSB 115.775.

[57] LBI.

poet and physician the nature of which we can only guess at, but it is difficult to know how seriously to take the claim that if only Dr. Hansy had accepted him, he would have gladly renounced beer.[58]

Altenberg understandably loathed Steinhof, and the fear of a return there haunted him for the rest of his life. Yet, as in Inzersdorf, so too in Steinhof he not only continued the work of assembling a new collection for publication, he also wrote fresh material, often of high quality.[59] The sadly lyrical "Der Rendezvous," dated 3 April 1913, was composed for the Munich journal *Jugend*, but never published. Even within the walls of his confinement Altenberg could still find the elements needed to fire his creative talents — nature and young girls. Above all, however, the text expresses first the impossibility of him realizing a relationship with the sort of girl who most attracted him, and second, the ensuing longing for a simple freedom in nature. It is published, probably for the first time, in appendix 2.

Altenberg's medical records in Steinhof are no longer extant, but some idea of his clinical condition can be gleaned from an essay in *Der Tag* of 21 September 1924 under the revealing pen-name "Custos." Probably written by someone treating Altenberg, besides describing life behind the walls it also gives a precise, if unintentionally funny, indication of his mental illness: an obsessive fear of constipation.[60] According to Custos, Altenberg had a legion of admirers and an army of female friends seeking to visit him in the Villa Austria, only the odd one of whom gained admission. This popularity made him happy, but when alone with those he trusted his mood swung and he would recite a litany of aches and pains; fear of being poisoned by the faithful warder Hennerbichler was a further concern. Altenberg's superficially good progress is confirmed in a letter from Alban Berg to Schoenberg on 16 April 1913. Berg had just made his teacher a present of *"Semmering 1912"*, having both bought a copy and received one from the author, and after a visit to the asylum he wrote that Altenberg was well and in good spirits. Berg intended going to Kraus's lecture that evening in the small hall of the Musikverein at which the satirist would read from *"Semmering 1912"*; it was even rumoured that Altenberg himself would appear to read some of his sketches.[61]

Ten days earlier, on 6 April, Bahr had written to Schnitzler concerning a letter in which Altenberg pleaded to be rescued from Steinhof. Perhaps remembering Altenberg's positive essay on him in the *Neues Wiener Journal* a year previously,[62] Bahr asked Schnitzler to intercede, offering help in any

---

[58] LBI

[59] For example: "Mein grauer Hut" (S^3 55), written on 8 March 1913 for Lilly St.(=Steiner); "Wasser im Garten" (N 85) written 27 March 1913.

[60] "Aus Peter Altenbergs düsteren Tagen," Kosler, *Peter Altenberg*, 178. A revealing portrait of everyday life inside Steinhof in 1919 can be found in Joseph Roth, "Die Insel der Unseligen. Ein Besuch in 'Steinhof'," *Das journalistische Werk 1915–1923*, ed. Klaus Westermann, (Cologne: Kiepenheuer and Witsch, 1989), 23–27.

[61] *The Berg-Schoenberg Correspondence. Selected Letters*, ed. Juliane Brand, Christopher Hailey and Donald Harris, (New York and London: W. W. Norton 1987), 173.

[62] Kosler, *Peter Altenberg*, 121–122.

way.[63] On 18 April Schnitzler replied that he too had received a letter from Altenberg, via Georg Engländer, also asking for help in getting out of Steinhof. Schnitzler had not seen Altenberg in over a year, but like Loos before him seriously doubted whether the poet was truly mad. Despite all the doctors had told him — and Schnitzler was himself a doctor — almost thirty years experience of Altenberg had made him skeptical about the genuineness of his insanity. Schnitzler considered Altenberg's release to be imminent, requiring neither a scandal nor an abduction.[64] In his diary for 20 April, Schnitzler noted visiting Steinhof, where Altenberg repeated his pleas for freedom. Schnitzler concluded that, as he had suspected, Altenberg was neither more nor less sane than he had ever been. He could stay locked up forever or be released immediately. Schnitzler was even invited to accept responsibility for Altenberg and accompany him to the Semmering for a few days, but this he refused to do.[65]

In a long letter to Bahr, written on 22 April after talking with Altenberg, his brother and his doctor, Schnitzler claimed to have gained a clear picture of the situation. Altenberg had been put in Steinhof initially because of alcohol-induced dementia, his subsequent paranoia being a consequence of the sudden and total abstinence from alcohol. Schnitzler found Altenberg to be mentally fresher than for a long time but agitated because he wanted to return to the Semmering. Schnitzler was sure his drinking would start up again, but the doctor in charge had nothing against Altenberg's release, as long as Georg Engländer assumed responsibility. Engländer would have preferred his brother return not to the Panhans, but to the Kurhaus, where he would be under modest medical supervision. Altenberg was now so institutionalized after five months in Steinhof that he even wanted to take his warder with him,[66] but Schnitzler told Bahr that he had observed none of the rumoured signs of degeneration. He reckoned that abstinence had done Altenberg good.[67] Schnitzler's coolly factual letter made no impression on Bahr, who replied with his own observations about Altenberg and withdrew the earlier offer of support.[68] On 25 April Schnitzler wrote to Bahr yet again with the news that Altenberg was to return to Dr. Hansy's detoxification center on the Semmering on Monday, 28 April, accompanied by his brother Georg.

Exactly two years after his release, Altenberg recalled the red motorcar driving up to the asylum to take him away to freedom, the heavy iron gates slowly opening and his brother enjoining him to be good. In a text revealing how much his self-destruction was a conscious act linked to his creativity,

[63] Daviau, *Schnitzler to Bahr*, 156.

[64] Ibid., 110.

[65] Arthur Schnitzler, *Tagebuch 1913–1916*, (Vienna: Akademie der Wissenschaften, 1983), 32.

[66] Altenberg later told Paula Schweitzer that Hennerbichler looked after him like a mother with a sick child (NF 321).

[67] Daviau, *Schnitzler to Bahr*, 110–111.

[68] Ibid., 155.

Altenberg writes that he would not be good, for it was a case of making up for seven months lost time behind prison walls. He would fall in love and go boozing, despite knowing that any recurrence of his alcoholism would be potentially lethal. He reported with childish pride:

> In derselben Freiheitsnacht war ich mit Anna, und trank 25 Flaschen Bier. Dann schrieb ich mein Buch "*Fechsung.*" (NF 222)[69]

> [That same night of freedom I was with Anna and drank 25 bottles of beer. Then I wrote my book "*Fechsung.*"]

In the posthumously published sketch "Der Bruder," the poet underscores the gulf separating him from the well-meaning, ever-concerned Georg Engländer, who apparently had no inkling of what was going on in Peter's head. Here again, Altenberg stylizes himself as a "poète maudit" for whom mental illness is something utterly natural. He claims that his demise is developing within him, as a matter of course, without any organic, insidious disease being present. There is something inherently destructive within him, and a brother's despair will not save him (N 45).

Altenberg had recovered well enough from his freedom binge to take the night-train to Trieste on 2 May 1913, accompanied by Adolf Loos and Bessie Bruce. His ecstatic reactions upon first seeing salt water are recorded in "Eindrücke" (S³ 217), and on the same day, 3 May, in a card to his brother Altenberg waxes lyrical about the laxative Rhamnin which was keeping both mind and bowels clear. Penciled in at the edge of the card is a note from Bessie that Peter is getting on marvellously.[70] Arriving in Venice on 4 May, he sent a string of happy postcards to Georg Engländer, including some written in late May as he toured through Padua, Levico, the Brenta valley and the Dolomites at the invitation of Frau Vallière (F 164). Ominously, however, a card from Venice dated 20 May 1913 suggests further money worries and an attachment not only to Rhamnin but also to the sleeping drug Paraldehyd, first prescribed to him in Steinhof. Both of them, he claimed, constitute "sacred" rejuvenation cures. It was the start of a spiraling addiction which, allied with his continuing alcohol abuse, would consume rather than rejuvenate him.[71]

An excellent swimmer, Altenberg took his first sea dip on 2 June, and two days later sent his brother a card describing sea-bathing as the most wonderful thing there is. Wearing Bessie Bruce's bathing costume, a white rubber cap and red raffia shoes,[72] he had himself photographed, hand on hip, in front of a wooden jetty. The picture is inscribed: "Show me how you are

---

[69] Anna may be Annie Weiß, who is mentioned in several cards written to Georg Engländer from Venice.

[70] GSE

[71] GSE. See also Springer, "Eine pathologische Skizze," 42–43.

[72] GSE

'built', and I shall tell you *who* you are."[73] Other photos of Altenberg and Kraus in their bathing suits, enjoying beach games on the Lido, suggest he lacked neither physical nor intellectual stimulation. In fact, Altenberg shared his holiday spot not only with Kraus and Loos but also with Georg Trakl, Ludwig von Ficker, Heinrich Mann, and Jakob Wassermann. Hermann Bahr celebrated his fiftieth birthday there, and in her delightful memoir Lotte Zavrel recalls that Altenberg was the darling of the beach, usurping Bahr who until then had been the "unchallenged lord of the sea and the isles" with his red and blue robes and Poseidon-like beard.[74]

For a memorable week in late August 1913, Venice played host not just to the *Brenner-Fackel* set but also to the "old guard" of the "Wiener Moderne" when S. Fischer and family shared their holiday with the Beer-Hofmanns and the Schnitzlers.[75] Altenberg mixed happily with them all.[76] His contacts with Trakl are recounted in two tantalizing snippets in *Nachfechsung*, where he shows little reverence for the dead by referring to "G. Tr." as a mediocre poet so entranced by Altenberg's diving abilities that he always addressed him as "Mr. Otter" Altenberg recalls feeling unable to return the compliment and address him as "Mr. Poet" (NF 177). In the other fragment we read what may be the transcript of a letter from Altenberg to Trakl linking athletic prowess, perhaps not Trakl's forte, with poetic creation:

> First show me that you can dive like an otter, do a dead straight hand-stand underwater, do a slow back-flip from the trampoline, walk backwards on stilts . . . like I can - - - and then I'll tell you whether or not you can *write poetry*. P.A. (NF 166)

Once again Altenberg displays here scant appreciation of a major figure not just in Austrian modernism, but European modernism as a whole. In *Vita Ipsa* Altenberg suggests that modern poets should all commit Harakiri on hearing Goethe's "Warte nur, balde ruhest Du auch!" (VI 22).

As in Vienna, Altenberg's bizarre Venetian exploits gave observers ample material for anecdotes. In her entertaining though inaccurate memoirs, which confuse Bessie Bruce with one of the Barrison sisters, the actress Tilla Durieux relates how some Viennese friends got together to provide Altenberg with a nurse, a pretty but coarse and ill-educated girl by the name of Bibiana Amon. Oblivious to the cultural treasures around her, Amon indulged her own enormous appetite while trying to prevent Altenberg from eating, on the grounds it was bad for his health. When he protested, she would gesticulate behind his back to the bemused waiters, tapping her brow to make the point clear. Yet again, his state of mind was willfully disregarded

[73] Historisches Museum der Stadt Wien, 94.618. Reproduced in *Otto Kallir, Ein Wegbereiter österreichischer Kunst*, (Vienna: Eigenverlag der Museen Stadt Wien, 1986), 47.

[74] Lotte Zavrel, "Peter Altenberg, wie ich ihn sah," *Vossische Zeitung*, 196 (1925): Unterhaltungsbeilage.

[75] Schnitzler, *Tagebuch 1913–1916*, 58.

[76] Brigitte B. Fischer, *Sie schrieben mir, oder was aus meinem Poesiealbum wurde*, (Munich: dtv, 1989), 39.

by those who set him up with this girl, who was herself exposed to the contempt of Altenberg's sophisticated companions. Durieux also describes a grotesque excursion by motorboat during which Bessie Bruce and Bibiana Amon came close to blows after Bibiana had suggested Bessie was a whore. All the while, the supposedly convalescent Altenberg cowered in a corner of the boot, whimpering that he felt sick and wanted to go home.[77]

Lotte Zavrel draws a vivid picture of this uncultured blonde girl, long-legged but pudgy with "schlampete Augen" [slovenly eyes] whose job it was to keep Altenberg sober. In Zavrel's recollections, however, Bibiana's name has been changed to Walpurga. Zavrel also tells a story about a boat trip, when Altenberg managed to catch the wrong vaporetto and instead of returning to the Lido ended up on an island housing the local mental asylum. Thanks to a German-speaking doctor he managed to extricate himself, exclaiming on his eventual return that he might have done better to stay there. Despite this reminder of a world he had just left, the early part of Altenberg's time in Italy appears to have been mostly happy and therapeutic, especially after a collection had raised enough money to return Bibiana to Vienna. By 10 September, however, things had gone sour, as this card to Georg Engländer confirms:

> Liebster Bruder, es geht mir nicht gut, weiß nicht, wie wegkommen. Schicke *300* Kr.! Venedig war die *schlimmste Idee! Man hat Freunde, pfui!*[78]

> [Dearest Brother, I am not well, don't know how to get away. Send *300* cr.! Venice was the *worst idea! And they say you've got friends?*]

In the revised version of *"Semmering 1912"* Altenberg commemorated his Venetian holiday with the last of his purportedly cyclical works. Called simply "Venedig," it is a cycle in name only. Disparate items are interrupted by a set of aphorisms and a throwback to the agonizing times of the recent past in "Sanatorium für Nervenkranke" (S 245). Other items written in and about Venice, which might have found a home in the cycle, are found scattered in his next book, *Fechsung*. In the "cycle" the city of Venice is hardly even a back-drop as the poet stammers out yet more agonies of unrequited longing for women he cannot have. Among them was the actress Mitzi Thumb, to whose charms he had succumbed totally. Thumb became a co-dedicatee of the revised book, figuring in pieces such as "Legende" (S 242), and later again in *Fechsung*. That Altenberg remained aware of reality emerges in a curt exchange with another woman who asks him who was the present object of his veneration. Mitzi Thumb, he answers, and she expresses surprise, enquiring whether his feelings were reciprocated:

---

[77] Tilla Durieux, *Eine Tür steht offen. Erinnerungen,* (Berlin: Non Stop Bücherei, 1954), 86–87; see also Hans Veigl, *Lokale Legenden. Wiener Kaffeehausliteratur,* (Vienna: Kremayr and Scheriau, 1991), 336. The subsequent career of Bibiana Amon, who became the lover of Anton Kuh amongst others, is related in Milan Dubrovic, *Veruntreute Geschichte,* (Vienna: Paul Zsolnay, 1985), 99–100.

[78] GSE

"Yes; she says she understands my passion!"
"That's all?!?"
"Yes, that's all!" (S 241)

Other titles like "Versäumtes Rendez-Vous," "Klage," "Jalousie" and "Verhängnis" perhaps indicate his true concerns in the city where "Gott Richard Wagner" breathed his last (S 217), but whose art treasures left him as cold as they did Bibiana Amon. As Altenberg wryly commented in *Fechsung*, people in Venice waste their money on old masters, churches and palazzi instead of concentrating on things which are more important: the blood-red, lilac-gray sunsets on the Lido and the folk costumes of the girls (F 50).

Altenberg's greatest pleasure was had at the beach, where he swam until his teeth chattered, watched the sunsets, admired women in varying states of undress and made a collection of seashells which he then characteristically gave away to a twelve-year-old girl, Martha-Maria (F 75). Simply letting sand slide through his fingers was a form of aesthetic ecstasy (S 219), and photographs of him playing beach-ball with Kraus reveal the pleasure he took in simply being at the seaside. He commemorates these days in "Le Lido," the very last piece in *"Semmering 1912"*. It is a collection of four smaller items, including a poem in French coolly relating how his emotional responses are most surely stirred by the young girls who endanger his sanity (S 247).

Venice having failed to provide the hoped-for recovery after the trauma of Inzersdorf and Steinhof, Altenberg now drank more than ever, his drug addiction became acute, and the sense of neglect was not assuaged by prestigious friends who sought his company. Ironically, however, examination of the cultural history of the dying Hapsburg Empire reveals that it was precisely at this period of well-publicized anguish that his renown would most clearly impact upon the work of creative artists whom posterity has ranked far higher than Altenberg himself.

6: Musical Postcards and Talking Apes

Altenberg and the "New Music" in Vienna

Like Altenberg himself, many of his friends and admirers felt he was famous for all the wrong reasons, but hindsight shows this assessment now requires revision. Although his personal problems did not diminish with age, the last half decade of his life did not lack professional recognition. In summer 1914 Altenberg was even nominated for the Nobel literature prize along with Arthur Schnitzler, but in the event no award was made that year. In contrast with Altenberg, who never referred to an honor which would have eased his money worries at a stroke, Schnitzler's reaction on hearing the news from Bertha Zuckerkandl was rather testy. In his diary for 1 August 1914 he shows no concern for great world events but expresses his own and his wife's disappointment at sharing the award, which had never before been split between two recipients.[1]

Although Schnitzler's irritation is understandable, it might not have been shared by the artistic community as a whole, where the impact of Altenberg's writing proved far more catalytic than Schnitzler's. This chapter therefore interrupts the narrative of Altenberg's career to focus attention upon the ways his work is reflected in some of the most innovative creations of the day: the short stories of Franz Kafka and the music of the Second Viennese School in general and the work of Alban Berg in particular.

Altenberg expressed his feelings about modernist art, literature and music in a letter to Loos, and they were not complimentary: "Deine Oskar Kokoschka- Else Lasker-Schüler- Arnold Schönberg Vorliebe beweisen (*sic*) genau den *Tiefpunkt* Deiner *geistig-seelischen Maschinerie*!"[2] [Your Oskar Kokoschka- Else Lasker-Schüler- Arnold Schönberg bias proves exactly the *nadir of your intellectual and spiritual machinery*!] Although Altenberg's own work challenged traditional aesthetic categories, his tastes generally reflected the increasingly conservative values of the assimilated German-Jewish bourgeoisie he hailed from. Intellectuals in late Hapsburg Austria did not easily tolerate opposing views, but for the court jester of their culture they clearly made an exception. In a culture so given to decorative artifice, Altenberg's love of nature, of children, of those unregarded everyday trifles from which he forged his poetic vision, had a particular appeal. For many he represented the true and the genuine. Hence even the extremely touchy Arnold Schoenberg seems to have taken no offense at Altenberg's unconcealed dislike of

---

[1] Arthur Schnitzler, *Tagebuch 1913–1916*, (Vienna: Akademie der Wissenschaften, 1983), 128.

[2] Willy Haas, "Aus unbekannten Altenberg-Briefen," *Forum* 8 (1961): 467–468.

"modern music."[3] Not only Schoenberg, but all the Viennese *Neutöner* knew Altenberg personally and, more importantly, reacted in a positive and often creative fashion to his writing.

Felix Greissle, son-in-law and student of Schoenberg, postulated in a Princeton lecture of 1959 that Altenberg's aphoristic brevity may well have influenced Schoenberg, Berg, and Webern in their predilection for attenuated musical forms.[4] Almost thirty years before that, David Josef Bach had ventured that the whole of Webern's work could be understood as the acoustic equivalent of *Wie ich es sehe*, a sort of "Wie ich es höre."[5] In spite of this, Altenberg's significance for this group of composers has attracted scant critical attention, and that mostly in the context of Alban Berg's Opus 4, *Fünf Lieder nach Ansichtskartentexten von Peter Altenberg*. It was their first performance at a concert conducted by Schoenberg in Vienna on 31 March 1913 which triggered off a riot and led to the occasion going down in musical history as the *Skandalkonzert*.

Despite an assertion to the contrary, Schoenberg never set Altenberg texts to music, nor, despite Bach's claim for the affinity between the two artists, did Webern.[6] This should not, however, be read as indifference on the part of either man. Despite Schoenberg's rocky finances he obtained in quick succession no fewer than six of Altenberg's books: *Bilderbögen des kleinen Lebens, Wie ich es sehe, Neues Altes, Pròdròmòs, "Semmering 1912"* and *Fechsung*.[7] By 1918 he apparently owned every book that Altenberg had published.[8] Furthermore, when reading other writers Schoenberg sometimes found the example of Peter Altenberg springing to mind, as in the following extract from Schopenhauer's *Parerga und Paralipomena* on the subject of authors and style (# 274.) Schopenhauer speaks of two sorts of book; where it is content-dominated:

> the characteristic feature is to be found in the *object*; and so the book can be important whoever its author may be.
> On the other hand, with regard to the What of a book, the characteristic feature is to be found in the author, the *subject*. The matters dealt with

---

[3] In conversation with the author, Edinburgh, June 1987, the anti-modernist Viennese composer Hans Gal condemned Altenberg as an embodiment of all that was wrong with Viennese coffeehouse culture.

[4] *Arnold Schoenberg and Wassily Kandinsky. Lectures, Pictures and Documents*, ed. Jelena Hahl Koch, trans. John C. Crawford, (London and Boston: Faber and Faber, 1984), 178, 201.

[5] David J. Bach, *Anton Webern zum 50. Geburtstag*, (Vienna: Verlag der IGNM [Sektion Österreich], 1934). Cited in Friedrich Wildgans, *Anton Webern*, trans. E. T. Roberts and H. Searle, (London: Calder and Boyes, 1966), 178.

[6] Michael P. Steinberg, "Jewish identity and intellectuality in fin-de siècle Vienna," *New German Critique*, 43 (1988): 28. For Webern's positive reception of Altenberg see Susanne Rode, *Alban Berg und Karl Kraus. Zur geistigen Biographie des Komponisten der "Lulu"*, (Frankfurt: Peter Lang, 1988), 100.

[7] Personal communication, Arnold Schoenberg Institute, University of Southern California.

[8] Hans H. Stuckenschmidt, *Arnold Schoenberg: His life and work*, trans. Humphrey Searle, (London and New York: Calder and Boyes, 1978), 183.

can be those that are accessible and known to everyone; but the form of interpretation, the What of the thinking, here imparts value to the book and is to be found in the subject. *And so if from this point of view a book is excellent and incomparable, so too is its author.* It follows from this that the merit of an author who is worth reading is the greater, the less this is due to the subject-matter.[9]

The highlighted sentence corresponds to underlining in Schoenberg's copy of the book, alongside which in the margin are inscribed two words: Peter Altenberg.

Some practical consequences of Schoenberg's interest in Altenberg may be audible in the *Drei Stücke* for chamber orchestra (1910) and the *Sechs kleine Klavierstücke* (1911), works whose composition coincided with the period when he was acquiring books by Altenberg. Although Schoenberg himself did not set Altenberg to music, it was also around this time that his disciples Alban Berg and Egon Wellesz did. Berg had set Altenberg as early as 1906 before turning to the picture postcard texts in 1912; Wellesz's setting of "Wie ein Bild" (WS 175) was performed in Budapest in 1910 in the presence of Bela Bartok and was instrumental in getting him a publisher in Budapest.[10] In the lapidary pieces for chamber ensemble and piano Schoenberg wrote music breathing the spirit of Altenberg, demonstrating particularly well that "synaesthesia of the arts in *fin de siècle* Europe which, through the crossing of boundaries and the mutual interchangeability of idiom, revealed many surprising relationships between painting, music, and literature."[11] In his desire to reduce music to its basics, Schoenberg reminds us not just of Altenberg's artistic practice but also of the programmatic call, in the introduction to *Wie ich es sehe*, for a new sort of literature to represent "l'huile essentielle de l'art, l'art bavard réduit en sobre silence" [the essential oil of art, garrulous art reduced to sober silence: WS X].

Schoenberg's intellectual debt to Kraus is well-known, but in the celebratory three-hundredth issue of *Die Fackel* Kraus showed his appreciation of the affinities between Schoenberg and Altenberg by printing on opposite pages the sketch "Widmung (Sommerabend in Gmunden)" and the manuscript facsimile of Schoenberg's Stefan George setting "Sprich nicht immer von dem laub" from *Das Buch der hängenden Gärten*.[12] Although Schoenberg chose to set other poets' works, his non-vocal miniatures seem often closer to Altenberg's literary manner than the gigantic orchestra in Berg's *Altenberg Lieder*.

At a personal level little is known of the relationship between Schoenberg and Altenberg, though their acquaintance may have gone back to the mid

[9] Arthur Schopenhauer, *Parerga and Paralipomena*, vol. 2, trans. E. F. J. Payne, (Oxford: Clarendon Press, 1974), 506.

[10] Egon Wellesz, *Wie ein Bild: Skizze von Peter Altenberg*, (Budapest: Rozsavolgyi, 1920).

[11] Nike Wagner, *Geist und Geschlecht. Karl Kraus und die Erotik der Wiener Moderne*, (Frankfurt: Suhrkamp, 1982), 37.

[12] Karl Kraus, *Die Fackel*, 300 (1910): 8–9.

1890s, when along with his future brother-in-law Alexander von Zemlinsky Arnold Schoenberg frequented the Café Griensteidl.[13] However, one exceptional, probably unique event is well-attested. When implored by Berg to support the public appeal in September 1911 on behalf of the near destitute Schoenberg, the miserly Altenberg, who disliked modern music, answered unequivocally and unreservedly: "Selbstverständlich und mit innerer Verpflichtung" [Naturally and with deep commitment].[14]

In 1918, shortly after the war had ended, and with only weeks to live, the ailing writer even travelled out to Mödling to visit Schoenberg at his home. What the stimulus for this visit may have been is not recorded, but it presumably betokens a mutual regard higher than that of Schoenberg's biographer who dubs Altenberg a loafer.[15] Writing to Berg shortly after the outbreak of hostilities in 1914, Schoenberg had mocked Altenberg's exaggerated enthusiasm for the war, expressed in a newspaper article entitled "Untergang des Franzosentums,"[16] but just how highly he thought of Altenberg emerged only after the writer's death. On 4 May 1923, fearing his friend Wassily Kandinsky might also have succumbed to Jew-hating, Schoenberg wrote an impassioned letter listing three Jews, all of whom happened to have been converted: Mahler, Altenberg and the composer himself:

> I ask: Why do people say that the Jews are like what their black-marketeers are like?
>
> Do people also say that the Aryans are like their worst elements? Why is an Aryan judged by Goethe, Schopenhauer and so forth? Why don't people say the Jews are like Mahler, Altenberg, Schoenberg and many others? [17]

Altenberg had been dead for almost seventeen years when Schoenberg's pupil Alban Berg succumbed to blood poisoning in December 1935 at the age of only fifty. In his graveside oration the writer Soma Morgenstern pointed out Altenberg's significance in the composer's life, claiming it went far beyond his role as poet of the Opus 4 songs. For Berg, he said, "was noble with the nobility of a new era which Peter Altenberg, its great prophet, had announced: with the nobility of naturalness."[18] Like Schoenberg, Berg owned practically every book by Altenberg; missing were just *Bilderbögen des kleinen Lebens* and *Ashantee*. Berg's relationship with Altenberg's writing had begun when Berg was still a very young man: in the summer of 1903, aged only eighteen, he wrote to Paul Hohenberg, expressing his delight that they

---

[13] Hans Graf, *Jede Stunde war erfüllt*, (Vienna and Frankfurt: Forum, n.d.), 153.

[14] Österreichische Nationalbibliothek, Musiksammlung, F 21 Berg 480–7.

[15] Stuckenschmidt, *Schoenberg*, 23.

[16] *The Berg-Schoenberg Correspondence. Selected Letters*, ed. Juliane Brand, Christopher Hailey and Donald Harris, (New York and London: W. W. Norton, 1987), 219.

[17] *Schoenberg and Kandinsky*, 79.

[18] Erich Alban Berg, *Der unverbesserliche Romantiker. Alban Berg 1885–1935*, (Vienna: Österreichischer Bundesverlag, 1985), 186.

shared the same literary tastes: Kraus and Altenberg.[19] In 1906 Berg wrote to his friend Watznauer of his fanatical love for nature as the basis of his existence. Many of the authors he had read evoked — or rather awakened — this reverence for nature and for this he thanked and venerated them, from Goethe through to Altenberg.[20]

Berg's personal acquaintance with Altenberg came about in 1906, thanks to his sister Smaragda, who counted as Altenberg's most refined female friend.[21] That same year Berg wrote the songs "Traurigkeit," "Hoffnung" and "Die Flötenspielerin" to words from *Was der Tag mir zuträgt* (WT 263–264). These minute texts — Altenberg calls them "Ganz kleine Sachen" — are already reminiscent in their concision of the picture-postcard texts Berg found six years later in *Neues Altes*. Although *Neues Altes* was not published until 1911, it is probable that the texts Berg chose for his songs date from around 1899–1900, exactly the same period as *Was der Tag mir zuträgt*. Probably unknown to Berg, the words of his early song "Die Flötenspielerin" also exist as a text Altenberg wrote on a picture-postcard.

When first published in the Munich journal *Jugend*,[22] "Die Flötenspielerin" was also illustrated, this time by a typically art-nouveau image of a girl playing what appear to be panpipes. More than a decade after Altenberg's death "Die Flötenspielerin" was republished in *Nachlese*, but whereas in *Was der Tag mir zuträgt* it is one of the "Ganz kleine Sachen," here it is specifically labelled as a picture-postcard text (NE 66). Thanks to Otto Kallir, the original postcard of the girl playing the shepherd's pipe is still extant. Dated 1899, it is addressed and dedicated to Emma Rudolf. On the reverse side is the poem, later slightly altered for publication in *Jugend* and *Was der Tag mir zuträgt*, where it was then presumably found by Berg.[23]

Thus, in a fashion impossible with the *Altenberg Lieder* proper, it is possible to follow here the cycle of a visual stimulus — itself representing a musical motif — leading to a verbal text leading to musical composition. Fortunately, the original manuscript of Altenberg's "Hoffnung" is also preserved,[241] but the words Berg found in *Was der Tag mir zuträgt* correspond only to the first stanza of the poem, occasioned by the death by cerebral hemorrhage of Alice Popper who, together with her sister Gusti, had the inspiration for the sketch "Neun und Elf" which opens *Wie ich es sehe*.[25]

[19] Rode, *Alban Berg*, 392. Despite this, Rode claims Berg's first indisputable reading of Altenberg was in May-June 1905 (99.)

[20] Rosemary Hilmar, *Alban Berg. Leben und Wirken in Wien bis zu seinen ersten Erfolgen als Komponist*, (Vienna, Cologne, and Graz: Böhlau, 1978), 38.

[21] Berg, *Der unverbesserliche Romantiker*, 181.

[22] *Jugend*, 24 (1900): 402.

[23] GSE

[24] GSE.

[25] The text of this poem can be found in Andrew Barker and Leo A. Lensing, *Peter Altenberg. Rezept die Welt zu sehen*, (Vienna: Braumüller, 1995), 407.

Although it remains conjectural whether Berg knew the circumstances surrounding the texts of his first Altenberg songs, of his intense occupation with *Was der Tag mir zuträgt* there can be no doubt. In his copy of the book, "Eine schweigende Runde" (WT 46) is covered with copious musical annotations which make clear that Berg associates his own subjectivity in counterpoint to his reading material.[26] His copy of *Vita Ipsa* is also covered with jottings and observations, an indication that Berg's interest did not wane over the years. As a young man the composer had harbored literary ambitions of his own, and it has even been suggested that Altenberg's singular style of punctuation, with its plethora of dashes, exclamation and question marks, had its effect upon Berg's literary manner.[27] At a thematic level Berg's handling of the complexities of female sexuality, above all in *Lulu*, reflects a fascination with a topic which obsessed early twentieth-century Austro-German culture and found repeated expression not only in Wedekind's work, but also in that of Berg's Viennese literary idols Karl Kraus and Peter Altenberg.

At the personal level there is no doubt that Berg was fascinated by Altenberg. Their paths crossed and re-crossed, most profoundly in Altenberg's feelings for the two women who for many years stood at the center of Berg's life: his sister Smaragda, and Helene Nahowski, whom Berg married in May 1911. Berg was well acquainted with Altenberg's obsession with Helene, for the poet was incapable of concealing his feelings about anything or anyone. In 1910–1911, after many months in Inzersdorf, Altenberg published homages to the soon-to-be Frau Berg in the third edition of *Märchen des Lebens* and then in *Neues Altes*, from which Berg then took the texts for his Opus 4 songs. The lyrical sketch "Besuch im einsamen Park" in *Märchen des Lebens*, soon reprinted in *Neues Altes*, and the poem "H. N." found only in *Neues Altes*, both refer to Altenberg's feelings for Helene during the time of his confinement.

The letters to Helene are now lost, but she must have fed his voracious appetite for picture-postcards, for in the early months of his confinement in Inzersdorf he sent a note thanking her for all the beautiful cards.[28] Dated 22 July 1910, it is preserved inside a copy of *Märchen des Lebens*, where Altenberg published "Besuch im einsamen Park," the sketch which pays tribute both to his passion for her and the effect she had upon him: "You came, Helene N., and everything came alive and blossomed forth" (ML[3] 225). Based on his experiences in Inzersdorf, where he was regularly visited by both Alban and Helene, "Besuch im einsamen Park" is a typically incandescent votive offering to an idolized woman soon to give herself to another man. That Alban and Helene ever found each other Altenberg ascribes solely to his own influence. In "Bekanntschaft," also published in *Neues Altes*, he

---

[26] Rode, *Alban Berg*, 19.

[27] Willy Reich, *The Life and Work of Alban Berg*, trans. Cornelius Cardew, (London: Thames and Hudson, 1965), 17–18.

[28] See also "Peter Altenberg als Sammler" (NA 191).

publicly (and perhaps preposterously) recalls shared conversations with both
Helene and the "noble youth" Alban, claiming that both sought his advice
on personal matters, and gave thanks to him for bringing them together (NA
88).

Berg's letters to his fiancée make several references to Altenberg, of
whom he never seems to have been in the least jealous. Frequently he is at
pains to establish parallels between himself and the poet, sometimes of a
touchingly trivial nature, as in the letter of 30 August 1909 where he establishes that they both bite their nails.[29] The best proof of Berg's positive assessment of the poet is of course his choice of texts for the Opus 4 songs.
This can be construed as the public recognition of Altenberg's role not only
in Berg's professional but also in his private life.

Berg began work on the songs in March 1912, finishing the first draft in
September, and while naturally mentioning his work in progress to Schoenberg, he could not initially pluck up the courage to show him the songs. Not
until 13 January 1913 did Schoenberg get to see them, having requested
from Berg two fairly short, fairly simple, orchestral songs for alto voice.[30] Despite Berg's uncertainties, above all in questions of orchestration, Schoenberg
apparently liked what he saw, greatly to Berg's relief. In a typically grovelling
letter of 17 January 1913 Berg expressed his relief at his teacher's approval
and his concern for the sick poet, whom he had recently visited in Steinhof:

> I saw Altenberg in Steinhof not long ago. His brother asked me to visit
> him. He's doing very poorly. The doctors call it paranoia. But it's an
> "inferno." He suffers dreadfully! Nonetheless, I hope he'll improve and will
> be able to work again.[31]

The riot during the first performance of the *Altenberg Lieder* on 31
March 1913 has gone down in musical history as a scandal comparable to
that caused by the premiere of Stravinsky's *Le sacre de printemps* in Paris just
a few weeks later. The concert's organiser Erhard Buschbeck found himself
in court after fisticuffs with the operetta composer Oscar Straus, who later
claimed that the thud of the punch was the most harmonious thing about
the whole concert.[32] Anton von Webern, who naturally had been present at
the concert, found the kerfuffle so distressing that he fled from Vienna to the
Adriatic resort of Portorose from where he wrote Berg a comforting letter
reminding him of a marvellous evening they had recently enjoyed with Al-

---

[29] For Altenberg's obsession with hands see Leo A. Lensing, "Peter Altenberg's Fabricated
Photographs," *Vienna 1900: From Altenberg to Wittgenstein*, ed. Edward Timms and Ritchie
Robertson, (Edinburgh: Edinburgh University Press, 1990), 47–72.

[30] *The Berg-Schoenberg Correspondence*, 140.

[31] Ibid., 145. For the original text see Rode, *Alban Berg* 18.

[32] Werner J. Schweiger: "Das Skandalkonzert im Wiener Musikverein," *Peter Altenberg
Almanach*, (Vienna: Löcker, 1987), 34–35. See also: David P. Schroeder, "Alban Berg und Peter
Altenberg: Intimate Art and the Aesthetics of Life," *Journal of the American Musicological Society*,
3 (1992): 261–293.

tenberg.[33] Reactions in the press were predictable. The anonymous critic "Veritas" of the *Wiener Mittags-Zeitung* dubbed Altenberg's texts "Afterpoesie" [anal poetry], a comment well up to the standard of a catcall during the concert itself, reported in the *Neues Wiener Tagblatt*, that all the idiots should be packed off to Steinhof.

It was common knowledge that Altenberg had only been permitted to leave the asylum in the company of a warder to attend the dress rehearsal in the morning. Yet while Altenberg might possibly have disapproved of the events at the concert, he probably would not have disagreed with the negative assessment of Berg's songs. Writing to Franz Schreker directly after the concert, he said before launching into praise of Schreker's wife that he understood nothing about "modern music." The composers which his "brainsoul" understood were Wagner, Wolf, Brahms, Dvořak, Grieg, Puccini and Richard Strauss.[34]

On 3 April, just three days after the *Skandalkonzert*, Altenberg composed a short prose sketch entitled "Alma" which can only refer to events he had witnessed at the dress-rehearsal. This sketch avoids any reference to Berg's settings of his words, concentrating instead on the frivolous reactions of Alma Mahler, a close friend of Alban and Helene Berg, during the rehearsal of her late husband's *Kindertotenlieder*. These songs were scheduled to conclude the public concert, but in the event had to be abandoned because of the rumpus caused by the *Altenberg Lieder*. The sketch depicts Alma Mahler dressed in widow's weeds, dallying with a young man while "the third Kindertotenlied wept" (F 231). In a few succinct lines Altenberg delivers a devastating cameo of Alma Mahler's facile reactions to the songs, which had eerily pre-dated the death of her daughter Anna Maria in 1906, an event which she apparently regarded as a punishment for their composition.[35] Although he is not named, the young man in the sketch can only be Oskar Kokoschka, whose affair with Alma Mahler was the talk of the town. As Altenberg well knew, he would be instantly recognized by the contemporary Viennese readership with a well-trained nose for scandal.[36] Altenberg's garrulous miniature was not, however, published until 1915, along with a dedication to Gustav Mahler conspicuously absent from the original manuscript.

---

[33] Hans Moldenhauer, *Anton von Webern. A chronicle of his life and works*, (London: Victor Gollancz, 1978), 172.

[34] *Peter Altenberg Almanach*, 35. Altenberg attended a performance of Schreker's ballet *Die Geburtstag der Infantin* which opened the Vienna "Kunstschau" of 1908. He praised the performance of the Wiesenthal sisters, cited Wilde as originator of the text, but failed to mention Schreker's name. His sole comment on the music is that it is "suitable" (B 124).

[35] Kurt Blaukopf, *Mahler*, (London: Allen Lane, 1973), 198. Blaukopf also numbers Altenberg among the "Mahler clique" in Vienna (219).

[36] The original manuscript is now in the WKA. The sketch was placed in an envelope addressed to "Herrn *Adolf Loos*, Architekt, für Oskar Kokoschka, Maler, Semmering an der Südbahn Hotel Panhans." It is not known whether Loos ever delivered the manuscript to Kokoschka.

The entire sketch, but especially the dedication, must have been intentionally provocative, especially as Alma Mahler had by then split with Kokoschka and taken up with the German architect Walter Gropius, a leading light in the Bauhaus movement. She went to law, and the sketch disappeared from all further editions of *Fechsung*.[37] Altenberg was obviously irritated by Alma's reactions, and though forced to withdraw the offending text, managed in effect to work it in to his next book *Nachfechsung* in the sketch "Hoher Gerichtshof." Not only does he gloss "Alma", he also provides an interpretation of his own sketch — it is concerned with the contrast between the ideal and life itself — and an assessment of Kokoschka's character: he is a nice, sympathetic young man (NF 157).

Although Altenberg reportedly told a correspondent he had been moved to tears by Berg's settings of his words,[38] the list of composers in his letter to Schreker is most revealing. They reflect his love for musicians who were modern, even "progressive," during Altenberg's formative years in the 1880s and 90s, but who, insofar as they were still alive (Puccini, Richard Strauss) had failed to go down the trail of modernism blazed by Schoenberg and his pupils. Earlier composers whom he venerated (especially Beethoven and Schubert) he fails to mention, and as usual for Altenberg, it is as if Mahler had never existed. In his musical appreciation Altenberg was thus fairly representative of the educated Viennese *Bildungsbürgertum* of the early twentieth century. The old Wagner-Brahms quarrel was now a thing of the past, as Altenberg realized when he said that Hugo Wolf was exceedingly important for the "development of the modern soul," but that Johannes Brahms was equally important (LA 289). However, even amongst musically receptive members of the non-musical avant-garde, developments in the New Music met with only minimal understanding. Hence of the trio Altenberg-Kraus-Loos, to which in the faction-ridden climate of Vienna the other triumvirate Schoenberg-Berg-Webern felt most drawn, Altenberg disliked modern music while Karl Kraus's musical sympathies seemed to stop with Jacques Offenbach; alone of the three only Adolf Loos fully supported the *Neutöner* and he, as was gleefully pointed out, was as deaf as a post.

Franz Kafka and Peter Altenberg

As the example of Franz Kafka shows, Altenberg's impact was felt not just in Vienna, but also in Prague. However, Kafka suffered so long from the ahistoricism of his critics that few attempts were made to see him in the context of literary or cultural history. Only in the 1980s did it begin to emerge how inappropriate it was to regard Kafka as an isolated genius whose works came out of thin air.[39] It is now obvious that the texture of Kafka's novels and sto-

---

[37] "Alma" is reprinted in Barker and Lensing, *Rezept*, 199–200.

[38] Gert Mattenklott, "Peter Altenbergs Postkarten," *Hofmannsthal Blätter*, 27 (1983): 91.

[39] Bert Nagel, *Kafka und die Weltliteratur. Zusammenhänge und Wechselbeziehungen*, (Munich: Winkler, 1983); Hartmut Binder, *Kafka. Der Schaffensprozeß*, (Frankfurt: Suhrkamp, 1983);

ries is indebted to world literature from Yiddish theater to French pornography, but only recently has it emerged how great the influence of contemporary Viennese intellectual debate was on Kafka's mindset. Kafka's library as described by Klaus Wagenbach nevertheless gives little indication of him possessing much of the literature produced on his doorstep, for apart from a healthy stock of works by his friend Max Brod, Kafka possessed little by other major Austro-German writers of the early twentieth century. There are three items by his fellow Prague writer Franz Werfel, but there is no Rilke, Bahr or Hofmannsthal, and no Beer-Hofmann, a writer whose strong interest in Jewish themes conceivably might have attracted Kafka. Theodor Herzl is represented by a single volume of his diaries dated 1922, and from the same year comes a copy of Stefan Zweig's *Jeremias*. Of Karl Kraus there remains no trace, although Kafka is known to have read *Die Fackel* avidly. Apart from Schnitzler's *Professor Bernhardi* the only Viennese writers represented are Anton Wildgans, Rudolf Kassner, Kraus's enemy Stefan Großmann — and Peter Altenberg. Altenberg, however, is represented by two substantial works, *Wie ich es sehe* (5th ed., 1910) and *Märchen des Lebens* (3rd ed., 1911).[40]

Superficial evidence for links between Kafka and Altenberg is surprisingly easy to come by. The Grabenhotel in the Dorotheergasse, where Altenberg lived on returning from Venice in autumn 1913, bears one of the many plaques in Vienna commemorating the cultural significance of a particular locus. The plaque informs passers-by that Peter Altenberg lived in this hotel between 1913 and 1919 and that Franz Kafka and Max Brod stayed there on several occasions. Of all the hostelries at their disposal, the two friends thus chose to stay at the modest lodgings of the writer synonymous with the Bohemian culture of the Kaffeehaus, notorious for his alcoholism, strange sexuality and Jewish self-loathing.

Whether Kafka met Altenberg during his stays at the Graben Hotel is not recorded, though common sense suggests the strong possibility of personal contact. The link would have been Max Brod, who first met Altenberg at the Cabaret Fledermaus. He recalls how *Ashantee* was a source of comfort to him as a young man,[41] recounting in his autobiography how Altenberg once offered to act as an intermediary between himself and Kraus during one of

Ritchie Robertson, *Kafka. Judaism, Politics and Literature*, (Oxford: Clarendon Press, 1987); Mark Anderson, *Kafka's Clothes. Ornament and Aestheticism in the Habsburg Fin de Siècle*, (Oxford: Clarendon Press, 1992). Anderson notes: "With his interests in reform clothing, vegetarianism, and physical culture, together with his cult of 'pure poetry', Altenberg provides an intriguing parallel to the '*Jugendstil*' Kafka." (25.) The present chapter is adapted from Andrew Barker, "Franz Kafka and Peter Altenberg," *Turn-of-the-century-Vienna and its legacy. Essays in honor of Donald G. Daviau*, ed. Jeffrey B. Berlin, Jorun B. Johns, Richard H. Lawson, (Vienna: Edition Atelier, 1993), 221–238.

[40] Klaus Wagenbach, *Franz Kafka. Eine Biographie seiner Jugend 1883–1912*, (Bern: Francke, 1958), 251–63; according to Hartmut Binder, Kafka's impecuniosity prevented him from buying many books until about 1911 ("Kafka und *Die neue Rundschau*," *Jahrbuch der deutschen Schiller-Gesellschaft*, 12 (1968): 96.)

[41] Josef Fraenkel, *The Jews of Austria*, (London: Valentine and Mitchell, 1967), 242.

their feuds.[42] Altenberg, however, refers neither to Kafka nor to Brod, and there are no references to Altenberg in Kafka's writing. On the other hand, in a conversation with Gustav Janouch from around 1920, Kafka reportedly made remarks indicating a positive attitude towards Altenberg:

> His little anecdotes reflect his entire life. And every step, every gesture he makes guarantees the veracity of his words. Peter Altenberg is a genius of trivialities, a strange idealist, who discovers the beauties of the world like cigarette-ends in the ashtrays of cafés.[43]

Despite such clues, previous critics have only rarely suggested possible links between the two authors.[44] Overall, the failure to examine the Kafka-Altenberg connection reflects a predominantly synchronic perception of literary worth; because Kafka is considered much more significant than Altenberg, it is assumed that in Kafka's day a similar judgment must also have applied. Kafka is important, so he is read; Altenberg is not, so his work remains mostly unavailable. Yet looking at Kafka's initial reception, it is difficult to overlook the references to Altenberg when critics were trying to formulate opinions about the radical novelty of Kafka's writing. As Jürgen Born remarks, they have an openness towards the texts which we no longer possess.[45] Perhaps later Kafka commentators have looked no further into the link with Altenberg because these reviews sometimes bear out later received value judgments; "ein etwas ramponierter Könner" [a rather tired old trooper] is one of the less flattering assessments of Altenberg by an early Kafka critic.[46]

Altenberg, it was felt, had not developed, his work was stuck in the groove of the prose miniature, the prose poem and the aphorism, while his personal crises of paranoid dementia and drug abuse made headline news. Should Wagenbach's catalogue of Kafka's library have tempted any researcher on "Kafka and World Literature," or even "Kafka and German Literature," into looking for evidence of Kafka reading Altenberg, neither *Wie ich es sehe* nor *Märchen des Lebens* seems to offer much. Yet can it be mere coincidence that several early reviewers of Kafka perceived similarities between the two writers? Could they have known things which today's critics do not? The answer is to widen the examination of Altenberg to works other than the surviving two from Kafka's library. After all, the list of Kafka's books was not compiled until ten years after his death, and is described by Wagenbach himself as fragmentary.[47]

---

[42] Max Brod, *Streitbares Leben, 1884–1968*, (Munich, Berlin, Vienna: F. A. Herbig, 1969), 116.

[43] Gustav Janouch, *Conversations with Kafka*, (London: André Deutsch, 1971), 79–80.

[44] Heidrun Graf-Blauhut, *Sprache: Traum und Wirklichkeit. Österreichische Kurzprosa des 20. Jahrhunderts*, (Vienna: Braumüller, 1983), 194; Hartmut Binder, *Kafka*, 96; W. G. Sebald, "Peter Altenberg, Le paysan de Vienne," (*Neue Rundschau* 100, no. 1 [1989]: 91–92).

[45] *Franz Kafka. Kritik und Rezeption zu seinen Lebzeiten 1912–1924*, ed. Jürgen Born, (Frankfurt: Fischer, 1979), 177.

[46] Ibid., 42.

[47] Wagenbach, *Franz Kafka*, 251.

1913 was the year both of Kafka's literary emergence and of Peter Altenberg's incarceration in Steinhof. In February, Brod's review of Kafka's *Betrachtung* mentioned Altenberg, but only to deny any similarity of Altenberg's work with Kafka's; in April Albert Ehrenstein finished his review with a comparison of Kafka and Altenberg. (In 1922 Ehrenstein produced an exquisite essay on Altenberg for Gustav Krojanker's *Juden in der deutschen Literatur*, which Kafka possessed). In June 1913 H. E. Jacob's review of *Der Heizer* first refers to Altenberg in the context of *Betrachtung*, while in August Paul Friedrich's review of *Betrachtung* starts by comparing Kafka with Peter Altenberg.[48] Given the miniaturist nature of Kafka's first publication, and the relative stature of the reluctant debutant with an established literary presence, the comparisons are not unduly surprising, especially as the title *Betrachtung* bears a generic similarity to *Wie ich es sehe*. Moreover, Altenberg was in the news in 1913, not just because of his confinement, but also as the author of the texts of Berg's *Altenberg Lieder* and their scandalous first performance. *Neues Altes*, the source of Berg's texts, was published in 1911, as was the edition of *Märchen des Lebens* in Kafka's possession. His copy of *Wie ich es sehe* dated from the year before. Assuming Kafka bought the books when they appeared, 1910–12 must have been a time when he took an interest in Altenberg. But here he was scarcely alone. Would it then be stretching credibility too far to suggest *Neues Altes* is a book Kafka might have known? After all, what modern student of Kafka glancing down the contents page of *Neues Altes* could fail to sit up on seeing consecutive sketches entitled "Der Affe Peter" (NA 73) and "Ungeziefer" (NA 75)?

"Der Affe Peter" is initially a series of reflections upon the tricks of the performing ape Peter, and the more general relationship between animals and their trainers. At the level of primary content there are thus obvious parallels between this text and Kafka's "Ein Bericht für eine Akademie." Both writers were fascinated by the circus,[49] and after his capture and shipment to Europe from the Gold Coast, Kafka's Rotpeter, the "Menschenaffe" who tries to be human, ends up as a circus performer just like Altenberg's ape Peter. In fact, Kafka's ape bears the name Rotpeter specifically to distinguish him from "the performing ape Peter who died not so long ago and had some small local reputation." Though Rotpeter despises Peter, he chooses an identical career:

---

[48] Born, *Franz Kafka*, 32.

[49] "Variété" (NA 33) also shows some affinities with Kafka's "Auf der Galerie." It should pointed out that Altenberg and Kafka may have drawn on common sources in their depiction of humanized apes. In the German Märchen tradition it is not unusual for animals to turn into people and vice versa. More specifically, there are two stories which show a similar pattern to that observable in Altenberg and Kafka: Wilhelm Hauff's "Der Affe als Mensch," and E. T. A. Hoffmann's "Nachricht von einem gebildeten jungen Mann."

> I said to myself: do your utmost to get onto the variety stage; the Zoologi-
> cal Gardens means only a new cage; once there you are done for.[50]

For many contemporary readers, the words "Der Affe Peter" would have
suggested a sketch about Peter Altenberg himself. The title is typical of the
mocking tones in which the author frequently wrote about himself, and in
which he was perceived by others. Parodying the popular perception of Altenberg around 1909, Robert Musil also resorts to animal similes:

> He's at his greatest when the object of derision. If a girl says to him: "Be a
> dear, Peter, the Baron wants to come to Paula tonight, lie down just this
> once in the servants' room," then Peter goes to the wonderfully beautiful,
> noble maid like a wise and kind elephant, like a serious and pensive tapier
> and gets into the servants' bed.[51]

On initial reading of "Der Affe Peter," however, it emerges that the Peter
referred to is not the expected Altenberg, but rather a performing human
ape, "really one of nature's miracles" (NA 73), whose apparently innate skills
and tricks entrance the narrator. After descriptions of Peter's accomplish-
ments come comments on the relationship between performing animals and
their human trainers. It is not always clear, though, whether the narrative
perspective is that of the ape or that of the narrator. Various comments on
dog-handlers and equestrian trainers, during which the ape Peter is no longer
discussed, are then interrupted with a recommendation:

> Mit einem der Menschenaffen wie Peter aber muß ein tiefes freundschaftli-
> ches echtes Verhältnis entstehen. Er speist nach der Vorstellung im Restau-
> rant wie ein wohlerzogener Mensch. (NA 74)
>
> [With one of the human apes like Peter there has to be a genuinely pro-
> found and friendly relationship. After the performance he eats in the restau-
> rant like a well-brought up person.]

The reader is thrown into confusion, for Peter's identity is no longer unambiguously that of the ape. Playing upon his penchant for talking about himself in his texts, Altenberg has deliberately thrown the question of identity
into doubt. For here is not a comment upon the needs of the ape Peter, but
rather a self-referential comment by the author Peter Altenberg, whose self-
identification with the performing ape bearing his name is overwhelming.
Such is his sense of insecurity and inferiority that he invites the confusion of
himself with something less than human, he perceives himself not as a true
"Mensch" but merely as a "Menschenaffe." Those in agreement with Ritchie
Robertson's analysis of "Ein Bericht für eine Akademie," which follows an
interpretation first suggested by Max Brod, may well find in Altenberg's

[50] Franz Kafka, *The collected short stories of Franz Kafka*, ed. Nahum N. Glatzer, (London:
Penguin, 1988), 257–258.

[51] Robert Musil, "P.A. und die Tänzerin," *Gesammelte Werke*, vol. 7, *Kleine Prosa, Aphorismen,
Autobiographisches*, ed. Adolf Frisé, (Reinbek bei Hamburg: Rowohlt, 1978), 714.

sketch from 1911 manifestations of the same quandary which exercised Kafka, that of Jewish assimilation into Gentile society.[52]

Hartmut Binder has pointed out that the *Prager Tagblatt* of 17 September 1908 carried a report of a performance by a trained ape called Konsul Peter. A day later the paper reported on his life outside the ring, exhorting readers to watch him eat in the theater restaurant after the performance. "It's just too hilarious," the report goes on, "when after eating like a well brought up person, with a grin he wipes his — let's call it mouth, with a serviette."[53] The verbal parallels with "Der Affe Peter" are clear and perhaps explicable. For many years Altenberg reported on cabaret and "Variété" for the *Wiener Allgemeine Zeitung*, hence it is very possible that, should this circus act have visited Vienna, Altenberg would have been present at a performance. He would also have been aware of the ape Peter's social habits. Indeed, he even seems to have been introduced to his "alter ego" personally, reporting how the ape offered him his hand, and even wanted to press it gently to his lips (NA 74). It is of course possible Kafka also read the *Prager Tagblatt*, though it is not very likely he would still have a copy from 1908 when composing his story in the summer of 1917. More likely is that he had a copy of *Neues Altes* available.

Binder finds strong echoes of Rotpeter's liking for alcohol in Karl Hagenbeck's *Von Tieren und Menschen* (1914) and we will recall that Rotpeter's account of himself begins with his capture by one of Hagenbeck's expeditions to West Africa. More persuasively still, Sebald quotes a passage from the sketch "Alkohol" in *Pròdrŏmŏs*:

> Alkohol füllt die schreckliche Kluft aus zwischen dem, was wir sind, und dem, was wir sein *möchten*, sein *sollten*! *Werden müssten*! Als der Affe erkannte, daß er ein *Mensch* werden *könnte*, begann er zu saufen, um den Schmerz seines Noch-Affe-Seins hinwegzuschwemmen. (P 119–120)

> [Alcohol fills the appalling abyss between what we are and what we should *like* to be, *should* be! *Ought to become*! When the ape recognised that he *could* become a human being he started to drink, to wash away the pain of still being an ape.]

Sebald concludes that this "contains the complete aetiology of Altenberg's own alcoholism which nightly helped him to his own metamorphoses."[54] He might have pointed out that the item in *Pròdrŏmŏs* following "Alkohol" is also concerned with the metamorphosis of ape into man. Cast in the form of a parable, it could be read as a reflection upon the ongoing debate within Western Jewry about assimilation, reflected in works as diverse in their recommendations as Herzl's *Der Judenstaat* and Rathenau's *Höre, Israel*! The parable, in a which an ape with a lighter skin than the others exhorts his fellow apes to walk upright, ends not quite with a "Bericht für eine Akademie,"

---

[52] Robertson, *Franz Kafka*, 164–165.

[53] Binder, *Kafka. Der Schaffensprozeß*, 299.

[54] Sebald, "Le paysan de Vienna," 92.

but with a "Broschüre" by an academic ape entitled "Die Décadence und ihre Gefahren" [Decadence and its dangers: P 120]

In Kafka's "Ein Bericht für eine Akademie" there is no such direct association of the author with the ape Rotpeter as in Altenberg's "Der Affe Peter." Kafka's story may be read not just as a disturbing reflection upon Jewish assimilation in general, but also as a commentary upon the experiences of a Jewish artist (viz. Franz Kafka) entering upon a public career in a non-Jewish environment. In the latter case, certain passages assume added significance in the light of Altenberg's biography at the time when Kafka was producing the prose miniatures of *Betrachtung*. Could it be that when the ape Rotpeter addresses the academicians, Kafka in typically self-accusatory terms obliquely acknowledges his debt to Altenberg?:

> And so I learned things, gentlemen. Ah, one learns when one has to; one learns when one needs a way out; one learns at all costs. One stands over oneself with a whip; one flays oneself at the slightest opposition. My ape nature fled out of me, head over heels and away, so that my first teacher was almost himself turned into an ape by it, had soon to give up teaching and was taken away to a mental hospital. Fortunately he was soon let out again.[55]

It is conceivable that with a characteristically exaggerated sense of guilt, Kafka reflects here upon his own early career, when his exposure to Peter Altenberg's writing coincided with Altenberg's well-publicized stays in various asylums from 1910 onwards.

In "Ein Bericht für eine Akademie," Rotpeter's nights are sweetened by a "semi-tamed female chimp" of whom he is more than a little ashamed because her wild ways are a constant reminder of his own proximity to the jungle. For Robertson this is a clear allusion to the embarrassment felt by Jews seeking assimilation when reminded of their near past by the exotically dressed *Ostjuden*.[56] Just as well-known as his problematic relationship with his mercantile Jewish background, which he tried to conceal by change of name and conversion to Christianity, were Altenberg's difficulties with women. This may have been known to Kafka, whose life was rich in similar problems. At the end of "Der Affe Peter" an attempt is made to re-establish a gap between Peter the ape and Peter Altenberg by changing the narrative stance from the third to the first person. The outcome is, however, exceedingly ambiguous:

> Die wunderbare Schimpansin Maja im Tiergarten, 1896, haßte jede Dame, die in meiner Gesellschaft oder gar in mich eingehängt ihr Zimmerchen betrat, und drängte sie weg, umarmte mich absichtlich stürmisch und liebevoll. Ich glaube, es war das einzige weibliche Wesen, das an mir ernstlich Gefallen fand. (NA 74)

---

[55] Kafka, *Stories*, 154. The most comprehensive survey of Kafka's animal figures is Karl-Heinz Fingerhut, *Die Funktion der Tierfiguren im Werk Franz Kafkas. Offene Erzählgerüste und Figurenspiel*, (Bonn: Bouvier, 1969). Fingerhut makes no reference to Altenberg.

[56] Robertson, *Franz Kafka*, 168–169.

[The wonderful chimpanzee Maja at the zoo, in 1896, hated every lady who entered her little room in my company or on my arm, pushed her away, embraced me in an intentionally ardent and affectionate way. I believe this was the only female creature to take serious pleasure in me.]

In the very year Richard Engländer made public his own "Verwandlung" into Peter Altenberg with the publication of *Wie ich es sehe* (1896) the unforgotten female chimpanzee saw in the changeling not homo sapiens, but a fellow ape. Her reactions, and Altenberg's ongoing memories, show that his attempts at assimilation failed. Maja is not fooled, and neither are "real" women. The outcome is sexual isolation, for in the eyes of the world he wants to live in, Peter Altenberg *is* "der Affe Peter."

Part of Altenberg's attractiveness for Kafka may have lain in the very openness with which he paraded neurosis and disappointment. Should Kafka indeed have known "Der Affe Peter," "Alkohol" and "Parabel" and drawn on aspects of them for his own story, this would provide a further ironic twist in the debate about Jewish assimilation to which "Ein Bericht für eine Akademie" is already an ironic contribution. The Darwinian notion of mimicry, seemingly exemplified in Rotpeter's desire to become human, "was frequently applied to the process by which Jews assimilated to their host society, shedding their Jewish traits and assuming the manners of their environment in a form of protective camouflage which, it was hoped, would eventually become second nature."[57] A charge often levelled at Jews by anti-Semites, however, and one of which Kafka will have been well aware, was that they were utterly derivative and uncreative. Otto Weininger, for example, believed that Jewishness was incompatible with the notion of genius. In response to Altenberg's texts, however, a Jewish genius, Kafka, may have produced one of his subtlest stories, one dealing with Jewish mimicry, in a derivative fashion. That Altenberg, the host for this parasitism (if such it is) was himself an anti-Semitic Jew is not without further irony. That "Ein Bericht für eine Akademie" was first published in Martin Buber's *Der Jude* is the crowning irony.

That Kafka was a literary magpie cannot seriously be doubted. His stories utilized, consciously or unconsciously, an astonishing array of written as well as personal material, and that Altenberg belonged to those sources seems confirmed by "Ungeziefer" which follows directly after "Der Affe Peter" in *Neues Altes.* Can it be just coincidence that there are two adjacent pieces referring to forms of metamorphosis, one featuring the "Menschenaffe" which is at the heart of Kafka's "Ein Bericht für eine Akademie," and the other revolving around the metaphor of the "Menschenwanze" [human bug], the dominant motif in "Die Verwandlung"? Coincidentally, at precisely the time Kafka composed "Die Verwandlung" in late 1912, Altenberg's confinement in Steinhof was making the news.

In compositional terms, "Die Verwandlung" predates "Ein Bericht für eine Akademie" by some years, and shows less response to Altenberg's texts

[57] Ibid., 165.

at a thematic level. Whereas in "Der Affe Peter" the stimulus from Altenberg's text to Kafka's appears demonstrable in terms of both theme and motif, in "Ungeziefer" the link is less direct, evident at the level of metaphor
and vocabulary rather than content. The derogatory term "krepieren," for
instance, which Kafka's Rotpeter applies to the ape Peter is used by Altenberg in "Ungeziefer," and it occurs again in "Die Verwandlung" when the
servant finds the dead Gregor Samsa: "Sehen Sie nur mal an, es ist krepiert;
da liegt es, ganz und gar krepiert!"[58] [Just look there, it's kicked the bucket;
it's lying there, it's absolutely kicked it!] In Kafka's work "Zimmer" [room]
is generally a metaphor for imprisonment, and in Altenberg's text the notions of a nocturnal insect and of vermin in a room are found side by side in
the same sentence. The text is short enough to reproduce in its entirety:

Ungeziefer
  Alle hatten sie gern, sie amüsierte, und war anders wie die meisten. Da-
her nützte man sie aus.
  Von Tag zu Tag sah sie schlechter aus, wie eine Besiegte in der Schlacht
des Lebens, die sich verwundet wegschleicht, hinter einem Busche zu
krepieren - - -.
  Da sagte der Dichter: "Nun, können Sie es mir nicht klagen?!"
  "Ich wohne, bitte, in einem Zimmer, wo Wanzen sind. Man erträgt alles tagsüber von den Menschen, und nachts benehmen sich die Wanzen
ebenso schamlos-feig und stören uns - - -. Da bricht man halt zusammen."
  Der Dichter machte eine Kollekte, steuerte aber selbst vorsichtig ein
Paket Insektenpulver bei.
  Er sagte: "Für *diese* Tiere gibt es Mittel; aber für die *Menschenwanzen*
gibt es keine. Ihre Nachtruhe ist nunmehr gesichert, Fräulein; aber *Tages-
ruhe* gibt es nicht. Da sind die *Menschenwanzen* unausrottbar an der Ar-
beit!" (NA 75)

[Vermin
  They all liked her, she was fun, and different from most of them. That's
why she was exploited.
  She looked worse by the day, like someone vanquished in the battle of
life who crawls away wounded to peg out behind a bush - - -.
  The poet said: "Now, can't you tell me about your woes?!"
  "If you please, I live in a room with bugs. By day you put up with everything from people, and by night the bugs are just as shameless and cow-
ardly and disturb us - - -. You simply cave in."
  The poet raised some money for her, but to be on the safe side he
added a packet of insect powder to it.
  He said: "You can do something about *these* creatures; but for *human
bugs* you can't do anything. Your night's rest is now secured, young lady;
but you'll get no rest by *day*. Then the *human bugs* are at work, and there's
no getting rid of them!"]

---

[58] Franz Kafka, *Sämtliche Erzählungen*, ed. Paul Raabe, (Frankfurt: Fischer 1973), 96.

Altenberg's "Ungeziefer" and Kafka's "Die Verwandlung" are very different sorts of writing, though both have as their subject the exploited individual. What Altenberg's text might well provide, however, is a link between the metaphor of "Ungeziefer" already used by Kafka prior to the writing of his story, and the unfolding and expansion of that metaphor into the central, dominant image of the story, the transformation of Gregor Samsa into a "Menschenwanze." This is not, of course, a term used by Kafka who, unlike his critics, scrupulously avoided any close definition of what it is that Samsa has outwardly become. In a fragment of 1910 Kafka had already used the "Ungeziefer" image to characterize a hermit, whilst a few months prior to the composition of "Die Verwandlung" Hermann Kafka had compared his son's friend Jizchak Löwy with vermin.[59] In German as in English the term "Ungeziefer" is unspecific, but in Altenberg's "Ungeziefer" he might conceivably have found the verbal connection which helped to trigger off his most celebrated narrative achievement.

The theme of both literal and metaphorical transformation which Altenberg adumbrates in "Der Affe Peter" and in "Ungeziefer" and which Kafka expands so greatly in "Ein Bericht für eine Akademie" and "Die Verwandlung" is also present in Kafka's "Ein Hungerkünstler." As the hunger artist's status declines, he increasingly resembles the other caged animals in the circus, eventually being carried out from his cage in the bundle of old straw, where, like an animal, he had slept and died. Similarities with the scene in "Die Verwandlung" where the dead vermin-Gregor is disposed of spring readily to mind, just as the theme of the cage provides a parallel with "Ein Bericht für eine Akademie." "Ein Hungerkünstler" is a late work (1922) yet it demonstrates the ongoing stimulus which Peter Altenberg's sketches provided for Kafka's literary creativity.

Published in 1909, *Bilderbögen des kleinen Lebens* contains the sketch with the most obviously Kafkaesque title, "Die Hungerkünstlerin", but like "Der Affe Peter" and "Ungeziefer," it is featured in none of the various Altenberg anthologies. The parallels between Altenberg's sketch and Kafka's story may be gauged from the following extended extract from Altenberg's "Die Hungerkünstlerin":

> Fräulein *Mrotek*, in *Berlin*, hungert bereits 16 Tage lang, in einem Kristallkasten, der Beobachtung ununterbrochen ausgesetzt.
>
> Irgendein merkwürdiges und unbekanntes Schicksal in ihrem jungen blühenden Leben muß ihr die Mahnung erteilt haben, wie ein "innerliches Wort Gottes", daß es ein besseres, ein reineres, ein seelischeres Leben gebe als das, das der in Verlogenheiten versunkene Alltagsmensch führe!
>
> Und so begann sie zu "*hungern*", d. h. ihrem Körper, dieser Edelmaschine allererster Ordnung, das zu *entziehen*, wessen er absolut nicht *bedarf*, sondern was ihn nur belastet und der "göttlichen Elastizität" beraubt! Fräulein Mrotek ist meine "*geistige Schwester*", denn sie führt das aus, in geistigen Erkenntnissen, was ich seit dreißig Jahren als die *Errettung* des

[59] Hartmut Binder, *Kafka. Der Schaffensprozeß*, 150.

Menschengeschlechtes erträumt habe - - die Befreiung vom schrecklichen Wahne des Wertes von *Nahrungsaufnahme*!!! Man kann nicht wenig genug essen, und Mastkuren sind *Teufelskuren*! Nahrung muß ein *unentrinnbares* tiefes Bedürfnis werden, nicht ein gemeines *Genußmittel*!

Es werde eine Art "religiöse Handlung", nicht ein "barbarisches Genuß-mittel", ein schändlicher Zeitvertreib! Nahrungsaufnahme ohne unent-rinnbares Bedürfnis danach, ohne daß sozusagen jede Zelle im Körper um Nahrungszufuhr gleichsam weint, ist ein *gemeines Verbrechen* physiologischer Natur! Wie göttlich ist der Wassertrunk, wenn man ihn *dringend* benötigt; aber wie direkt *widerstehend,* wenn man ihn *nicht nötig* hat! (B 167–168)

[Fräulein Mrotek in Berlin has already been starving herself for 16 days under constant supervision in a glass case.

Some remarkable and unknown twist of fate in her young, blossoming life must have warned her, like an "inner word of God," that there is a better, a purer, a more spiritual life than that led by ordinary people, mired in their mendacities.

Thus she began to "*starve,*" i.e. to *withdraw* from her body, that noble mechanism of prime order, that which it does not absolutely require, which rather merely weighs it down, robs it of its "divine elasticity"! Fräulein Mrotek is my "*spiritual sister,*" for through her spiritual insights she carries out what for the past thirty years I have dreamed of as the *salvation* of the human race - - liberation from the appalling delusion about the value of *ingesting food*!!! One cannot eat too little, eating cures are the *devil's cures*! Food must become a deep and inescapable necessity, not a *common means of gratification*!

May it become a sort of "religious act," not a "barbaric means of gratification," a disgraceful pastime! Intake of food without an inescapable need for it, without so to speak every cell in one's body as it were weeping for an influx of food, is a *common crime* of a physiological nature! How divine is a drink of water when *urgently* required; but how absolutely *perverse* if *not necessary*!

Let it be thus in everything, in everything!]

Altenberg, like Kafka, was obsessed by questions of food and diet, and his views on dietary abstinence often seem echoed in Kafka's diaries. *Pròdrŏmŏs*, in which Altenberg most consistently expresses his view on health and nutrition, appeared in the same year as Jens Peter Müller's *Mein System*, a book which similarly propounds a complete "Body Culture"; it was one which made a profound impact upon Kafka.[60] Altenberg's "Die Hungerkünstlerin" is merely one of many texts which record his obsession with fasting, but what makes it particularly interesting in the context of Franz Kafka, and beyond the similarities of title, is its linking of starvation with the artistic process itself. People, says Altenberg, demand instant gratification; they refuse to allow things to mature in their own time and way. This is something which a

[60] Anderson, *Kafka's Clothes*, 77–84.

woman carrying a child for nine months knows all about, as does "jeder Künstlerorganismus, der kein Scharlatan ist" [every artistic organism which is not a charlatan: B 168].

Despite all their differences in narrative tone and technique, the parallels between the two texts are self-evident, Altenberg's text concluding with a particularly Kafka-like paradox. Fräulein Mrotek wishes to teach people that one can long for food for thirty days but remain cheerful: "Sie wird es aber nur denen beweisen, die es auch ohne sie schon wissen - " [However, she will only be able to prove this to those who already know it without her - : B 168]. This surely finds an echo in Kafka's words: "Versuche, jemandem die Hungerkunst zu erklären! Wer es nicht fühlt, dem kann man es nicht begreiflich machen." [Just try to explain to anyone the art of fasting! Anyone who has no feeling for it cannot be made to understand it.][61]

Altenberg's text makes no reference to the panther, which at the end of Kafka's story replaces the dead starvation artist. However, a further link with Altenberg is nonetheless possible, for *Bilderbögen des kleinen Lebens* contains a sketch entitled "Du hast es so gewollt," a maudlin piece about disappointed love, in which the following lines, stylistically incompatible with the rest of the sketch, appear:

> *Sahst du den schwarzen Panther in seinem Käfig manchmal mit dem gelben Blick des Wahnsinns rastlose seine Achter schleichen?! Sahst du ihm?!* (B 94)

> [*Did you see the black panther in his cage with the yellow look of madness restlessly pacing out his figures of eight?! Did you see him?!*]

If Altenberg is as significant for Kafka as I believe him to be, his impact can be located on several fronts. Of the receptivity of Kafka's creative imagination to literary stimuli there can be no doubt, and this chapter has shown some possible models and sources for Kafka in Altenberg's work. Of Kafka's fascination with confessional literature there can also be no doubt, and here too Peter Altenberg would seem to have displayed in a very public way doubts and uncertainties which also plagued Kafka. Altenberg was at least as famous for the public performance he made of his life as he was for his writing, and this will have been no secret to Kafka. Thus Altenberg's rejection of commerce for art (his father's firm was very similar to that of Hermann Kafka) his public agonizing over his racial origins, his health, diet and sexual failures might well have struck a chord in a writer who in a less ostentatious way played out his inner agonies in the public realm of the printed page.

[61] Kafka, *Sämtliche Erzählungen*, 170; *The collected stories*, 276.

7: War and Late Loves

Fechsung

Regardless of either his own predicament or that of the world, Altenberg continued to write, fall for young women and be the source of anecdotes. On the day when Franz Ferdinand was assassinated in Sarajevo, Altenberg declared that there might be something to worry about if the heir to the British throne had been killed.[1] By October he had changed his tune, as Berg wrote to Schoenberg after reading "Untergang des Franzosentums." There Altenberg derided the French as "sham-romantics and heartless megalomaniacs in this earthly madhouse"; the insanity of the Russians he considered temporary and curable by the "world-psychologist." The French, however, were incurably mad because they suffered from the syphilis of false patriotism.[2]

Although his initial view of the war must have offended Kraus, Altenberg's noisy patriotism did not extend to him taking up arms. Berg recounts Altenberg's fear of being called up, and how, to comfort him, Adolf Loos asked whether he had ever seen a sixty-year-old recruit. "No," Altenberg exclaimed tearfully, "but generals!!!"[3] In May 1916, with relations between Kraus and Altenberg at a low ebb, the satirist informed his lover Sidonie Nádherný that Altenberg would have rather returned to Steinhof than don a uniform. He had it from a reliable source that Altenberg had gone to Steinhof when war broke out and implored the director to provide him with written confirmation that he was under treatment and therefore exempt from the draft. This, according to Kraus, merited at least five of Altenberg's exclamation marks.[4]

Having comfortably escaped call-up, Altenberg began recording his reactions to the war in ways which often, but not always, confirmed his position in the loyalist camp occupied by most Austrian writers. He also continued writing erotica such as "Les romanticismes de la réalité. 1914," an explicit

---

[1] Siegfried Trebitsch, *Chronicle of a life*, trans. Eithne Kaiser and Ernst Wilkins, (London: Heinemann, 1953), 218–219. Trebitsch was responsible for introducing George Bernard Shaw to German audiences.

[2] *The Berg-Schoenberg Correspondence. Selected Letters*, ed. Juliane Brand, Christopher Hailey, and Donald Harris, (New York and London: W. W. Norton, 1987), 219. The provenance of this essay has still to be determined.

[3] Ibid.

[4] Karl Kraus, *Briefe an Sidonie Nádherný von Borutin 1913–1936*, vol. 1, ed. Heinrich Fischer and Michael Lazarus, (Munich: dtv, 1977), 332.

depiction of heterosexual activity viewed from the female perspective.[5] His reactions to world events can be judged first in *Fechsung*, published in the spring of 1915. This was followed a year later by *Nachfechsung*. Both volumes reveal the author's contradictory stance vis-à-vis the carnage in Europe.

The intended title for *Fechsung* had been *Sammelsurium 1914* (NF 182), a title similar in shape to *"Semmering 1912"*, but where this was focused in time and space, *Sammelsurium 1914* would have been an admission of his diffuse responses to the war. His publisher reportedly wrote to the author:

> You want to call your new book "Sammelsurium 1914" [1914 Scrapbook]?! One shouldn't make oneself smaller than one already is, my dear Peter! If even you consider your work a "scrapbook," what about the folks out there? So let's stick with your title *"Fechsung."* Of course nobody knows what it means, but that might entice a few people to bite. They don't always have to be *carp*!
> Yours in constant friendship
> S. Fischer (NF 182)

More evidence of Fischer's paternalistic concern, as well as of the author's work practices, is revealed in *Nachfechsung* when Altenberg cites another letter from his publisher. When he continued sending fresh manuscripts on a daily basis after dispatching the bundle of manuscripts for *Fechsung*, his "revered publisher" wrote telling him to stem his insidious productivity, for it was in his own interests to keep the cost down to four marks (NF 260). Fischer remained true to his word, the cheaper version costing four marks, the dearer one five marks (NF 199).

When the book finally appeared as *Fechsung*, an arcane Austrian word meaning harvest, it hinted at autumnal qualities not only in its author, but also in the civilization at the core of his writing. In further contrast to *"Semmering 1912"*, *Fechsung* bore no personal dedications. These reappeared in the even more autumnally-tinged *Nachfechsung* where, along with a belated dedication of *Fechsung* to Klara Panhans (NF 88), we also find an item "Widmung meines Buchs '*Fechsung*' an K. K." Here at least, perhaps in an attempt to recapture the satirist's sympathy, Altenberg aligns himself fully with Kraus, claiming that they should march together like Danton and Robespierre (NF 24). Just who is Danton, and who Robespierre, is not made clear! The belated publication of the memorial to Annie Kalmar "Wie Genies sterben" (NF 252) would also indicate a desire to ingratiate himself with Kraus, who was now going for months at time without seeing him.[6]

For more than a hundred pages *Fechsung* presents a medley of short items on long familiar topics. In lieu of the hoped-for new edition of *Pròdròmòs*, the book opens with a "Nachtrag zu Prodromos" (F 9–30) reflecting alongside the usual dietary tips the resentments he harbored against the regimes in Steinhof and Inzersdorf. Utterly familiar, too, is the work's fo-

---

[5] The unpublished manuscripts in the Munich Stadtbibliothek are only partially in Altenberg's hand.

[6] Unpublished postcard from Kraus to Otto Janowitz, 13 November 1915 (WSB 167.363.)

cus upon the women of the moment: these include Mitzi Thumb,[7] an unnamed 15-year-old (possibly Albine Ruprich) and most importantly Paula
Schweitzer, who until her marriage and move to Innsbruck in the summer of
1917 played a role similar to that played earlier by Helga Malmberg. As
usual, *Fechsung* is full of hints for middle-class young women in their relationships with men, and full of Altenberg's observations on these relationships. In *Nachfechsung*, the author characterizes its predecessor as being
about the nature of the female soul, which is generally absent, and laxatives.
Both, Altenberg claimed, would survive the war (NF 160).

Other recurring elements in *Fechsung* are a concern with members of his
family and the days of his youth. We also find a whimsical readiness to poke
fun at his own image. In "Das Leben," one of several pieces inspired by
Venice, Altenberg for once even ironizes his adoration of young girls to
show how they exploit him (F 56). *Fechsung* also refers frequently to Adolf
Loos,[8] with whom Altenberg's personal relationship had become strained
towards the end of 1913 when he accused the architect of competing for the
affections of Esthère Vignon.[9] It deteriorated again in 1914 when "der
heimtückische Hund Loos" [the malicious dog Loos] was blamed for the
withdrawal of the monthly *Rente* which Julius Muhr paid Altenberg.[10] It
took a further nose-dive towards the end of 1915 when Loos introduced
him to the clairvoyant Raphael Schermann, a Viennese bank clerk whose
phenomenal powers were the talk of the Kraus-Loos clique. Unfortunately,
Schermann predicted difficulties ahead in Altenberg's relationship with his
beloved — perhaps this did not require clairvoyance at all — whereupon Altenberg took to cursing Loos daily before meals.[11]

Biographically, *Fechsung* is most significant for the way Altenberg pays
tribute to a new soul mate, the teenager Paula Schweitzer, whose acquaintance was made after she wrote effusive birthday greetings in March 1914.
This letter Altenberg simply reproduces as the text "55 Geburtstag" (F 86).
Earlier, in "Ständchen," there is the first full reference to the woman whose
name would be featured heavily over the next few years (F 72). Her significance for *Fechsung* was, in his view, considerable: "An Paula Sch.: Ich

---

[7] Thumb herself had a fine (if untranslatable) turn of phrase, which Altenberg was glad to record:
"Peter, du bist der Ausrufer in der Praterbude des Lebens" (F 33).

[8] See "Nester" (F 31); "Stammtisch" (F 60); "Italien" (F 61); "Café Capua" (F 61); "Reforma-
tionszeitalter" (F 76); F 123, "Quod licet (F 137); "Dilemma" (F 139); "Werdet einfach!" (F
218).

[9] WSB 160.467. See Gustav Jagersbacher's caricature "Die Tobsucht wegen Esthère Vignon,
1913" in *Otto Kallir-Nirenstein. Ein Wegbereiter österreichischer Kunst*, (Vienna: Eigenverlag der
Museen der Stadt Wien, 1986), 47.

[10] WSB 160.469.

[11] Unpublished postcard from Kraus to Janowitz, 13 November 1915, WSB 167.363. See the
satirical sketch "Graphologie" (NF 9) which refers to Schermann, and also Norbert Jacques, *Mit
Lust gelebt. Roman meines Lebens*, (Hamburg: Hoffmann and Campe, 1950), 334. Jacques recalls
Altenberg's contempt for Kraus, whom he called "eine jüdische Giftnudel und galizischen Klein-
krämer" (240).

schenke Ihnen, Fräulein, mein Buch. Es ist nicht *für Sie* geschrieben, aber *aus Ihnen heraus!*" [To Paula Sch.: Young lady, I present you with my book. It is not written *for you*, but *out of you!*: F 259]. However, in parallel with his growing concern with the role of Jews in the war, Altenberg was unpleasantly conscious of Paula's "Jewish soul,"[12] just as he had been of Helga Malmberg's "lovingly Christian soul."[13]

What both women had in common, beyond their extraordinary devotion to Altenberg, was their insufficiency in his eyes. As with Helga, so too Paula was physically not his ideal type, and he did not hesitate to say so in print, with a brutality that has lost none of its power. He tells her, and the world, that for all her mental and spiritual qualities she will never achieve her ambition of being "mysterious," "magical" or "different." For that she would need the body, hands and feet of "A. M.", the actress Annie Mewes (NF 83, 146). Only the "intelligence and the soul" of Paula Schweitzer can be counted among the list of his "ideals," along with Klara Panhans. With the listing of this trinity, which only omits mention of his mother, comes confirmation that no single female could hope to encompass the range of Altenberg's complex physical and emotional requirements.

Altenberg's strained relationship with Kraus during this period dominates a splendidly unhinged letter to S. Fischer dated 15 February 1915, complaining about Kraus's plans to bring out a sanitized anthology of his works. Altenberg was most unhappy with Kraus's undertaking which, he contends, had *degraded up* ["*hinauf degradiert*"]:

> den größten tiefsten weisesten und zugleich einfachsten *Neuerer aller* modernen *Lebens-Anschauungen* zu einem großen *Lyriker* und *feinen Stimmungsmaler* à la Lilienkron (*sic*).

> [the greatest, profoundest and at the same time simplest *innovator* in *all* modern philosophies of life to a great *lyric poet* and sensitive *mood-painter* à la Liliencron.]

Nor is this the end of Altenberg's self-assessment within the scheme of modern literature and thought, for he also regards himself as someone who had accurately and simply summarized the teachings of Nietzsche, Strindberg, Ibsen and the Romantics.[14]

A major source of tension between Kraus and Altenberg was doubtless the latter's inconsistent stance towards the hostilities. Whereas Altenberg's initial response was immediate, bellicose and flag-waving, Kraus did not break his long silence until the essay "In dieser großen Zeit" of December 1914. As his response to the bombardment of Rheims cathedral, Kraus countered with the magnificent rhetorical question-statement "Wann hebt die größere Zeit des Krieges an der Kathedralen gegen Menschen!" [When

[12] WSB 115.785.
[13] WSB 203.448.
[14] WSB 199.208, 1–5.

does the greater time of war begin, that of the cathedrals against people!]^{15}
Altenberg, on the other hand, lent his signature to the "Aufruf zur Würde"
[Call to Dignity] in the Munich *Kritische Rundschau*, defending the need to
bomb the cathedral and condemning the foreign press for portraying the
Germans as a barbarian horde.^{16}

Perhaps more typical of Altenberg's writing on the war, which has generally been regarded as paralleling Kraus's critical position, is "Krieg." This
sketch moves steadily away from the external apparatus of the tragedy to the
war within ourselves. The blank-verse opening, with its echoes of martial
rhythms, is especially arresting:

> Krieg, Krieg und Krieg!
> Und Greueltaten!
> Kinder werfen auf speisende hungrige Helden,
> am Mittagstisch neugierig sie umstehend, Handgranaten!
> Krieg und Krieg! (F 134–135)

> [War, war and war!
> And atrocities!
> Inquisitive children, surrounding hungry heroes
> at the lunch table, throw handgrenades on them!
> War and war!]

Alluding perhaps to the bombardment of Rheims Cathedral, "Krieg"
notes the destruction of cultural monuments while also asking why mankind
requires cultural monuments at all when what it really needs is soup (F 135).
Having moved from the world stage to the domestic privations of the war,
the text finally shifts to the timeless questions of individual ethics, exorting
readers to wage war on the enemy within: Altenberg's targets are our weakness and stupidity, habit, luxury, prejudice, inner cowardice and mendacity
(F 135–136). This ascetic ending aligns "Krieg" with a wider concern of
Fechsung, indeed of Altenberg's oeuvre as a whole, one which yet again
demonstrates his proximity to Loos and Kraus.

Like Kraus, Altenberg also suffered censorship during the war. With Altenberg, however, it bordered on the farcical, as a letter of 21 March 1916
from Max Macher of the *Wiener Allgemeine Zeitung* demonstrates: it informed him that the censor had confiscated his review of a piece called *Frau
Eva* because it used words like "Kanaille" [riff-raff] and "Mistviecher"
[bitches]. Macher had received confidential advice from "higher sources"
that reviews had to be strictly factual and that any deviations would be cut
mercilessly.^{17} At same time as receiving his rebuff from the censor, Altenberg
published a contribution in the *Kriegsmappe 1916* of the Schutzverband
deutscher Schriftsteller, an association for protecting the rights of German

---

^{15} Karl Kraus, *Die Fackel* 404 (1914): 4.

^{16} Manuscript in the Monacensia section of the Munich Stadtbibliothek.

^{17} GSE.

authors. Here too he stresses how little one should expect from the war as a means of radically changing things for the better: how can one expect dum-dum bullets suddenly to produce "Buddhistische Lebensreinheit" [Buddhist purity of life: LA 46]?[18]

Writing from the safety of Vienna about a cruel and unjust world war (F 132), Altenberg, who lost a cousin in battle (NF 288), is often at his best when able to catch the tone of ordinary people's anxieties und suffering. "Kaffeeküche" (F 261) depicts the fears of a Viennese kitchen maid who only knows her lover has been wounded but has no other details. "Die 'Taube'" ironically describes the aerial bombing of Paris on 22 September 1914; a French model turns to a colleague and remarks: "Cochon d'alboche, il fait kaka sur nous!" [Pig Kraut, he's crapping on us!: F 222]; in "Die junge Gattin" (F 252) Altenberg assumes the voice of a woman whose husband is dying in battle, whilst "Verwundetenspital" (F 254) demonstrates his sensitivity towards the victims of war.

Occasionally, Altenberg's scorn at the futility of the suffering boils over to produce work with a moral intensity worthy of Kraus himself. One of the most powerful achievements is "Kriegshymnen" with its telling use of Viennese vernacular at the outset. Here is the voice of the people, whose experience of war's reality has stripped bare the clichés of the official media:

> Kriegshymnen san net schlecht. Gar net schlecht!
> So Worttrompeten, Wortetrommeln, Wortgeratter:
> Auf in den Kampf, auf in den Tod! Zum Siege!
> Doch *schmerzlicher* dient man dem Vaterlande
> mit einem Leberschuß, einem Schuß in die Niere,
> in die Nabelgegend! . . .
> Der Krieg begeistert jeden schon *von selbst*!
> Was braucht man da noch Trommeln und Trompeten?!?
> Jedoch im heiligen Frieden wird wieder alles
> *schlapp* und *müde*
> und trottet fort in *schäbigem* Geleise!
> In *Friedenszeiten*, Dichter, Philosophen,
> rufet die Menschen *wach* und *auf*
> zu Lügelosigkeit, Einfachheit, Askese und
> vornehmer Gesinnung *durch* und *durch*!
> Auf daß ein nächster Krieg *unmöglich*
> werde und sein *Schreckenslärm*,
> und ebenso *Kriegshymnen-Blech*! (F 207–208)

> [War hymns ain't bad at all. Not bad at all!
> Like, bugles of words, batteries of words, chatter of words!
> To battle, to death! to victory!

[18] Ernst Fischer, *Der "Schutzverband deutscher Schriftsteller", 1909–1933*, (Frankfurt: Buchhändler-Vereinigung, 1980), 162–163.

But it's more *painful* to serve the fatherland with a
bullet in the liver
a bullet in the kidneys, in the umbilical! . . .
War is *its own* inspiration
Who needs drums and bugles?
Yet in the sacred peace everything goes
slack and *tired* again,
trotting along its
shabby track!
In *times of peace*, ye poets and philosophers,
wake and *shake* the people up,
to truth, simplicity, asceticism and
a noble attitude *through* and *through*!
So that a future war becomes *impossible*
and its *terrifying din*
and its rubbishy war-hymns as well!]

Despite all we know about Altenberg, it is still bewildering that the writer of "Kriegshymnen" could publish in the same volume "Romantik der Na-men! - U9" celebrating the submarine U9's sinking of the cruisers HMS *Aboukir, Hogue* and *Crecy*. Resorting first to the sort of language excoriated in "Kriegshymnen," Altenberg then lists by name the entire crew of the ship before claiming that there was now a new word in history to set alongside Thermopylae, Waterloo, Sedan: U9 (F 202). Altenberg eventually had sec-ond thoughts about "Unterseeboot-Spielerein" [U-Boat games], regarding them as nursery romps of a completely immature humanity (LA 331).

Also to be set against "Romantik der Namen - U9" is "Politik" (F 262). This addresses specifically French jingoism, but by implication home-grown chauvinism as well, with its wry reference to well-known German obsessions. Its ironic call for tolerance in war sits uneasily with the instant patriotism of "Romantik der Namen - U9." Every nation, Altenberg insists, would like its "Plätzchen an der Sonne" [little place in the sun], but:

Sich *vertragen*, ist immer noch das beste
Lebensgeschäft, das man auf dieser Lebensbörse
effektuieren kann!

[*Tolerating* one another is still the best business one can do in the stock-market of life!: F 262][19]

Although Altenberg was unable to ignore the war and its consequences, a great (initially perhaps the greater) part of him would rather have done just that. In "Der Sommer," a contribution to a collection whose profits went to the Austrian Red Cross, he muses on some earthenware vases in his room

---

[19] A variant on "Politik" entitled "Kriegsphilosophie von Peter Altenberg (Ein öffentlicher Vortrag)" appeared in the propaganda sheet *Wieland* 1, 6, (1915): 10. See Fritz Schlawe, *Litera-rische Zeitschriften 1910–1933*, (Stuttgart: Metzler, (1972), 28.

which are filled with lilac thistles. Stuck in Vienna, he dreams of the thistles growing in the heat of the sun, the butterflies landing on them, the stream alongside and the white, dusty country lane. The date is Sunday, 8 August 1915; with care and attention the thistles will last for a month, by which time it will be September and the end of another summer he has not experienced:

> Und dennoch *erlebt*!
> In Ton-Vasen, im Zimmer, in Wien,
> Ja, ich vergaß ganz, daß auch Weltkrieg ist!
> *Schuster*, bleib bei deinem Leisten
> *Dichter*, bei den Wiesen-Disteln!
>
> [But *experienced* nevertheless!
> In earthenware vases, in my room, in Vienna.
> Yes, I totally forgot there was a World War!
> *Cobbler*, stick to your last,
> *Poet*, stick to your thistles!][20]

Surprisingly, the first text devoted specifically to the war in *Fechsung* does not occur until "Kriegszeiten" (F 126), and it is symptomatic that Altenberg focuses here on its effects upon the ordinary civilian population. Not for him the sham exchange of letters between Bahr and Hofmannsthal, with its pretense that Hofmannsthal was serving in the trenches when all along he was safe and warm in Vienna. Altenberg is concerned with the effects of diet and poverty, but he is far from immune to the public orthodoxies of the times. Thus "Zum Heldentode des Dr. Frank (Die Einigkeit)" (F 130) is not even by Altenberg, but is simply reproduced from a newspaper clipping. The effect which this German Socialist parliamentarian's death had upon the author was nevertheless considerable: it led to his unambiguous affirmation of Social Democracy. Altenberg now contended that a poet who was not a Social Democrat was not a poet at all. Frank's heroic death has been of more service to the "party," that is to *humanity*, than his life (F 254).[21]

In a new departure, for Altenberg had never been involved in party politics, the programmatic "Poeta," with its obvious reference to Friedell's *Ecce Poeta*, also opens with a similar fanfare: "A poet who is not a *Social Democrat . . . is not a poet . . . He is not a doctor for *sick* humanity, therefore not a poet!*" (F 233). Given the ultra-loyal responses of the German and Austrian Socialist parties in the war, this was hardly revolutionary stuff, and in a further text culled from a newspaper, Altenberg reproduces "Der letzte Wille eines deutschen Prinzen" (F147), a typical example of conformist, nationalistic war reporting.

---

[20] *Österreichs Geist und Schwert. Ein Gedenkbuch aus ernster Zeit*, ed. Clara Körber, (Leipzig: Verlag der Dürr'schen Buchhandlung, 1915), 32. Besides "Der Sommer" this book also contains "Der Frosch" (32–33), a rather feeble allegory about "doing one's bit" for the Fatherland. Neither item was reprinted in book form.

[21] The coloured lithograph which inspired the text is now in the Historisches Museum der Stadt Wien, I.N. 94901.

Much to Altenberg's dismay, *Fechsung* made little impact, its reception in Vienna being especially muted. As he bitterly noted in *Nachfechsung*, not one of the major Viennese newspapers even mentioned it (NF 199). Otto Zoff in the Viennese arts periodical *Der Merker* was downright hostile: the book was supposed to be a harvest, but was merely a sign that Altenberg had ground to a halt; his concentrated forms now lacked any artistic quality whatsoever.[22] Max Herrmann-Neiße, on the other hand, in an extensive review for the Zürich periodical *Der Mistral*, takes the contradictions of *Fechsung* in his stride. Unlike Zoff, he reckons *Fechsung* to be a "faultless jewel."[23] Quoting the end of "Kriegshymnen," the critic contends that *Fechsung* should become "eine Fibel der Schwertlos-Tapfren" [a primer for the swordless brave] and closes his review with a quotation about Altenberg from Lasker-Schüler, his "heavenly blood-sister before God" whom Altenberg, however, regarded as an "edle Hochstaplerin und Nichtskönnerin" [noble confidence trickster and incompetent.][24] For Herrmann-Neiße, Altenberg is a prophet and revolutionary whose background has led him to write Viennese just as Ibsen writes Norwegian: "in short, without blasphemy, a condensed Strindberg!"[25]

Altenberg may well have read this review, given his acquaintance with Walter Serner, the editor of *Der Mistral*, and a seminal figure in the development of Dadaism.[26] In *Nachfechsung*, however, he challenges Herrmann-Neiße's assessment by explicitly stating "My name is *Altenberg* and not *Strindberg*" (NF 304), as well as distancing himself from Strindberg on another occasion in the book (NF 167). We may recall here Altenberg's comment that, unlike Strindberg, he did not succumb to woman, but neither is he unremittingly hostile to them.

The relative critical neglect of *Fechsung* and the author's patent disappointment at its reception are constant themes in *Nachfechsung*, which concerns itself with its predecessor to a quite unusual degree. Thus Walter Reiz's hostile review of the earlier book in *Der Berner Bund* is adroitly turned to his advantage when Altenberg recounts a lady telling him that this will simply encourage her to go buy the book (NF 44). On another occasion he addresses his disappointment with self-deprecatory humour:

> "Ich glaube, die Herren Journalisten haben mein letztes Buch 'Fechsung' gar nicht gelesen!?"
> "O sicherlich, Peter!"

---

[22] *Der Merker*, 6 (1915): 645.

[23] Max Herrmann-Neiße, *Die neue Entscheidung. Aufsätze und Kritiken*, (Frankfurt: Zweitausendeins, 1988), 320–322. Note also the very positive general review of Altenberg by Hans Leybold in *Die Aktion* 5, nos. 7–8, (1915): 73–80.

[24] WSB 160.399.

[25] Herrmann-Neiße, *Die neue Entscheidung*, 321–322.

[26] Werner J. Schweiger, *Der junge Kokoschka. Leben und Werk 1904–1914*, (Vienna and Munich: Christian Brandstätter, 1983), 263. See also Andrew Barker and Leo A. Lensing, *Peter Altenberg. Rezept die Welt zu sehen*, (Vienna: Braumüller, 1995), 122–131.

"Du Idealistin, du!"
"Sie müssen sich überzeugen, ob es nicht *doch* vielleicht schwächer ist
als die früheren Bücher!" (NF 177)

[I believe the gentlemen of the press have not read my latest book
"*Fechsung*" at all!?
"Of course they have, Peter!"
"Oh, what an idealist you are!"
"They had to convince themselves it perhaps really *was* feebler than the
earlier books!"]

A similar wry humor informs "Observer,"[27] in which Altenberg recounts his
delight at finding that no less than the *Mercure de France* had reproduced
"the *most radical*, profoundest, most special sections" from the "Nachtrag
zu 'Prodromos'," only to conclude the extracts with: "Fortunate France, this
is *one* poet you truly don't have to envy the Germans" (NF 26).

Another of Altenberg's strategies to counter neglect was simply to quote
what sympathetic critics had written. "Ein mir nicht ganz unsympathisches
Referat" (NF 153) reproduces an unidentified but positive notice which presumably reflects Altenberg's assessment of the way his writing has in fact developed. The anonymous critic observes how steeply the lyrical input has
declined since *"Semmering 1912"*, the delicate prose poem "Der Vorfrüh-
ling" (F 130) now standing out as an exception (NF 154).[28] He further
notes how Altenberg used to be more literary, more gracious, more soulful,
more flexible, whereas today his manner is harder and clearer.
"Buchbesprechung" reproduces Hans Georg Richter's long piece from the
Leipziger Tageblatt (NF 199). Richter's view of Altenberg as an ideal Christian must have been music to his ears, and Altenberg would certainly have
agreed that his books were not read widely enough. Richter's insight into the
essentially oral quality of his best work is also noteworthy: Altenberg is a
"Kaffeehausgenie" whose best work could have been spoken to a friend late
at night as the café emptied (NF 199).

The feeling that Altenberg no longer had anything to say, articulated by
Zoff and acknowledged by the poet himself whilst at the same time he disputed it (NF 183–184), may indicate why the traditional channels for promoting literature were no longer effective in the case of *Fechsung*. Hence
Altenberg was forced to resort to demeaning self-promotion in *Nachfechsung*, even quoting verbal responses from personal friends and acquaintances
such as Paula Schweitzer and Elisabeth Muhr (NF 109), as well as from the
twenty-one year-old cadet Felix Ressek, who went on to become Johannes
Urzidil's physician in New York:

Cadet Ressek: "Mr. Altenberg, I was eight months in the war. I had
two books with me in the trenches. Your '*Fechsung*' and the bible!"

[27] The "Observer" was a Viennese agency specialising in press cuttings.

[28] Consistent with his new strategy, Altenberg also uses *Fechsung* to plug *"Semmering 1912"* (F
164).

"Very nice, very kind! But why the *bible*?!" (NF 175)[29]

Nachfechsung

When *Nachfechsung* came out in March 1916 it bore a dedication to Paula Schweitzer, who achieved after two years' service a distinction denied Helga Malmberg after seven. Given, however, that *Nachfechsung* contains some of the most offensively anti-woman texts Altenberg ever published, this may be a doubtful honor. Although the title *Nachfechsung* suggests a sequel to *Fechsung*, and indeed both volumes bear as a motto versions of Lessing's dictum "Reader, how do you *like* me?!/ Reader, how do *I* like *you*?!," the photographic frontispieces of the two books emit very different signals. Whereas *Fechsung* displays the behatted author in relaxed half-profile, clad in the light-colored casual clothes worn in many of the Venice photographs,[30] *Nachfechsung* projects a sternly patriotic image. Taken in 1914 by Anton Josef Třcka, a young associate of Egon Schiele, the picture presents the calm, very bald author facing the camera directly, hand on temple and decked out in a dark jacket and striped bow tie with an array of patriotic badges pinned to the lapels. Underneath is a message in Altenberg's hand exhorting "good patriots" to "*verlernen, umlernen, zulernen!*" [unlearn, to learn anew, to learn more.] Kraus's reactions to all this are summed up in his terse description of Altenberg as a "Kriegshanswurst mit Abzeichen" [bellicose clown with badges].[31] Indeed, a letter from Kraus of 13 November 1915 to Otto Janowitz, serving in Dalmatia, suggests that Altenberg went around constantly in such attire: Kraus notes that on Altenberg's chest (and on his hotel door!) there are war badges, placards with "Gott strafe" etc. whose numbers swell with those of the hostile powers.[32]

Uniquely amongst Altenberg's works, it is possible to trace the genesis of *Nachfechsung* with some precision. A letter to his sister reveals that his longest book took only six months to write.[33] Fischer was equally quick off the mark: after the manuscript was sent off to Berlin on 12 October 1915,[34] Altenberg got word of its safe arrival on 16 October, and on 25 October he re-

[29] In a text in the Leo Baeck Institute, dated 26 July 1915, Altenberg pays tribute to Ressek's devotion to him. Born in Prague in 1894, Ressek died in New York in 1957.

[30] Ernst Darmstaedter, *Peter Altenberg zum Gedächtnis*, Munich (1927). One hundred privately published copies of this pamphlet were produced for the Gesellschaft der Bücherfreunde in Munich.

[31] Karl Kraus, *Briefe an Sidonie Nádherný von Borutin 1913–1936*, vol. 1, ed. Heinrich Fischer and Michael Lazarus, (Munich: dtv, 1977), 332.

[32] WSB 167.363. The photographic frontispiece to *Nachfechsung* also confirms the suspicions of Else Lübcke, a German reader of *Die Aktion*, who had recently read a report of him attending the theatre wearing "shiny uniform buttons" and beaming down at the audience from the center balcony (*Die Aktion*, 5 [1915]: 186).

[33] GSE

[34] "Kalendarium," GSE.

ceived the first set of corrections. True to form, he must have kept on sending work after submitting the "finished" text to Fischer, for the last item is
dated 4 November 1915 (NF 347). Moreover, it is difficult to square Altenberg's assertion about the speed with which he completed *Nachfechsung* with
this description of his working habits in the poem "Dichten":

> Ich schreibe oft Wochen lang nichts.
> Das ist richtig, ich kann es nicht leugnen.
> Ich bin faul, es fällt mir nichts ein.
> Und dann schreibe ich plötzlich, aber ganz plötz-
> lich dreißig Zeilen. Die sind mir eingefallen,
> ins Herz, ins Gehirn nämlich hinein.
> Auf mich kann man sich nicht verlassen,
> oft verläßt mich, wie gesagt, für viele Monate,
> die ganze sogenannte Dichtergestaltungskraft. (NF 281–282)

> [For weeks I often write nothing
> That is correct, I cannot deny it.
> I am lazy, I get no ideas.
> And then suddenly, but quite sudden-
> ly I write thirty lines. They have entered into my head,
> my heart, my brain that is.
> You cannot rely upon me,
> all my so-called creative power deserts me, as I said,
> for months on end.]

As in *Fechsung*, so too in *Nachfechsung* Altenberg does not hesitate to
make extensive use of work from pens of other writers. In *Nachfechsung*,
however, he goes beyond reviews citing his own work, including what is by
far the longest single item in the book: an extract from Leopold Ziegler's
Der deutsche Mensch. To Kraus's disgust Altenberg also filched Felix Salten's
review of Helene Thimig's performance in *Das Käthchen von Heilbronn* (NF
263), and equally to Kraus's displeasure, he quoted verbatim one of General
Dankl's military orders (NF 289). For Kraus, apt use of others' words was
the most devastating form of satire, so he can hardly have objected to Altenberg's use of quotation per se. What irked him was the utterly unsatirical
purpose they served in *Nachfechsung*. Salten was someone Kraus simply despised; Dankl's italophobic text is saber-rattling of the crassest kind. Writing
to Sidonie on 17 May 1916 Kraus reports:

> Saw by chance yesterday P. A.'s book which I'm supposed to have made
> derogatory comments about. Now I'm doing it for real. Between sketches
> the poor fool reprints absolutely anything which has *pleased* him: e.g. one
> of General Dankl's orders against Italy. Without adding a word! As litera-

ture by P. A.! I was so totally disgusted that I walked past his pavement table without saying hello.[35]

This letter refers to an earlier incident when Kraus received an outraged letter from Altenberg after some supposedly derogatory remarks about *Nachfechsung*, which Kraus at that juncture had not even read. On 18 April, the day after Kraus received this "rabiater Ausfall" [rabid outburst] he wrote to Sidonie admitting that he had not seen Altenberg for half a year but had much enjoyed himself composing a reply, a copy of which he also sent to Loos. The amused condescension of Kraus's tone is unmistakable; Altenberg had become little more than a figure of fun for Kraus and friends.[36] Sadly, no copy of this letter has survived, although Kraus himself stressed its importance because it made absolutely clear his relationship with Altenberg.[37] However, Kraus's letter of 17 May became the matrix upon which he built an extensive critique of Altenberg in *Die Fackel* of 2 August 1916.[38]

Meanwhile, the more Kraus read of *Nachfechsung*, the more dismayed he grew at its indiscriminate and indiscreet revelations. Sidonie Nádherný and her exquisite estate at Janowitz in Bohemia were of paramount importance in Kraus's life, and the thought horrified him that, because of some inconsequential words of Loos, who alone of Kraus's Viennese friends had visited Janowitz, they could be transmuted into one of Altenberg's instant sketches. Writing to Sidonie on 22 July, he related in a state of considerable agitation that he had warned Loos how a delinquent like Altenberg could create a finished sketch out of a shout. Before sending the signed copy of his next book off to Janowitz, Kraus claimed he would have to check closely whether the name N. appeared in a sketch amongst the ranks of the non-payers or "worthless women" whom Herr K. K. admires.[39]

Kraus's disquiet about Altenberg's garrulous exposure of private relationships must be seen in the wider context of his concern for what he regarded as Altenberg's exploitation by the press. He expressed his complex reactions to Altenberg in the *Fackel* essay "Hunde, Menschen, Journalisten," whose catalyst was Altenberg's sketch "Die Hunde-Steuer" which had appeared in the *Prager Tagblatt* of 29 June 1916. It is an unconsidered and flippant trifle in which Altenberg shows scant understanding of human-canine relationships. He concludes that a general love of animals is an indication of highest humanity whereas private love for a private animal makes the human heart stupid, depriving it of the strength one owes to human beings (NF 344). Kraus, however, loved dogs, and particularly Bobby, Sidonie's large Leonberger. The resulting disagreement led to an important analysis of Altenberg's work. In spite of everything, Kraus continues to rate the writing of this "bunte Dreeinigkeit aus Falstaff, Heiland und Harpagon" [bright trinity of

---

[35] Kraus, *Briefe an Sidonie*, 331.

[36] Ibid., 326.

[37] Ibid., 328.

[38] Karl Kraus, *Die Fackel*, 431–436 (1916): 6–12.

[39] Karl Kraus, *Briefe an Sidonie* 351.

Falstaff, Saviour and Harpagon][40] above that of Schnitzler, Bahr and Hofmannsthal, blaming the dross not on Altenberg's irresponsibility and defi-
cient logical, artistic and social awareness,[41] but on the editors who exploit his
financial neurosis. Kraus is less concerned with protecting dogs against the
people who want to send them off to the pound than with protecting the
poet from the editors who deliver him to the printer.[42]

In many respects Kraus's essay, which at base is indulgent of Altenberg,
elaborates the same points made in the essay he wrote in 1909 to commemorate Altenberg's fiftieth birthday. Altenberg is a writer out of control:
masterpieces occur cheek by jowl with rubbish; that is an inescapable fact
which has to be grasped in order to understand Altenberg's writing in all its
humanity and not merely as a series of artistic fragments.[43]

Kraus had to contend not only with "Die Hunde-Steuer," which Altenberg, undeterred, re-published in *Vita Ipsa* as "Die Hundesteuer" (VI 302),
but also with the wildly misogynistic "Der 40fache Frauenmörder" in which
the victim is condemned and the perpetrator commended. First published in
the *Prager Tagblatt* of 23 May 1916,[44] this sketch turned up again in *Mein
Lebensabend* (LA 28), but as he did not have a say in the final editing, Altenberg may not have been responsible for its inclusion. Kraus wrote to Sidonie
condemning the "rabid sketch," wondering whatever had become of the
"Dichter der Frauenseele" [poet of the female soul]. Should Altenberg require proof of his insanity to prevent him being called up, this sketch would
suffice.[45] In his *Fackel* essay Kraus concludes that there is now a duty to pro-
tect "a delightful man and often venerated poet."[46] The solution would be to
enshrine literary prizes in the statute books, so that Altenberg would not
need recourse to newspaper publication. For Kraus, just as important as the
protection of animals is that of poets.[47] No prizes were instituted, and the
question of Altenberg, dogs and the *Prager Tagblatt* refused to go away.

In the issue of *Die Fackel* published on April Fools' Day 1917 Kraus
again felt constrained to take Altenberg to task for an article in the Prague
journal where he had concluded that it was criminal to expend one's emotions on dogs. Rather one should send the money spent annually on one's
mongrel to a children's charity.[48] Kraus took this as a jibe against himself,
pointing out how often he gave money to children's charities, and repeating
his call for literary prizes to obviate the need for Altenberg to publish such
stuff. Kraus concludes his weary lament by commenting that future biogra-

[40] Karl Kraus, *Die Fackel*, 431–436 (1916): 8.

[41] Ibid.

[42] Ibid.

[43] Ibid., 9.

[44] Karl Kraus, *Briefe an Sidonie*, 336.

[45] Ibid.

[46] Karl Kraus, *Die Fackel*, 431–436 (1916): 11.

[47] Ibid., 12.

[48] Karl Kraus, *Die Fackel*, 454–456 (1917): 38.

phers will not wish to miss such incidents. He, however, wishes for a time when there will no longer be a *Prager Tagblatt* to print Altenberg's sketches.[49] This advice has been heeded, and Kraus's wish has come true.

A final postscript to this episode appeared soon after Altenberg's death when Kraus published the sketch "Bully," written on 25 August 1918, to prove that Altenberg did, after all, like dogs.[50] Altenberg's own reactions to the affair may be judged from an unpublished manuscript entitled "In Sachen der 'Fackel' des *Karl Kraus*" which is either a transcript of an item in the *Prager Tagblatt* or, as is more likely, Altenberg's pastiche of what he would like to have read there:

> Unser Leserkreis und wir sind es *sehr zufrieden*, daß *Peter Altenberg* uns seit geraumer Zeit, *völlig unaufgefordert*, seine *kleinen* großen "Splitter des Lebens selbst" zur Verfügung stellt, und der Versuch, dem 58 jährigen kranken Dichter ein litterarisches und "ein wenig auch ökonomisches" Absatzgebiet in wenig geschmackvoller Art zu untergraben, ist als *gescheitert* zu betrachten!
>
> Die *Redaktion* des "Prager Tagblatt"[51]

> [We and our readers are *very pleased* that for some time now, and entirely of his own accord, *Peter Altenberg* has placed at our disposal his *small* great "Splinters of life itself." The rather tasteless attempt to undermine a literary outlet which is "also slightly profitable" for the ailing 58-year old poet is to be regarded as a *failure*!
>
> The *Editor*, "Prager Tagblatt"]

Like *Fechsung*, *Nachfechsung* was not widely reviewed, perhaps because, like Adolf Loos, people were not sure what to make of the work. In *Mein Lebensabend*, Altenberg claims that Loos told him that he did not know whether *Nachfechsung* was good or awful; he only knew that for the next ten years he would not need to read any modern books (LA 163). Altenberg tried to compensate for the continuing lack of critical response by reprinting Hans Wantoch's review of *Nachfechsung* in *Vita Ipsa* (VI 55). This must have delighted Altenberg, as it described him as absolutely pure, kindness itself, and totally understanding. Closer reading would, however, have revealed reservations on the reviewer's part. As near to Christ as Altenberg is for Wantoch, he recommends new readers not to begin with *Nachfechsung* but with earlier works, as these contain better examples of his views on life and hygiene, of his will to spiritualization and of his view of woman's duality as saint and prostitute. Wantoch implies that *Nachfechsung* is prolix, and that the image of the "Fleisch-Extrakt im Liebig-Teigel" no longer applies. Though happy to talk in generalities about Altenberg, Wantoch avoids critical contact with the specific content of *Nachfechsung*. He even excepts Altenberg from aesthetic categorisation altogether: the book is neither good

[49] Ibid.
[50] Karl Kraus, *Die Fackel*, 508–513 (1919): 13–14.
[51] GSE

nor bad, for Altenberg's work does not come under these aesthetic categories. It stands above them (VI 55).

Upon reading other reviews one wonders with how much care *Nachfechsung* has been read. In the *Berliner Tagblatt*, for instance, it is claimed
that all the old wisdom is present, only deeper and more transfigured,
warmer and more human.[52] Can the reviewer have read those virulent, even
violent texts which demonstrate how little Peter Altenberg could now be regarded as a modern counterpart to the medieval poet Frauenlob? That neither this reviewer, nor Ludwig Ullmann in the *Wiener Allgemeine Zeitung*,[53]
nor indeed Kraus, saw fit to draw attention to them merely demonstrates the
extent to which misogyny was institutionalised in Altenberg's culture:

> Die "körperlich ideale" Frau ist die *gefährlichste* natürlich, denn es ist am
> schwersten sie zu *verachten*! (NF 105)

> [The "physically ideal" woman is the *most dangerous*, of course, for it is
> hardest to *despise* her!]

Or:

> Warum man soviel über die Frauen *nachdenkt*?! Weil man sie *braucht*, weil
> man sie *unbedingtest braucht*! Eigentlich sollt' man ja *ebenso* viel über seinen
> *Nachttopf* nachdenken. (NF 105)

> [Why do we give women so much thought?! Because we need them, be-
> cause we absolutely and unconditionally need them! Actually we ought to
> think just as much about our chamber-pot].

Or again:

> Frauen sollte man überhaupt sogleich vernichten, sobald sie *irgend* eine
> *Initiative* ergreifen! Wenn sie aber einen "geliebten?!?" Mann wegen poli-
> tischer Sachen *rächen*, *schützen* wollen, sollte man aus ihnen "Hundefutter"
> in einer *Hackmaschine* machen! *Arme Hunde* aber! (NF 37)

> [Women should actually be annihilated as soon as they take *any initiative*!
> If for political reasons they wish to *avenge*, *defend* a "beloved?!?" man, they
> should make "dog food" out of them in a *mincing machine*! But the *poor
> dogs*!]

These are extreme, but typical examples of an important strand in *Nachfechsung*. Altenberg claims Paula Schweitzer is the only woman he has ever
respected (NF 24); he sings her praises on numerous occasions, even claiming that she has had the same effect upon him as St. Peter's has on Roman
Catholics: she has made him pious (NF 55). Evidence for this piety is as
weak as his efforts to respect Schweitzer's feelings. For example, Altenberg

---

[52] This review is appended to the 12.-15. edition of *Wie ich es sehe* (1919.)

[53] Ullmann claims in a review dated 18 April 1916: "Peter Altenberg litt und leidet in seiner
Beziehung zum Verständnis der Mitwelt an der deutschen Vorliebe für geschlossene äußere
Ordnung, für das Reglement." ("Der neue Altenberg," *Wiener Allgemeine Zeitung*, 11406
(1916): 3–4)

had known a girl named Albine Ruprich (b. 1900) since she was eleven (NF 220), and by the age of fourteen she was posing nude for him.[54] In *Nachfechsung* Altenberg prints successively what purports to be a parting letter to him from Albine and a text entitled "Paula" in which he not only hints at a tendency to violent behaviour, but speculates that Paula sees in him a replacement for her dead father (NF 220). Even more crassly, he couples a "Brief an Paula" with an item entitled "An A. R." (NF 334–335). In the letter to Paula he tells her that she is the best example of womanhood in the world, combining the highest intelligence with the highest sexuality (NF 334). This is followed by a declaration in which Ruprich is thanked by Altenberg for giving him her beautiful body and lovely soul (NF 335).

As with Helga Malmberg, it is not easy to deduce from the printed texts the precise nature of the relationship between Altenberg and Schweitzer, but letters in a private collection are extremely graphic in their genital references. In the same collection, an inscribed card mounted with clippings of the hair from Paula's head, armpits and pudenda leaves little to speculate about. Evident though it is that Altenberg exploited Paula to the hilt, in "Klage" he bemoans the tragically risible fate of being born male and reveals a coprophiliac desire not only to be "used," but to be sullied by her. This profoundly self-abasing document requires no further elucidation:

> Oh, oh, weshalb bin ich nicht lieber als ihr weißes liebes Nachttöpfchen auf die Welt gekommen?
> Als ihr weißes zartes Batisthöschen?!
> Als ihre weiße Lilienmilch-Seife?!
> Als ihre weiße Badewanne?! (NF 42)

> [Oh, oh, why did I not come into the world as her dear little white potty?!
> As her soft white linen panties?
> As her white lily-milk soap?!
> As her white bath tub?!]

On the occasions when Altenberg quotes Paula directly, we gain the impression of a person with considerable insight into his work. Whatever his earlier reputation as a liberator, Altenberg's call for a recognition of the female soul is not politically revolutionary; indeed, his view that woman's ultimate role is to facilitate the development of the male and that women need men to unlock their souls for them is profoundly reactionary.[55] Paula dares to suggest that the omniscient Altenberg has not really understood the nature of female aspirations, though she herself is unable to find the answer:

> Paula Sch. said to me: "The sum of your nine books is that woman *wants something other than* - - - than what man wants from her!

---

[54] Images are reproduced in Hans Bisanz, *Mein äußerstes Ideal: Altenbergs Photosammlung von geliebten Frauen, Freunden und Orten* , (Vienna and Munich: Christian Brandstätter, 1987), 94; *Traum und Wirklichkeit*, (Vienna: Eigenverlag der Museen der Stadt Wien, 1985), 326.

[55] See also "Erkenntnis der Maria B." (NF 126–127).

"What is it she wants then?!"
"If only one knew!" (NF 149)

Presenting now the flip side of the coin, there are, however, indication enough in *Nachfechsung* of a relationship of real substance between Altenberg and Paula Schweitzer. They appear to have been telepathically close (NF 104), and it says much for Schweitzer's regard for Altenberg that despite the indiscreet revelations of their intimate moments she remained with him for many months after the publication of *Nachfechsung*. One of several texts by Paula herself included in both *Fechsung* and *Nachfechsung* is the letter she wrote on his fifty-sixth birthday, setting out the parameters of their relationship. In a style much influenced by her friend — as Altenberg smugly pointed out — she recalls the letter of a year previously which had established their relationship. Breathless with adoration, she sees herself as subservient to his "Dichtergeist" [poetic spirit]. In this gushing abdication of her individual identity, which resembles nothing so much as a teenage crush, she sees herself as no more than the realization of Altenberg's wishes (NF 275).

From the page of Paula's diary in *Nachfechsung* we can presume that Altenberg himself wishes us to know more precisely why she gave herself to him in the way she did. We learn that her father had died from "S." (syphilis?) when she was thirteen, and although Altenberg clearly represents some sort of father substitute, it is even clearer that Schweitzer harks back to the late nineteenth century world of decadence and accursed poets: she has inherited her father's sick nerves but is content that her sick, indescribably sensitive soul, is the inheritance she suffers from. Her father was sick, and so is she (NF 319).

Whereas Altenberg made a token effort to conceal his morally and legally questionable relationship with Albine Ruprich through use of her initials — the age of consent in Austria-Hungary was then fourteen — he felt no such constraints when expressing his feelings for actresses. By the time *Nachfechsung* came out his passion for Mitzi Thumb had faded; she had been replaced by the young and still unknown Annie Mewes, who won his heart on 12 October 1915 when he saw her in Gogol's *Eine Heiratsgeschichte* at the Volkstheater (AB 43–44). In "Hymne" he demonstrates that at the age of fifty-seven he can still react as he did aged twenty, when he fell for Marie Renard in *Manon*; but a new irony has now entered his writing. Publicly, he professes to realize that writing incoherent letters to idealized and distant love-objects merely makes them conceited and bored, but he cannot help himself: "Alter Esel, gibst du keine Ruhe?!" [You old ass, won't you be quiet?: NF 322]. Inevitably, he wrote Mewes a string of intimate love-letters which showed his capacity for unreciprocated passion undimmed by the passage of time. They were subsequently reprinted in *Das Altenbergbuch*.[56]

As will be apparent, *Nachfechsung* displays a constant awareness of the problems arising from male-female relationships; like *Fechsung* it is relatively

---

[56] The original letters are in the Bayerische Staatsbibliothek, Munich. Mewes's personal copy of *Das Altenbergbuch* is in a private collection in England.

lacking in lyrical elements, and there is an equally strong emphasis on collo-
quially-expressed mini-texts, often tinged with humor, which have been
"listened from life." Altenberg's parasitic tendency to include writing by
authors other than himself is even more pronounced than in *Fechsung*, yet
the collection also includes a handful of technically innovative texts which
must challenge the notion that Altenberg's writing made no advances.

As Christian Schad recalls, Altenberg was in frequent contact with Walter
Serner and the emergent Dadaists in Switzerland. Indeed, Altenberg's work
was read at early meetings of Dada in Zürich in 1916,[57] and a text such as
"Der Geist der Familie," an aural collage composed entirely of sound snippets, has a decidedly Dada-like character. Only with the snide reference to
Kraus are we suddenly brought back to Altenberg's habitual Viennese ambience and his strained and distanced relationship with the satirist:

> "Welchen *Zweck*, bitte, hat das?!" "*Dieser* Verkehr?! Pardon, da ist mir
> schon lieber, *gar keiner*!" "Ich möchte *noch später* nach Hause kommen an
> deiner Stelle!?" "Von einem Extrem ins *andere*!" "Große Freuden erlebt
> man mit euch, das muß ich schon sagen!" "Wie geht's? Den Verhältnissen
> angemessen!" "Was der Arzt *sagt*, ist!" "Ja, es ist gegen ihn nichts *einzu-
> wenden, aber - -*." "Dieser *Kraus* muß ein *verbitterter* Mensch sein!" (NF
> 280)

> ["What *purpose*, if you please, has that?!" "*This* contact?! Pardon me, I'd
> rather there were *none at all*!" "If I were you I'd rather get home *even
> later*!?" "From one extreme to the *other*!" "One experiences great pleasure
> with you, that I have to say!" "How's it going? Appropriate to the circum-
> stances!" "What the doctor *says*, goes!" "Yes, I've no *objections* to him,
> *but - -*." "This *Kraus* must be an *embittered* person!"]

In "Koketterie" Altenberg successfully employs a strict interior monologue
technique to depict the loosely-connected thoughts of a woman, unhappily
in love and on the point of tears (NF 283). In "Ein Brief, von mir geschrieben, an mich, von einer anderen" he toys with the question of gender and
identity, adopting the persona of his sister in order to write to himself (NF
292).[58] In these texts at least, Altenberg showed that the artistic spark still
glowed within him.

---

[57] Barker and Lensing, *Rezept*, 125–126.

[58] Other examples where Altenberg adopts a female persona are ML 127, 130; NF 39, 188, 319;
N 35, 37. See Geoffrey Broad, "The Didactic Element in the Works of Peter Altenberg," Ph.D
diss., Otago, 1980, 64.

8: The Final Years

Vita Ipsa

The grim coda to Altenberg's life encompassed not only personal calamity, but also the disintegration of the Dual Monarchy. His perpetual financial worries were, however, temporarily alleviated in 1916 when a deal with Alfred von Schebek, of Schloß Hodkov near Zbraslavic in Central Bohemia, raised 1,000 crowns for the manuscripts of *Fechsung* and *Nachfechsung* (at that time there were roughly eight crowns to the U.S. dollar.) The manuscripts arrived safely on 18 September 1916 and went straight into Schebek's library, by which time Altenberg and Schweitzer had enjoyed six weeks on holiday at Weyer an der Enns in Upper Austria, with excursions to Eisenerz and Leoben in Styria.[1] This holiday in the "Gesäuse," when for the first time in three years Altenberg escaped the summer heat of Vienna, appears to have been genuinely happy. On returning to the city, however, a nervous crisis confined him to his room for eight weeks. Looking back on this period at the very end of his life, Altenberg recalled a feeling of being buried alive, a fate even worse than that of Frank Wedekind and Gustav Klimt, both of whom had died in the course of 1918 (LA 292).

Despite his illness, the late autumn of 1916 was at least partially enlivened by an infatuation with a Hilde Berger, who worked in a fashion salon at the celebrated 40 Neustiftgasse, built by Otto Wagner in 1909–1910. However, thoughts of death were never far away when in late spring 1918 he published *Vita Ipsa*, with its memoirs of happier times. Thus, the genial recounting of the vacation in "Sommerreise" (VI 84) leads directly on to "Mein Begräbnis" (VI 86) in which, instead of wreaths, Altenberg requests donations to children's charities.[2] In similar vein, "Mein Testament," written in 1917, publicly declares Paula Schweitzer to be Altenberg's universal beneficiary (VI 118). With some percipience he recognizes the importance of his photograph albums for posterity, even foreseeing the day when Schweitzer might become rich: after all, he writes with deadpan humor, "ein bißchen Optimismus *gehört* zum Leben, wenn man gestorben ist" [a bit of optimism is a *necessary part* of life when you are dead: VI 119]. He fantasises about the nation buying his estate for 25,000 crowns, little knowing that a decade later the state would turn down his effects, supposedly for lack of space. It is not

---

[1] WSB 115.762; 115.801; 116.819. See also letters in the GSE and VI 112.

[2] An account of the actual funeral appears in Karin Michaelis, *Das heilige Feuer. Schicksale und Menschen*, (Dresden: Carl Ressner, 1930), 279–280.

hard to guess his reaction to a single inscribed postcard by Altenberg today
costing several thousand schillings at Viennese antiquarians.

When *Vita Ipsa* came out it bore a personal dedication to Frau Dr. Paula
Deman-Schweitzer (*sic*) who had become, rather suddenly, the wife of a
Regimental Doctor Demant (shades of the tragic Jewish regimental doctor
Demant in Joseph Roth's *Radetzkymarsch!*) How Paula came to meet and
marry her husband, who was already the father of an infant daughter,
emerges somewhat cryptically in *Mein Lebensabend*. There Altenberg recounts how he married off his "sacred blond friend with the most ideal boy's
legs" to one of his deepest and most understanding admirers, the deeply
melancholic regimental doctor Dr. D. who had spent a year in solitary confinement in Siberia (LA 292). Anton Kuh believed Altenberg had simply
grown tired of Schweitzer, and that in the end he was relieved to see her go.[3]
In a letter to "Dr D." dated 9 June 1917, Altenberg refers to Demant's
"new young girl friend" as "the anti-whore," something rare enough in a
woman for it to be worthy of comment (LA 99). Paula departed Vienna for
married life in Innsbruck on 31 July 1917 (VI 144), and in compensation
Altenberg dreamt of taking a thirteen-year-old girl on a trip to the Schneeberg, to show her the peace of the mountains amidst a world he considered
stupid, uncouth, and ugly (VI 145).

The sudden change in her status seemingly took even Schweitzer by surprise. This emerges from a letter she wrote to a girl-friend, which Altenberg
had somehow obtained, but which he had no qualms about publishing (VI
208). The elegiac, deeply dejected "Sonntag der Einsamkeiten," dated 1 July
1917, nevertheless alludes to problems in their relationship, hardly surprisingly given an age gap of almost forty years:

> Ich bin durch Leid, Selbstbesinnen, Angst, Dich zu verlieren nun zum
> Dichter geworden für Dich . . .
> Drei Jahre lang warst Du die "Photographie meines geistig-seelischen
> Ich", die ewig besorgte Mütterliche, die ergebenst Schwesterliche,
> die grenzenlos lautlos Duldende . . . nie, nie, nie mich eigentlich je
> enttäuschend; . . .
> und ich "besann mich nicht,"
> daß ich, Alter, Kranker, Armer, Ungetreuer, Gleichgültiger, allzu Wil-
> lenstärker,
> ein Milliardär war, durch Dich.
> Nun aber besinn' ich mich!
> Sei gegrüßt, Paula! Wenn auch zu spät. (VI 230)

[Through suffering, self-reflection, fear of losing you, I have now become a poet for you . . . For three years you were the "*photograph* of my
intellectual and spiritual self," *the ever the caring mother, the most devoted sister*, boundlessly and silently suffering . . . never, never, never, ever actually
letting me down; . . . and I "didn't realise" that I, old, sick poor, unfaithful,

---

[3] Anton Kuh, *Luftlinien. Feuilletons, Essays und Publizistik*, ed. Ruth Greuner, (Vienna: Löcker,
1981), 464.

indifferent, all too self-willed, was thanks to you a millionaire. But now I realise! I send you my greetings, Paula! Even if they come too late.]

The inability — or refusal? — to spell Paula Demant's married name correctly in the dedication of *Vita Ipsa* may reflect Altenberg's unreadiness to accept the radically changed circumstances he appears to have willingly engineered. The ensuing loneliness doubtless contributed to his rapid decline. During 1917 the deaf sculptor *cum* poet Gustinus Ambrosi (1893–1975) who in February 1915 had celebrated Altenberg in verse, completed an outstanding bronze bust of the poet which well captures his condition. Infinitely sad, with an aura of suffering wisdom, the downcast eyes of the poet avoid all contact with the observer. Of the sculptor, Altenberg cryptically remarked that Sisyphus must have smelled like Ambrosi.[4] Writing to his publisher Kurt Wolff on 7 August 1917, Franz Werfel, who had moved to Vienna to work for the Kriegspressequartier and had lodgings beside Altenberg in the Graben Hotel, noted that although he appeared very sane indeed, he was living in terribly unsettled circumstances and seemed very ill.[5] From now on little went right for Altenberg, and even Paula Demant's decision to name her baby son Peter proved scant consolation, for he had naturally hoped she would give birth to a girl.[6]

Altenberg's personal dedication to his former companion, inscribed in her copy of *Vita Ipsa*, is back-dated to Innsbruck, October 1917, when the poet had left Vienna to visit the couple at home in Tyrol, apparently at Paula's urgent behest (LA 107). He left Vienna on 2 October 1917, in the company of Paula and shared a compartment with the working class Socialist writer Alfons Petzold. A tactless item in *Mein Lebensabend* suggests that the Demants' marriage was less than idyllic: Altenberg records a remark attributed to "Dr. D", who claimed that an unhappy marriage with somebody like "P. Sch." was still better than a supposedly happy one with anyone else (LA 48).[7] In the same volume, a deft pen sketch of Paula, cigarette in hand, hatless, with open-necked blouse might well indicate someone for whom conventional marriage in the provinces would have proved irksome after life in the capital with somebody as outré as Altenberg (LA 52). The public dedication in *Vita Ipsa* signals also a desire to restore a relationship which had come under great strain during the month he spent with the newlyweds in Innsbruck.

[4] The bust is in the Gustinus Ambrosi Museum at 1a Scherzergasse, in Vienna's 2nd district. See Franz Renisch, *Gustinus Ambrosi*, (Vienna: Österreichische Galerie, 1990), 816–817.

[5] *Kurt Wolff. Briefwechsel eines Verlegers 1911–1932*, ed. Bernhard Zeller and Ellen Otten, (Frankfurt: Heinrich Scheffler, 1966), 117.

[6] Photographs of Paula and infant son are preserved in the GSE.

[7] It is not known what became of the marriage. However, the now Paula Oberländer was living in Cernauti-Czernowitz in Romania in the early 1930s (WKA). She visited the restored Peter Altenberg room in Otto Kallir's Neue Galerie on 11 September 1931 (*Otto Kallir-Nirenstein. Ein Wegbereiter österreichischer Kunst*, [Vienna: Eigenverlag der Museen der Stadt Wien, 1986], 43.) Her eventual fate, and that of her child, is unknown.

One source of the tension must have been Altenberg's bourgeoning passion for the seventeen-year-old Alma Ptaczek, a Christian girl from an originally Tyrolean family whom he first met in 1916 (LA 118–119, 123) and who would later publish under the name of Alma Holgersen.[8] When Altenberg met her she was studying piano at the Academy in Vienna with the great Emil Sauer. The daughter of a retired senior civil servant, her blond hair and boyish figure were calculated to arouse his passion, to which he gave free vent in letters written whilst visiting Paula Demant in Innsbruck. From these letters,[9] it appears that Ptaczek was in many respects a substitute for Demant-Schweitzer. He is even crass enough to tell her she was a more beautiful version of Paula, whom he rails against for the "crimes" she has committed against him. Predictably, he declares Ptaczek to be his sole heir in the event of his death, inheriting the contents of his room and the annual income from his books, which he claims is about 5,000 crowns per annum.[10] She declined the honour because her parents would never have permitted it.

On 1 October 1917, the day before leaving Vienna for Innsbruck, Altenberg wrote hymnically about Ptaczek (LA 105), yet on 3 October he apostrophized the recently-married Paula Schweitzer (*sic*) with a rash of exclamation marks: "Ich liebe Dich!!!!!!!" (LA 107). A letter of 16 October to his confidant and adviser Emil Franzos, whose importance along with that of his art-loving wife Lotte was now considerable, shows the poet's mind once more in a fragile and febrile state. Keeping confidences was not a priority:

> Unter dem Siegel *tiefster Verschwiegenheit* Herr Dr D . . . ..hat mir heute . . . das ihn lange bedruckende Geständnis gemacht, daß Paula seit Wochen es in *raffinirt geschickter* Art bei ihm *versuche,* seine Freundschaft, *Verehrung, Anerkennung,* ja *Begeisterung,* für mich als Menschen *und* Dichter, zu *untergraben,* zu *vernichten,* ja fast *unmöglich* zu machen, um "freie Hand" zu bekommen und ihre *jüdische Seele* von meiner Gewaltherrschaft endgiltig befreien, und vor allem über ihn eine größere Gewalt zu bekommen, da er bisher an *meiner* "Geistigkeit" und "Persönlichkeit" einen Rückhalt hatte!!!
> Ihr verzweifelter und körperlich *todeskranker*
> Peter Altenberg][11]

> [Under the seal of *deepest secrecy* Dr. D . . . ..confessed something which had long been troubling him, that in her *crafty clever way* Paula had been *trying* for weeks to *undermine, destroy,* make virtually *impossible* his *friendship, veneration, acknowledgement,* indeed *enthusiasm* for me as a person

---

[8] Dietmar Grieser, *Eine Liebe in Wien,* (St Pölten and Vienna: Verlag Niederösterreichisches Pressehaus, 1990), 145–152. Grieser gives her age as 21 (147). The author has unearthed many valuable details about their relationship, but both his chronology and details of Altenberg's life should be treated cautiously.

[9] Extracts of the correspondence are cited in Grieser, *Eine Liebe,* 148–150.

[10] Ibid. 151. See, however, WSB 115.771 where he claims his income is down to 2,000 Crowns a year.

[11] WSB 115.785.

and poet, so as to gain a "free hand" and to liberate at last her *Jewish soul* from my tyranny and above all to gain greater power over him because he previously had found support in *my* "intellectuality" and "personality"!!!.
Your desperate and mortally sick
Peter Altenberg.]

Another letter to Franzos, postmarked Innsbruck, 17 October 1917, contains more imprecations against Paula, but letters in this mode were becoming commonplace as Altenberg discovered enemies everywhere. The printed page cannot convey the anguished multiple underlinings which characterize these tortured manuscripts:

> Paula hat mich aus *entsetzlich-Strindbergischen* Gründen hierher *gelockt*, um "*ihre Macht zu erweisen*", läßt mich jetzt hier, in der *fremden Stadt*, den *Todeskranken*, vollkommen mir selbst und meinem *schrecklichen Schicksale* überlassen!
>
> Ich flehe *Sie* an, *erretten* Sie mich aus der *entsetzlichen* Lage, in die eine *alleregoistischste* Frau einen *unglückseligen gläubigen Dichter* gebracht hat!
>
> *Erretten* Sie mich aus diesem *schauerlichen* Egoismus. P. A.= Péché! Man hat mich nur hergelockt, um "dem *Anderen*" zu beweisen, *wie* wertvoll man selbst sei, *pfui*.
> Ihr verzweifelter
> Peter Altenberg[12]

> [Paula has *tempted* me here for *appallingly-Strindbergian* reasons in order to "*demonstrate her power*," and now here in this *strange city* she abandons me, a *mortally sick man*, completely to my own devices and my *terrible fate*!
>
> I implore *you*, *deliver* me from the *appalling* situation into which a *totally self-centred* woman has delivered an *unhappy trusting poet*!
>
> *Save* me from this *dreadful* self-centredness. P. A = Péché! I was *only* lured here in order to prove to "the *other man*" *how* valuable one is oneself, *ugh*.
> Your desperate
> Peter Altenberg]

In this same month of October 1917, Kraus made space in *Die Fackel* not only to attack in epigrammatic verse the antics of Hofmannsthal, Bahr, Dehmel and Hauptmann, but also to praise an old friend in need:

> P.A.
> Klarer als solche wohlerzogene Dichter
> hast du im Nachtlokal und bei der Flasche
> die halbe und die ganze Welt erfaßt.

---

[12] WSB 115.786. Altenberg's almost comic distress contrasts most oddly with a postcard the Demants sent Lotte Franzos on 16 October, thanking her for the marvellous work by Klimt which had arrived that day and which together with Peter they had sat and admired all morning in the café (WSB 116.225). Emil and Lotte Franzos were obviously good friends to more than Altenberg.

Du steckst das ganze Taggelichter
von Dichtern und Bürgern in die Tasche
wiewohl du andres drin noch lieber hast.

[P. A.
More clearly than such well-bred poets
you grasped in the night clubs and in your cups
the demi-monde and the whole world.
You stick the whole diurnal rabble
of poets and burghers into your pocket
though you'd rather have something else there.][13]

Altenberg returned the compliment in *Vita Ipsa* with "Wie ich mir Karl Kraus 'gewann'" (VI 165), as well as his own sparing epigram:

K. K. - - - Mundus?
Etsch!
Noch lange nicht!
Ein geniales Teilchen. (VI 159)

[K. K. - - - A world?
Rubbish!
Not by a long chalk!
An inspired particle!]

By late 1917 Altenberg needed all the support he could muster; many passages in *Vita Ipsa* show him on the point of conceding, with often paranoid hyperbole, that his battle might be lost. In "Der Verlust," inspired by the "dead poet-hero" Hans Leybold's essay on him in *Die Aktion*,[14] Altenberg admits he sees no happy and hopeful future, no way out of life's many labyrinths. With what he describes as a surfeit of creative power, he had created ten substantial tomes, but now, alas, his "Lebens-Maschinerie" [vital machinery] simply functions in the same way as that of everyone else: he no longer notices anything particularly remarkable, he has lost his spiritual reserves (VI 137).

In the absence of Paula, whose goodness and maturity radiate from the pages of *Vita Ipsa*, Altenberg's life finally collapsed under the combined effects of alcohol, sleeping potions, and a bad fall in late 1917, when he suffered a compound fracture of his left wrist.[15] This fall marks the beginning of the end, but not of his need to write. Indeed, the months of Altenberg's demise are richly documented, both in published autobiographical texts and extant manuscripts such as the diary-like "Inventar- und Merk-Büchlein" where the meticulous concern with day-to-day finance, down to the price of

---

[13] Karl Kraus, *Die Fackel*, 472–473 (1917): 21.

[14] Hans Leybold, "Wege zu Peter Altenberg," *Die Aktion*, 5 (1915): 73–80.

[15] The death of the test pilot Karl Josef Saliger on 16 July 1917 was a further factor in Altenberg's gathering gloom. See WSB 115.815.

the last picture-postcard, is recorded alongside the practical concerns of a literary life. We learn, for example, that despite his injury, Altenberg's productivity stretched the capacity of his publisher to the limit. He takes a lordly line with Fischer, whose schedules manifestly could not keep pace with the supply of texts:

> Monday, 11. /2. 1918 granted permission to Mr S. Fischer, Berlin W 57, Bülowstraße 90 to publish my new book *Vita Ipsa* in 2 parts, No.I at *Easter*, No. II *in the autumn.*[16]

The notebooks confirm that Altenberg's reputation for financial prudence was more than anecdotal. They expose not merely a pathological penny-pincher, but one who by tallying his belongings found a tangible reality in a world spinning out of control. They document a life whose most private moments now scarcely deviated from the image projected in the published work. Pathetically, the absent Paula remained central to his financial plans. He now cut a sadly isolated figure, although his money worries were probably more imagined than real. One entry records the gift on 8 August 1917 of 1,157 crowns from a Frau Dr. R., which had all been spent by 15 September, on which day he received a 3,000 crowns advance from Fischer for *Vita Ipsa* (these manuscripts would eventually go to the collector Alfred von Schebek in June 1918.)[17] Nevertheless, the accounts show September 1917 as a month of crisis. Neither the purchase of four photographs of naked children for five crowns nor the receipt of corrections for *Vita Ipsa* on 22 September provided him with any joy. When setting out for Innsbruck on 2 October Altenberg's frame of mind was already deeply disturbed, and any euphoria at being with Paula again was merely temporary.

Vita Ipsa, yet more confessional than its immediate predecessors, proves a vehicle for Altenberg's obsession with providing guidance to a benighted mankind. However, he can no longer conceal a contempt for "the herd" (VI 13) which is tantamount to misanthropy: "I do not *hate* people, for *that* would be *ignorant*, I *despise* them, I *deride* them! (VI 15). As usual when talking of people, Altenberg really means the mendacious strategies of bourgeois behavior in the realms of sex, marriage, child-rearing, friendships and careers. To be a bourgeois woman means falling for the blandishments of luxury and ornamentation (VI 35), whereas Paula, servants, waitresses and young girls escape Altenberg's censure. Enemy nations do not, although they figure less than in *Nachfechsung*. England is a criminal and selfish shopkeeper, Italy and France are "misguided, sham-romantic countries, easily aroused to false enthusiasm," Russia a genius lacking leadership, "gleichsam ein Goethe in einem 2 Mark-Bordell verkommen" [going to seed as it were like a Goethe in a down-market bordello: VI 16]. With Paula Schweitzer, Altenberg ceremonially burnt Maeterlinck's *La Vie de l'abeille*, hitherto one

---

[16] GSE

[17] Many letters detailing the break-down in sales of his books and his ensuing income from Fischer are preserved in the WKA.

of his "life-bibles," an incident which was, of course, transmuted into a sketch, "Das Autodafé" (VI 91).

This silly incident, and idiocies like the tirades against Italy, have to be set against such writing as "Die 'dienende Klasse', im Weltkrieg" where the ability to record the thoughts and experiences of humble, anxious people remains as acute as ever (VI 102). People still responded to his writing, and as he remarked in a letter to Max Oppenheimer, he was probably the only person to receive alms from the front.[18] One of the book's most effective items is the tiny cameo "Die Mutter," where the poet's capacity for empathetic understanding is undiminished. The prolix projections of the Peter Altenberg persona give way to taut, unsentimental prose as the artist describes the thoughts of an anxious mother whose son has been called back from leave to fight on the Italian front:

> Heute morgens ist der Franz weggefahren.
> Urlaub unterbrochen.
> Telegramm von der Isonzo-Front:
> Einrücken!
> Gestern abends hat er nichts gegessen
> Ich habe in der Nacht einen leichten "Brech-
> Durchfall" gehabt.
> Er wollte nicht, daß man ihn auf die Bahn begleite.
> Ich sah dem "Einspänner" nach, bis ich nichts
> mehr sah. (VI 38)

> [Franz went off this morning.
> Leave cancelled.
> Telegramme from the Isonzo-front.
> Report back!
> Last night he ate nothing
> In the night I had a mild attack of vomiting and
> diarrhoea.
> He didn't want me to accompany him to the station.
> I watched the trap until I couldn't see it any more.]

"Die Mutter" is, however, untypical of the work as a whole. If Altenberg really were writing about "life itself," then *Vita Ipsa* would relate far more than it does to the dark days of a war-sick city. As Herbert Ihering noted in a belated review in the *Berliner Börsen-Courier* of 31 January 1919, by which time Altenberg was dead, not only was he repeating himself, and "repetition is powerless,"[19] but Altenberg and the world had now drifted apart. In his early work, poet and world had been one, but this harmony was now lost, superseded by concern with presenting a minutely detailed spiritual portrait of "P. A.". Like Goethe, mentioned approvingly on several occasions in *Vita*

---

[18] *Berliner Tagblatt* 286, 19 June 1927. Reprinted in Andrew Barker and Leo A. Lensing, *Peter Altenberg. Rezept die Welt zu sehen,* (Vienna: Braumüller, 1995), 342.

[19] Herbert Ihering, "Theater, Musik und Kunst. Peter Altenbergs letztes Buch," *Berliner Börsen-Courier* 51, 31. 1. 1919. Reprinted in Barker and Lensing, *Rezept,* 296–297.

Ipsa, Altenberg pretends to an Olympian pose now that life's battles are supposedly behind him:

> Es ist vorüber . . .
> Das wilde Wetter meiner Seele hat sich verzogen.
> Heiter wird es und rein,
> Nur hie und da ein leichter Wolkenschleier. (VI 63)

> [It is past . . .
> The stormy weather of my soul has dispersed.
> It is bright and clear,
> only here and there a a thin veil of cloud.]

Nobody who knew Altenberg would have been fooled, for as Ihering noted, the more world and poet grew apart, the noisier and more violent both became. The music disappeared as depictions of the persona displaced the work of the poet. Nevertheless, Alban Berg read *Vita Ipsa* with great seriousness, making copious annotations in the margins of his copy, and not surprisingly, reacting positively to texts such as "Kunstgewerbliches" showing Altenberg's continuing adherence to the Loos-Kraus aesthetic:

> Mein Tintenfäßchen ist aus braunem Glas, fabelhaft leicht zu reinigen, kostet 2 Kronen, und heißt noch dazu "Bobby", also jetzt "Robert". Es ist daher ein Kunstwerkchen, es erfüllt seinen Zweck, stört Niemanden und ist schön braun. (VI 48)

> [My little inkwell is made of brown glass, fabulously easy to clean, costs 2 crowns, and moreover is called "Bobby," well, "Robert" nowadays. It is thus a little work of art, it fulfils its purpose, disturbs nobody and is a beautiful brown.]

In Berg's copy of *Vita Ipsa* a single word is inscribed beside this not unironic passage: "Loos."[20] Altenberg's desire for simplicity in life and art remains undiminished, the "*simplicities* and the *power* of a Mozart, a Beethoven" (VI 121) remain an artistic ideal. In "Ehrgeiz" and "Speisehaus Prodromos. Ein unerfülltes Ideal" (VI 72) he weaves fantasies of turning the banks of the Danube at Klosterneuburg into a huge nature reserve and building a primitive hotel whose menu would be all you might expect from the author of *Pròdròmòs*.

Despite its constant strictures against ornament, *Vita Ipsa* also reveals Altenberg's return to the world of jewelry design and manufacture, continuing earlier attempts with the "P. A.-Kollier." Besides designing blouses for Paula (VI 79) he applied to patent his "Donau-Kiesel," polished stones taken from the Danube, with 20% of the profits to go as a "patriotic gift" to those blinded in the war (VI 65).

A noteworthy feature of Ihering's review is its final paragraph, which enlarges upon the commonplace observation about Altenberg as a Viennese

---

[20] This inkwell is now in the Historisches Museum der Stadt Wien, 94.605–1, 2.

Socrates by pointing out the fundamentally oral nature of his achievement.[21]
Ihering believed that those who experienced the latter-day Altenberg would
instantly recognize the "fanatically ecstatic, fanatically ironic, fanatically flirta-
tious tone of the homilies addressed to his drinking companions." Unlike
any previous book, *Vita Ipsa* must be judged according to the modulations
of the speaker of the texts, but according to Ihering, although it contained
the gestures and intonation of Altenberg, it had hardly any of his soul. When
written down, Altenberg's coffeehouse language lost some of its genius, but
even in its inferior guise it contained more fantasy and humorous insight into
people than in the collected poetic works of *fin de siècle* Vienna.

Altenberg would probably have agreed with Ihering's strictures about
Young Vienna, for in "Stimmung" he expresses contempt for the generation
of 1900. Altenberg's is a holistic but also mechanistic approach to life and
art; the need for "Stimmung," the buzz-word of literary decadence, is dis-
missed in a favourite phrase as a "Lebenslüge" [sham]. Can he have forgotten the exquisite evocations of mood in the "See-Ufer" sketches?:

> Es gibt nur "*somatische*" Ursachen, *alles* Geistige, Seelische ist nur eine *not-
> wendige* Konsequenz der *Gesamt-Maschinerie*. Bessere die Schräubchen, die
> Ventile aus, und die "Stimmung" kommt von selbst! Wenn die
> "Maschinerie" *prompt* funktioniert, funktionieren auch Geist und Seele
> *promptest*! (VI 105)

> [There are only "*somatic*" causes, *everything* intellectual, spiritual, is merely
> a *necessary* consequence of the *total-machinery*. Improve the screws and
> valves, and the "mood" will come by itself! If the "machinery" functions
> *promptly*, then mind and soul will also function *most promptly*!]

By now Altenberg's sympathy for the literature of impressionism was
limited, although *Vita Ipsa* refers favorably to Schnitzler's *Dr Gräsler,
Badearzt* which appeared in 1917 (VI 38). Altenberg's interest in the painter
and poet Uriel Birnbaum (1894–1956) and his "Abenteurer" cycle points to
a sympathetic awareness of expressionism (VI 70–71), as does the association
with Franz F. Kocmata and his journal *Ver!*, subtitled with a possible allusion
to Adolf Loos's *Das Andere*, "auf daß der moderne Geist in Allem und
Jedem zum Ausdruck komme" [So that the modern spirit might gain expression in each and everything]. The first issue of *Ver!* came out in Vienna
in August 1917, opening with Kocmata's interview with Altenberg in which
the poet spoke slightingly of England, the very mention of which made him
incandescently angry.[22] Altenberg's influence upon *Ver!* was considerable. In
"Die Menschen" (LA 275) he claims to have given Kocmata the title for the

[21] W. B. Spinnen, "Die Seele in der Kritik. Zur zeitgenössischen Rezeption Peter Altenbergs,"
M.A. diss., Münster, 1983, 115; Arnold Hollriegl, "Peter Altenberg in Elysium," *Vossische
Zeitung*, 25 January 1919, has an imaginary meeting in heaven between Altenberg and Socrates.
Altenberg described himself as a "modern Socrates" (in inverted commas!) in a letter to Lotte
Franzos of 22 January 1915 (WSB 115.789).

[22] Hedwig Prohaska, "Peter Altenberg. Versuch einer Monographie," Dr. Phil. Diss., Vienna,
1948, 187–188.

journal, suggested its green cover and exercise-book format and donated five free sketches. Considerably indebted to *Die Fackel* — the June 1918 volume was dedicated to Kraus — *Ver!* survived until its thirty-third issue in February 1921, which was devoted to Altenberg's memory.

In December 1917 Altenberg suffered the fall from which he never recovered fully. Bad times were thus made worse. He aged rapidly, his "elasticity" deserted him, his incapacity isolating him further in a city which charmed him less and less. In June 1917 he had even applied for a residence permit to go and live in Gmunden (LA 262). For nearly five months he was effectively out of circulation (LA 268), confined to the hotel room his brother called a "Vorgrab" [early grave: LA 263] and he his "Sarg-Kabinett" [coffin room: LA 287].

As Altenberg's world caved in around him, one solution was to seek what he termed regeneration cures in such hardy stand-bys as laxatives and footbaths. Unfortunately, these harmless remedies were offset by an increased reliance on alcohol and paraldehyde, now regularly taken at forty times the dose originally prescribed in Steinhof. As if isolation and pain were not enough, Altenberg received a further blow with the death of Gustav Klimt on 6 February 1918. For once, instead of him relating the event immediately and exclusively to his own plight, Klimt's passing inspired a heartfelt tribute from the self-obsessed writer, inscribed on the mount of one of Klimt's drawings and dated 21 February 1918. From this eulogy we nevertheless realize that the artist Altenberg admired was not the sexually-charged painter of female nudes, but the landscape artist in whose withdrawal from the world Altenberg discovered a parallel with himself. The tribute closes with the simple, but heartfelt words: "Gustav Klimt, Du warst ein Mensch!!! [Gustav Klimt, you were a real human being!!!][23]

The Evening of my Life: *Mein Lebensabend*

Altenberg did not live to see the publication of *Mein Lebensabend*, whose opening pages come close to a consequential autobiography in sketch form. In light, graceful prose he reviews his parents, scenes from childhood, education and his first love, a twelve-year-old girl with whom he played hide and seek around the Theseus-Temple in the Volksgarten (LA 6). The relaxed, playfully ironic mood of these pages does not, however, last. The urge to recapture the past, eliciting sketches comparable with his best, simply could not withstand the dark realities of his life's end: physical and mental capitulation to drugs and alcohol amid the collapse of the Austro-Hungarian Empire.

The handsome photograph album Altenberg received from Paula Demant for his birthday on 9 March 1918 contains numerous examples of his

---

[23] Alice Strobl, *Gustav Klimt*, vol. 5, *Gustav Klimt 1862–1918. Zeichnungen*, (Vienna: Albertina, 1962), 252. A slightly different translation of this text appears in Fritz Novotny and Johannes Dobai, *Gustav Klimt*, (Boston, New York: Graphic Society, 1967), 393. For the impact of Klimt's death see also the unpublished text "Fernwirkung" in the Bibliotheka Jaglionensis, Kraków.

support for the final throes of the Austrian war effort and his love of the House of Hapsburg. Altenberg was far more bourgeois than he would ever have admitted to himself. The album's dedication also confirms Paula's enduring love for him. Though married and living far away, she maintains, somewhat implausibly, that nothing has changed since their first contact. She even claims that everything is exactly the same as it was on 9 March 1914.[24]

Several of Altenberg's photograph albums are still extant, in Austria, Germany and the United States,[25] and as detailed examination has revealed, they are far from being haphazard images inserted into the albums as the spirit moved him.[26] They have their own narrative and pictorial structures, inspired by concerns that are identical or similar to those that inspired Altenberg's written texts. Often inscribed by Altenberg himself, the images in the final album of 1918 are arranged to express his concern with the passage of the war, the relationship between the self and nature, the impact of war upon the natural world, and more specifically, his relationship with Paula Demant.[27]

Although his last book appeared as *Mein Lebensabend* in the spring of 1919, the proofs which Altenberg received in late November 1918 are stamped not with that title, but with "Vita Ipsa II."[28] The published title was presumably validated by a text written on All Souls Day, 2 November 1918, in which Altenberg wishes only to live long enough to see what he knows will be his last book, to be called "Mein Lebensabend" (N 146.) The following day the Austro-Hungarian monarchy effectively ceased to exist when it unwillingly signed the cease-fire a week before its German allies. Altenberg's expectation that his book would appear at Christmas with a print run of around 4,000 was thus dashed both by his own deepening crisis and that of the world in general (LA 259). When *Mein Lebensabend* did appear in March 1919, the first print run of 8,000 was a record for an Altenberg text, Fischer rightly calculating that the author's recent death would prove a spur to increased sales.[29]

The memories of happier days with which *Mein Lebensabend* opens soon yield to the dismal chronicle of Altenberg's last six months, making it the darkest and most self-absorbed of all his works. However, the extent to which the inclusion of much of the morbid and chronologically confused material is the work of the anonymous editor cannot now be ascertained. What is certain, is that *Mein Lebensabend*, garnished with a melancholy and

[24] Altenberg spent the evening of his fifty-ninth birthday at the cinema watching an Erna Morena movie with Paula's then-husband Dr. Demant and his cousin Lotte.

[25] The only album in a public collection, "Semmering 1912," was acquired by the WSB 1994.

[26] Barker and Lensing, *Rezept*, 169–190.

[27] Of the two albums in the WKA, the first, begun on 15 September 1915, is dominated by images contrasting war with nature, the second, started in Innsbruck on 17 October 1917, during his stay with Paula, reflects his passion for Alma Ptaczek. This album would appear to be the direct predecessor of the 1918 album in the GSE.

[28] GSE

[29] Spinnen, diss, 124.

world-weary portrait of the author, differs considerably from "Vita Ipsa II." A Fischer Verlag memo, probably in Polgar's hand, dated 21 February 1919, details excisions from Altenberg's manuscript: those with blue pencil through them are contained in *Mein Lebensabend*, those penciled out had been considered unsuitable.[30] It may also be significant that *Mein Lebensabend* includes the text "Versöhnung," describing how after a long estrangement "P. A.", whose initials are capitalized, makes his peace with Polgar, "a. p.", whose initials are small-lettered (LA 122). Thus Polgar himself may well have prepared *Mein Lebensabend* for publication, prior to officially editing *Der Nachlaß*, completed in the winter of 1921, but only published in 1925. The surviving galley proofs of "Vita Ipsa II," which Altenberg saw, diverge considerably from the published *Mein Lebensabend* and illustrate the limited extent to which the form of *Mein Lebensabend* as published can be ascribed to Altenberg alone.

Re-emerging into life in the spring of 1918 after five months on his sickbed (LA 268), Altenberg's thoughts were never far from suicide. Lacking the resolve to take his own life, he railed incessantly against the curse of addiction, chronicling in detail the euphoria of various regeneration cures, these invariably followed by relapses and depression. The cure detailed in his diary on 19 June explains why, for alongside a large number of eggs it consisted of a litre of white wine and six glasses of plum brandy! Interspersed with texts cursing paraldehyde are others where Altenberg appears petulantly proud of his addiction to this "heilige Schlafmittel" [sacred barbiturate: LA 231]. Using an image which perversely attempts to portray the poison as natural, he even contends that to renounce paraldehyde would be like asking a darting trout to try out stagnant pond water (N 127). He was also well aware of the appalling effect wine had on him — it would indirectly lead to his death — yet he continued drinking it in vast amounts as a spur to creativity (LA 238).

In a letter of December 1918, sent by registered express mail, Altenberg inquired of his vintner how much seventeen bottles per week of riesling would cost.[31] In "Trebern" — the title refers to a brand of schnaps — he boasts that in the absence of talent, stimulants alone have made him into a poet (LA 239). And it is in such texts, playing again the role of the *poète maudit*, that he claims to have given guidance to girls and young women (LA 239). On 11 June 1918 he recorded the experience of a night without barbiturates, when in place of paraldehyde he continually drank Upper Austrian riesling. Perceiving himself as a certain candidate for death (LA 243), he objectively assesses his life as the "inescapable tragedy of ego and at the same time a comedy" (LA 244). The wine may well have aided his creativity, for "Die Nacht ohne Schlafmittel" belongs to the better items in the book. The next day he declared he was writing his final sketches for the enlightenment of others (N 145), two days after that on 14 June he recorded how toothache had struck him for the first time in his life. The refrain here, as so often

[30] GSE
[31] GSE

in *Mein Lebensabend*, is the need to hang on until his sixtieth birthday on 9 March 1919.

As ever in times of stress and distress, Altenberg found solace not just in drink, but in self-effacing young women ready to pander to his ego and his oddness. Alma Ptaczek was still exercising his thoughts on 14 June, as he noted in the birthday album he had received from Paula, and on 15 June he wrote a tribute to the blonde, eighteen-year old Else Körber who in February had left her job in a bakery to look after him (LA 248). On June 16 he inscribed a copy of *Vita Ipsa* for one Poldi Kühhaß, a postal worker in the Bräunerstraße in Vienna. With his customary effusion he tells her that her hands, arms, hair and figure make her a "P.-A. Ideal" whom he must serve from the depth of his being (LA 251). Perhaps on this day too he received the letter dated 15 June which an Alma Mandl sent from Klobenstein near Bolzano, telling him that since reading *Vita Ipsa* her every day and hour had been filled with admiration and gratitude for the poet.[32] Again on 16 June he recorded in "Besuch" the thoughts of one Henriette H. who looked upon him as the sheet anchor of her life (LA 252).

A seemingly profound cure was effected on 26 June 1918, four days after the composition of "Krisen," in which Altenberg claims again to have overcome a six-month long crisis (LA 229). A consultation with his admirer the professor of psychiatry and Nobel laureate Julius Wagner von Jauregg (1857–1940) had convinced him that his extraordinary lifestyle allowed but two possibilities: delirium or cancer (LA 282, 287). Faced with the prospect of an imminent return to the padded cell (LA 261) it seems that he astonished Jauregg with his miraculous ability to cure himself instantly of the paraldehyde addiction which had intensified since abusing the drug to dull the pain of his fractured wrist. Perhaps, however, the real reason for Altenberg's apparently instantaneous cure lay in Jauregg's notorious use of electric shock treatment on the soldiers under his care at the psychiatric division of the Allgemeines Krankenhaus in Vienna. Jauregg even reported Altenberg's case in a lecture to his colleagues, for such a swift recovery was inexplicable and hitherto unknown.

Since 26 June Altenberg had also regained his "earlier elasticity, as if saved through a mystery, through physiological Christianity" (LA 288). In his diary for that day Altenberg announced a new regeneration cure after a sudden "deliverance" had taken place between 10 a.m. and 2 p.m., a claim to be treated with caution, for similar cures were now coming thick and fast (N 146). Those of 22 and 26 June were preceded by one on 26 May, when Altenberg had written to Emil Franzos claiming that he would not be re-entering the sanatorium because he was completely cured since renouncing paraldehyde.[33] Yet on 24 May he had noted he was "completely destroyed" and could not even summon the courage to kill himself. On 25 May he concluded that his life was absolutely lost (N 145). Georg Engländer must have

[32] GSE
[33] WSB 115.767.

set little store by such repeated "cures," for Altenberg reported to Franzos in the autumn that there was imminent danger that his brother would take steps to deprive him of his liberty. Referring proudly to himself as the author of *Vita Ipsa*, which had gone through seven impressions within a few months, he is in no doubt about what he wants: "I demand my *absolute* personal freedom, at *my own* peril! . . . I wish to find perdition alone and in my own fashion."[34]

Altenberg's feeling that the "cure" of 26 June was genuine was bolstered by the receipt the next day of 1,000 crowns from Schebek for the sale of manuscripts. The interrelationship between biography, literary texts and the photograph album is particularly marked at this juncture, where the photograph album acts as a sort of scrapbook *cum* diary. On a single page are mounted the remittance note for Schebek's money and a cheap tear-off calendar slip dated Saturday 29 June and subtitled "Pet. u. Paul" — the Feast of St. Peter and St. Paul, names who symbolism cannot have escaped Altenberg. Partly covering the calendar date is a printed receipt for the Apotheke zum schwarzen Bären in the Graben, the pharmacy where Altenberg obtained the drug from which he now considered himself delivered. Inscribed underneath the calendar slip are the words "Feiertag in jeglicher Hinsicht! PA" [Feast day in every respect! PA]. Beneath this verbal collage Altenberg has mounted two photographs. On the left is a demure female nude with the inscription "*Idealer* Leib! PA" [Ideal body! PA], to her right a photograph of the costumed Grete Wiesenthal in a pose quite reminiscent of the anonymous nude model, whose full-frontal photograph appears elsewhere in the album. Underneath both photographs is a rural landscape, inscribed in Altenberg's hand "Nach dem Gewitter!" [After the storm!]. On this page we are invited to follow Altenberg's own (mistaken) interpretation of his fantasies and witness his sense of relief that a particularly trying period in his life had reached a satisfactory denouement.[35]

This led to some bizarre flights of fancy, most notably a letter to Grete Wiesenthal on 1 July, in which Altenberg confidently announced his intention of partnering her on the occasion of his sixtieth birthday (LA 288). His imagination ran riot as he set out the scenario, himself in silk Lido-cap and Lido-bathing suit, bare-footed and in shorts. Between her individual numbers, which Altenberg would accompany with gestures, he would perform solo Ashanti dances. He would also compose the rhythms, which any competent Kapellmeister could set for orchestra in five minutes. To finish with, he intended to dance a six-step with her.[36]

Such temporary relief from a depression was further helped by Professor Viktor Hammerschlag's recommendation of a new "sacred" laxative, guar-

---

[34] WSB 115.770.

[35] This page is reproduced in Barker and Lensing, *Rezept*, 188.

[36] A translation also appears in Harold B. Segel, *The Vienna coffeehouse wits*, (West Lafayette: Purdue University Press, 1993). Altenberg says he will also dance with Grete at Ronacher's night club in October (LA 293).

anteed to keep him youthful for years (LA 228–229). Now making the best of the harsh times, which also saw the withdrawal of the free supper he had enjoyed at Ludwig Domansky's Hotel Residenz since May 1915 (NF 331), Altenberg even claimed that the privations of war, which by July 1918 had reduced him to a diet of potatoes, possessed a rejuvenating effect, not just physically but also spiritually and intellectually (N 118). However, his letters to Lotte Franzos and her husband Emil, whom he dubbed the "only Philistine who was not a Philistine,"[37] disclose Altenberg still exploiting their tolerance and support up to and beyond the limit. Along with Georg Engländer, Else Körber and Victor Hammerschlag, the Franzos's had stood by Altenberg during the problems triggered by his broken wrist, whereas the rest, he felt, had let him down (LA 272).

As the war took its toll, the failure of such friends and patrons as Julius Muhr and Ernst von Lieben to pay their *Renten* in the accustomed manner further upset Altenberg's fragile equilibrium. He was most particular not just about the amount paid, but also about the method of payment, especially as his earnings from Fischer were in decline. A letter to Franzos of 21 June 1917 says that Muhr was unwilling to pay a fixed *Rente*, insisting rather on guaranteeing a sum of 1,000 crowns over the year as a whole. The importance of such money can be judged from a letter to Franzos claiming that Altenberg's total income from S. Fischer for the year 1917 had been 2,000 marks.[38] His resentment stoked by paranoia, ferocious diatribes ensued; the language in letters to Franzos written in 1918 betrays a fearful anger. Ernst von Lieben is a monster, inhuman, a Satan,[39] Julius Muhr is an indecent Jewish devil and lunatic who has maliciously persuaded Lieben to suspend his financial support.[40]

A closely related obsession in the summer of 1918 was the desire to reach his sixtieth birthday on 9 March 1919, and to organise a collection to celebrate it. A typescript draft for the appeal, doubtless composed by Altenberg himself, claims his right to demand such a modest tribute of gratitude from the human race to which he has donated, and is still donating, infinitely more than it can give him back.[41] To Siegfried Jacobsohn in Berlin Altenberg wrote pleading for yet another public appeal on his behalf, this time in the columns of the influential journal *Die Weltbühne*. The refrain is unchanging: his economic circumstances are desolate, but the chutzpah turns to comically servile flattery when he informs Jacobsohn that his periodical is the only one he loves.[42]

---

[37] WSB 115.789.

[38] WSB 115.771.

[39] WSB 115.756.

[40] WSB 115.760.

[41] WSB 116.221.

[42] Hedwig Prohaska, "Peter Altenberg. Versuch einer Monographie," Dr. Phil. Diss., Vienna, 1948, 210.

Emil Franzos, now placed at the pivot of Altenberg's financial ambitions, had the temerity to suggest that any monies raised should be placed in to a fund from which he could then draw regular interest. The response was both anxious and choleric, for Altenberg regarded this not as sensible financial management but as the equivalent of certifying him mentally incapable, and this would be the same as murdering him.[43] Franzos's initially gentle response to this letter was to remind Altenberg on 6 July that so far not a single penny had been collected, but his frayed patience is all too clear as he suggests Altenberg is active enough to take charge of his own affairs and organize the collection in the manner he thinks most appropriate.[44] Whereupon the poet turned to Lotte Franzos, begging her to dissuade her husband from leaving him in the lurch. His letter contains the crudest emotional blackmail: should Franzos shift the responsibility for the appeal back on to Altenberg himself, then he would have no option but to return to paraldehyde.[45]

The following day Altenberg's free supper was withdrawn, and his diary betrays a rather different response than that noted above: he now experiences the "complete organic collapse of his nervous system and the most profound melancholy" (N 145). By 19 July he had gone to pieces again, nearly immolating himself by falling asleep in bed with a lighted cigarette (N 132). Repeated protestations to have stopped smoking were as hollow as claims he had overcome drug addiction.

Although the war was making terrible inroads into the lives of every Austrian citizen, *Mein Lebensabend* reveals even less about it than its predecessors. Only rarely do we find texts with the power of the sketch "Natural-Wirtschaft" (LA 272). In terms reminiscent of Kraus, Altenberg relates an incident, reported in the *Reichenberger Tagespost*, where a soldier entered a brothel in Graz and offered thirty eggs and a half kilo of butter in exchange for sexual services. Two girls accepted the barter. The next day an officer and a detective appeared enquiring about the theft of eggs and butter from the battalion. The girls admitted receiving the foodstuffs, and were locked up for 48 hours. This powerful text is, however, an exception. Absorbed in himself, Altenberg continues to inhabit as far as possible the world of yesterday.

On 13 July he conjured up the magical world of the Vienna Stadtpark, its "fairytale trees, fairytale shrubberies, fairytale paths" which are far more conducive to good health than any cure in the spa at Karlsbad, Franzensbad or Teplitz. The reduced circumstances of everyday life in the capital are reflected in an elegiac lament for a lost world: where, the poet asks, is the elegant handcart made of varnished light brown wood, formerly used for spraying the dusty paths in summer? How can they possibly curtail this activity? It doesn't cost much to employ a lad to go out and "lay the dust which

---

[43] WSB 115.801.

[44] WSB 115.801.

[45] WSB 115.773.

murders the lungs" (LA 307). For all its delicacy, this passage betokens a loss of contact with life in a society on the brink of collapse.

Equally revealing is the short text "Bemerkungen zu einem 'politischen Attentate'" (LA 58) which does not even specify that it was evoked by the murder in 1916 of the Austrian Minister President Karl von Stürgkh by Friedrich Adler, son of the Socialist leader Viktor Adler. The text contents itself with setting the scene for the coming assassination in a Viennese restaurant, detailing what was on the menu — ironically it was a "meat-free day" — and ending lamely with the observation that nobody knew what was about to take place. Yet even this trifle of a text on a momentous issue did not escape Altenberg's attention, for he wrote a letter to the Fischer Verlag noting the failure to return his manuscript along with his other "Oktober-Skizzen." The tone is only partially ironic as he requests the return of a text for which he possesses no copy: on no account should this be lost to the "world" (Altenberg's own quotation marks.)[46] The general level of Altenberg's political engagement seems well captured in an anecdote which went the rounds shortly after the assassination: Altenberg decided that Adler really must have been insane because he had paid for his meal before pulling the trigger. In the ensuing commotion, he asks, who would have stopped to consider whether the bill had been settled?[47]

Reared in an age of elegance and plenty, Altenberg could not envisage the new utilitarianism. By 3 August he felt "completely abandoned, isolated and pushed into the corner" (N 132). 8 August was even worse, "a miserable, grey suicidal day" (N 133), and he plunged into an ever deeper depression, exacerbated because he felt that critical recognition of *Vita Ipsa* had failed to materialize. An exception was the periodical *Ver!* which printed a review which Altenberg felt was lenient, decent, and just (LA 276). Personal letters of recognition for *Vita Ipsa* (N 133) can only have been partial compensation, though Altenberg still set great store by the sort of letter he received in early August from an Alice Pilzer, telling him that her lonely life on the Hungarian puszta was enriched by reading his books.[48]

For the most part, however, Altenberg's last summer was fraught with misery. In a letter to Lotte Franzos on 19 June he had revealed his intention of spending July and August in the Salzkammergut resort of Bad Aussee, as if the summer rituals of the old world were still to be observed. By escaping from Vienna he hoped to find the "peace, ideal peace and freedom from

---

[46] GSE

[47] Peter Haage. *Der Partylöwe, der nur Bücher fraß. Egon Friedell und sein Kreis*, (Hamburg: Claassen, 1971), 76.

[48] Barker and Lensing, *Rezept*, 45–46.

care" as well as the proper food such as eggs — a main ingredient in the "regeneration cure" — which were now hard to obtain in the city.[49] He did not make the trip, and it is unlikely he ever again saw the lakes and hills of his beloved Salzkammergut.

---

[49] WSB 115.799.

9: Epilogue

Death in Vienna

In the late summer of 1918 Vienna was hit by the Spanish flu epidemic which added still further to the European death toll. Although he was untouched by the disease, Altenberg's depression was deepened by the premature death of so many non-combatants. Increasingly, his thoughts concentrated on his own mortality. Morbidity being part of his mental make-up, this was nothing new. Nevertheless, an altogether more genuine sense of desolation and impending demise imbues his writing from now on. Many self-excoriating texts have survived from his last months, displaying a cool-headed realism and brutal frankness which still shock the reader. Altenberg knew the end really was in sight; he was prepared for it, and able to write about the experience. His confidence was nevertheless severely shaken, for when the *Berliner Börsen-Courier* requested an item for their jubilee edition on 1 October 1918, he could merely reply that he was concerned night and day with the ending of his own unbearable existence.[1]

He now felt desperately alone, surrounded by ignorant people barely belonging to the same species as himself (N 135). So disillusioned and misanthropic had he grown that he even wished flu upon the "people" (Altenberg writes "Menschen [?!?]") around him (N 136). The desire to see his sixtieth birthday, and to have this milestone properly remunerated, grew increasingly at odds with his growing wish for death, and for once even he saw the contradiction. The birthday became an irrelevance as he reviewed the "unnatural" deaths of so many friends and acquaintances, all of them "lebensfähiger" [more vital] than himself (N 130). He now found little point in living to see the appearance of his last book (N 135). Many believed that in the end Altenberg had grown so alienated that he consciously willed his demise, thereby committing a sort of suicide. Astonishingly, despite his appalling abuse of stimulants, he remained sound in body if not in mind, leading Anton Kuh to conclude that he was simply unable to adapt to the new realities of post-Imperial Vienna.[2]

Political and natural catastrophes helped stoke feelings of despair, but Altenberg's reactions to the historical and environmental cataclysm of late 1918, as to the prospect of death itself, were coloured by obsessions long

---

[1] Hedwig Prohaska, "Peter Altenberg. Versuch einer Monographie," Dr.phil diss., Vienna, 1948, 53.

[2] Anton Kuh, *Luftlinien. Feuilletons, Essays und Publizistik*, ed. Ruth Greuner, (Vienna: Löcker, 1981), 464–465.

predating the present malaise. Thus the death of the sixteen-year old Jewish girl Trude Klebinder on 4 September had to be bent into the shape of Altenberg's own version of reality. Taking the newspaper announcement of her death, he proceeded to reconstruct his own text out of it. Her particular case is generalized under the title "Alltägliche Tragik," the familiar Trude becomes the more formal Gertrude, and a cause of death, Spanish flu, is inserted where in the original notice none was given. In addition, all references to her Jewishness are excised.[3] On All Saints Day, when the cult of the dead is observed with especial fervor in Austria, Altenberg simply copied out the death notice of Alfred Kerr's young wife Inge, who had died, aged 21, on 23 October 1918, entitling it "Tragödie des Daseins. Allerheiligen 1918."[4] Yet another text entitled "Allerheiligen 1918" speculates upon his own death which he expects to occur as soon as his next birthday has passed (N 146–147). Two days later, the Austro-Hungarian empire itself died, but Altenberg seems to have been too preoccupied to notice the event.

This already intense concern with individual mortality, in counterpoint to the collapse of the very state itself, was further heightened by the deaths of Egon Schiele and wife at the end of October. In the posthumously published "Die Spanische Grippe" Altenberg evokes their premature end, concluding of Egon Schiele that he was a good painter, that is to say, someone who was special and different (N 114). In a text dated 2 November (All Souls Day) Altenberg tried again to come to terms with the death of an artist whose expressionist excesses obviously unsettled him. Influenza may have relieved Schiele of his "tortured ambitions," but Altenberg was unconvinced that the artist would ever have achieved anything "naturally." Just how "unnatural" his own life and work had been seems to have escaped Altenberg as he apostrophizes the dead painter who time and again had drawn girls who were abnormal, deformed and virtually half-starved rather than the "genuinely dematerialised ideals" of Altenberg's own Dante-esque fantasies. Implicitly comparing the painter with himself, Altenberg concludes that Schiele's idealism had no power and that his power was lacking in idealism (N 136–137)[5]

Although he was now painfully aware of his own mortality, the old Altenberg, capable of "the most profound enthusiasm for things worth enthusing about" (N 141) could still briefly be reactivated. On 7 November, seeing a shop-girl at work in a delicatessen transformed him not just into an enraptured youth, but back into "P. A." himself, effusive, enthusiastic and "wunschlos" [contented: N 138].[6] Such lack of self-insight is untypical of Altenberg's writing in general, and of his last work in particular. The well-rehearsed, formulaic, hyperbole is given a final airing as his vision transforms the girl from a shop assistant slicing salami into a saint whom he worships.

---

[3] GSE

[4] GSE

[5] For a more detailed examination of Altenberg's responses to Schiele see Barker and Lensing, *Rezept*, 107–111.

[6] See also "Die Bedienerin," LA 340, where he writes in similar vein.

His passion is, however, conditional; no longer can he forget the circumstances which prevent the "old" Altenberg from giving free rein to his feelings. It may seem like a return to earlier ways, but there is even more artifice
than usual in "Die Bedienerin," composed on 9 November to acknowledge
how sickness has dampened the ardor which made him the writer he once
was (LA 340). In truth, his boundless enthusiasm, lunatic passion and crazy
idealism had been sapped not just by illness, narcotics, alcohol and despair,
but by the grimness of the age itself.

The tone of much of Altenberg's last writing mixes the genuinely tragic
with the maudlin and outraged. He complained of isolation — and certainly
in the last months of his life we hear nothing of old friends like Kraus and
Loos — but his condition continued to attract the foremost medical men of
the day. After Werner von Jauregg it was the Freudian rebel Alfred Adler's
turn to treat the ailing poet. However, the consultation was brief and unsuccessful, to judge from the letter Altenberg sent Bela von Gomperz on 2 December excoriating the "jüdische *und* christliche *Lausbuben*" [Jewish *and*
Christian *rascals*] who have exploited him for twenty years: "You see how
the psychiatrist Alfred Adler *immediately* left me in the lurch!!! He knows
why!!!"[7]

Altenberg also continued firing salvoes of panic and despair at Lotte and
Emil Franzos. His concerns are familiar ones: misery at his addiction to paraldehyde, the necessity of financial patronage, his forthcoming birthday, and
the terrible prospect of being readmitted to the asylum. The tone and vocabulary of these letters is unwavering. Nevertheless, they are not just cries
from the heart, but consciously composed epistolary texts whose bold and
confident calligraphy contrasts markedly with the sentiments expressed. A
letter of 10 December is typical, but typographic conventions fail to evoke
the manic multiple underlinings of the word *Todesnöten*, where the clichéd
expression "in Todesnöten" — in a desperate situation — regains the force
of its original meaning:

> An Frau Dr Lotte Franzos!
>
> Hilfe! Erbarmen! Es ist doch schließlich ganz gleichgiltig, *was* daran
> schuld ist!
>
> Ich flehe Sie und Ihren von mir *geliebten* Mann um Errettung aus ei-
> nem "Schlafmittel-Abgrunde." Vergönnen Sie mir noch das *letzte* Ergebnis
> eines 60. Geburtstages.
>
> In Todesnöten
> Ihr verzweifelter Peter Altenberg.[8]

[Help! Mercy! In the last resort it is entirely irrelevant *what* is to blame. I
implore you and your husband, whom I *love*, for deliverance from the
"barbiturate-abyss." Grant me the *final* outcome of a 60th birthday. In
mortal anguish, your desperate Peter Altenberg.]

---

[7] WSB 206.692.

[8] WSB 115.774.

A further letter to Lotte Franzos, dated 13 December, again screams for help, its tenor typical of Altenberg's correspondence in the final months of his life:

> Ein "Sanatorium" ist direkt ein Mord, nein, ein *Meuchelmord*, da diese *verbrecherischen Idioten* von meiner pathologisch-exzentrischen Organisation nicht die geringste Ahnung haben können, und einen Menschen wie mich mit ihrer *bequemen-schamlosen* Schablone ermorden . . . *Helfen Sie mir*!!![9]

> [A sanatorium is simply murder, no, it's *assassination*, for these *criminal idiots* cannot have the faintest inkling of my pathologically-eccentric organisation and are murdering a person like me with their *conveniently-shameful* clichés . . . *Help me*!!!]

December 1918 witnessed a further downward lurch, but no letup in the need to record in writing his worsening state of mind and body. It is as if Altenberg were taking his own case notes, addressing himself as often as not in the second or third person. On 13 December this self-dialogue concluded: "Du stehst vor . . . vor Deinen eigenen *unüberbrückbaren* Abgründen" [You stand . . . before your own *unbridgeable* abysses: LA 352–353]. The same day he wrote to Lotte Franzos that he was lost, but that it was nobody's fault but his own.[10] On 14 December Altenberg composed a text marked by repetitive, pathos-ridden parataxis which expressed the fear that a bite from a possibly rabid stray dog would prove fatal. The shifting perspective, always avoiding the first person, and a desperate search for objectivity, typify this last phase in Altenberg's career. At times it is not even clear whether the subject of the discourse is Altenberg or the dog, and as with all great and true clowns, the effect is to induce laughter and pity in almost equal measure:

> Ein Hund beißt ihn, ein verlaufener, kleiner Hund. Ist er krank, ist er gesund, Niemand weiß es, Niemand kann es erkennen. Er erwartet sein Schicksal, Niemand kann ihm irgendwie helfen. Der Hund hat ihn gebissen. Das Schicksal droht über Deinem unglückseligen Haupte. Wirst Du schrecklich untergehen oder nicht?!? Beides ist möglich. Das frißt an Dir bei Tag und bei Nacht. Nie hört es auf, es zerrüttet Dich, gegen Deinen Willen. Ein Hündchen hat dich gebissen, bei Nacht. Niemand weiß es, ob er gesund oder krank war. Du lebst seitdem unter einem schauerlichen Schicksale, Niemand vor allem kann Dich erretten. (LA 355)

> [A dog bites him, a little stray dog. Is he sick, is he healthy, nobody knows. Nobody knows, nobody can tell. He awaits his fate, nobody can help him in any way. The dog has bitten him. Fate hangs threateningly over your unhappy head. Will you perish appallingly or not?!? Both are possible. It's eating away at you day and night. It never stops, it is shattering you, against your will. A little doggy has bitten you, at night. Nobody knows whether he was healthy or sick. Since then your life is governed by an appalling fate, for nobody can save you.]

[9] WSB 115.775.
[10] WSB 115.775.

It is with this tragicomic cry *de profundis*, a tortured self-analysis confronting the ultimate isolation of every existence, that the editor brings *Mein Lebensabend* to a close. As Altenberg himself noted, neither friends, nor doctors, nor drugs can substitute for self-help: our only crutches are our mind and our soul, and nothing else. (LA 357).

Thanks to the remarkable detail in which Altenberg chronicled his demise, the onset of death can be traced to 1 a.m. on 19 December 1918. On the morning of 19 December the bronchial catarrh which had plagued him in early adulthood now recurred. He finishes with the words of Horace: "Sunt certi denique fines" [Everything has its limits: N 127]. On 20 December 1918, in a text originally entitled "Die Rettung", he still salutes, without a hint of irony, the virtues of "mens sana in corpore sano" (N 138).[11] On 21 December, however, he recorded briefly and coolly how two days earlier he had knocked over a full glass of wine onto his bed linen and slumbered on in the icy wetness with the windows wide open. At 1 a.m. on 23 December Altenberg announced the end of his life as a poet and as a human being before launching an attack of unparalleled ferocity upon his mother and father, sick parents of a sicker son (N 141). The birthday which only two days earlier he had still anticipated seeing (N 126) becomes part of the quasi-obituary of a "living corpse," written in the third person (N 141).

Yet life of a sort went on. He wrote to Lotte Franzos on 23 December telling her he would be at the Stadt Brünn restaurant on Christmas Eve at 6 o'clock sharp;[12] Christmas Eve was a "sacred day" day not for its religious connotations, but because it was spent in the company of Alma Ptaczek. The seemingly endless Christmas Day was spent alone, writing to Ptaczek to thank her.[13] This last, lonely Christmas was itself then later recorded in the unpublished "Mein Weihnachtsabend 1918." There had been no visitors, no gifts, "no distinctive walking stick or glass or clay vase, nothing at all." The "living corpse" motif occurs again, but thanks to a new and safe sleeping medication called Brom Ural, available without prescription, Altenberg claims to have slept properly for the first time in fourteen months, that is, since his return from Innsbruck, his accident and spiraling addiction. In a mood of reconciliation the poet concludes this was a Christmas gift of far greater value than anything he might have received from friends. It was the "gracious gift of a benevolent fate."[14]

On 27 December Altenberg was in the company of friends, but on returning home in the evening he yet again he evoked the formula of the living corpse to describe his condition, reciting the names of those who had remained staunch to the end. However, their efforts at help met with a ferocious misanthropy: Josephine K., Johanna St., Járo Fürth, the Gomperz brothers und Else Körber had stuck by this "living, crippled, breathing

---

[11] Alfred Kerr, "Dem toten Peter Altenberg," *Die neue Rundschau* 30, no. 3 (1919): 339.

[12] WSB 115.803. See also the unpublished text "Mein Weihnachtsabend" (GSE.)

[13] *Volkszeitung*, Klagenfurt,17 February 1980, 11.

[14] GSE

corpse," but their advice was brushed aside with contempt. Their failure to get to the bottom of him reduces them to "Mörder mit guten Absichten" [well-intentioned murderers: N 142].

The last text of any substance from Altenberg's pen, dated Sunday, 29 December, underlines the inevitable isolation of each individual's departure from the world. Altenberg's leave-taking is fittingly set in the apparently sociable milieu of a Viennese café. Surrounded by friends, he is fully alert to the ironies of his situation. Drinking raspberry cordial tea, hot chocolate and coffee, eating ham sandwiches, they dole out advice to a drug addict who is beyond their help. By now a semi-detached onlooker upon his own last days, Altenberg still had enough energy to turn his demise into prose. This last text is typically formulaic, yet at the very end he conjures up an image of striking freshness. Once again, we note the use of the third person:

> die Sorge seiner wenigen wirklichen Freunde glitt bereits an ihm ab wie Quecksilberkügelchen von einer Glasplatte! (N 143–144)
>
> [the concern of his few real friends slid off him like pellets of mercury from a plate of glass]

In the schizophrenic manner so typical of his last months, and not without a dash of self-pity, the writer takes leave not so much from his friends as from himself: he bids farewell to the unhappy poet who had given his soul to everyone and who had been the cause of his own demise (N 144).

All that survives after this are a few letters to friends such as Karl Hollitzer regarding illustrations for a possible book to celebrate his sixtieth birthday. Anton Kuh reports the receipt a postcard on 6 January imploring his help in getting a sugar baron to join the list of people giving him *Renten*. By now, however, Altenberg had disappeared from circulation, and towards 9 p.m. on 6 January some concerned friends went to his room in the Graben Hotel. There they found him in a delirious state. An ambulance took him to the Allgemeines Krankenhaus in the Alser Straße where, on the assumption that he had taken an overdose of paraldehyde, his stomach was pumped. When this produced negative results, and his temperature rose to 40 degrees, it was discovered that in fact he had advanced pneumonia (N 148). He died on 8 January 1919, just two months short of his sixtieth birthday. His last words were "Pfui - Leben!" [What the hell - live!][15]

The funeral was fixed for 11 January, and at 4 p.m. on a bitterly cold winter's evening Peter Altenberg was lowered into a municipal grave of honour at the Vienna Zentralfriedhof. Posthumous respectability had come with remarkable swiftness. A death mask had been taken by Alexander Jaráy,[16] and a report of the poet's appearance in his coffin describes a face which had finally found more peace and happiness in death than it ever had in life.[17] De-

---

[15] Andrew Barker and Leo A. Lensing, *Peter Altenberg. Rezept die Welt zu sehen*, (Vienna: Braumüller, 1995), 330.

[16] Eugen Thurnher, *Neue Deutsche Biographie*, (Berlin, Duncker and Humblot, 1953), 213–214.

[17] Prohaska, diss., 57–58.

spite the weather, the time of the year, and the times themselves, hundreds turned out for his Catholic funeral at which aristocrats rubbed shoulders with tramps, artists with peddlars, rabbis with priests.[18]

Karl Kraus, who had hardly figured in Altenberg's last months, read the generous oration for the "Narr, der uns Normen gab" [fool who set our standards].[19] Others were less generous, with some especially vicious obituaries appearing in the Nationalist and anti-Semitic press. In 1920 Kraus felt compelled to gather together these depressing documents in *Die Fackel* under the title "Peter Altenberg und die Christen."[20] Yet the disturbing ambivalence of Altenberg's own position (and Kraus's too) on the Jewish question can be seen in the Altenberg material Kraus chose to publish in *Die Fackel* in the spring of 1919.[21] The first items are Kraus's graveside oration, separate copies of which were sold in aid of Altenberg's favorite children's charity, followed by a poem where Kraus not only draws attention to the fact that the dead writer had changed his name, but also *inter alia* to his dog-like empathy:

> Dies Auge sah den Herzen auf den Grund
> und fühlte Schmerz und Liebe mit dem Hund.

> [This eye saw to the bottom of the heart
> and felt pain and love with the dog.]

Following this comes the sketch "Bully," composed on 25 August 1918, in which Altenberg speaks approvingly of a dog. All this might be regarded as the satirist simply wanting the last word in their long-running squabble about dogs, but the final item opens up deeper issues. Kraus presents a lithographic reproduction of a letter from Altenberg, written in 1914, in which the poet launches an anti-Semitic tirade against the Jewish elements in Austrian literature, requesting Kraus to annihilate them.[22] In a linking paragraph between "Bully" and this intemperate letter, Kraus draws a comparison between his dead friend's ability to evoke the nature of man's best friend, and the antics of the "Köter", the (Jewish) mongrels of the Viennese press who, in Kraus's view, had so exploited Altenberg.

When the details of Altenberg's will were revealed, many were astonished and even embittered to learn of the fortune which the perennially impecunious *Schnorrer* had managed to accrue. According to Anton Kuh, Altenberg bequeathed 107,834 crowns to the Viennese children's charity Kinder-Schutz- und Rettungs-Gesellschaft. But those who took offense at the extent

---

[18] Karin Michaelis, *Das heilige Feuer. Schicksale und Menschen*, (Dresden: Carl Ressner, 1930), 279–280.

[19] Peter Altenberg, *Auswahl aus seinen Büchern von Karl Kraus*, (Vienna: Anton Schroll, 1932), 521.

[20] Karl Kraus, *Die Fackel*, 546–550 (1920): 41–44.

[21] Ibid., 508, (1919): 8–14.

[22] Barker and Lensing, *Rezept*, 258. Kraus conceals the identity of the specific target of Altenberg's abuse, Ludwig Ullmann.

of Altenberg's wealth had, in Kuh's opinion, simply failed to understand the essence of the man: his goal had been to live as a true poet in complete independence, free from care and compromises. What is more, as an inspired dietician he had also wanted to live until he was 130 years old. Without amassing a fortune, how could these two goals ever be achieved?[23]

Dead, but not forgotten

Despite the attentions of the anti-Semitic press, numerous warm tributes were published in the immediate aftermath of Altenberg's death, their praise for his achievements masking the isolation of his last days. On 19 January a memorial concert was held, at which a brass ensemble from the Vienna Opera played music from *Götterdämmerung*, Friedell read an address and leading actors and actresses recited from Altenberg's works.[24] The proceeds went towards the erection of a graveside monument and the children's charity mentioned in Altenberg's will. Later in 1919 a memorial was even erected to his memory in the arcades at Vienna University, then a hotbed of German nationalist sentiment.[25] Efforts were also soon afoot to realize Adolf Loos's design for the grave, a huge wooden cross, dwarfing the stone monuments alongside, and possibly overstating the apostate Jew's commitment to Christianity. As Altenberg had himself requested, the grave bore the inscription "Er liebte und sah" [He loved and saw], an epitaph which perhaps does less than justice to one of Vienna's more impassioned haters.

Once more concerning himself with Altenberg, Kraus played a major role in the fund-raising as well as keeping his friend's memory alive through public readings from his work.[26] Egon Friedell's contribution was to orchestrate the many contributions to *Das Altenbergbuch*, a title possibly inspired by Else Lasker-Schüler's *Das Peter Hille Buch*, her similar tribute to an author regarded by many as Altenberg's Berlin counterpart. In February 1921 the thirty-third and final edition of Franz Kocmata's *Ver!* was devoted to Altenberg's memory. Besides an important evaluation of Altenberg by Egon Erwin Kisch, it also contained a tribute from Erich Mühsam, intended for *Das Altenbergbuch* but turned down by Friedell on the grounds of decorum. Mühsam concluded that it was time for Altenberg's fellow-countrymen to stand before his grave and feel ashamed of the fate that had befallen him through their neglect and misunderstanding.[27]

The volume of *Ver!* was probably intended as competition for *Das Altenbergbuch*, its mostly young authors contrasting with the better-known and

---

[23] Kuh, *Luftlinien*, 463.

[24] Among those performing were his long-time friend Gertrude Barrison, Maria Mayen, Alice Lach, Karl Etlinger, and Karl Forest, brother of Lina Loos.

[25] Max Grunwald, *Vienna*, (Philadelphia: Jewish Publication Society of America, 1936), 529.

[26] Christian Wagenknecht, "Die Vorlesungen von Karl Kraus. Ein chronologisches Verzeichnis," *Kraus Hefte*, 35–36 (1985): 1–30.

[27] Erich Mühsam, "Gedenkblatt für Peter Altenberg," *Ver!*, 33 (1921): 358.

more established contributors to Friedell's volume. Many were so-called *Aktivisten*, whose political commitment stood in such sharp contrast to the world of the Café Griensteidl, in which Altenberg's first work had appeared. The activity surrounding Altenberg was by now quite intense. An edition of his letters, edited by Georg Engländer, was expected to come out in the Fischer Verlag in 1921,[28] but this did not appear. Neither, for the time being, did Polgar's edition of *Der Nachlaß*.

This collection of mostly late texts, including diary-like texts from Altenberg's last weeks as well as a long essay by Polgar himself (N 149–154),[29] was prepared at the request of Georg Engländer, who had assumed responsibility for his brother's papers. Despite Polgar's claims to have made no changes to the manuscripts apart from correcting spelling errors and excluding some wartime items he felt Altenberg himself would have wanted suppressed, the editing was not as neutral as Polgar maintains. Some texts in *Der Nachlaß* had previously been published by Alfred Kerr in March 1919,[30] and comparison reveals that cuts were made. Polgar also republished texts from *Das Altenbergbuch* and the third edition of "*Semmering 1912*". Indeed, there are several obviously pre-war texts in *Der Nachlaß*, relating in particular to Altenberg's relationship with Anna Konrad and the months in the Inzersdorf sanatorium.

One such is "Die Seidenfetzerln" (N 11), a text admired by both Kraus and the exiled Viennese writer Felix Pollak, who cited it in his critical demolition of Alexander King's English-language version of Altenberg's writing which appeared in the USA in the early 1960s. Describing "Die Seidenfetzerln" as one of Altenberg's most famous and enchanting stories, Pollak tries to communicate the magic of the piece through resumé, much as Bahr and Hofmannsthal had done on Altenberg's début nearly seventy years before:

> It tells of a little thirteen-year-old girl who showed Peter a few colored silk dress swatches which she had obtained from a girl-friend who worked in a tailor shop. 'Which one is the most beautiful?' asks the girl. Whereupon the elderly poet writes a short letter to a fashion store asking for a box of colored silk snippets, and when he receives the box, gives it to his little friend. The girl calls all her playmates together and after school they all sit on a dusty grass patch at the roadside and admire their hostess' treasures. When the sun goes down leaving 'blood-red zigzag lines' in the clouds . . ., they depart and the girl says to Peter: 'Tonight I'll sleep well and dream sweet, sweet dreams, but not of you but of your beautiful silk pieces.' That is all, but in Altenberg's way of telling it, it is sheer poetry."[31]

---

[28] "Briefe an St. Gr.," *Das Tagebuch* 1, no. 48 (1920): 1543.

[29] This a was reprint of the obituary notice in *Der Friede* 53, no. 3 (1919): 18–19. In 1919 Polgar published the story "Marthas Genesung" evoking Altenberg's memory: *Simplicissimus* 24, no. 35 (1919): 490, 502f.

[30] Alfred Kerr, "Dem toten Peter Altenberg," 329–335.

[31] Felix Pollak, "A case of literary blasphemy," *Southwest Review*, (1964): 89–91.

While Friedell, Polgar, and Kocmata remembered the dead poet through acts of commemorative celebration, other aspects of the remembrance of Peter Altenberg revealed the depths to which cultural politics had sunk in post-war Austria. *Die Neue Freie Presse*, as part of its running feud with Kraus, had intended to ignore Altenberg's death altogether, for the simple reason that Kraus gave the eulogy. Its change of mind came about only upon hearing that the municipality of Vienna was to bestow a grave of honour upon Altenberg.[32] In the event, the Socialist city fathers were represented neither at the funeral nor at the unveiling of his grave monument.[33] In 1920 Kraus also had to withstand a withering attack on his probity in Franz Werfel's drama *Spiegelmensch* where, without mentioning the satirist by name, Werfel assassinates the character of his former champion. The hero Spiegelmensch declares to the audience that he knows a great contemporary who, after eulogising his dead friend, then turned to the assembled mourners to enquire what sort of an impression he had made.[34]

Kraus's relationship with Friedell was also probably strained when *Das Altenbergbuch* was compiled, for it contains nothing by Kraus, to whom many of its contributors, for example Hofmannsthal, Bahr, Salten, were in any case anathema. Furthermore, Kraus had attacked Friedell in the *Fackel* of July 1920 for his readiness to propagate the Altenberg anecdotes which Kraus believed served only to demean the country's greatest poet.[35] A more charitable view would be to regard these anecdotes as good Jewish jokes, which may be why Kraus disliked them so much. Early in 1921 Kraus became embroiled in a lawsuit, which dragged on until the end of 1924: he was accused of trying to make money by selling copies of the Altenberg funeral oration. In reality the booklets had been sold to benefit the memorial fund. Throughout 1922 and 1923 Kraus toiled to raise money for Altenberg's grave marker, and when he finally closed the appeal in June 1923, the account stood at 11,288,267 crowns.[36] In mid-October Kraus announced an Altenberg Festival to commemorate the unveiling of the monument, and this event took place on 15 November 1923. However, nearly 300,000 crowns remained unspent, and in the spirit of Altenberg himself, the money was devoted to his favorite children's charity.[37]

The grave monument aside, the most tangible sign of Kraus's ongoing concern for the dead poet is the very fine anthology *Peter Altenberg. Auswahl aus seinen Büchern* which finally appeared in the Anton Schroll Verlag in Vienna in 1932. Originally entitled "Das Buch der Bücher von Peter Altenberg," this anthology, in whose production Sigismund von Radecki played a

[32] Reprinted in Raoul Auernheimer, "Peter Altenberg," *Das ältere Wien. Bilder und Schatten*, (Leipzig and Vienna: E. P. Tal, 1920), 160–167.

[33] Karl Kraus, *Die Fackel*, 668–675 (1924): 147.

[34] Franz Werfel, *Spiegelmensch. Magische Trilogie*, (Munich: Kurt Wolff 1920), 187–188.

[35] Karl Kraus, *Die Fackel*, 546–550 (1920): 38.

[36] Karl Kraus, *Die Fackel*, 608–612 (1922): 50–51.

[37] Karl Kraus, *Die Fackel*, 649–656 (1924): 71.

considerable part, was intended for publication with the Fischer Verlag.[38]
Given Kraus's strained relationship with Fischer and most of his Austrian
authors apart from Altenberg, it is surprising that he had agreed to work for
Fischer in the first place. Presumably he did so in response to their commitment to his friend's work, and after the anthology, proposed in 1925 by
Fischer's chief reader Oskar Loerke, had failed to materialize. Unfortunately,
however, Kraus's involvement coincided with a vicious feud with Alfred Kerr,
one of Fischer's most lucrative authors, and an admirer of Altenberg to boot.
After much unpleasantness, Kraus withdrew from the project, unwilling to
publish in the same house as Kerr, who was infinitely more valuable to
Fischer than Kraus. When the anthology finally appeared in Vienna, with
Fischer's permission, the proceeds went to Altenberg's heirs and the same
children's charity to which he had bequeathed his fortune.

A further indication that Peter Altenberg retained a faithful following in
post-war Vienna was the opening in 1927 of an Altenberg exhibition organized by the pioneering art dealer Otto Kallir-Nirenstein (1894–1978.) Kallir,
who owned the Neue Galerie in the Grünangergasse, had acquired Altenberg's papers and inscribed photographs after the death of George Engländer in 1927. According to Anton Kuh, Altenberg's brother had guarded Faf-
ner-like over the *Nachlaß*, numbering, ordering and cataloguing it with an
archivist's avarice.[39] Kallir then generously offered this horde to the city of
Vienna, but the gift was declined, ostensibly because there was no available
space for it.[40] On 10 November 1929 Kallir went a step further and opened
his reconstruction of Altenberg's last room at the Grabenhotel to the public:
only the bed was missing, kept by the hotelier as a souvenir. The writer Rudolf Huppert read a tribute, the Burgtheater actress Maria Mayen recited
Altenberg texts, Erika Dannbacher read from unpublished letters, and Elsie
Altmann-Loos recounted, inevitably, Altenberg anecdotes.[41] The room remained in situ until 1938, when under the onslaught of National Socialism
Kallir shifted his gallery first to Paris and then to New York. In 1950, many
items from the Altenberg room were acquired by the Historisches Museum
der Stadt Wien, where they have since lain in store, occasionally exhumed for
retrospective exhibitions on *fin de siècle* Vienna.

The tenth anniversary of Altenberg's death in 1929 saw further efforts to
keep alive his memory. Kraus organized Altenberg festivals in Berlin in October 1928 — this when his feuding with Kerr was at its height — and in Vienna in February 1929. Franz Glück, who was soon to begin collecting
Altenberg letters for publication, recorded the impact which Kraus still made

[38] WSB Druckschriftensammlung, Akten Samek C 147.951.

[39] Anton Kuh, "Peters Bruder," *Hamburger Fremdenblatt*, 112 (1927): 5. Kuh reports that two
years earlier he had offered the "Altenberg-Galerie" to Paul Cassirer.

[40] Oskar Bendiener, "Peter Altenberg — Erinnerungen," *Berliner Börsenzeitung* 72, no. 122
(1927).

[41] *Otto Kallir-Nirenstein. Ein Wegbereiter österreichischer Kunst,* (Vienna: Eigenverlag der Museen
der Stadt Wien, 1986), 37–38. The final photograph album of 1918 contains inscribed images of
Elsie, whom he inevitably found very attractive.

when reading Altenberg. After attending a reading on 8 February, he noted that Kraus's performance had itself been "a new work of art," the "noblest memorial for someone who will live forever."[42]

Marie Mauthner's collection *Die Nachlese*, published in 1930, was significant less for the quality of the texts than for her important biographical essay prefacing the collection, and the fine reproduction of photographs from the Altenberg Gallery. Mauthner was not a competent transcriber of her brother's manuscripts, and her decision to include material rejected by Polgar for *Mein Lebensabend* and *Der Nachlaß* is questionable. Without doubt, however, the biggest puzzle at this time was the non-appearance of Glück's edition of Altenberg's correspondence, announced as early as 1932 by Anton Schroll, publisher of Kraus's anthology. By means of a small advertisement inserted in the anthology, Schroll invited readers to subscribe to a volume of around 480 pages which promised to be a kind of epistolary biography. On 8 January 1934 Glück read from the collection at the Institute of Architects on the fifteenth anniversary of Altenberg's death. The proceeds from the reading were intended for the appeal for Adolf Loos's grave, situated only a few yards from Altenberg's in the Zentralfriedhof. A leaflet announced that the letters would appear in the autumn of that year, accompanied by many illustrations and facsimiles.

After the civil war of February 1934, however, the artistic climate in Austria was so changed that publication of Glück's volume became untenable. The First Republic was riven with internal differences and prey to a pincer movement from Nazis both inside and outside the land. This was even more the case in 1936, when Glück offered the collection of letters to the Bermann-Fischer Verlag in Vienna. The reply he received from Gottfried Bermann-Fischer was unequivocal in its belief that the times no longer suited the appearance of such a volume.[43] Glück went on to become the post-war director of the Historisches Museum der Stadt Wien, acquiring Altenberg material from Otto Kallir for his collection for the symbolic sum of 8,000 schillings.[44] After Glück's death the Deutsches Literatur Archiv at Marbach am Neckar acquired some items from his estate, but the whereabouts of the Altenberg letters remained unclear. It is now known, however, that the letters making up the unpublished volume are still extant, having passed into the possession of a private collector in Germany.[45]

Given that circumstances in Austria were less than conducive to civilized artistic discourse, the level of interest in Altenberg around the fifteenth anni-

---

[42] WSB Druckschriftensammlung L 137.759. Partially quoted in Susanne Rode, *Alban Berg und Karl Kraus. Zur geistigen Biographie des Komponisten der "Lulu"*, (Frankfurt: Peter Lang, 1988), 429.

[43] WKA.

[44] *Otto Kallir-Nirenstein*, 42.

[45] According to information in the WKA, the edition was ordered chronologically and contained many very early letters to Bertha Lecher and Ännie Holitscher. It would appear that Glück's editorial work went only as far as 1910. The considerable correspondence relating to the gathering of the material is in this archive.

versary of his death in 1934 remained surprisingly high. Days after the brief but bloody civil war, an old acquaintance of Altenberg's, the educationalist and reformer Genia Schwarzwald, was advertized to give a reading of his work organized by Richard Lanýi, publisher of *Nachlese*. In a letter reeking of the fear which the lurch to fascism had unleashed in many sections of the Viennese intellectual community, Friedell wrote to Lanýi on 22 February, supposedly on behalf of a sizeable group of people, requesting that the planned reading be cancelled. Friedell had been happy enough to include a piece by Schwarzwald in *Das Altenbergbuch*, but he now cited her lack of moral legitimation to read from the works of a writer such as Altenberg. Even though the event was ostensibly for charity, Friedell claimed that people were offended that the proceeds would go into Schwarzwald's pocket.

As the letter proceeds, however, it becomes obvious that this objection is a pretext for something far more disturbing. Friedell refers to strong trends in youthful circles against people like Schwarzwald, and is fearful that "Zwischenfälle" [incidents] might well occur should the planned reading go ahead. He tells Lanýi, whom he praises for the efforts he has already made on Altenberg's behalf, that it is his wish, and that of many others, that Peter Altenberg should not be dragged into this discord.[46] Friedell's call for appeasement shows how much Austria had changed since his friend's death, and how bleak the future was for the works of a writer like Altenberg, the very essence of a "degenerate" artist, in the Europe of the 1930s. For the next eleven years, cultural politics would be debated with slogans and jackboots.

Only on the other side of the Atlantic was there still chance to celebrate a writer whose world was soon to disappear forever. Thus in 1935 the American-Austrian Alexander King paid a theatrical tribute to Altenberg with *A Profound Bow to the Memory*, a *Lesestück* presented for one evening only at the Mercury Theatre in New York before 1,500 people. The performance even attracted the attention of the *New York Times* critic Brooks Atkinson.[47] Four years later, with once-Imperial Vienna now the provincial capital of Hitler's Ostmark, hundreds of Altenberg's letters, postcards and manuscripts, rescued initially from Vienna to Paris, found a safe refuge in Otto Kallir's new Galerie St. Etienne in Manhattan. It was the privilege of working with these manuscripts some forty years later which provided the impetus for this study.

---

[46] WSB 213.796.

[47] *Alexander King presents Peter Altenberg's evocations of love*, (New York: Simon and Shuster, 1960), 161.

Appendix 1

Altenberg published work in the following periodicals:

Der Brenner
Deutsche Bühnen-Genossenschaft
Deutsche Monatshefte
Deutsche Rundschau
Dramaturgische Blätter
Entwicklung
Das Forum
Frauen-Zukunft
Der Friede
Illustrierte Frauenzeitung
Der liebe Augustin
Liebelei
März
Münchner Salonblatt
Österreichische Rundschau
Pan
Patriotisches Extra-Blatt der Bühnen-Künstler
Revolution!
Die Rheinlande
Der Ruf
Die Schaubühne
Simplicissimus
Sirius
Das Stichwort
Das Tagebuch
Der Sturm
Das Theater
Ver!
Wieland
Wiener Rundschau
Die Zeit

Sources:

Thomas Dietzel, Hans-Otto Hügel, *Deutsche literarische Zeitschriften 1880–1945*, (Munich: K. G. Saur, 1988).

Paul Raabe, *Die Zeitschriften und Sammlungen des literarischen Expressionismus*, (Stuttgart: Metzler, 1964).

Appendix 2

Der Rendezvous

So gieng er denn 27 Abends in den Anstaltsgarten hinaus mit seinem Pfleger-Freund Josef Hennerbichler. Die Sträucher hatten noch keine Blätter, aber goldgelbe Blüten, lila, rosa. Auf den Wiesen waren weißgelbe Primeln, duftlose, und auf Felsblöcken schon goldgelbe duftende. Weit zog sich die braune Mauer hin. Ein Kind erkletterte mit nackten weißen Beinen geschickt eine weiße Birke, um über die Mauer hinüber zu schauen. Gärtner arbeiteten. Eine Pflegerin wünschte: Guten Abend! In der Ferne sah man den Rauch der Stadtbahnzüge. Das 15-jährige Kindermädchen kam nicht. Sie kam nicht und sie kam nicht. Es wurde dunkel und kühl. Sie kam nicht und sie kam nicht. Das war das große tiefe Ereignis in dem weiten kühlen Garten: *Sie kam endgiltig nicht!*

Am nächsten Tage sagte sie: "Weshalb waren Sie gestern nicht im Garten?! Ich habe Sie erwartet - - -."

"Ich war zu krank, um auszugehen - - -," erwiderte er.

Dann sagte er: "Ich *war* im Garten und *habe* gewartet."

Sie sagte: "Ich kauerte hinter einem Busche und sah Sie gehen, stehen, suchen, warten! Da traute ich mich nicht Sie zu stören durch meine unansehnliche Persönlichkeit - - -."

Dann sagte sie: "Und übrigens, hätte es denn *noch* schöner werden können?!?"

Der Garten wurde dunkel und kühl. Er sah nicht mehr die lange braune Mauer, die sich herumzog. Er glaubte im Freien zu sein, frei zwischen Wiesen, Hügeln, Wäldern, in einer zarten friedlichen und gütigen Welt - - -!

[The Rendezvous

So he went out into the sanatorium garden at 6.30 in the evening with his nurse-friend Josef Hennerbichler. The bushes still bore no leaves, only golden yellow blossom, lilac, pink. On the lawns there were yellowy white primroses, scentless, and on boulders the golden yellow ones were already giving off scent. The brown wall stretched into the distance. A child with bare white legs skillfully climbed a silver birch to look over the wall. Gardners were at work. A nurse said "Good evening!" In the distance could be seen the smoke of the suburban railway trains. The 15-year old girl did not come. She did not come, and she did not come. It grew dark and cool. She did not come and she did not come. That was the great, profound event in the large cool garden: *She simply did not come!*

The next day she said: "Why weren't you in the garden yesterday?! I was expecting you - - -."

"I was too sick to go out - - -," he replied.

Then he said; "I *was* in the garden and I *did* wait."

She said: "I crouched behind a bush and watched you walking, standing, searching, waiting! Then I didn't dare disturb you with my unappealing personality - - -."

Then she said: "And anyway, could it possibly have been *any* more beautiful?!?"

The garden grew dark and cool. He no longer saw the long brown wall winding its way around. He believed he was on the outside, free amongst meadows, hills, woods, in a gentle, kind and peaceful world - - -!]

(Manuscript in the Galerie St. Etienne)

Works Cited

Albertsen, Elisabeth. "Ea oder die Freundin bedeutender Männer. Porträt einer Wiener Kaffeehaus-Muse." *Musil Forum* 5 (1979): 138–139.

Altenberg, Peter. *Expedition in den Alltag. Gesammelte Skizzen 1895–1898*, ed. Werner J. Schweiger. Vienna and Frankfurt: Löcker and Fischer, 1987.

Anderson, Mark. *Kafka's clothes. Ornament and aestheticism in the Habsburg Fin de Siècle*. Oxford: Clarendon Press, 1992.

Auernheimer, Raoul. *Das ältere Wien. Bilder und Schatten*. Leipzig and Vienna: E. P. Tal, 1920.

Bahr, Hermann. *Studien zur Kritik der Moderne*. Berlin: Fischer, 1894.

Bahr, Hermann. *Secession*. Vienna; Wiener Verlag, 1900.

Bahr, Hermann. *Dialog vom Tragischen*. Berlin: Fischer, 1904.

Bahr, Hermann. *Tagebuch*. Berlin: Paul Cassirer, 1909.

Bahr, Hermann. *Prophet der Moderne. Tagebücher 1888–1904*. Ed. Reinhard Farkas. Vienna: Böhlau, 1987.

Barker, Andrew. "'Die weiseste Ökonomie bei tiefster Fülle.' — Peter Altenberg's *Wie ich es sehe*." In *Studies in Nineteenth Century Austrian Literature*. Ed. Brian O. Murdoch and Mark G. Ward. Glasgow: Scottish Papers in Germanic Studies, 1983.

Barker, Andrew. "'Der große Überwinder'. Hermann Bahr and the Rejection of Naturalism." *The Modern Language Review* 78 (1983): 617–630.

Barker, Andrew. "'Unforgettable People from Paradise!': Peter Altenberg and the Ashanti visit to Vienna of 1896–7." *Research in African Literatures* 22 (1991): 57–70.

Barker, Andrew. "'Ich hasse die Retouche.' Altenberg's letter to Arthur Schnitzler, July 1894." *Modern Austrian Literature* 25 (1992): 256–272.

Barker, Andrew. "Franz Kafka and Peter Altenberg." In *Turn-of-the-century-Vienna and its legacy. Essays in honor of Donald G. Daviau*. Ed. Jeffrey B. Berlin, Jorun B. Johns, Richard H. Lawson. Vienna: Edition Atelier, 1993.

Barker, Andrew and Leo A. Lensing. *Peter Altenberg: Rezept die Welt zu sehen. Kritische Essays. Briefe an Karl Kraus. Dokumente zur Rezeption. Titelregister der Bücher*. Vienna: Braumüller, 1995.

Beer Hofmann, Richard. Papers at the State University of New York, Binghamton.

Berg, Alban. *Briefe an seine Frau*. Munich and Vienna: Albert Langen and Georg Müller, 1965.

Berg, Erich Alban. *Der unverbesserliche Romantiker. Alban Berg 1885–1935.* Vienna: Österreichischer Bundesverlag, 1985.

Binder, Hartmut. *Kafka. Der Schaffensprozeß.* Frankfurt: Suhrkamp, 1983.

Binder, Hartmut. "Kafka und *Die neue Rundschau.*" *Jahrbuch der deutschen Schiller-Gesellschaft* 12 (1968), 94–111.

Bisanz, Hans. *Mein äußerstes Ideal: Altenbergs Photosammlung von geliebten Frauen, Freunden und Orten.* Vienna and Munich: Christian Brandstätter, 1987.

Blaukopf, Kurt. *Gustav Mahler.* Trans. Inge Goodwin. London: Allen Lane, 1973.

Blei, Franz. *Schriften in Auswahl.* Munich: Biederstein, 1960.

Böckel, Fritz. *Detlev von Liliencron im Urteil zeitgenössischer Dichter.* Berlin: Schuster und Loeffler, 1904.

Born, Jürgen, ed. *Franz Kafka. Kritik und Rezeption zu seinen Lebzeiten 1912–1924.* Frankfurt: Fischer, 1979.

Boyer, John W. *Cultural and political crisis in Vienna. Christian Socialism in power, 1897–1918.* Chicago and London: The University of Chicago Press, 1995.

Brandes Georg, and Arthur Schnitzler. *Ein Briefwechsel.* Ed. Kurt Bergel. Bern: Francke, 1956.

Braun Prager, Käthe. "Seien Sie barmherzig mit mir ... Ungedruckte Briefe Peter Altenbergs an seine erste Braut Aennie Holitscher." *Neues Österreich* 3 August 1958, 13–14, 10 August 1958, 19.

Broad, Geoffrey. "The Didactic Element in the Works of Peter Altenberg." Ph.D diss., Otago, 1980.

Brod, Max. "Peter Altenberg: 'Märchen des Lebens.'" *Die Gegenwart* 37 (1908): 350.

Brod, Max. *Streitbares Leben, 1884–1968.* Munich, Berlin, Vienna: F. A. Herbig, 1969.

Carr, Gilbert C. "Großstadt und Kaffeehaus in der Wiener Literatur um 1900." In *Deutsche Literatur in sozial-geschichtlicher Perspektive.* Ed. Eda Sagarra. Dublin: Trinity College, 1989.

Castle, Eduard. "Peter Altenberg." *Radio Wien* 5 (1929): 229–30.

Chapple, Gerald, and Hans H. Schulte, eds. *The turn of the century. German literature and art 1890–1915.* Bonn: Bouvier, 1981.

Dehmel, Richard. *Ausgewählte Briefe aus den Jahren 1902 bis 1920.* Berlin: Fischer, 1923.

Dickens, Charles. "Mugby Junction." *Christmas Stories.* London: Chapman and Hall, 1894

Dietrich, Margret, ed. *Hermann Bahr Symposion; "Der Herr aus Linz."* Linz: LIVA, 1987.

Dittmann, Ulrich. *Erläuterungen und Dokumente. Thomas Mann "Tristan."* Stuttgart: Reclam, 1983.

Döblin, Alfred. *Schriften zu Ästhetik, Poetik und Literatur*. Olten and Freiburg: Walter, 1989.

Döblin, Alfred. *Kleine Schriften I. Ausgewählte Werke in Einzelbänden*. Ed. Anthony W. Riley. Olten and Freiburg: Walter, 1982.

Doderer, Heimito von. *Die sibirische Klarheit: Texte aus der Gefangenschaft*. Ed. Wendelin Schmidt-Dengler and Martin Loew-Cadonna. Munich: Biederstein, 1991.

Darmstaedter, Ernst. *Peter Altenberg zum Gedächtnis*. Munich, 1927.

Dubrovic, Milan. *Veruntreute Geschichte*. Vienna: Paul Zsolnay, 1985.

Durieux, Tilla. *Eine Tür steht offen. Erinnerungen*. Berlin: Non Stop Bücherei, 1954.

Falckenberg, Otto. "Peter Altenberg, der Redakteur." *Freistatt* 5 (1903): 891.

Ficker, Ludwig von. *Briefwechsel 1909–1914*. Salzburg: Otto Müller, 1986.

Fingerhut, Karl-Heinz. *Die Funktion der Tierfiguren im Werk Franz Kafkas. Offene Erzählgerüste und Figurenspiel*. Bonn: Bouvier, 1969.

Fischer, Brigitte B. *Sie schrieben mir, oder was aus meinem Poesiealbum wurde*. Munich: dtv, 1989.

Fischer, Ernst. *Der "Schutzverband deutscher Schriftsteller", 1909–1933*. Frankfurt: Buchhändler-Vereinigung, 1980.

Fischer, Jens Malte. *Fin de Siècle: Kommentar zu einer Epoche*. Munich: Winkler, 1978.

Fischer, Samuel and Hedwig Fischer. *Briefwechsel mit Autoren*. Ed. Dierk Rodenwald and Corinna Fiedler. Frankfurt: Fischer, 1989.

Fischer, Wolfgang G. *Gustav Klimt and Emilie Flöge. An artist and his muse*. London: Lund Humphries, 1992.

Fontana, Oskar Maurus. "Peter Altenberg auf dem Semmering." *Der Merker* 4 (1913): 959–960.

Foster, Ian. "Altenberg's African Spectacle *Ashantee*." In *Theatre and Performance in Austria. From Mozart to Jellinek*. Ed. Ritchie Robertson and Edward Timms. Edinburgh: Edinburgh University Press, 1993.

Fraenkel, Josef. *The Jews of Austria*. London: Valentine and Mitchell, 1967.

Friedell, Egon. *Ecce Poeta*. Berlin: Fischer, 1912.

Friedell, Egon. *Kleine Porträtgalerie*. Munich: Beck, 1953.

Friedell, Egon. *Abschaffung des Genies. Essays bis 1918*. Ed. Heribert Illig. Vienna and Munich: Löcker, 1982.

Friedell, Egon. *Das Friedell-Lesebuch*. Ed. Heribert Illig. Munich: Beck, 1988.

Fülleborn, Ulrich. *Das deutsche Prosagedicht: zur Theorie und Geschichte einer Gattung*. Munich: Wilhelm Fink, 1970.

Furness, Raymond S. *Wagner and Literature*. Manchester: Manchester University Press, 1982.

Gay, Peter. *Freud, Jews and other Germans: Masters and victims in modernist culture*. New York: Oxford University Press, 1978.

Goethe, Johann Wolfgang von. *Werke in zwei Bänden*. Ed. Richard Friedenthal. Munich: Knaur, 1953.

Gilman, Sander L. *On Blackness without Blacks: Essays on the image of the Black in Germany*. Boston: G. K. Hall, 1982.

Goldschmidt, Hans E., ed. *Quer Sacrum: Wiener Parodien und Karikaturen der Jahrhundertwende*. Vienna and Munich: Jugend und Volk, 1976.

Graf, Max. *Jede Stunde war erfüllt*. Vienna and Frankfurt: Forum, n. d..

Graf-Blauhut, Heidrun. *Sprache: Traum und Wirklichkeit. Österreichische Kurzprosa des 20. Jahrhunderts*. Vienna: Braumüller, 1983.

Greve, Ludwig, and Werner Volke, eds. *Jugend in Wien. Literatur um 1900*. Marbach: Deutsche Schillergesellschaft, 1987.

Grieser, Dietmar. *Eine Liebe in Wien*. St. Pölten and Vienna: Niederösterreichisches Pressehaus, 1989.

Großmann, Stefan. *Ich war begeistert. Eine Lebensgeschichte*. Berlin: Fischer, 1930.

Grunwald, Max. *Vienna*. Philadelphia: Jewish Publication Society of America, 1936.

Haage, Peter. *Der Partylöwe, der nur Bücher fraß. Egon Friedell und sein Kreis*. Hamburg: Claassen, 1971.

Haas, Willy. "Aus unbekannten Altenberg-Briefen." *Forum* 8 (1961): 467–468.

Halbe, Max. *Jahrhundertwende*. Munich and Vienna: Langen and Müller, 1976.

Habermas, Jürgen "Ein philosophischer Intellektueller." In *Über T. W. Adorno*. Ed. J. W. Adorno. Frankfurt: Suhrkamp, 1968.

Hamann, Richard, and Jost Hermand. *Impressionismus*. Munich: Nymphenburger Verlagshandlung, 1972.

Hardin, James, and Donald G. Daviau, eds. *The Dictionary of Literary Biography*, vol. 81, *Austrian Fiction Writers 1875–1913*. Detroit: Bruccoli Clark Layman, 1989.

Heine, Heinrich. *Deutschland ein Wintermärchen*. Stuttgart: Reclam, 1977.

Hermand, Jost. *Der Schein des schönen Lebens. Studien zur Jahrhundertwende*. Frankfurt: Athenäum, 1972.

Herrmann-Neiße, Max. *Die neue Entscheidung. Aufsätze und Kritiken*. Frankfurt: Zweitausendeins, 1988.

Hiller, Kurt. *Leben gegen die Zeit*, vol. 1, *Logos*. Reinbek bei Hamburg: Rowohlt, 1969.

Hilmar, Rosemary. *Alban Berg. Leben und Wirken in Wien bis zu seinen ersten Erfolgen als Komponist*. Vienna, Cologne, Graz: Böhlau, 1978.

Hoffmann, Edith. *Kokoschka: Life and work.* London: Faber and Faber, 1947.

Hofmannsthal, Hugo von. *Gesammelte Werke in Einzelausgaben. Aufzeichnungen.* Ed. Herbert Steiner. Frankfurt: Fischer, 1959.

Hofmannsthal, Hugo von, and Arthur Schnitzler. *Briefwechsel.* Ed. Therese Nickl and Heinrich Schnitzler. Frankfurt: Fischer, 1964.

Hofmannsthal, Hugo von, and Richard Beer-Hofmann. *Briefwechsel.* Ed. Eugene Weber. Frankfurt: Fischer, 1972.

Holm, Korfiz. *ich klein geschrieben. Heitere Erlebnisse eines Verlegers.* Munich: Langen, 1932.

Ihering, Herbert. "Theater, Musik und Kunst. Peter Altenbergs letztes Buch." *Berliner Börsen-Courier* 51, 31 January 1919.

Janouch, Gustav. *Conversations with Kafka.* London: André Deutsch, 1971.

Johnson, Uwe. *"Wo ist der Erzähler auffindbar?" Gutachten für Verlage 1956–1958.* Ed. Bernd Neumann. Frankfurt: Suhrkamp, 1992.

Johnston, William M. "Martin Buber's literary début: 'On Viennese Literature' (1897)." *The Germanic Quarterly* 47 (1974): 556–566.

Just, Klaus G. *Von der Gründerzeit bis zur Jahrhundertwende. Geschichte der deutschen Literatur seit 1871.* Bern: Francke, 1973.

Kafka, Franz. *Sämtliche Erzählungen.* Ed. Paul Raabe. Frankfurt: Fischer 1973.

Kallir, Jane, and Hans Bisanz, eds. *Otto Kallir, Ein Wegbereiter österreichischer Kunst.* Vienna: Eigenverlag der Museen Stadt Wien, 1986.

Kassner, Rudolf. "Peter Altenberg: 'Was der Tag mir zuträgt.'" *Wiener Rundschau* 5 (1901): 75.

Kaszynski, Stefan H., and Sigurd Paul Scheichl, eds. *Karl Kraus, Ästhetik und Kritik: Beiträge des Kraus Symposions Poznan.* Munich: Edition Text + Kritik, 1989.

Kerr, Alfred. "Dem toten Peter Altenberg." *Die neue Rundschau* 30 (1919): 329–342.

King, Alexander. *Alexander King presents Peter Altenberg's evocations of love.* New York: Simon and Shuster, 1960.

Köhn, Eckhardt. "Stenograph des Wiener Lebens. Großstadterfahrung im Werk Peter Altenbergs." *Sprachkunst* 17 (1986): 22–37.

Kokoschka, Oskar. *Briefe,* vol. I, *1905–1919.* Ed. Olda Kokoschka and Heinz Spielmann. Düsseldorf: Claassen, 1984.

Körber, Clara, ed. *Österreichs Geist und Schwert. Ein Gedenkbuch aus ernster Zeit.* Leipzig: Verlag der Dürr'schen Buchhandlung, 1915.

Kosler, Hans Christian, ed. *Peter Altenberg: Leben und Werk in Texten und Bildern.* Munich: Matthes and Seitz, 1981.

Köwer, Irene. *Peter Altenberg als Autor der literarischen Kleinform.* Frankfurt: Peter Lang, 1987.

Kraus, Karl. *Die Fackel*. Vienna: Verlag "Die Fackel", 1899–1936.

Kraus, Karl. *Die demolirte Literatur*. Vienna: Bauer, 1897.

Kraus, Karl. *Die chinesische Mauer*. Frankfurt: Fischer, 1967.

Kraus, Karl. *Briefe an Sidonie Nádherný von Borutin 1913–1936*, 2 vols. Ed. Heinrich Fischer and Michael Lazarus. Munich: dtv, 1977.

Krojanker, Gustav, ed. *Juden in der deutschen Literatur*. Berlin: Welt-Verlag, 1922.

Kuh, Anton. "Peters Bruder." *Hamburger Fremdenblatt* 112 (1927): 5.

Kuh, Anton. *Luftlinien. Feuilletons, Essays und Publizistik*. Ed. Ruth Greuner. Vienna: Löcker, 1981.

Lensing, Leo A. "Peter Altenberg's fabricated photographs. Literature and photography in fin-de-siècle Vienna." In *Vienna 1900: From Altenberg to Wittgenstein*. Ed. Edward Timms and Ritchie Robertson. Edinburgh: Edinburgh University Press, 1990.

Lensing, Leo A. "Scribbling squids and the Giant Octopus: Oskar Kokoschka's Unpublished Portrait of Peter Altenberg." In *Turn-of-the-century Vienna and its legacy. Essays in Honor of Donald G. Daviau*. Ed. Jeffrey B. Berlin, Jorun B. Johns, Richard H. Lawson. Vienna: Edition Atelier, 1993.

Leybold, Hans. "Wege zu Peter Altenberg." *Die Aktion* 5 (1915): 73–80.

Loos Adolf. *Theory and Works*. Milan: Idea Books Edizioni, 1982.

Loos, Lina. *Du silberne Dame Du. Briefe von und an Lina Loos*. Ed. Franz Theodor Csokor and Leopoldine Ruther. Vienna and Hamburg: Zsolnay, 1966.

Lorenz, Albert. *Wenn der Vater mit dem Sohne*. Vienna: Deuticke, 1952.

Malmberg, Helga. *Widerhall des Herzens. Ein Peter Altenberg-Buch*. Munich: Langen and Müller, 1961.

Mann, Thomas. *Tagebücher 1918–1921*. Ed. Peter de Mendelssohn. Frankfurt: Fischer, 1979.

Mattenklott, Gert. "Peter Altenbergs Postkarten." *Hofmannsthal Blätter* 27 (1983): 72–91.

McGrath, William. *Dionysian art and populist politics in Austria*. New Haven: Yale University Press, 1974.

Mendelssohn, Peter de. *S. Fischer und sein Verlag*. Frankfurt: Fischer, 1970.

Michaelis, Karin. *Das heilige Feuer. Schicksale und Menschen*. Dresden: Carl Ressner, 1930.

Minutes of the Vienna Psychoanalytical Society 2 (1908–09). Trans. H. Nurnberg. New York: International Universities Press Inc., 1967.

Mitterer, Felix. *Der Narr von Wien: Aus dem Leben des Dichters Peter Altenberg. Ein Drehbuch*. Salzburg: Residenz, 1982.

Moldenhauer, Hans. *Anton von Webern: A chronicle of his life and works*. London: Victor Gollancz, 1978.

Monson, Karen. *Alban Berg: A biography*. London; Macdonald and Jane's, 1980.

Mühsam, Erich. "Gedenkblatt für Peter Altenberg." *Ver!* 33 (1921): 358.

Mühsam, Erich. *Ausgewählte Werke*, vol. 2, *Publizistik, Unpolitische Erinnerungen*. Ed. Christlieb Hirte, Berlin: Volk und Welt, 1978.

Mühsam, Erich. *In meiner Posaune muß ein Sandkorn sein. Briefe 1900–1934*. Ed. Gerd W. Jungblut. Vaduz: Topos, 1984.

Mulot-Déri, Sibylle. *Sir Galahad: Portrait einer Veschollenen*. Frankfurt: Fischer, 1987.

Musil, Robert. *Prosa, Dramen, Späte Briefe*. Ed. Adolf Frisé. Reinbek bei Hamburg: Rowohlt, 1957.

Musil, Robert. *Gesammelte Werke*, vol. 7. Ed. Adolf Frisé. Reinbek bei Hamburg: Suhrkamp, 1978.

Musil, Robert. *Tagebücher*. Ed. Adolf Frisé. Reinbek bei Hamburg: Rowohlt 1976.

Musil, Robert. *Briefe*, vol. 1. Ed. Adolf Frisé and Murray G. Hall. Reinbek bei Hamburg: Suhrkamp, 1981.

Nagel, Bert. *Kafka und die Weltliteratur. Zusammenhänge und Wechselbeziehungen*. Munich: Winkler, 1983.

Nebehay, Christian M. *Gustav Klimt: Zeichnungen und Dokumentation*. Vienna: Galerie Christian Nebehay, 1968.

Nielsen, Erika, ed. *Focus on Vienna 1900*. Munich: Wilhelm Fink, 1982.

Nienhaus, Stefan. *Das Prosagedicht im Wien der Jahrhundertwende. Altenberg — Hofmannsthal — Polgar*. Berlin and New York: de Gruyter, 1986.

Nordau, Max. *Degeneration*. London: Heinemann, 1895.

Oppenheimer, Max. "P. A. Text und Zeichnung." *Berliner Tagblatt* 286, 19 June 1927.

Pascal, Roy. *From Naturalism to Expressionism. German Literature and Society 1880–1918*. London: Weidenfeld and Nicholson, 1973.

Pinthus, Kurt. "Peter Altenberg, 'Semmering 1912.'" *Beiblatt der Zeitschrift für Bücherfreunde* 5 (1913): 71–72.

Pollak, Ilse. "Über Else Feldmann." *Literatur und Kritik* 279 (1993): 193–194.

Prohaska, Hedwig. "Peter Altenberg. Versuch einer Monographie." Dr.phil diss., Vienna, 1948.

Polgar, Alfred. "Marthas Genesung." *Simplicissimus* 24 (1919): 490, 502–503.

Polgar, Alfred. *Kleine Schriften*, vol. 4. Ed. Marcel Reich Ranicki and Ulrich Weinzierl. Reinbek bei Hamburg: Rowohlt, 1984.

Pollak, Felix. "A case of literary blasphemy," *Southwest Review* (1964): 89–91.

Przybyszewski, Stanisław. *Ferne komm ich her ....* Leipzig and Weimar: Gustav Kiepenheuer, 1985.

Raabe, Paul, ed. *Expressionismus. Der Kampf um eine literarische Bewegung.* Munich: dtv, 1965.

Reich, Willy. *The Life and Work of Alban Berg.* Trans. Cornelius Cardew. London: Thames and Hudson, 1965.

Renisch, Franz. *Gustinus Ambrosi.* Vienna: Österreichische Galerie, 1990.

Rilke, Rainer Maria. *Werke in drei Bänden,* vol. 1, *Gedicht-Zyklen.* Frankfurt: Insel, 1966.

Rilke, Rainer Maria. *Sämtliche Werke,* vol. 3, *Jugendgedichte.* Frankfurt: Insel, 1959.

Rilke, Rainer Maria. *Sämtliche Werke,* vol. 5, *Worpswede, Rodin, Aufsätze.* Frankfurt: Insel, 1965.

Rider, Jacques Le. *Modernity and crises of identity. Culture and society in fin-de-siècle Vienna.* Trans. Rosemary Morris. New York: Continuum, 1993.

Riemerschmied, Werner. "Peter Altenberg." *Literatur und Kritik* 12 (1977): 593.

Robert, Marthe. *From Oedipus to Moses. Freud's Jewish Identity.* Trans. Ralph Mannheim. New York: Anchor Press, 1976.

Robertson, Ritchie. *Kafka. Judaism, Politics and Literature.* Oxford: Clarendon Press, 1987.

Rode, Susanne. *Alban Berg und Karl Kraus: Zur geistigen Biographie des Komponisten der "Lulu".* Frankfurt: Peter Lang, 1988.

Rößler, Karl. *Das Lebensfest.* Berlin: Fischer, 1906.

Rosten, Leo. *The Joys of Yiddish.* London: Penguin, 1976.

Roth, Joseph. *Das journalistische Werk 1915–1923.* Ed. Klaus Westermann. Cologne: Kiepenheuer and Witsch, 1989.

Rukschcio, Burkhardt, ed. *Für Adolf Loos: Gästebuch des Hauses am Michaelerplatz. Festschrift zum 60. Geburtstag.* Vienna: Löcker, 1985.

Rukschcio, Burkhardt, ed. *Adolf Loos.* Vienna: Graphische Sammlung Albertina, 1989.

Rukschcio, Burkhardt and Schachl, Roland. *Adolf Loos: Leben und Werk.* Salzburg and Vienna: Residenz, 1987.

Salten, Felix. *Das österreichische Antlitz.* Berlin: Fischer, 1910.

Salten, Felix. "Aus den Anfängen. Erinerrungsskizzen." *Jahrbuch deutscher Bibliophilen und Literaturfreunde* 18–19 (1932–1933): 45.

Sandgruber, Roman. "Wiener Alltag um 1900." In *Ornament und Askese im Zeitgeist des Wien der Jahrhundertwende.* Ed. Alfred Pfabigan. Vienna: Christian Brandstätter, 1985.

Schaefer, Camillo. "Peter Altenberg." *Literatur und Kritik* 96–97 (1975): 426.

Schaefer, Camillo. *Peter Altenberg. Ein biographischer Essay.* Vienna: Freibord, 1981.

Schaefer, Camillo. *Peter Altenberg, oder, Die Geburt der modernen Seele.* Vienna: Amalthea, 1992.

Schaukal, Richard von. *Über Dichter.* Munich and Vienna: Langen and Müller, 1966.

Schaukal, Richard von. *Um die Jahrhundertwende.* Munich and Vienna: Langen and Müller, 1965.

Schlawe, Fritz. *Literarische Zeitschriften 1910–1933.* Stuttgart: Metzler, 1972.

Schmidt-Dengler, Wendelin. "Das Ende am Anfang. Zu unbekannten Texten Doderers aus der Frühzeit." In *Internationales Symposion Heimito von Doderer. Ergebnisse.* Vienna: Niederösterreich-Gesellschaft für Kunst und Kultur, 1986.

Schmujlow-Claasen, Ria, and Hugo von Hofmannsthal. *Briefe, Aufsätze, Dokumente.* Ed. Claudia Abrecht. Marbach: Deutsche Schillergesellschaft, 1982.

Schneider, Karl Ludwig, and Gerhardt Burckhardt, eds. *Georg Heym. Dokumente zu seinem Leben und Werk.* Munich: Heinrich Ellermann, 1968.

Schnitzler, Arthur. *Tagebuch 1879–1892.* Vienna: Akademie der Wissenschaften, 1987.

Schnitzler, Arthur. *Tagebuch 1893–1902.* Vienna: Akademie der Wissenschaften, 1989.

Schnitzler, Arthur. *Tagebuch 1903–1908.* Vienna: Akademie der Wissenschaften, 1991.

Schnitzler, Arthur. *Tagebuch 1909–1912.* Vienna: Akademie der Wissenschaften, 1981.

Schnitzler, Arthur. *Tagebuch 1913–1916.* Vienna: Akademie der Wissenschaften, 1983.

Schnitzler, Arthur. *Tagebuch 1920–1922.* Vienna: Akademie der Wissenschaften, 1993.

Schnitzler, Arthur. *Das Wort.* Ed. Kurt Bergel. Frankfurt: Fischer, 1966.

Schnitzler, Arthur. *The letters of Arthur Schnitzler to Hermann Bahr.* Ed. Donald G. Daviau. Chapel Hill: University of North Carolina Press, 1978.

Schnitzler, Arthur and Otto Brahm. *Der Briefwechsel.* Ed. Oskar Seidlin. Tübingen: Niemeyer, 1975.

Schnitzler, Arthur and Richard Beer-Hofmann. *Briefwechsel 1891–1931.* Ed. Konstanze Fliedl. Vienna: Europa Verlag, 1992.

Schoenberg, Arnold and Alban Berg. *The Berg-Schoenberg Correspondence. Selected Letters.* Ed. Juliane Brand, Christopher Hailey, Donald Harris. New York and London: W. W. Norton, 1987.

Schoenberg, Arnold and Wassily Kandinsky. *Lectures, Pictures and Documents.* Ed. Jelena Hahl Koch, trans. John C. Crawford. London and Boston: Faber and Faber, 1984.

Schoenberg, Barbara Z. "The Art of Peter Altenberg. Bedside Chronicles of a Dying World." Ph.D diss., U. C. L. A., 1984;

Schoenberg, Barbara Z. "'Woman Defender' and 'Woman Offender'. Peter Altenberg and Otto Weininger. Two Literary Stances vis-à-vis bourgeois Culture in the Viennese 'Belle Epoque.'" *Modern Austrian Literature* 20 (1987): 51–69.

Schoenberg, Barbara Z. "The influence of the French prose poem on Peter Altenberg." *Modern Austrian Literature* 22 (1989): 15–32.

Schopenhauer, Arthur. *Parerga and Paralipomena*, vol. 2. Trans. E. F. J. Payne. Oxford: Clarendon Press, 1974.

Schroeder, David P. "Alban Berg und Peter Altenberg: Intimate Art and the Aesthetics of Life." *Journal of the American Musicological Society* 3 (1992): 261–293.

Schweiger, Werner J. "Wiener Literatencafés. VI. Ein Dichter wird entdeckt." *Die Pestsäule* 10 (1974): 945–947.

Schweiger, Werner J. "Peter Altenberg als Varietékritiker." *Parnaß* 2 (1982): 24–29.

Schweiger, Werner J. *Wiener Werkstätte. Kunst und Handwerk 1903–1932.* Vienna: Christian Brandstätter, 1982.

Schweiger, Werner J. *Der junge Kokoschka. Leben und Werk 1904–1914.* Vienna and Munich: Christian Brandstätter, 1983.

Schweiger, Werner J., ed. *Peter Altenberg Almanach. Lese-Heft des Löcker Verlags.* Vienna: Löcker, 1987.

Sebald, W. G. "Le Paysan de Vienne. Über Peter Altenberg." *Die Neue Rundschau* 100 (1989): 75–95.

Segel, Harold B. *Turn-of-the-century cabaret: Paris, Barcelona, Berlin, Munich, Vienna, Cracow, Moscow, St. Petersburg, Zürich.* New York: Columbia University Press, 1987.

Sekler, Eduard F. *Josef Hoffmann: The architectural work. Monograph and catalogue of works.* Princeton N.J.: Princeton University Press, 1985.

Sheppard, Richard, ed. *Die Schriften des Neuen Clubs 1908–1914,* 2 vols. Hildesheim: Gerstenbergverlag, 1980, 1983.

Simpson, Josephine M. N. *Peter Altenberg: A neglected writer of the Viennese Jahrhundertwende.* Frankfurt: Peter Lang, 1987.

Spiel, Hilde. *Vienna's Golden Autumn, 1866–1938.* London: Weidenfeld and Nicolson, 1987.

Spinnen, Burkhard. "Die Seele in der Kritik. Zur zeitgenössischen Rezeption Peter Altenbergs." M.A. diss., Münster, 1983.

Spinnen, Burkhard. *Schriftbilder. Studien zu einer Geschichte emblematischer Kurzprosa.* Münster: Aschendorff, 1991.

Spinnen, Burkhard. "Idyllen in der Warenwelt. Peter Altenberg's *Pròdrŏmŏs* und die Sprache der Werbung." *Zeitschrift für Literaturwissenschaft und Linguistik* 22 (1992): 133–150.

Springer, A. "Peter Altenberg. Eine pathographische Skizze." *Wiener Zeitschrift für Suchtforschung* 1 1977–78): 41–46.

Stefan, Paul. "Der Semmering und Peter Altenberg." *Neue Zürcher Zeitung,* 1 June 1913.

Steinberg, Michael P. "Jewish identity and intellectuality in fin-de siècle Vienna. Suggestions for a historical discourse." *New German Critique* 43 (1988): 3–33.

Steiner, Rudolf. *Gesammelte Aufsätze zur Literatur 1884–1902.* Dornach: Rudolf Steiner-Verlag, 1971.

Sternheim, Carl. *Briefwechsel mit Thea Sternheim, Dorothea und Klaus Sternheim.* Ed. Wolfgang Wendler. Darmstadt: Luchterhand, 1988.

Stieg, Gerald. *Der Brenner und Die Fackel.* Salzburg: Otto Müller, 1976.

Stratz, C. H. *Naturgeschichte des Menschen.* Stuttgart: Ferdinand Enke, 1904.

Strutz, Joseph. "Der Mann ohne Konzessionen. Essayismus als poetisches Prinzip bei Altenberg und Musil." In *Robert Musil. Essayismus und Ironie,* ed. Gudrun Brokoph-Mauch. Tübingen: Francke, 1992.

Stuckenschmidt, Hans Heinz. *Arnold Schoenberg. His life, work and world.* Trans. Humphrey Searle. New York: Schirmer, 1978.

Szittya, Emil. *Das Kuriositätenkabinett.* Leipzig: Kurt Wolff, 1922.

Szittya, Emil. *Ausgedachte Dichterschicksale.* Paris: Les Ecrivains Réunis, 1928.

Thurnher, Eugen. *Neue Deutsche Biographie.* Berlin: Duncker and Humblot, 1953.

Timms, Edward. "Peter Altenberg — authenticity or pose?" In *Fin de siècle Vienna.* Ed. Gilbert J. Carr and Eda Sagarra. Dublin: Trinity College 1985.

Timms, Edward. *Karl Kraus. Apocalyptic satirist. Culture and catastrophe in Habsburg Vienna,* New Haven and London: Yale University Press, 1986.

Traum und Wirklichkeit. Wien 1870–1970. Vienna: Eigenverlag der Museen der Stadt Wien, 1985.

Trebitsch, Siegfried *Chronicle of a Life.* Trans. Eithne Wilkins and Ernst Kaiser. London: Heinemann, 1953.

Tucholsky, Kurt. *Gesammelte Werke,* vol 1. Ed. Mary Gerold-Tucholsky and Fritz J. Raddatz. Reinbek bei Hamburg: Rowohlt, 1960.

Veigl, Hans *Lokale Legenden. Wiener Kaffeehausliteratur.* Vienna: Kremayr and Scheriau, 1991.

Vergo, Peter. *Art in Vienna 1898–1918. Klimt, Kokoschka and their comtemporaries.* London: Phaidon, 1981.

Wagenbach, Klaus. *Franz Kafka. Eine Biographie seiner Jugend 1883–1912.* Bern: Francke, 1958.

Wagenknecht, Christian. "Die Vorlesungen von Karl Kraus. Ein chronologisches Verzeichnis." *Kraus Hefte* 35–36 (1985): 1–30.

Wagner, Nike. *Geist und Geschlecht. Karl Kraus und die Erotik der Wiener Moderne.* Frankfurt: Suhrkamp, 1982.

Wagner, Nike. "Theodor Herzl oder das befreite Wien." *Die Zeit*, 5 April 1985, 73–74.

Wagner, Nike. "Theodor Herzl und Karl Kraus." In *Theodor Herzl und das Wien des Fin de Siècle*. Ed. Norbert Leser. Vienna: Böhlau, 1987.

Wagner, Peter. "Peter Altenbergs Prosadichtung. Untersuchungen zur Thematik und Struktur des Frühwerks." Dr.phil diss., Münster, 1965.

Wassermann, Jakob. *Die Geschichte der jungen Renate Fuchs*. Berlin: Fischer, 1910.

Weiß, Walter, and Eduard Beutner, eds. *Literatur und Sprache in Österreich der Zwischenkriegszeit*. Stuttgart: Hans-Dieter Heinz, 1985.

Wellesz, Egon. *Wie ein Bild: Skizze von Peter Altenberg*. Budapest: Rozsavolgyi, 1920.

Werba, Robert. "Ein Außenseiter der Theaterkritik. Peter Altenberg und das Wiener Theaterjahr 1898–99." *Maske und Kothurn* 20 (1974): 163–190.

Werfel, Franz. *Spiegelmensch. Magische Trilogie*. Munich: Kurt Wolff, 1920.

Werkner, Patrick. *Physis und Psyche. Der österreichische Frühexpressionismus*. Vienna and Munich: Herold, 1986.

Werkner, Patrick. *Egon Schiele. Art, sexuality and Viennese modernism*. Palo Alto: Society for the Promotion of Science and Scholarship, 1994.

Werner, Arthur. "Redakteur Peter Altenberg." *Der österreichische Zeitungshändler. Presse und Vertrieb in Österreich* 10 (1967): 17–20.

Wildgans, Friedrich. *Anton Webern*. London: Calder and Boyars, 1966

Wolff, Kurt. *Briefwechsel eines Verlegers 1911–1932*. Ed. Bernhard Zeller and Ellen Otten. Frankfurt: Heinrich Scheffler, 1966.

Wunberg, Gotthart, ed. *Das junge Wien: Österreichische Literatur- und Kunstkritik 1887–1902*, vol. 2. Tübingen: Niemeyer, 1976.

Wysocki, Gisela. *Peter Altenberg: Bilder und Geschichten des befreiten Lebens*. Munich and Vienna: Hanser, 1979.

Zavrel, Lotte. "Peter Altenberg, wie ich ihn sah." *Vossische Zeitung*, 196 (1925): Unterhaltungsbeilage.

Žmegač, Viktor. *Geschichte der deutschen Literatur vom 18. Jahrhundert bis zur Gegenwart*, vol. 2, 2. Königstein im Taunus: Athenäum, 1980.

Žmegač, Viktor, ed. *Deutsche Literatur der Jahrhundertwende*. Königstein im Taunus: Athenäum, 1981.

Zohn, Harry. *"... ich bin ein Sohn der deutschen Sprache nur..." Jüdisches Erbe in der österreichischen Literatur*. Vienna and Munich: Amalthea, 1986.

Zweig, Stefan. *Die Welt von gestern: Erinnerungen eines Europäers*. Stockholm: Bermann-Fischer, 1947.

Index

Adler, Friedrich 222
Adler, Viktor 222
Adorno, Theodor Wiesengrund xi
Akademischer Verband für Literatur
  und Musik 87, 142
Aktion, Die 44, 137, 210
Allesch, Ea von. See: Emma Rudolf
Allesch, Johann von 80

Altenberg, Peter
And the arts:
  Anthologies xiii–xv 235
  Aphorisms 108–9
  Aural quality of writing 47–48, 67–
    69, 150, 204, 213–14
  Cabaret 123–131
  Cinema 40, 117
  Correspondence xiv–xv, 234–35
  Dada 84, 95, 204–5
  Expressionism 39, 112–13, 115,
    214
  Extrakt theory 35–36, 93–94, 96,
    99–101, 118, 168
  Frauenkult 10–12, 77–78, 87–92,
    113–14, 118, 188, 202–3
  French literature 39, 41, 48–50
  Impressionism xvi, 29–33, 38–45,
    113, 214
  Literary beginnings 24–30
  Literary manifestos 43–44, 93, 97,
    132, 150
  Modernism xi, 40–42, 69, 116,
    163, 166–67
  Music and musicians xii, 7, 86–88,
    100, 166–173
  Naturalism 35, 40–41, 44, 96–97,
    116
  Neo-Romanticism 116
  Painting 116–118, 135–39, 156–
    57, 215, 225
  Photography 32–34, 44, 80–81,
    92, 96–98, 116–18, 154–55,
    216, 219, 235
  Short forms xii, xvii–xviii, 34–37,
    39–42, 51–62, 93–94, 108–9,
    125
  Theater criticism 74–77
  Ver! 214–16, 222, 231–32
Portrayed in literature:

Egon Friedell: Altenberg anecdotes
  86, 129–30
Eduard Keyserling: *Nicky* 82
Thomas Mann: *Tristan* 83–84
Robert Musil: "P.A. und die
  Tänzerin" 124–26; *Der Mann
  ohne Eigenschaften* 126
Max Oppenheimer: Altenberg anec-
  dotes 84
Alfred Polgar: "Marthas Genesung"
  232
Karl Rößler: *Das Lebensfest* 106–7
Arthur Schnitzler: *Das Wort* 103–
  105; "Der Tod des Gabriel"
  105
Jakob Wassermann: *Die Geschichte
  der jungen Renate Fuchs* 83
*Portrayed in drawing, painting and
sculpture:*
  Gustinus Ambrosi 207
  Carl Hollitzer 124
  Gustav Jagerspacher 99
  Oskar Kokoschka 73, 135–38
  Max Oppenheimer 136–37
Texts set to music:
  Alban Berg: "Die Flötenspielerin,"
    "Hoffnung," "Traurigkeit" 170;
    *Fünf Lieder nach Ansichtskarten-
    texten von Peter Altenberg* 171–
    73
  Hanns Eisler: *Hollywood-Liederbuch*
    xii
  Egon Wellesz: *Wie ein Bild* 168
Biography:
  Addiction 140, 150, 158–60, 161–
    162, 165, 215, 217–19
  Christianity 2–3, 19, 84, 149, 180,
    189, 195, 218, 226, 230–31
  Dietary views 14, 93–94, 107-8,
    115, 185–6, 187
  Education 10, 16
  Engländer family 5–9, 188
  Funeral 229–31
  Homosexuality 14, 90–91, 152
  Jewishness and Judaism xvi, 1–5,
    13–14, 23–25, 43, 75–76, 84,
    90, 107, 113, 134, 137, 180–
    81, 189, 224, 230–32, 233
  Heinz Lang, suicide of 103–4
  Munich 81–86, 106

Mental illness 140–46, 150–55, 157–165, 218, 226–28
Nobel Prize for literature xvi, 166
Politics 60–62, 193, 222, 235–37
Race and racism 64–71
Pseudonym 1–2, 11–12, 14–16, 43, 49
Sexuality xi, 11–15, 35–36, 38–39, 78–81, 90–92, 113–16, 121–23, 150–53, 157–58, 185, 201–4
Slovakia 120–21
Venice 162–65
War 186–87, 189–93, 197, 214
Relationships with girls and women: see under:
Bibiana Amon; Smaragda von Berg; Hilde Berger; Cäcilia Brandstätter; Bessie Bruce; Sonja Dungjersky; Ilna Ewers; Ännie Holitscher; Annie Kalmar; Anna Konrad; Elsie Körber; Bertha Lecher; Lina Loos; Helga Malmberg; Líoschka Maliniewich; Annie Mewes; Helene Berg; Klara Panhans; Alma Ptazcek; Emma Rudolf; Albine Ruprich; Paula Schweitzer; Mitzi Thumb; Esthère Vignon; Olga Waisnix; Annie Weiß; Grete Wiesenthal

Altenberg, S. 94
Altmann-Loos, Elsie 234
Ambrosi, Gustinus 207
Amon, Bibiana 163–65
Andrian, Leopold von 23
Annunzio, Gabriele d' 23
Ansorge, Konrad 87
Atkinson, Brooks 236
Auernheimer, Raoul 233

Bach, David Josef 46, 167
Bahr, Hermann 21 23, 25, 28, 33, 38, 40, 42, 62–66, 75–76, 99, 101, 107, 112, 115, 138, 142–43, 159–61, 163, 175, 193, 199, 209, 232–33
Balzac, Honoré de 132
Bamberger, Viktor 84

Barrison, Gertrude 112, 124–25, 129, 143, 147, 231
Bartels, Adolf 26
Bartok, Bela 168
Baudelaire, Charles 39, 41, 48, 126, 146
Beer-Hofmann, Richard 8, 10, 21, 25–27, 62, 65–66, 68, 84, 127, 163, 175
Beethoven, Ludwig van 174, 213
Bendiener, Oskar 234
Berg, Alban xi, xv, 18, 21, 91, 132, 160, 166–74, 177, 186, 213
Berg, Helene 132, 147–48, 171–73
Berg, Smaragda 90, 122, 170–71
Berger, Hilde 205
Bermann-Fischer, Gottfried 235
Berliner Börsen-Courier 214
Berliner Börsenzeitung 234
Berliner Lokalanzeiger 135
Berliner Tagblatt 201, 214
Berner Bund, Der 194
Berton, Pierre 76
Billroth, Theodor 7
Binder, Hartmut 179
Birnbaum, Uriel 214
Bisanz, Hans 154
Bisson, Alexandre 77
Blei, Franz xix, 127, 139
Bleibtreu, Karl 114
Born, Jürgen 176
Brahm, Otto 1, 102
Brahms, Johannes xviii, 7, 173–4
Brandes, Georg xx
Brandstätter, Cäcilia 158
Brecht, Bert xii
Brehmer, Arthur 94
Brendel, Ulrik. See: Leopold Liegler
Brenner, Der xv 153
Broch, Hermann 80
Brockdorff, Rolf Baron 29, 88
Brod, Max 66, 131–32, 175–76, 178
Browning, Elizabeth 115
Browning, Robert 115
Bruce, Bessie xv, 99, 104, 119, 162–64
Bruckner, Anton 28
Buber, Martin 64, 181
Bukovac, Vlado 95
Bülow, Reichskanzler Fürst 150

Buschbeck, Erhard 172
Busson, Paul 98

Canciani, Alfons 95
Canetti, Elias 80, 108
Cassirer, Paul xi, 102, 137
Castle, Eduard 113
Chekhov, Anton 45, 59
Cody, Buffalo Bill 64
Csokor, Franz Theodor 91, 95, 119
Custos 160
Czegka, Bertha 73
Czeschka, Carl Otto 128, 143

Dankl, General 197
Dannbacher, Erika 234
Dante 159, 225
Darwin, Charles 40
Dehmel, Richard xvii, 42, 53, 142–43,
    209
Delvard, Marie 123–24, 126, 129
Demant, Dr. 206, 208, 216
Demant, Paula. See: Paula Schweitzer
Dickens, Charles xvii
Döblin, Alfred xvi, 112, 126, 143
Doderer, Heimito von 15, 68, 103,
    108
Domansky, Ludwig 220
Dönges, Pauline 87
Dörmann, Felix 1
Dungyersky, Sonja 156–57
Durieux, Tilla 164
Dvořak, Antonin 173

Ebermann, Leo 3
Eckstein, Bertha 28
Eckstein, Fritz 28
Ehrenstein, Albert xvii, 4, 107, 177
Eisler, Hanns xii
Engländer, Georg xiv, xv, 8–9, 82, 84,
    92, 98, 101, 120, 123, 140, 157,
    159, 161–62, 164, 218–19, 232,
    234
Engländer, Gretl 8, 158
Engländer, Marie 8, 10, 13, 18, 20,
    235
Engländer, Moriz 4, 9, 16, 65, 93,
    185
Engländer, Paulina 6–9, 16

Etlinger, Karl 231
Ewers, Hans Heinz 122
Ewers, Ilna 122
Extrapost, Die 74, 76, 81

Fackel, Die 2, 20, 27, 75, 77–78, 90,
    94, 96, 111, 134–35, 141, 143–44,
    146, 168, 175, 198, 233
Falckenberg, Otto 94, 97
Falke, Gustav 98
Feldmann, Else 152
Ficker, Ludwig von 153, 163
Fischer, Hedwig 27–28, 82
Fischer, Samuel xiv-xv, 1, 26–28, 48,
    65, 69, 76, 84, 102–3, 133–35,
    143, 151, 153, 159, 163, 187,
    189, 197, 211, 216, 220, 234
Fischer Verlag xiii, xiv, 27–28, 31, 49,
    103, 106, 109, 119, 134–35, 149,
    219, 222, 232, 234
Fließ, Wilhelm 11, 91
Fontana, Oskar Maurus 153–54
Forest, Karl 231
Frank, Friede 158
Franz, Ferdinand Archduke 186
Franzos, Emil 159, 208–10, 218–20,
    226
Franzos, Lotte 158–59, 209, 214,
    220–2, 226–28
Frauenlob 201
Freistatt 95, 97
Fremden-Blatt 132
Freud, Sigmund xvi, xix, 4, 88, 92,
    114
Friede, Der 232
Friedell, Egon xviii, 1–2, 10, 13, 29,
    31, 38–39, 41, 43–44, 48, 60, 86,
    91, 104, 108, 110, 121, 123, 126–
    30, 133–34, 143–44, 155–56, 158,
    193, 231–35, 236
Friedrich, Paul 177
Fries, Emil 141
Fürth, Járo 228
Fjaestad, Gustaf 117

Gal, Hans 167
Galahad, Sir. See: Bertha Eckstein
Gay, Peter 4
Gebhardt, E. von 3

George, Stefan xviii, 40, 44, 53, 112, 116, 168
Ghega, Carl von 155
Gilman, Sander 70
Girardi, Alexander 77, 143
Glück, Franz xv, 235–6
Goethe, Johann Wolfgang von xii, xix, 31, 39, 63, 129–30, 133, 146, 163, 169–70, 211–13
Gogh, Vincent van 137
Gogol, Nikolai 203
Goldmann, Paul 75
Gomperz, Bela von 226, 228
Graf, Max 4, 65, 74
Greissle, Felix 167
Grieg, Edvard 173
Grieser, Dietmar 208
Grillparzer, Franz 6, 9, 52, 108
Gropius, Walter 174
Großmann, Stefan xiv, 2, 5, 18, 28, 77, 84, 104, 125, 175
Guilbert, Yvette 123
Günsberg, Dr. 155

Habermas, Jürgen xi
Haeckel, Ernst 4
Hafner, Josef 98
Hagenbeck, Karl 179
Halbe, Luise 82
Halbe, Max 8, 81, 84, 139
Hamburger Fremdenblatt 234
Hammerschlag, Viktor 219–220
Hansy, Dr. 160–61
Hansy, Resa 159
Hardekopf, Ferdinand 112
Harden, Maximilian 1
Hartleben, Otto Erich 81, 84
Hauer, Karl 84
Hauff, Wilhelm 177
Hauptmann, Gerhart 35, 40, 74, 102, 142, 209
Hauser, Arnold 43
Hegel, Georg Wilhelm Friedrich xix
Heimann, Moritz 66
Heine, Heinrich 43, 93, 142
Hennerbichler, Josef 160–61
Henry, Marc 124, 126–27, 130
Herrmann-Neiße, Max 194
Hermand, Jost 83
Herzl, Theodor 3, 14–15, 175, 179

Hesse, Hermann 143
Heym, Georg 112–13
Heymann, Walther 142
Hille, Peter 231
Hiller, Kurt xix 112
Hitler, Adolf xvi, 236
Höflich, Lucie 36
Hoffmann, E.T.A. 177
Hoffmann, Edith 135
Hoffmann, Josef 99, 128, 130–31, 139, 143
Hofmannsthal, Hugo von xvi, xviii, 10–11, 21, 23, 25, 38, 43, 45, 50, 57, 62–65, 71, 74–77, 82, 84, 101–4, 107–8, 116, 142–43, 159, 175, 193, 199, 209, 233
Hohenberg, Paul 169
Holbein, Hans 14
Holgersen, Alma. See: Alma Ptazcek
Holitscher, Ännie 19–20, 70, 235
Holitzscher, Arthur 83
Hollitzer, Carl 124, 229
Hollriegl, Arnold 214
Holm, Korfiz 82, 84–85
Holz, Arno 21, 45
Honus, Ilci 158
Horace 228
Horn, Risa 19, 96-97
Huppert, Rudolf 234
Huysmans, Joris-Karl 48–50, 62, 96

Ibsen, Henrik 20, 72, 89, 189, 194
Ihering, Herbert 214–16

Jacob, H.E. 177
Jacobsohn, Siegfried 133, 220
Jacques, Norbert 188
Jagerspacher, Gustav 99, 170, 188
Jandl, Ernst 68
Janikowski, Ludwig von 136, 141
Janowitz, Otto 187-8, 197
Janouch, Gustav 176
Jaráy, Alexander 229
Jauregg, Julius Wagner von 218, 226
Jean Paul 102, 154
Jews in Vienna 23–24
Johnson, Uwe xi, 60, 108–9, 135, 150
Johnston, William M. 108
Jordan, Eduard 15
Jude, Der 181

Jugend 160, 170
Jung Wien. See: Young Vienna

Kafka, Franz xi, xiv, xvi, 8, 108, 115,
 166, 174–85
Kafka, Hermann 183, 185
Kainz, Josef 142
Kallir, Otto 170, 234–35, 236
Kalmar, Annie 76–80, 81, 86, 141,
 187
Kandinsky, Wassily 169
Karczewska, Irma 99
Kassner, Rudolf 86, 175
Kaszýnski, Stefan 108
Kerr, Alfred xi, 1, 13, 53, 68, 75, 83,
 102–3, 143, 154, 225, 228, 232,
 234–35
Kerr, Inge 225
Keyserling, Eduard von 82, 85
Kidderminster Times 104
Kinder-Schutz- und Rettungsgesell-
 schaft 231
King, Alexander 232, 236
Kírínovic, Víctora 120–21
Kisch, Egon Erwin 231
Klebinder, Trude 225
Kleen, Tysa 95
Klein-Löw, Stella 11
Klimt, Gustav xi, 3, 90, 99, 115, 117,
 126, 138–39, 205, 209, 215
Kocmata, Franz F. 214–16, 231–33
Köhn, Eckhardt 44
Kokoschka, Oskar xi, 72, 103, 122,
 128–29, 135–38, 153, 157, 159,
 166, 173
Konrad, Anna 132, 144–51, 232
Körber, Else 218, 220, 228
Kosel, Hermann Clemens 97
Kraus, Karl xiv–xvi, xviii, 1, 11, 13, 15,
 21–22, 25–28, 40, 42, 44, 47, 70–
 71, 75, 76–79, 82, 86–89, 92, 94–
 97, 99, 109, 111, 116, 121, 126–
 27, 129, 133, 135–39, 141–46,
 153, 160, 163–64, 168, 174, 186–
 91, 197–201, 204, 209–10, 213,
 215, 221, 230–31, 233–35
Krauss, Friedrich 95, 98
Kritische Rundschau 190
Krizwanek, R. 77
Krohn, Charlotte 188

Krojanker, Gustav 177
Kuh, Anton 164, 224, 229–31, 234
Kühhaß, Poldi 218

La Rochefoucauld, Alexandre de La
 108
Lach, Alice 231
Lang, Edmund 99, 103
Lang, Erwin 103, 129
Lang, Greta. See: Greta Wiesenthal
Lang, Heinz 103–5
Lang, Ida 85
Lang, Marie 99, 103
Lanýi, Richard 236
Lasker-Schüler, Else 126, 166, 194,
 231
Lecher, Bertha 10, 14–16, 18, 23, 235
Lecher, Emma 15
Lecher, Luise 10
Lecher, Zacharias Konrad 10
Lensing, Leo A. 136–38, 154
Lessing, Gotthold Ephraim 197
Lessing, Theodor 13, 83
Leybold, Hans 44–45, 194, 210
Lichtenberg, Georg Christoph 108
Liebelei 29, 88
Lieben, Ernst von 157–58, 220
Liebermann, Max 103
Liebig & Co 36, 93–94
Liegler, Leopold 153
Liliencron, Detlev von 47, 189
Liljefors, Bruno 33
Loerke, Oskar xiv, 234
Loewenson, Erwin 112
Löffler, Berthold 130
Loos, Adolf xi, xv, 4, 8–9, 11, 13, 44,
 73, 87, 90-91, 93, 95–96, 99,
 100–1, 103–4, 109, 114, 119–20,
 135, 138, 142–45, 156, 161–63,
 173–74, 188, 198, 200, 213–14,
 231, 235
Loos, Lina 13, 19, 77, 91, 93, 102–4,
 119, 129, 155, 231
Lorenz, Albert 18
Lorenz, Adolf 15–16
Lorenz, Konrad 15
Loris. See: Hugo von Hofmannsthal
Löwy, Jizchak 183
Lübcke, Else 197
Lueger, Karl 15, 90

Lunzer, Heinz 48, 134
Lunzer, Viktoria 48

Mach, Ernst 32, 42
Macher, Max 190
Machlup, Frau 158
Macleod, Fiona. See William Sharp
Macpherson, James 39
Maeterlinck, Maurice 50, 114
Mahler, Alma 79, 156–57, 173
Mahler, Anna Maria 173–74
Mahler, Gustav 18, 87, 144, 169, 173–74
Maliniewich, Lióschka 157–58
Mallarmé, Stéphane 39, 48, 132
Malmberg,˙Helga 31, 35, 79–80, 92, 119–24, 137, 140–149, 189, 197, 202; *her letters to Kraus* 140–45
Mandl, Alma 218
Mann, Heinrich 53, 137, 163
Mann, Thomas 45, 53, 83–84, 102, 124
März 112, 146
Marx, Karl 40
Mauthner, Fritz 102
Mauthner, Marie. See Marie Engländer
Maupassant, Guy de 63
Mayen, Maria 231, 234
Menzel, Simon 126
Mercure de France 195
Merker, Der 194
Messer, Max 66
Mestrović Ivan 95
Mewes, Annie 189, 203
Meyerbeer, Giacomo 93
Michaelis, Karin 205, 230
Mistral, Der 194
Mitterer, Felix xi, 91
Mombert, Alfred 43
Monatsschrift für Turnwesen 110
Morena, Erna 216
Morgenstern, Soma 169
Morris, William 70
Mozart, Wolfgang Amadeus 213
Muhr, Elisabeth 195
Muhr, Julius 188, 220
Mühsam, Erich xvi, 125–28, 133, 231–2
Müller, Jens Peter 184

Musil, Robert xi–xii, 7, 80, 108, 113, 124–26, 178
Musset, Alfred de 49

Nádherný, Sidonie von 186, 197–199
Nagy, Kamilla von 158
Nahowski, Helene. See: Helene Berg
Nestroy, Johann xvii
Neue Freie Presse 41, 233, 104
Neue Reich, Das 2
Neue Rundschau, Die xi, 14, 134
Neue Zürcher Zeitung 155
Neues Wiener Journal xiii, 97–98, 141, 160
Neues Wiener Tagblatt xiii, 142
New York Times 236
Nietzsche, Friedrich 40, 45, 53, 70, 87- 88, 107–8, 134, 189
Nobel Prize for Literature xvi, 166
Nordau, Max 1, 61–62
Novalis 39, 132

Obertimpfler, Lina. See: Lina Loos
Offenbach, Jacques 174
Oppenheimer, Max 83, 136–37, 214
Orlik, Emil 143

Pagin, Ferdinand 98
Pan 146
Panhans, Klara 150–52, 154, 187, 189
Perscheid, N. 95
Petzold, Alfons 207
Pfemfert, Franz 44, 137
Pilzer, Alice 222
Pindar 63
Pinthus, Kurt xi, 112, 153
Polgar, Alfred xi, xvi, 1, 30, 39, 77, 79, 101, 104, 120, 126, 129–30, 144, 217, 232–3, 235
Pollak, Felix 232–3
Popper, Alice 24–25, 170
Popper, Auguste 24–25, 170
Prager Tagblatt xiii, 179–80, 198–200
Przybyszewski, Stanisław xvii, 13–14
Ptazcek, Alma 208, 216, 218, 228
Puccini, Giacomo 173–74

Radecki, Sigismund von 234
Raimund, Ferdinand xvii

Rakaric, Anka 147
Rasch, Wolfdietrich 83
Rathenau, Walther 102, 179
Reich, Willi xv
Reinhardt, Max 1, 142–45
Reiss, Erich xiv
Reiz, Walter 194
Renard, Marie 203
Ressek, Felix 195-6
Reuter, Gabriele 143
Richter, Hans Georg 195
Rilke, Rainer Maria 71-72, 80, 112,
    126, 175
Rimbaud, Arthur 39
Robertson, Ritchie 180
Roda, Roda 98
Roessler, Arthur xv
Rolland, Romain xvi
Roller, Alfred 87
Rosegger, Peter 10
Rößler, Karl 105–6
Rosten, Leo 26
Roth, Joseph 52, 206
Ruch, Hannes 124
Rudolf, Emma 77, 79–82, 85–86, 88,
    122, 147, 170
Rudolf, Theodor 79
Ruf, Der 153
Ruprich, Albine 155, 202–3
Ruskin, John 70

Saliger, Karl Josef 210
Salomé, Lou Andreas 79
Salten, Felix 1, 18, 21, 26–28, 84,
    124, 130, 134, 197, 233
Salus, Hugo 98
Sassmann, Hanns 134
Sauer, Emil 208
Schad, Christian 204
Schaubühne, Die xiv, 27, 146
Schaukal, Richard von xviii–xix, 94, 98,
    125, 133, 143
Schebek, Alfred von 205, 211, 219
Scherbart, Paul 98
Schermann, Raphael 188
Schiele, Egon xv, 52, 138, 151, 197,
    225
Schiller Foundation Weimar 119
Schlaf, Johannes 21, 42, 45
Schlager, Ludwig 8

Schließmann, Hans 49
Schnitzler, Arthur xi, xvi–xviii, 1, 8, 10,
    16, 19–22, 25, 27, 29–31, 33, 37,
    55, 59, 64–65, 74, 84, 97, 101,
    104–5, 108, 119–20, 124, 127,
    140, 142, 159–61, 163, 166, 175,
    199, 214
Schnitzler, Olga 67, 104
Schoenberg, Arnold xii, xv, xviii, 4, 21,
    160, 166–69, 172, 186
Schönherr, Karl 16
Schopenhauer, Arthur 167–69
Schreker, Franz 173
Schroll, Anton xv, 235–36
Schubert, Franz 3, 7, 80, 138, 174
Schujlow, Wladimir 75
Schujlow,-Claasen Ria 82
Schutzverband deutscher Schriftsteller
    190
Schwarzwald, Genia 145, 236
Schweitzer, Paula 7, 161, 188–89,
    195–96, 201–3, 205–13, 216
Sebald, W.G. 179
Sedelmayr, Sophie 87
Seligmann, A.F. 42
Senders, Tini 101
Serner, Walter 137, 194, 204
Servaes, Franz 76
Sharp, William 11
Shaw, George Bernard 5, 98
Simon, Charles 76, 136
Simplicissimus 34, 137, 141, 146, 154,
    232
Skeene [?] 80
Socrates 214
Spinoza, Baruch 3
Spitzer, Daniel 41, 48–50
Springer, A. 141
Stefan, Paul 153, 155
Stekel, Wilhelm 110
Steiner, Lilly 158
Steiner, Rudolf 66
Sternberg, Wilhelm 143
Sternheim, Carl 111
Stifter, Adalbert 108
Stoessl, Otto 110
Stonborough-Wittgenstein,
    Margaretha 139
Straus, Oscar 172
Strauss, Richard 102, 173–74

Strauß, Rudolf 29
Strindberg, August 12, 88–89, 132, 189, 194, 209
Stürgkh, Karl von 222
Sturm, Der 113, 146, 154
Szeps, Moritz 142
Szittya, Emil xvi, 92

Tagebuch, Das xv, 232
Tann-Bergler, Ottokar 97–98
Täubele, Emma. See: Emma Rudolf
Theater, Das 35–36
Thimig, Helene 197
Thoma, Ludwig 143
Thumb, Mitzi 1, 158, 164, 188, 203
Timms, Edward 1, 90
Tolstoy, Leo 74
Trakl, Georg 163
Třcka, Anton Josef 197
Trebitsch, Siegfried 5, 186
Tucholsky, Kurt 129

Ullmann, Ludwig 134, 201, 230
Unger, Ilke Maria 98
Urzidil, Johannes 195

Vallière, Frau 158, 162
Ver! 214–16, 222, 231–32
Ver Sacrum 33
Verlaine, Paul xi
Vignon, Esthère 188

Wage, Die 153
Wagenbach, Klaus 175–76
Wagner, Ernst 95
Wagner, Otto 159, 207
Wagner, Richard 14, 39, 86–89, 165, 173–74
Waisnix, Olga 16, 19–20
Walden, Herwarth 1, 35, 113, 121, 143, 136–38
Wantoch, Hans 200
Wärndorfer, Fritz 98, 119, 123, 130, 127
Wassermann, Jakob 82, 124
Webern, Anton 21, 46, 167, 172
Wedekind, Frank 86, 111, 124, 126, 129, 171, 205

Weininger, Otto 12–14, 78, 91, 114, 181
Weiß, Annie 162
Wellesz, Egon 168
Werfel, Franz xiv, 4, 175, 207, 233
Wieland 192
Wiener Allgemeine Zeitung xiii, 72, 98, 129, 146, 154, 179, 190, 201
Wiener Mittags-Zeitung 173
Wiener Rundschau 66
Wiener Werkstätte 98, 119, 123, 127–28, 145
Wiesenthal, Else 129, 173
Wiesenthal, Grete 76, 103, 129, 173, 219
Wilde, Oscar 1, 173
Wildgans, Anton 175
Wolf, Hugo 28, 99, 173–4
Wolff, Kurt xiv, 207

Young Vienna 18–23, 64, 67, 78, 94, 214

Zavrel, Lotte 163–64
Zeit, Die (Hamburg) xii
Zeit, Die (Vienna) 25, 62, 66
Zeit im Bild 153
Zeitung, Die (London) 106
Zemlinsky, Alexander von 4, 169
Ziegler, Leopold 197
Žmegač, Victor 108
Zoff, Otto 194
Zola, Emile 44–45, 117
Zöllner, Rudolf 6
Zuckerkandl, Berta 166
Zukunft, Die 62
Zweig, Stefan 23, 52, 55, 71